Rethinking the Cold War

In the series
Critical Perspectives on the Past,
edited by Susan Porter Benson,
Stephen Brier, and
Roy Rosenzweig

Edited by Allen Hunter

Rethinking the Cold War

Temple University Press / Philadelphia

Temple University Press, Philadelphia 19122
Copyright © 1998 by Temple University (except Chapter 6 copyright © 1998 by Brenda Gayle Plummer). All rights reserved
Published 1998
Printed in the United States of America

♾ The paper used in this book meets the requirements of the American National Standard for Information Sciences—
Permanence of Paper for Printed Library Materials, ANSI Z39.48-1984

Text design by William Boehm

Library of Congress Cataloging-in-Publication Data

Rethinking the Cold War / edited by Allen Hunter.
p.   cm.—(Critical perspectives on the past)
Includes bibliographical references.
ISBN 1-56639-561-5 (cloth. : alk. paper). — ISBN 1-56639-562-3 (pbk. : alk. paper)
1. Cold War. 2. World politics—1945–   . I. Hunter, Allen, 1944–   . II. Series.
D843.R437   1998
909.82—DC21   97-11618

Acknowledgments

I have benefited from the collaboration, advice, and assistance of many people and I would like to thank a number of them here. Tom McCormick co-organized the conference from which these essays derive and commented on an earlier draft of the introduction. Michael Barnett, Barbara Forrest, Lucy Mathiak, David Myers, Francisco Scarano, David Tarr, and Joseph Thome also served on the conference organizing committee. Financial support for the conference came from the Goethe Institute of Chicago, the Wisconsin State Historical Society Library, and a number of funds and programs at the University of Wisconsin: the Anonymous, Knapp and Nave funds, Office of International Studies and Programs, Center for International Cooperation and Security Studies, Goldberg Center, and the office of the Chancellor.

At the Havens Center I've had the privilege and pleasure of working with a number of terrific people who provided crucial help in organizing the conference and editing this book. They include Debra Armes, Karen Bassler, Carin Bringelson, Barbara Forrest, Steve Halebsky, Rob Mackin, Laura McEnaney, Brian Obach, Nancy Plankey, Meera Seghal, and Greg White.

Regarding the contributors to the volume, from whom I have learned a tremendous amount in the editing process, my thanks for their flexibility and patience.

Other friends helped me through many conversations about the Cold War, domestic U.S. history, and international politics. They include Linda Gordon, who gave me a lengthy set of critical comments on an earlier version of the introduction, Rosalyn Baxandall, Jeremy Brecher, Elizabeth Ewen, Stuart Ewen, Edward Friedman, Lewis Leavitt, Arthur MacEwan, Jim Riker, Gay Seidman, Bob Sutcliffe, David Trubek, and many of the visiting scholars who have been in residence at the Havens Center.

I join a number of the authors in this volume in appreciating the high quality of the work of Patricia Sterling, the copy-editor.

The effects of the Cold War on human society and the natural environment will stretch untold generations beyond our era. This book is dedicated to its past, present, and future victims. I'd like to think of this volume as a small fraction of the work that needs to be done to get at the truths of the era and contribute to minimizing its deleterious effects on the lives of billions around the globe.

Contents

Part II Decentering the Cold War: Looking South

Part III Explaining the End of the Cold War

Part IV Disciplined Knowledge and Alternative Visions

Introduction

The Limits of Vindicationist Scholarship

Allen Hunter

The end of the Cold War should have been the occasion for sustained critical inquiry into its significance. For nearly half a century the confrontation between the United States and the Soviet Union dominated world politics and gave a geopolitical focus to the broader conflict between capitalism and communism. It absorbed major portions of the budgets of both superpowers. It set priorities in science and technology. And, especially because of the threat of nuclear annihilation, it cast a shadow across politics and everyday life. The bipolar conflict so thoroughly shaped U.S. political culture and scholarship that there was little critical thought about its scope, origins, and consequences. The end of the Cold War, a historic moment itself resonant with multiple meanings, thus invited imaginative and open-ended historical and political analysis and numerous major questions: Who won? Who lost? What was won? At what cost for whom was victory attained? Could the Cold War have ended sooner? How? Under what circumstances and whose auspices? Could the United States have pursued a less costly arms race? How was the Cold War influenced by, and how in turn did it contribute to, the transformations of the global economy under way since the early 1970s? What are the lasting influences of the Cold War? The questions could be extended to include many domestic features of the United States and other countries.

Unfortunately, narrow intellectual horizons formed during the Cold War have constrained analyses since its end, and too little intellectual inquiry has taken place. The dominant response assumes that since the United States won, critical research and reflection are unnecessary. It is understandable, if regrettable, that in the midst of the Cold War it was difficult to secure standpoints outside its paradigm of neatly aligned binary oppositions: United States/Soviet Union, West/East, capitalism/communism, freedom/tyranny, good/evil. Important features of domestic and international politics since World War II were thereby understood within a framework in which the East-West confrontation was not only all-encompassing but also heavily laden with a moralistic politics. To understand why we have not moved further away from those confining assumptions, it is useful to consider how the Cold War has been approached in the mainstream political culture.

Vindicationism

In the fall of 1989, particularly once the Berlin Wall had been joyously smashed apart, many U.S. scholars, journalists, and politicians began to articulate an interpretation of the Cold War which portrayed the U.S. victory as vindicating earlier U.S. foreign policy. It is incontrovertible that the United States emerged the victor, but viewing victory as vindication claims more than mere triumph. Out of a narrative framed by an "us" versus "them" dichotomy, the "vindicationist" frame, as I call it, shapes an integrated reading of the entire Cold War era, not just its denouement.[1] Briefly: The United States prevailed because it was right; the Soviet Union lost because it was wrong and inefficient. As aggressor, the Soviet Union bears responsibility for initiating and perpetuating the Cold War, a war that could have been avoided only if the United States had evaded its moral obligation to defend freedom. The United States, however, did accept that obligation, responded appropriately to the Soviet threat, maintained vigilance against that hostile and dangerous enemy, and ultimately prevailed. The United States bears responsibility neither for initiating the Cold War nor for perpetuating the Cold War system. It had no reasonable alternative to participation in the struggle. Moreover, in the vindicationist interpretation the end of the Cold War demonstrates the superiority of the American political and economic system, not only because we won but because our former enemies now embrace our economic and political values. The world is better off because the United States met the challenge.

This vindicationist interpretation of Cold War history is the official national history. As President George Bush put it in his January 1990 State of the Union address, "For more than 40 years, America and its allies held communism in check and ensured that democracy would continue to exist."[2] In December 1992 Bush even more expansively proclaimed, "The Soviet Union did not simply lose the Cold War. The Western democracies won it. I say this not to gloat but to make a key point. The qualities that enabled us to triumph in that struggle—faith, strength, unity, and above all, American leadership are those we must call upon now to win the peace."[3]

I use the term "vindicationism" to denote this narrative of political, economic, moral, military, and foreign policy victory. It is the continuation of what diplomatic historians during the Cold War considered the orthodox or traditional account, which it develops and encompasses. The orthodox position held that U.S. foreign policy after World War II was a defensive response to the Soviet threat. Critics of orthodoxy, known as revisionists because they sought to revise that account, focused on the domestic sources of U.S. involvement.[4] The orthodox account of the origins of the Cold War was defined soon after it began, by diplomats and elite foreign policymakers turned authors such as Herbert Feis and Louis J. Halle, who, of course, supported U.S. foreign policy.[5] In historian Richard Melanson's succinct summary: "The orthodox account of the origins of the Cold War rested on three chief contentions: (1) that Soviet ambition and intransigence had by 1945 triggered the Cold War; (2) that the American reaction, though perhaps belated, was 'the essential response of free men to communist aggression'; and (3) that the United States committed no major avoidable foreign policy mistakes in meeting the Soviet challenge."[6]

Vindicationism presents itself both as a reprise of and a final conclusion to the debate about who was responsible for the Cold War, both a perspective on history and a commentary on historiography. It holds, first, that victory vindicates the U.S. role in the Cold War and, second, that scholars and politicians whose writings and actions supported the United States in the Cold War were right and the revisionists wrong. Arthur Schlesinger Jr., one of the original orthodox scholars, has been a leading critic of revisionism both during and after the Cold War.[7] Vindicationist authors—including William Hyland, Jeane J. Kirkpatrick, John Lewis Gaddis, and R. C. Raack—may seem a diverse lot, but they share a basic view about responsibility for the Cold War, even if they differ over particular interpretations and policies.[8]

The vindicationist narrative is, of course, not entirely homogeneous. Its several versions involve slightly different players and different arguments for why "we" won, what the Cold War was, and what it was about. "We" refers, alternatively, to Republicans, conservatives, the United States, the West, defenders of freedom and democracy, proponents of capitalism; "they," variously, to Stalin, the USSR, the Eastern bloc, purveyors of totalitarianism, communists. Different sets of players created different (if obviously related) versions of the Cold War with different issues at the center, different chronologies, and different sources of "our" victory. Commentators credited different individuals, groups, or forces with the victory. Some credited Republicans, conservatives, or Reagan in particular;[9] others pointed to a bipartisan commitment to containment or to NATO.[10] Still others cited broader political and economic forces. For conservative political scientist and activist Jeane Kirkpatrick it was democratic capitalism. For *New York Times* writer Thomas Friedman the end of the Cold War "derived from a single fact: the triumph of capitalism over Communism."[11] For *New York Times* columnist A. M. Rosenthal the Cold War was a conflict not between "armed camps or even economic systems but between slavery and freedom."[12]

A number of vindicationism's claims appear obvious, commonsensical, or compelling, at least at first glance. Given that the end of the Cold War followed the tremendous 1980s arms buildup in the United States, it seems reasonable to conclude that the nuclear arms race spent the Soviets into the ground. The nuclear arms race (as the crucial element of the geostrategic conflict at the core of the Cold War) kept the peace by making hot war too horrific and thus creating the time and space necessary for other forces to erode Soviet aggressive intentions and capacities. Moreover, since the Cold War ended when Soviet policy decisively changed while U.S. policy remained broadly consistent, it is intuitively reasonable to assume that the Soviet Union's foreign policy had sustained the Cold War. Indeed, containment theory—first articulated in 1947 by George Kennan—appears to have been proved right: if the United States sustained a foreign policy that could stop or contain Soviet aggression long enough, then the expansionary tendencies fed by communist ideology would wane, and the Cold War could subside. And the Cold War did end when Mikhail Gorbachev instituted changes in those aspects of the Soviet regime which were viewed as most threatening to the United States. Internationally, he retreated from maintaining an empire and politico-military control over Eastern Europe: he withdrew troops from Afghanistan, and he made it clear that the Soviet Union would not use force to maintain friendly regimes in Eastern Europe. Domestically, he turned away from rigid authoritarianism and a command economy: he instituted *glasnost* and *perestroika*, which signaled the liberalization of Soviet economic and political systems. Today the Soviet Union no longer exists, and the new sovereignties formally embrace electoral democracy and capitalism. Thus U.S. political and military strategy enabled not only a political and economic victory but a moral one as well.

Not all U.S. political commentary or scholarship about the Cold War fits within this vindicationist frame, but it has been the dominant American interpretation since 1989, even influencing critical interpretations by sustaining the position critics argue against.[13] Its influence reflects the fact that it was constructed not primarily in the academy but through networks linking some academics, policymakers and analysts, political commentators, and members of elite economic and political circles. Scholars who became part of these elite networks generally have come to view their own research and writing as valuable to existing policymakers, and this view in turn has encouraged them—at times perhaps unconsciously—to conform their work to specific and narrow policy questions. This approach has been reinforced through formal and informal networks that provide them with access to policy circles and thus an opportunity to become part of the conventional wisdom. As a result, the vindicationist scholars have been disproportionately likely to experience the rewards of foundation grants, publication or republication of their articles in policy journals, and access to the media. Those scholars who move between the worlds of scholarship, policymaking and analysis, and political commentary become the main bearers of scholarship into the public domain. Participation in these networks becomes intellectually formative, a consequence being that its members tend to ask questions useful to those in power.[14]

Although critics of U.S. foreign policy have had a considerable impact in the historical profession, and some of their particular findings have become the focus of public debate, they have not contributed much to debates in elite circles over fundamental interpretations of U.S. foreign policy. It is largely those authors with conventional views, such as John Lewis Gaddis and Arthur Schlesinger Jr., rather than critics such as Walter LaFeber or Richard J. Barnet, whose articles will appear in *Foreign Affairs,* who are called upon to contribute to elite policy discussions, and who are considered to produce opinions and knowledge relevant to pundits, even though many foreign policy critics are themselves articulate as well as prolific authors.[15] Critics have been less often silenced than marginalized and labeled as irrelevant to pressing policy questions. Consequently, their views are seldom the basis for far-reaching debates about future policy choices; they receive less foundation support, and their views are rarely elicited by the media. Uncomfortable facts about U.S. policies or U.S.-supported regimes are occasionally reported in the mainstream press and acknowledged in vindicationist discourse, but such facts are generally treated as exceptional, not characteristic of U.S. foreign policy. A mid-1980s review in the *New York Times Book Review* is paradigmatic of the ideological assumptions that marginalize dissident voices. Alan Tonelson (at the time an associate editor of the liberal journal *Foreign Policy*) criticized Noam Chomsky's *Turning the Tide: U.S. Intervention in Central America and the Struggle for Peace*, for "debating points that are factually valid, but useless as guides to American policy."[16] His assumption—that criticism of U.S. policy is relevant only to the extent that it helps politicians decide how they should pursue the national interest—narrows the political or intellectual space available for approaches that do not assume the perspective of existing American interests. As a result those discussions of the Cold War which are most integrative and broad are marginal, whereas those which are more narrow and tightly focused on issues relevant to immediate policy questions are consolidated via repetition and resonance with the immediate concerns of politicians and pundits.[17]

Reasonable as the vindicationist account seems in some respects, there are both methodological and substantive problems with its arguments. Methodologically, it characteristically offers findings as conclusions that ought to be stated as hypotheses or, at best, interpretations. Such claims include the stabilizing role of nuclear weapons—a claim that Charles Kegley and Shannon Blanton critically dissect in their essay in this book—and the centrality of Stalin's commitment to expansion as the essential cause of the Cold War.[18] Indeed, a major problem with vindicationism is its readiness to take as conclusive those views that fit its presuppositions, and its manifest lack of interest in questions that challenge its narrow framework.

The substantive errors that result from these limited assumptions and biases remain largely unanswered in popular discourse, even though the collapse of the Soviet Union means there is less need on the part of political elites to maintain ideological unity on Cold War issues. First among these substantive errors is the notion that the USSR was always primarily responsible for initiating and perpetuating the Cold War, and the U.S. always reacting to manifest threats.[19] It is as if narratives and causal questions about who did what first could not be separated from moral and ideological questions, making any suggestion of U.S. initiative or Soviet nonaggression a sign of disloyalty.[20]

Another widespread vindicationist approach, fitting all U.S. foreign policy and the actions of smaller states and national liberation movements aspiring to statehood into the bipolar Cold War frame, originally grew out of anticommunism. Anticommunism routinely condensed all forms of dissent from "our way of life" into a powerfully unified "other." The belief that bipolarity defined the Cold War still contributes to blurring important distinctions between the nuclear arms race, the larger East-West politico-military conflict, and political economic dimensions of that conflict. Foregrounding the nuclear arms race suggests a much greater degree of equivalence between the two superpowers than does consideration of military forces and political economic power overall; it obscures the larger imbalance in strength and capacity of the Soviet Union and the United States.[21] Autonomous United States interests or nationalist interests in other parts of the world fade from view, and the behavior of all states and of dissenters within states is constructed as either pro- or anti-American, pro- or anti-Soviet. Nor does vindicationism invite questions about social and political forces that escaped containment or definition within this bipolar frame. As Cary Fraser argues in this volume, the lack of attention to these other dynamics means that crucial post–World War II developments such as decolonization (as in South Asia and much of Africa), revolution (as in China and Cuba), nationalism (as in Vietnam) were accorded less historical autonomy than some analysts feel they deserve.[22] Thus, for example, nationalist anticolonial revolutionary movements, as in Vietnam or Angola, were viewed as part of the East-West, communism-capitalism struggle; viewing them in that manner helped legitimate policies which, in turn, generally forced proponents of such movements to choose between those two sides. Belief in bipolarity also meant that forces such as nationalism, which came to the fore in the process of, and contributed to, the dissolution of the Soviet empire, received inadequate scholarly or policy attention.

By exaggerating the extent to which the superpower geopolitical conflict defined the Cold War and the Cold War constituted the whole post–World War II international order, the vindicationist frame cuts the Cold War off from history and marginalizes attention to continuities in U.S. foreign policy not part of a narrowly defined Cold War. Failure to attend to long-term trends in the U.S. pursuit of political and economic objectives, in turn, sustains the image of the Cold War as a fixed bipolar system. This imagery encourages overlooking those ways in which the end of the Cold War was not a decisive watershed for all global developments, a point made by Ronen Palan's essay in this volume.[23]

Vindicationism assumes that the USSR, not the United States, was responsible for driving the arms race; that options for lessening the danger of war always lay with the Soviet Union; that its systematic intransigence, not similar patterns on the part of the United States, prolonged the Cold War.[24] Presenting the arms race in this way contributes to the view that deterrence worked, that nuclear weapons were crucial in keeping the peace, and that nothing the United States could have done would have ended the Cold War earlier—or at least that the dangers of appeasement far outweighed any potential benefits. Placing responsibility for perpetuating the arms race on the other side, of course, helped legitimate military spending.

It also enables politicians and political commentators to apply lessons from the Cold War through the use of historical analogies. In the vindicationist view Munich is the appropriate analogy, with its lesson that the U.S. should never be militarily unprepared or psychologically or politically unwilling to meet force with force (the arms buildup before World War I is not invoked as a counter-example).[25] Vindicationists ignore evidence that the arms race did little to preserve the peace between the superpowers but, rather, led to continued nuclear proliferation, increased the potential for terrorists to gain access to weapons-grade nuclear materials, and created vast amounts of nuclear waste that remains difficult to dispose of.

Above all, vindicationism has failed to explore variations in political systems within the Eastern and Western blocs and has rejected without examination alternatives to those blocs. The vindicationist frame downplays the extent to which both superpowers suppressed such alternatives domestically, within their spheres of interest, and globally.[26] Vindicationists have been less likely than others to entertain the hypothesis that Soviet and Eastern European dissidents were attracted not just to the United States but to European social democratic welfare states.[27] And, being inattentive to various possible alternatives to communism, they assume that the best and only alternative for the former Soviet Union and the rest of the world is to adopt American models of free market capitalism and a two-party electoral system as rapidly as possible; there is no third way.[28]

Revisionism

In the 1960s a body of revisionist scholarship sharply criticized the orthodox position, stressing that dynamics within the United States—not just or primarily an external military threat—set the terms of U.S. foreign policy both before and during the Cold War. Although some of this work presented a mirror image of orthodoxy by portraying the Soviet Union as the innocent party, merely responding to threats from the United States and its allies, that was not a main feature of revisionism. In fact, one of the best and most widely read revisionist texts, Walter LaFeber's *America, Russia, and the Cold War*, argues that there were domestic roots to the foreign policies of both countries.[29] Revisionism is more open to the criticism of having been inattentive to the realist view that the nature of the interstate system, more than domestic imperatives, determines foreign policies of nation-states.[30] But the vindicationist frame makes it difficult to understand Cold War revisionist scholarship correctly. Three problems with vindicationist dismissals of revisionism stand out: (a) assuming that revisionism is only about blaming the United States and defending the Soviet Union (b) missing revisionism's call for critical, independent inquiry; and (c) failing to acknowledge the revisionist identification of continuities in U.S. foreign policy.

Vindicationists argue as though anything that damns the USSR refutes revisionism. But in fact the revisionist critique of orthodoxy grew not out of a defense of the Soviet Union but out of analyses of the domestic sources of a U.S. foreign policy that had promoted the open-door policy and expansion since the late nineteenth century. For instance, new evidence confirming yet again the horrors of Stalin and Stalinism—based on autobiographies and memoirs of former Soviet officials as well as new archival findings—is presented (prematurely at best) as incontestable evidence against revisionist claims that Stalin was responding to projections of U.S. economic and political power.[31] The vindicationist perspective consistently downplays the greater structural power of the United States in the world in order to present the Soviet Union as the Cold War's prime mover. By focusing only on specific political actions rather than larger strategic anxieties, and by suggesting that the U.S. vision of world order was not only self-interested but broadly beneficial, vindicationists can acknowledge that the United States pursued a global open-door policy after World War II without reckoning with the significance of that policy for the origins of the Cold War.[32] The vindicationist focus on Soviet actions advances the attitude that to investigate U.S. actions other than as responses to the USSR is to minimize the Soviet threat. The United States, seeking open doors for economic ventures and believing that its own economy in particular and the world economy as a whole would best be served by free trade and investment in an open capitalist world economy, would have found Soviet control over its closed Eastern European bloc a threat, whether or not it took an expansionist stance toward Western Europe. Yet as Carolyn Eisenberg, Mary Kaldor, and Harriet Friedmann all show in their essays in this volume, a measured and balanced analysis of relevant political and economic forces in constructing and sustaining the Cold War need not rest on apologetics for Stalin or the Soviet Union.

These misreadings of revisionism follow as much from the political standpoint of vindicationism as from its historical findings. Its political standpoint is aligned with the U.S. foreign policy establishment. During the Cold War the focus on the Soviet threat within a bipolar system meshed with anticommunism to lead many defenders of the United States to attack its critics for favoring the Soviet Union. They missed the extent to which many criticisms of the United States sought to escape the binary oppositions that the Cold War enforced. Whereas revisionists—especially William Appleman Williams, as Paul Buhle explains in his essay in this volume—analyzed U.S. history in their search for alternative futures, vindication-ist commentators tended to view their efforts as evidence that they were soft on communism.[33] Other commentators critical of the Cold War as a system but with impeccable anticommunist credentials were also misinterpreted—as Jeffrey Isaac argues here in his essay on Hannah Arendt. Although some revisionists—and some antiwar activists who drew on revisionist scholarship—were uncritical of U.S. enemies (primarily Vietnamese communists, China, and the Soviet Union), revisionism was always more animated by a search for alternatives *within* America than for alternatives *to* America. Recently, that critical spirit has led scholars such as Thomas McCormick to shift from a focus on the internal sources of U.S. for-eign policy to a focus on the way those forces in the U.S. economy contribute to the construction of a world system, and Bruce Cumings to engage in a thorough study of the domestic sources of the Korean war, itself set in a comprehensive con-text.[34]

Finally, as part of their general lack of interest in the domestic sources of U.S. foreign policy, vindicationists have not confronted revisionist accounts of the Cold War as part of long-term patterns of U.S. foreign policy. Revisionism's ur-text, William Appleman William's *The Tragedy of American Diplomacy* (1959), was only partly about the Cold War; it was offered less as an explanation of U.S. Cold War diplomacy than as a sweeping historical analysis of the sources of U.S. expansion. The vindicationist claim that the end of the Cold War eroded any legitimacy for revisionism is answered by Walter LaFeber in his contribution in this volume. Sim-ilarly, Ronen Palan's essay—based in the subfield of International Relations the-ory known as International Political Economy, not revisionist diplomatic his-tory—highlights continuities of U.S. economic power during and after the Cold War.

Both the vindicationist emphasis on Soviet aggression and the early revisionist focus on inexorable U.S. expansionary tendencies overlook the power and histor-ical agency of other actors, whether other nation-states or national or transna-tional social movements, which have affected foreign policy. Essays in this collec-tion by Cary Fraser, Brenda Gayle Plummer, and Ian Roxborough explore and demonstrate the power of analytic frames that escape both bipolarity and a singu-lar emphasis on the U.S. as an imperial power. By sustaining a limited debate that most revisionists have abandoned, vindicationists narrow the range of questions considered worth studying.

Moreover, the vindicationists have erroneously assumed that the end of the Cold War ipso facto undermines revisionist claims. True, the Cold War ended when the Soviet Union gave up its (purported) dreams of expansion, ceased controlling Eastern Europe, entered into serious arms control negotiations with the United States, and softened its authoritarian rule at home. Clearly the West won. But systemic triumph does not necessarily mean, as vindicationism assumes, that the victorious side deserves credit for all the steps that led from nuclear stalemate to the collapse of one of the parties. Indeed, it takes nothing from the victory of capitalism over communism to consider the possibility that it was Soviet rather than U.S. initiatives that broke out of the confines of nuclear deterrence.[35] None of these differing interpretations are incompatible with the revisionist emphasis on the causal force of dynamics within the United States.

The essays in this volume exemplify the critical spirit of revisionism without being bound by its substantive concerns. They invite a rethinking of what the Cold War was, how fully it defined the decades after World War II, what forces sustained it and led to its demise. The essays do not share a single analytic or political position; they derive from different disciplines and contrasting approaches within disciplines. Some work within the coordinates of U.S. diplomatic history (LaFeber, Lairson, Eisenberg), others in the nexus between social or intellectual history and foreign policy (Bernstein, Plummer, Isaac, Buhle). Some consider the Cold War as an aspect of the interstate system (Fraser, Kaldor); others approach their topic from the field of international political economy (Roxborough, Friedmann, Palan) or of strategic studies (Cox, Kegley and Blanton). They do not propose a single alternative perspective but offer interpretations of a range of core Cold War themes. In doing so they expand the range of topics and approaches relevant to evaluating the significance of the Cold War.

Creating the Cold War

The essays in Part I provide three perspectives on the forces that created and sustained the Cold War. Walter LaFeber focuses on continuities in the domestic dynamics of U.S. foreign policy; Carolyn Eisenberg analyzes the role the division of Germany played in the U.S.-Soviet conflict; and Thomas Lairson dissects the relationship between bipolarity and globalism in U.S. Cold War foreign policy. They illustrate several of the themes just discussed: that the U.S. foreign policy did not simply respond to external threats, that pursuing its own goals, not just countering Soviet initiatives, led to its global strategy.

It is fitting that LaFeber's essay, which places the U.S. contribution to the Cold War in the context of a century of U.S. imperial expansion and military action, opens the volume. While setting his own scholarly agenda, he has maintained a fidelity to the core historiographical and ethical concerns that animated William Appleman Williams, in whose memory the conference from which these papers derive was convened. Those concerns include the ideological and economic dynamics and political and cultural consequences of empire in American history. LaFeber adds new insights to twin themes in Williams's work: the continuity of the expansionist dynamic in U.S. history, and the attendant aggrandizement of presidential power.

Against those who conclude that the U.S. victory in the Cold War reveals the intellectual poverty of revisionism, LaFeber argues that U.S. expansion in pursuit of its economic interests remains a powerful explanation for U.S. foreign policy before, during, and after the Cold War.[36] Thus the end of the Cold War does not constitute a major fault line in redefining U.S. global purpose. Although he does not deny the repressiveness of the Soviet regime, LaFeber does not locate the main source of U.S. foreign relations after World War II in American response to Soviet behavior. He is an "internalist" who believes that U.S. policy was and is primarily driven by domestic forces that predated and now postdate any Soviet threat.[37] If there had been no Soviet Union or Cold War, the United States and Russia would still have had expansionist, imperial foreign policies, although what exact course each would have taken is obviously unknowable.[38] With the Cold War and the USSR gone, the U.S. global presence is changing, not disappearing.[39]

LaFeber argues that since McKinley's presidency a century ago, expansionism has contributed to the aggrandizement of the federal government, in particular the executive branch and the presidency. He confronts us with the irony that as suffrage and electoral democracy were legally extended to women early in the century and practically enabled for blacks with the Voting Rights Act of 1965, the shift in control over the "ultimate question of using military force" from Congress to the president entailed a reduction of democratic control over the crucial life-and-death question of military engagement. The historic contribution of foreign policy in building the American state has been neglected. The same conservative politicians who attack liberals as statists for building the welfare state have been equally responsible for creating the warfare state by supporting the power and prominence of the executive branch of government via support for military spending and domestic surveillance operations. But conservatives have not been alone in neglecting the role of foreign policy in state-building. Most scholars who have analyzed the growth of the U.S. state, liberal and radical as well as conservative, have focused primarily on domestic sources. LaFeber thus contributes to theorizing the origins of the national security state. Whereas Richard J. Barnet and others locate the growth of the national security state in the Cold War era itself, LeFeber traces its origins back to the turn of the century and explains its growth in terms of economic expansion, in contrast to Barnet and others who have stressed the state-centered interests and motivations of national security managers.[40]

Carolyn Eisenberg is critical of the conventional wisdom about the role the U.S. played in constructing the Cold War in Central Europe, its *locus classicus*. She focuses on the middle-to late 1940s to explain why the United States bears more responsibility than the Soviet Union for the division of Germany—an event militarily, economically, politically, and ideologically important in the early Cold War, yet one that has received little scholarly attention.[41] Eisenberg finds that its division was an American decision, supported by the British and opposed by the Soviets. At the end of World War II, U.S. policymakers with roots in New Deal liberalism sought dramatic reforms to denazify the polity, break the power of economic cartels, strengthen labor, and push through land reform; the more conservative officials, who won the debate, held that the general revival of European capitalist economies should take precedence. They sought reforms sufficient to break the power of those Nazi economic institutions that inhibited a free market but not so thorough as to "reduce the incentives of the German capitalist class." They believed that the level of reparations the Soviets demanded would weaken Germany, whereas economic integration of the three Western zones in a divided Germany would give the United States the power to shape a growing, open economy.[42]

Once in place, the division of Germany led to the consolidation of the geostrategic dimension of the Cold War, and many "offensive Soviet behaviors" in Western Europe were direct responses to Soviet exclusion from West Germany. Eisenberg shows in a concrete historic circumstance how the broad imperatives of U.S. policy led to conflict with the Soviet Union and contributed to constructing the terms of bipolarity. Support for her analysis comes from the fact that a similar shift took place in U.S. policy toward reform in Japan: an emphasis on democratization shifted to an emphasis on sustaining the economic growth the United States sought for Japan in Asia. The United States was intent on building strong economies in its recently defeated enemies, both Japan and Germany, even if that entailed forsaking thorough reforms of those societies.[43]

According to Thomas Lairson, post–World War II U.S. foreign policy was global in scope and not defined by participation in bipolar conflict. He argues this case by clarifying the significance of "credibility" for U.S. policy. For U.S. officials "credibility" was "an image of reliability" indicating that the United States had the political will to support its commitments as well as the military might to confront enemies and provide protection for (and some degree of control over) its allies.

Lairson argues that "credibility" derived from U.S. pursuit of global hegemony, not the bipolar conflict with the Soviet Union. Those with whom he takes issue, in particular John Lewis Gaddis, have argued that credibility helped erode the distinction between America's vital interest—containing its military equal, the Soviet Union—and its secondary interests. The erosion of that distinction in turn led the United States to overextend its global commitments because, with the distinction between primary and secondary concerns blurred, credibility became a global concern. Lairson responds that bipolarity is conceptually unable to deal with the significantly greater economic, political, and military power of the American-led Western bloc. Shifting the analytic frame from bipolarity to a structural analysis of the United States as a hegemonic power makes it possible to "specify the lines of causation between the structure of the international system and the perceptions, calculations, and actions of national leaders." Understood in this way, credibility can be shown to have become "the 'glue' holding the system together." Shifting from the conventional focus on bipolarity to dynamics internal to the U.S. political economy offers a better explanation for the generally acknowledged importance of "credibility" in strategic thought.

Decentering the Cold War

Moving even further from the vindicationist frame, the essays in Part II argue that the Cold War was not uniquely defined by the confrontation between the United States and the Soviet Union, or postwar history completely defined by the Cold War itself. For Ian Roxborough, phases of capitalist development were influenced but not determined by the Cold War; for Brenda Gayle Plummer, Cold War politics intersected with U.S. racial politics in a mutually determining fashion; Cary Fraser even more radically disrupts conventional views by arguing that bipolarity and hegemony are both analytic constructs that exaggerate the role of major powers in post-1945 international relations.

For Fraser even the broadest definitions of the Cold War do not encompass all the relevant actors. His line of inquiry challenges many assumptions of International Relations theory, especially as constructed in the context of the Cold War.[44] In particular, his essay lends historical substance to critiques of realism.[45] He argues that International Relations theory's stress on bipolarity, nations as unitary actors, and system stability all constrain explanations of the origins, course, and demise of the Cold War. The bipolar focus diminishes the importance of European states in creating the Cold War system. Bipolarity and the assumption of stability have blinded much International Relations theory to the importance of Third World states since the end of World War II, both as sources of change in the international order and as powers exploiting the bipolar conflict for their own ends. The stress on stability and the assumption that nations are unitary actors make it harder to factor in the importance of political, cultural, and economic dynamics within East European civil societies in precipitating the crisis of the bipolar order. Significantly, for Fraser it also follows that nuclear weapons were less able to control events than most International Relations theorists anticipated.

Roxborough's essay complements Fraser's in arguing that the Cold War's influence on Latin America is best understood in terms of domestic developments there as well as U.S. pressure. Most critics of U.S. foreign policy focus on military intervention and show that the history of U.S. intervention long preceded the threat of communism. Most defenders of U.S. policy toward Latin America justify it by reference to the threat of Soviet-instigated communist subversion. In contrast, Roxborough looks at the interactions between domestic politics in Latin America and the U.S. role in shaping but not determining Latin American political economy. He agrees with other commentators that between the end of World War II and the late 1940s a shift in U.S. policy toward Latin America took place as the United States sought to reframe political conflict from democracy versus dictatorship to capitalism versus communism.[46] That shift shaped Latin American postwar economic strategies and political compromises by emphasizing economic growth and its requisites. Building on industrial development during World War II, Latin American countries adopted an economic growth strategy of import substitution industrialization (ISI): that is, industrializing by domestically manufacturing products that had been imported. At first the ISI strategy involved a class compromise in which organized labor and the left, including Communist Parties, collaborated with the national bourgeoisies with whom they shared a "common interest in industrialization." The outcome of U.S. involvement was not the destruction but the rightward reconstruction of the political coalitions that supported ISI. Shared hostility toward communism helped traditional Latin American elites and the United States forge anticommunist hemispheric security pacts, split radical unions, and strengthen unions' more conservative elements.[47]

These internal and external influences led to a shift toward conservatism in Latin America but not an embrace of the hard right. Labor was weakened but not completely suppressed. Ironically, the post–Cold War period, notwithstanding the pervasive rhetoric of democratization, is proving less friendly to labor than when it was contained under the sign of anticommunism. The triumph of the neoliberal economic model coinciding with the end of the Cold War and associated with the rhetoric of constitutional democracy has not been favorable to labor. In the 1940s foreign and elite domestic forces combined within Cold War imperatives to split unions so that labor could be incorporated as a "responsible" junior partner in the ISI growth strategy; in the 1990s foreign and elite domestic forces are combining to shut labor out as a political force.

Plummer sees Fidel Castro's stay in Harlem in September 1960—when he visited New York to address the UN—as a dramatic moment that brings together "several strands of Cold War history." By focusing on connections between foreign policy and racial dynamics within the United States, she provides another example of the ways in which social forces other than bipolarity contributed to the Cold War system. Arguing that Castro's visit to Harlem "joined foreign and domestic policy considerations [and] helped keep U.S. race relations on the international docket," Plummer enriches our understanding of the Cuban Revolution as a "watershed" in Cold War history and of the influence of transnational racial dynamics on U.S. foreign policy and international relations more generally. Both U.S. policy elites and black civil rights leaders consciously linked the Cuban Revolution to U.S. racial politics; U.S. policymakers found that the Cuban Revolution focused their attention on decolonization and newly independent states in Africa and Latin America. It also restimulated interest in foreign affairs on the part of leading African Americans. Castro's presence in Harlem linked decolonization abroad to racism in the United States, a linkage that Cubans consciously sought. The linkage was not lost on American blacks or political elites, for the Cuban Revolution took place at a crucial moment in race relations in the U.S.: the civil rights movement had registered some successes, but segregation was still a major factor in the diplomatic corps, Congress, and many northern cities.

Theories that situated blacks as an internal colony in the United States aligned civil rights with antiimperialist struggles in the Third World, just as Castro, even as his ties to the USSR were growing, aligned Cuba with the Afro-Asian nonaligned bloc. Although not all black Americans were sympathetic to the Cuban Revolution, many welcomed Castro's presence in Harlem as he tacitly "colluded with black Americans" to focus political attention on the oppression of people of color in the United States and elsewhere. Plummer's essay complements Fraser's on the role smaller powers can play in defining the international political terrain and highlights the role of domestic politics in constructing the interactions between bipolarity and U.S. hegemonic practices. In doing so it contributes to two literatures: one that analyzes the mutual influences of Cold War foreign policy and the politics of civil rights,[48] and one that analyzes the role of domestic ethnic and racial influences on foreign policy.

Explaining the End of the Cold War

The essays in Part III stress the inadequacies of Soviet and strategic studies to anticipate or explain the end of the Cold War; providing explanations at variance with conventional wisdom, they show how definitions of the Cold War and explanations of its demise are intimately connected. Michael Cox explores the failure of Western scholarship to predict the Soviet collapse. Charles W. Kegley Jr. and Shannon Lindsey Blanton provide an internal methodological critique of leading conventional explanations for the stability of the bipolar East-West confrontation. Mary Kaldor, Harriet Friedmann, and Ronen Palan expand outward to resituate the Cold War within an international political economy that helped define but was not confined by the structures of the Cold War.

Cox explains why the Soviet crisis was predicted by hardly anyone, especially in the field of Soviet Studies. He adduces several dimensions to the "collective failure" of the discipline. Academic knowledge stresses specialized research, and many academics are discouraged from asking big questions. It is a safer bet to predict the continuity of social systems than their fragility. Individual and collective interests as well as intellectual habits led many specialists to stress Soviet continuity; after all, Cox reminds us, reporting on the Soviet threat provided a livelihood for many Western academics, journalists, and intelligence officers. Soviet strength was exaggerated in part because maintaining support for military spending depended on assessments stressing Soviet strength, not weakness.

In particular, the thesis that totalitarian regimes were stable and unchangeable from within because all bases of internal dissent were suppressed helped legitimate high levels of defense spending and a militant U.S. foreign policy. In the 1980s some scholars of Soviet politics made just the opposite argument: Totalitarianism was brittle and unstable but was being replaced by modest amounts of political pluralism, which was increasingly the source of system stability. The conservative hard-line emphasis on the fragility of the Soviet Union, used to legitimate increasing military budgets as a fiscal weapon to spend the Soviets into the ground, Cox argues, turns out to have been more accurate than the liberal stress on system stability as a rationale for not engaging in an economically motivated arms race.

Just as insights are gained from analyzing the construction of intellectual frameworks in fields like Soviet Studies, so are there benefits from doing internal critiques of those frameworks, as Kegley and Blanton show. Political realists reject criticisms of state-centered strategies as utopian, and hard-line critics of the Soviet Union can reject as naive policy proposals that do not start with the basic assumption that the Soviet Union was a threat. In response, Kegley and Blanton argue that prevalent explanations for the supposed "long peace" are internally flimsy. Through not alone in questioning orthodox views of deterrence, their essay provides a fine-grained internal critique of the logic of several leading explanations for the stability of bipolarity. Given the millions of people killed since World War II in conflicts precipitated or prolonged by Cold War imperatives, they argue that by any reasonable definition the Cold War was not a period of institutionalized stability. Nor are explanations of that purported stability consistent with each one another: Theories grounding "the long peace" in bipolarity are at odds with those finding that the U.S. used its strategic supremacy to maintain the peace.[49] Furthermore, each explanation considered alone is logically faulty, has little or no evidence to support it, or is so abstract that it cannot readily be proved or disproved.

Since more stringent criteria can reasonably be applied in evaluating policies after the fact than in the heat of debate, their essay is less a criticism of policy rationales offered during the Cold War than a criticism of the way they have since been marshaled to bolster support for post–Cold War military strategies. By demystifying conventional explanations of the role of geostrategic conflict, their essay helps clear the ground for explanations of the end of the Cold War not founded on the "myths" they have identified.

The essays by Kaldor, Friedmann, and Palan pursue several explanatory routes. Kaldor and Friedmann identify changes in the political economy of the East-West bloc system as the source of the demise of the Cold War. For Kaldor the distinctive feature of the Cold War was the creation of ideologically and economically integrated blocs through which the United States and the Soviet Union each used threats of the "other" to legitimize itself. As the number of states proliferated after World War II (largely as a consequence of decolonization), Kaldor contends that nation-states were increasingly inadequate for integrating the international political order. She contrasts nation-states and blocs: Territoriality integrates states; ideology integrates blocs. A growing cultural homogeneity among bloc elites tended to override otherwise divisive national identities. In the West, unity was partially based on the shared language of nuclear strategy and macroeconomic management, in the East, on Marxism-Leninism. Through unified political and military command systems, blocs overcame the problems of coordination and collective action that characterize state alliances.

Kaldor finds that analyzing the Cold War as a bloc system helps explain both its persistence and its demise. Whereas most approaches to the international political economy focus on the complementarities and tensions between nation-states and transnational economic flows, Kaldor argues that during the Cold War the bloc system, not the nation-state, was the crucial political institution. Less interested in explaining the origins than the persistence of the Cold War, she argues that it was an "imaginary war" used to fashion blocs in a period when the nation-state was becoming outmoded.[50] By removing some of the impediments to global economic organization posed by nation-states, the bloc system was functional for reproducing Fordist forms of mass production and mass consumption. But blocs proved to be inflexible as political systems. Kaldor finds that the decline of rapid economic growth and the emergence of new, post-Fordist forms of production created strains: They both sped up global economic integration in ways not easily contained within the bloc system and stimulated new forms of decentralization also inhibited by blocs. As they lost their function, blocs lost credibility, and imaginary war scenarios of nuclear deterrence became less compelling.

Friedmann provides a carefully reasoned account of how changing economic transactions between the blocs and within the Eastern bloc brought about resistance to Soviet domination over its bloc "allies," paving the way for *perestroika* and contributing to the end of the Cold War. Like Kaldor, she focuses on the historically specific forms that state socialism and Western capitalism assumed in the bloc system, attending more to the conjunctural economic and political dilemmas that state socialist systems confronted than to what might be termed fundamental, systemic contradictions in socialist regimes.

Friedmann and Kaldor agree that blocs do not replace nation-states but provide overarching political structures that more or less successfully subordinate national interests. Friedmann clarifies why the nation-bloc tension was more rigid and explosive in the East than the West. What she calls Warsaw Pact Socialism was created in the late 1940s to draw East European economies into a Soviet-led bloc as an alternative to the Marshall Plan. The USSR sought to break economic intercourse with Western Europe by creating Soviet-led industrialization in the East but was never able to do so successfully because bloc-wide versus national autarkic strategies were in tension. At first the Soviets imposed autarkic national economic growth. But they also sought to impose a bloc-wide "socialist division of labor" and treated as treasonous governments that sought their own national routes. Latent tension between bloc-wide policies and national autarky impeded central planning, and from 1970 on, that tension was increasingly constitutive of economic and political life in the Eastern bloc. East European countries following national routes to growth sought to strengthen ties with Western Europe, seeking especially loans and new technologies. Even before the 1982 Mexican default that "initiated the capitalist debt crisis," Western banks began to tighten up their loans to Eastern Europe as they worried about the viability of those economies. The economic crises in Eastern Europe that followed the change in Western banking strategies created space for the "popular mobilizations that broke the chain of Party rule in the bloc," as increasing economic linkage with Western Europe eroded the bloc's formal political institutions.

Increased economic ties with the East also led some West European countries to seek eased East-West relations. Thus, Friedmann concludes that the "links across blocs" were "major sources of tension within blocs." Against the conventional wisdom that containment worked, Friedmann's essay suggests that it helped the solidity of the Warsaw bloc, and that more open economic and political relations with the East could have precipitated *perestroika,* or an equivalent, earlier.

Kaldor and Friedmann lead us onto the terrain of international political economy, Ronen Palan sustains that focus, but whereas they explain the Cold War system in terms of political economic dynamics, Palan decenters the Cold War. His work cuts against the tendency of most scholars, especially diplomatic historians and international relations theorists, who assume the central role of the Cold War in structuring the interstate system. He believes that the Cold War was not at the core of the post–World War II international system and that its end will not prove to have been a major watershed in the history of the international order. He argues that U.S. hegemony has been such a central feature of the world order that the restructuring of the U.S. domestic political economy, more than the loss of its external enemy, is propelling the restructuring of the global economy.

Given the role U.S. hegemony played in the past half-century, Palan recognizes the role of states in forging an interstate order but also stresses the roles of international organizations, transnational capital flows, and domestic dynamics in providing cohesion to and tension within the postwar Pax Americana. He identifies three levels in the Pax Americana: the world market, the interstate system, and U.S. military and economic power as the "hegemonic articulation of power that held together the other two levels." The interactions between these levels created "both centripetal and centrifugal tendencies." But he does not believe that the end of the Cold War itself will prove decisive in tilting the balance between these tendencies, because he locates the system's core dynamic in domestic U.S. political conflict. Palan does not believe that trilateralist coordination can dampen centripetal forces because "the more serious challenge to the Pax Americana emanates from the very core, from the American state." Neither of the two main groups in the United States—the protectionist or the unilateral globalist—is likely "to be impressed by the trilateral solution."

Disciplined Knowledge and Alternative Visions

The essays in Part IV demonstrate that the Cold War contributed more significantly to forming knowledge and intellectual life in the second half of this century than is often realized. Michael Bernstein explores its influence on the construction of economics knowledge. It is not particularly controversial that the Cold War stimulated research in fields such as area studies, strategic studies, and the basic sciences.[51] It is more controversial to argue, as Bernstein does, that the Cold War not only contributed funding and legitimacy to particular fields of scholarly endeavor but significantly influenced the very construction of knowledge in many fields.[52] Bernstein, an economic historian versed in economic theory, finds that social networks forged during World War II were important in shaping economics during the Cold War. He is less interested in demonstrating the conservatizing influence of anticommunism on the economics profession—itself an important topic—than in analyzing the influences on economic thought of the development of economics-based methods for controlling large-scale mobilizations in World War II and the Cold War.

Besides showing that new developments in economics such as game theory, input-output analysis, and national income accounting methods owe part of their power and prestige within the profession to their use by government, Bernstein further argues that the military uses of economics "had a decisive impact on the theoretical trajectory of the discipline"; in particular, the construction of game theory and the spread of its influence in economics owe much to the role it played in the Cold War, especially in constructing highly formalized two-person games to simulate the nuclear dimension of strategic conflict. As physicists came to have positions of prominence in the Cold War because of their role in developing nuclear weapons, so did economists and the formal properties of their discipline come to be influential in strategic studies as game theory was developed.

Yet Cold War assumptions were challenged by some scholars and public intellectuals, as Jeffrey Isaac and Paul Buhle make clear in their respective essays on Hannah Arendt and William Appleman Williams, whose influential scholarship flourished during the period.[53] Because of differences in background and intellectual approach, mid-Western diplomatic historian Williams and German emigré philosopher Arendt may seem an unlikely pair with which to conclude this volume. Arendt was the preeminent theorist of totalitarianism and an implacable critic of the Soviet Union; Williams was consistent in his opposition to U.S. expansion and the growth of the American national state. Yet both dissented from the terms of the Cold War itself and located alternatives to its centralized imperial states in local democratic political association.

To better understand the significance of Isaac's argument about Arendt and Buhle's about Williams, it is worth considering the reception of the two scholars' ideas in different political contexts. Because she included Stalinism as well as Nazism in her definition of totalitarianism, Cold War anticommunists saw Arendt as an ally, and many radical critics of U.S. foreign policy tended to shy away from her views. In the early 1950s theories of totalitarianism were politically mobilized in the United States to shift animus from Nazi Germany to Stalinist Soviet Union. Yet partisan political use does not in itself discredit theory. Moreover, it is wrong to think that Arendt framed her theory of totalitarianism in an East-West dichotomy. Drawing on her essays as well as her sustained political theory, Isaac holds that Arendt cannot be categorized simply as an anticommunist critic of Soviet totalitarianism. Rather, resisting simple political categorization, she was "a radical political thinker who rejected the terms of the Cold War."

Arendt saw totalitarianism as a pathology of Western modernity, growing out of imperialism, anti-Semitism, and mass politics, but she did not believe that the democratic and the totalitarian were neatly separated between West and East, as did most Cold War scholarship. She not only opposed McCarthyism but saw it as the leading edge of broader repressive tendencies in U.S. political culture. And though she rejected authoritarian tendencies in Third World national liberation movements and in Marxism, she did not oppose revolution itself. Whereas anticommunist liberals opposed Marxism and revolution, in part through their association with each other, she was supportive of revolutionary impulses and rejected U.S. hostility, in the name of anticommunism, to Third World revolution.

Because of Arendt's focus on the democratic promise of political activism in civil society, East European dissident intellectuals felt an affinity of purpose and temperament with her. By contrast, it is among the ironies of the Cold War that few of these dissidents found intellectual sustenance in the work of William Appleman Williams. Because they were understandably unreceptive to explanations of the Cold War not centered in the brutalities of Stalinism and Soviet domination, few were sympathetic to sustained criticisms of U.S. foreign policy.[54] They perceived explanations rooted in U.S. domestic factors as minimizing not only Soviet responsibilities for the Cold War but Soviet perfidy more generally. Yet analytically and historiographically there is no necessary conflict between Williams's focus on the domestic sources of U.S. foreign policy and opposition to authoritarian state socialism within the Soviet Union or its domination of Eastern Europe. Indeed, his criticisms of empire and defense of local and regional autonomy might have resonated with some of their own concerns before the collapse of the Soviet

Union, and his insights into the market could have helped alert them to the risks of forsaking control over the process of integration into the global economy.

In the concluding essay, historian and biographer Paul Buhle stresses Williams's continuing relevance to scholarship and social criticism after the Cold War. Against liberal and conservative defenders of American Cold War policy who interpret the end of the Cold War as conclusive evidence of the wrongheadedness of revisionist interpretations of diplomatic history, Buhle—like LaFeber—agrees with Williams that U.S. expansion preceded the Cold War, and is likely to continue unless Americans heed Williams's call for an alternative to empire.

Although some of Williams's critics considered him an apologist for the USSR because he focused on the domestic roots of U.S. expansion, his concern was not with excusing Soviet politics but with explaining U.S. history. He took no comfort from the USSR but sought to distance himself from many things done in the United States in the name of anticommunism. In his opposition to the centralized state, for instance, he aligned himself more with conservatives than with liberals (or communists) and like some conservatives, Buhle argues, searched for alternatives to U.S. imperial expansion in communities capable of controlling their own local economies. Enlarging upon Williams, Buhle stresses that control over economic expansion is essential not only for the well-being of human communities but for the preservation of the earth's ecology. Precisely because the vindicationism accompanying the end of the Cold War has tended to marginalize critical views of U.S. economic policies as well as of political and military policies, Buhle would have us read Williams not only for his analysis of expansion but for his historically grounded insights into possible alternatives.

The kinds of critical inquiry that Arendt and Williams called for can take place within and especially against any of the disciplines in which conventional wisdom has found comfort. By addressing audiences other than policy elites and raising questions outside the dominant frame during the height of the Cold War, Arendt and Williams helped clear intellectual space for critical scholars after the Cold War. Both serve as models for the independent and rigorous thinkers needed today.

Notes

1. Scholars trace the term "frame" to Erving Goffman, *Frame Analysis: An Essay on the Organization of Experience* (New York: Harper & Row, 1974). It is especially used today by social movement and communications theorists. A frame "refers to an interpretive schemata [*sic*] that simplifies and condenses the 'world out there' by selectively punctuating and encoding objects, situations, events, experiences and sequences of actions within one's present and past environment" (David A. Snow and

Robert D. Benford, "Master Frames and Cycles of Protest," in *Frontiers of Social Movement Theory*, ed. Aldon D. Morris and Carol McClurg Mueller, [New Haven: Yale University Press, 1992], 137). In themselves frames are neither objectionable nor avoidable, but they are not natural; they are socially constructed in institutionally, culturally, and historically specific contexts that are inseparable from the operative social relations of power. At issue, then, is how frames are constructed. Gaye Tuchman, *Making News: A Study in the Construction of Reality* (New York: Free Press, 1978), analyzes the role that reporters themselves play, in the context of the papers they work for, in constructing the frames they use. Todd Gitlin, *The Whole World Is Watching: Mass Media in the Making and Unmaking of the New Left* (Berkeley: University of California Press, 1980), explains that frames are ideologically constructed in contexts of uneven power, that those contexts need to be explained, and that then we need to ask, "What difference do the frames make for the larger world?" (7). I argue that social networks of journalists, policymakers, and scholars are among the settings in which political and economic elites exercise their power in constructing foreign policy frames.

2. *Historical Documents of 1991* (Washington, D.C.: Congressional Quarterly, 1992), 811.

3. Speech at Texas A&M University, December 15, 1992, *Foreign Policy Bulletin* 3 (January–April, 1993): 48.

4. The historiographical debate about the Cold War has been covered in numerous essays, among them, J. Samuel Walker, "Historians and Cold War Origins: The New Consensus," in *American Foreign Relations: A Historiographical Review*, ed. Gerald K. Haines and J. Samuel Walker (Westport, Conn.: Greenwood Press, 1981); Geir Lundestad, "Moralism, Presentism, Exceptionalism, Provincialism, and Other Extravagances in American Writings on the Early Cold War Years," *Diplomatic History* 13 (Fall 1989): 527–45; Anders Stephanson, "The United States," in *The Origins of the Cold War in Europe* ed. David Reynolds (New Haven, Conn.: Yale University Press, 1994).

5. See, e.g., Herbert Feis, *Churchill, Roosevelt, Stalin: The War They Waged and the Peace They Sought* (Princeton, N.J.: Princeton University Press, 1957); Feis, *Between War and Peace: The Potsdam Conference* (Princeton, N.J.: Princeton University Press, 1960); Feis, *The Atomic Bomb and the End of World War II* (Princeton, N.J.: Princeton University Press, 1966); and Louis J. Halle, *The Cold War as History* (New York: Harper & Row, 1967).

6. Richard A. Melanson, *Writing History and Making Policy: The Cold War, Vietnam, and Revisionism* (Lanham, Md.: University Press of America, 1983), 43.

7. See Arthur Schlesinger Jr., "Origins of the Cold War," *Foreign Affairs* 46 (October 1967): 22–52; and Schlesinger, "Some Lessons from the Cold War," *Diplomatic History* 16 (Winter 1992): 47–53.

8. See William G. Hyland, *The Cold War: Fifty Years of Conflict*, 2d ed. (New York: Times Books, 1991); Jeane J. Kirkpatrick, "Beyond the Cold War," *Foreign Affairs* 69 (Winter 1989–90): 1–16; John Lewis Gaddis, *The United States and the End of the Cold War: Implications, Reconsiderations, Provocations* (New York: Oxford University Press, 1992); R. C. Raack, *Stalin's Drive to the West, 1938–1945: The Origins of the Cold War* (Stanford, Calif.: Stanford University Press, 1995). Gaddis is listed here and considered part of the "vindicationist school" even though he sought to transcend the orthodox-revisionist debate and named his new perspective "post-revisionism." But in the post–Cold War context postrevisionism no longer exists as a separate interpretive strand, and he is clearly closer to current versions of orthodoxy than to revisionism. This position is clear in his latest book, published after this essay was written, *We Now Know: Rethinking Cold War History* (New York: Oxford University Press, 1997). He draws on new archives and documentary evidence made available through the very useful Cold War International History Project based at the Woodrow Wilson International Center for Schol-

ars, Washington, D.C., which Gaddis himself was instrumental in initiating. But he uses them to answer questions that cannot be answered by reference to new facts alone, as he seems to assume. It makes sense that this book, aimed at stating the centrist common sense, is a Council on Foreign Relations book, even if the Council also publishes more heterodox volumes on occasion. See, e.g., *Arming the Future: A Defense Industry for the 21st Century*, ed. Ann Markusen and Sean Costigan (New York: Council on Foreign Relations, forthcoming).

9. Peter Schweizer, *Victory* (New York: Atlantic Monthly Press, 1994), argues that Reagan won the Cold War; Jay Winik, *On the Brink: The Dramatic, Behind-the-Scenes Saga of the Reagan Era and the Men and Women Who Won the Cold War* (New York: Simon & Schuster, 1996) claims that a small set of neoconservative policy advisers in the Reagan administration did it; Adam Meyerson, "The Battle for the History Books: Who Won the Cold War?" *Policy Review* 52 (Spring 1990): 2–3, credits conservatives; Leslie Gelb, "Who Won the Cold War?" *New York Times*, August 20, 1992, Op-Ed, critically reports on a claim at the 1992 Republican Convention that the Republican Party deserves credit. The most extended conservative argument, to my knowledge, is Patrick Glynn, *Closing Pandora's Box: Arms Races, Arms Control, and the History of the Cold War* (New York: New Republic, Basic Books, 1992), which breaks with vindicationism. Glynn is less interested in claiming victory for the United States than in attacking Wilsonianism, appeasement, and arms control as characteristic of most Democrats and too many Republicans, and "a seemingly permanent part of the political landscape in Western democracies" (368).

10. Gelb, "Who Won the Cold War?"; Craig R. Whitney, "NATO, Victim of Success, Searches for a New Strategy," *New York Times*, October 26, 1991.

11. Jeane J. Kirkpatrick, "Exit Communism, Cold War and the Status Quo," *Imprimis* 20 (January 1991): 3; Thomas L. Friedman, "There's a New Era. Then There's the Middle East," *New York Times*, July 28, 1991.

12. A. M. Rosenthal, "Victors in the Cold War," *New York Times*, June 10, 1990.

13. Vindicationism represents the "bias of the center," a term that media critic Jeff Cohen uses to clarify that centrists as well as critics from the left and right have a point of view; the center is not, by virtue of being between other perspectives, any more true or adequate. See Cohen, "The Centrist Ideology of the News Media: Propaganda from the Middle-of-the Road," *Extra!* October–November 1989: 12–14. Two useful overviews of the Cold War since 1989 which initially respond to the orthodox, vindicationist approach are H. W. Brands, *The Devil We Knew: Americans and the Cold War* (New York: Oxford University Press, 1993); and Edward Pessen, *Losing Our Souls: The American Experience in the Cold War* (Chicago: Ivan R. Dee, 1993). One of the purposes of this volume is to break with the orthodox-revisionist debate from the Cold War era without denying the importance of many of the issues that animated it.

14. International Relations theorists have been applying the concept of "epistemic communities" to networks of experts or scientists who share views on particular truths or methods for arriving at knowledge. See, e.g., *International Organization* 46 (Winter 1992), special issue edited by Peter M. Haas. Fruitful as it may be for some purposes, this approach does not address interactions between experts and others with shared beliefs and interests who work together; hence, it misses the ways in which experts' networks are structured by and constitute relations of power. For an approach that explicitly addresses the construction of knowledge frames in social networks within which scholars collaborate with governmental officials in contexts structured by elites, see Charles Thomas O'Connell's analysis of the origins of Soviet Studies as influenced by the Cold War in "Social Structure and Science: Soviet Studies at Harvard" (Ph.D. diss., University of California—Los Angeles, 1990).

15. This is what Jeff Cohen calls the "echo effect," whereby those messages propagated by mainstream elites or well-funded corporate public relations campaigns will reverberate across diverse media outlets. The likelihood that a message gets echoed is a function less of its inherent worth than of its overlap with elite frames or the extent to which the echo effect is consciously created by political or corporate strategists. For instance, John Lewis Gaddis's 1992 address as president of the Society for Historians of American Foreign Relations appeared first as "The Tragedy of Cold War History" in the society's journal *Diplomatic History* 17, no. 1 (1993): 1–16, and then in a slightly different version in *Foreign Affairs* 73, (January–February 1994): 142–54. *Diplomatic History* publishes a politically diverse range of scholarly articles, as illustrated by those collected in *The End of the Cold War: Its Meanings and Implications*, ed. Michael J. Hogan (New York: Cambridge University Press, 1992), which first appeared as two special issues of *Diplomatic History*.

16. Alan Tonelson, "Institutional Structure Blues," *New York Times Book Review*, April 13, 1986, 28.

17. It is instructive in this regard to compare *Foreign Affairs*, the most important and establishment foreign policy journal, published by the elite, centrist Council on Foreign Relations; *Foreign Policy*, a liberal journal; and *World Policy Journal*, a left-liberal publication. Since 1989 *Foreign Affairs* has not really sought to explain why the Cold War ended or shed new light on its historical significance. It publishes articles addressed to sitting elites, especially in the U.S. State and Defense Departments, and has not addressed, for example, the domestic costs of the Cold War. *Foreign Policy* has been more expansive in its historical and analytical reach and has carried articles about the domestic costs of the Cold War as registered, for instance, in threats to civil liberties, constrictions of democracy, and environmental degradation. *World Policy Journal* offers the broadest analyses of the Cold War and has published articles calling for more dramatic cuts in defense spending than current economic and political elites will entertain. Some of its articles contain proposals not only relevant to current policymakers but also of use to groups seeking to redirect foreign policy, even if that reorientation challenges the legitimacy of core elites.

18. Schlesinger, "Some Lessons from the Cold War." asserts that nuclear weapons kept the Cold War cold. Gaddis, "The Tragedy of Cold War History," 4, argues that Soviet archives, revealing new depths to the horror of Stalinism, are forcing us to recognize how hard it is "to separate any aspect of [Soviet history] from the baleful and lingering influence of this remarkable but sinister [Stalin]." Yet Russian historians Vladislav Zubok and Constantine Pleshakov, who do not take a back seat in denouncing Stalin as a tyrant or Soviet leaders generally as butchers, argue that tempting as it may be to blame Stalin totally for the Cold War, the historical evidence is not so simple; see their *Inside the Kremlin's Cold War: From Stalin to Khrushchev* (Cambridge, Mass.: Harvard University Press, 1996). Melvyn P. Leffler "Inside Enemy Archives: The Cold War Reopened," *Foreign Affairs* 75 (July–August, 1996): 120–35, is skeptical of vindicationists' claims that new Soviet and Eastern European archival materials sustain their view of the Soviet Union as singularly responsible for initiating the Cold War.

19. This is the approach taken in, e.g., Hyland, *The Cold War*. With years of service as a senior official on the National Security Council and in the State Department, Hyland was editor of *Foreign Affairs* when he wrote this book.

20. On moralism in U.S. foreign policy historiography, see Lundestad, "Moralism."

21. Thomas McCormick, e.g., views the Cold War as "merely a subplot" of America's post–World War II hegemonic project. See the preface to the second edition of his *America's Half-Century: United States Foreign Policy in the Cold War* (Baltimore, Md.: Johns Hopkins University Press, 1995), VIII–XVIII. Similarly, Richard Falk writes, "It is important to contrast the 'bipolarity' of geopolitics

in the Cold War with the 'unipolarity' of geoeconomics during the same span of years"; see his "Theory, Realism, and World Security," in *World Security: Trends and Challenges at Century's End*, ed. Michael T. Klare and Daniel C. Thomas (New York: St. Martin's Press, 1991), 12.

22. A good historical overview that treats a broad range of historical dynamics without reducing them to functions of the Cold War is T. E. Vadney, *The World since 1945* (New York: Penguin Books, 1987).

23. Vindicationists are not alone in exaggerating the Cold War as a distinct period of history cut off from past and future international relations. See Martin Walker, *The Cold War: A History* (New York: Henry Holt, 1994). In addition, the current interdisciplinary fascination with globalization is seldom grounded in analyses of the Cold War and its contribution to current political economic trajectories. In part this is due to the separation of scholarship about the Cold War from that of the history of capitalism. For an instance of this separation, see Eric Hobsbawm, *The Age of Extremes: A History of the World, 1914–1991* (New York: Pantheon Books, 1994).

24. See, again, Hyland, *The Cold War*.

25. The core of the Munich analogy is "aggression unchecked is aggression unleashed" and will lead to general war, as Yuen Foong Khong puts it in *Analogies at War: Korea, Munich, Dien Bien Phu, and the Vietnam Decisions of 1965* (Princeton, N.J.: Princeton University Press, 1992), 175. For a sustained history critical of U.S. politicians for their internationalism and accommodationism in which the relevance of the Munich analogy is a constant, see Glynn, *Closing Pandora's Box*. The question of Cold War analogies is also addressed in Brands, *The Devil We Knew*, 222, and in John Lewis Gaddis's generally astute "International Relations Theory and the End of the Cold War," *International Security* 17 (Winter 1992–93): 5–58.

26. See, e.g., Fred Inglis, *The Cruel Peace: Everyday Life and the Cold War* (New York: Basic Books, 1991); Mary Fulbrook, *The Divided Nation: A History of Germany, 1918–1990* (New York: Oxford University Press, 1992); Geoffrey Hawthorn, *Plausible Worlds: Possibility and Understanding in History and the Social Sciences* (New York: Cambridge University Press, 1991).

27. See Fred Halliday, "Interpreting the Cold War: Neither Geostrategy nor 'Internalism,'" *Contention* 4 (Fall 1994): 49–66.

28. This is the argument of Francis Fukuyama, "The End of History?" *National Interest*, no. 16 (Summer 1989): 3–18, and Fukuyama, *The End of History and the Last Man* (New York: Free Press, 1992). It is also developed in a more scholarly fashion in Seymour Martin Lipset, "No Third Way: A Comparative Perspective on the Left," in *The Crisis of Leninism and the Decline of the Left: The Revolutions of 1989*, ed. Daniel Chirot (Seattle: University of Washington Press, 1991).

29. Walter LaFeber, *America, Russia, and the Cold War, 1945–1992*, 7th ed. (New York: McGraw-Hill, 1993).

30. Charles Maier develops this point in "Revisionism and the Interpretation of Cold War Origins," *Perspectives in American History* 4 (1970): 313–47.

31. In addition to Gaddis, "The Tragedy of Cold War History," and Hyland, *The Cold War*, see Raack, *Stalin's Drive to the West;* Jacob Heilbrun, *"The Revision Thing,"* New Republic, August 15, 1994, 31–4, 36–9; Wilson D. Miscamble, "The Foreign Policy of the Truman Administration: A Post–Cold War Appraisal," *Presidential Studies Quarterly* 24 (Summer 1994): 479–95; and Douglas J. Macdonald, "Communist Bloc Expansion in the Early Cold War: Challenging Realism, Refuting Revisionism," *International Security* 20 (Winter 1995–96): 152–88. Arguments against this position include Zubok and Pleshakov, *Inside the Kremlin's Cold War;* and a review essay by Melvyn P. Leffler, "Was the Cold War Necessary?" *Diplomatic History* 15, (Spring 1991): 265–75; and Leffler, "Inside Enemy Archives."

32. Schlesinger's "Origins" and "Some Lessons" acknowledge that the United States was

committed to a liberal capitalist international order. Antirevisionist Gideon Rose, in "The New Cold War Debate," *National Interest*, no. 38 (Winter 1994–95): 89–96, also recognizes that the United States not only responded to Stalin but pursued its own internationalist vision. An implicit point of contention between revisionists and their critics is whether that U.S. vision was benign and globally beneficial. If revisionists have at times been silent about those circumstances in which U.S. hegemony benefited other nations (or at least economic and political elites in those countries), it is more the case that defenders of the U.S. vision of global order have ignored the extent to which international economic systems are not structured by apolitical market transactions, and the extent to which that vision entailed extensive structural power to construct and sustain it. They do not address the structural dimension of power in the global system. For a typology and analysis of power in the global system, see Stephen Gill and David Law, *The Global Political Economy: Perspectives, Problems, and Policies* (Baltimore, Md.: Johns Hopkins University Press, 1988).

33. See Peter Novick, *That Noble Dream: The "Objectivity Question" and the American Historical Profession* (New York: Cambridge University Press, 1988); and Bruce Cumings, "'Revising Postrevisionism,' or, The Poverty of Theory in Diplomatic History," *Diplomatic History* 17 (Fall 1993): 539–69.

34. McCormick, *America's Half-Century*; Bruce Cumings, *The Origins of the Korean War: Liberation and the Emergence of Separate Regimes, 1945–1947* (Princeton, N.J.: Princeton University Press, 1981); and Cumings, *The Origins of the Korean War*, vol. 2, *The Roaring of the Cataract, 1947–1950* (Princeton, N.J.: Princeton University Press, 1990).

35. For a compelling argument along these lines see Michael MccGwire, *Perestroika and Soviet National Security* (Washington, D.C.: Brookings Institution, 1991).

36. Not all commentators share this judgment. Peter Collier writes of the work of the historian William Appleman Williams that his "'60s revisionism—especially after the fall of communism—seems only slightly less antique than the whiggery of Thomas Babington Macaulay" (in "Falling for Fidel," *Washington Post Book World*, April 10, 1994).

37. For a similar emphasis on internal dynamics, see Benjamin C. Schwarz, "The Arcana of Empire and the Dilemma of American National Security," *Salmagundi*, nos. 101–2 (Winter–Spring 1994): 182–211. The emphasis on internal economic imperatives is currently complemented by the work of some critical international relations theorists who analyze the discursive formation of foreign policy and contend that Cold War anticommunism focusing on the Soviet Union was due less to unmediated perceptions of a Soviet threat than to an aspect of national identity formation grounded in naming external enemies. See David Campbell, "Global Inscription: How Foreign Policy Constitutes the United States," *Alternatives* 15 (1990): 263–86; and Campbell, *Writing Security: United States Foreign Policy and the Politics of Identity* (Minneapolis: University of Minnesota Press, 1992).

38. I write "exact course" because clearly many features of post–World War II U.S. foreign policy would have been in place without the Cold War, even though their particular configuration would have been different. Decolonization and the North-South tension, the contraction of the British empire, the U.S. stress on an open world economy, the emphasis on productivity and economic growth, and the forging of the international economic institutions of the Bretton Woods system would all have gone forward without a Soviet challenge. See, e.g., Nassau Adams, *Worlds Apart: The North-South Divide and the International System* (London: Zed Books, 1993), on how the international economic institutions were shaped, but not constituted, by Cold War bipolarity.

39. Not all critics of U.S. foreign policy after the Cold War share LaFeber's views about the lengthy history of empire. For instance, in *The Imperial Temptation: The New World Order and Amer-*

ica's Purpose (New York: Council on Foreign Relations Press, 1992), Robert W. Tucker and David C. Hendrickson, while worrying that the United States will opt for an imperial policy that they see foreshadowed in the Gulf War, nevertheless view the U.S. role in the Cold War as among the nation's shining moments.

40. See Richard J. Barnet, *The Roots of War* (1972; New York: Penguin Books, 1973). Others who attribute the growth of the national security state to Cold War foreign policy include William Blum, *Killing Hope: U.S. Military and CIA Interventions since WW II* (Monroe, Maine: Common Courage Press, 1995); and Melvyn P. Leffler, *The Specter of Communism: The United States and the Origins of the Cold War, 1917–1953* (New York: Hill & Wang, 1994). For an argument that domestic influences—including a commitment to private market capitalism and a hostility in the political culture to permanent military mobilization—militated against the creation of a full Cold War garrison state, see Aaron L. Friedberg, "Why Didn't the United States Become a Garrison State?" *International Security* 16 (Spring 1992): 109–42.

41. Neglect of this question continues. For instance, *Daedalus* 123 (Winter 1994), an issue devoted to "Germany in Transition," has numerous essays about Germany and the relationship of the reunified Germany to its past. Yet as if to confirm Eisenberg's point, none of those essays address the origins of the division.

42. Revisionists are not alone in stressing the search for growth-oriented open markets under U.S. hegemony. Charles Maier, "The Politics of Productivity: Foundations of American International Economic Policy after World War II," in his *In Search of Stability: Explorations in Historical Political Economy* (New York: Cambridge University Press, 1987), refines William Appleman Williams's point that the United States projects abroad its vision of the good life at home: "The stress on productivity and economic growth arose out of the very terms in which Americans resolved their own organization of economic power" (123). See as well G. John Ikenberry, "Creating Yesterday's New World Order: Keynesian 'New Thinking' and the Anglo-American Postwar Settlement," in *Ideas and Foreign Policy: Beliefs, Institutions and Political Change*, ed. Judith Goldstein and Robert O. Keohane (Ithaca, N.Y.: Cornell University Press, 1993), 57–86. Neither essay considers bipolarity a significant factor in determining U.S. (or, in the case of Ikenberry, British and U.S.) policy initiatives. Ikenberry does not mention the Soviet Union or the Cold War at all; Maier cogently notes that although the economic rationale for U.S. policies was modified by the geostrategic Cold War conflict, "it also logically continued the politics of productivity. Both were efforts to align universalist aspirations with United States preponderance" (141). Mark Rupert, *Producing Hegemony: The Politics of Mass Production and American Global Power* (New York: Cambridge Univeristy Press, 1995), also argues that after World War II the United States sought hegemonic control over an open world economy within which bipolarity was played out.

43. See John W. Dower, *Japan in War and Peace: Selected Essays* (New York: New Press, 1993); Michael Schaller, "Securing the Great Crescent: Occupied Japan and the Origins of Containment in Southeast Asia," *Journal of American History* 69 (September 1982): 392–414, and Schaller, *The American Occupation of Japan: The Origins of the Cold War in Asia* (New York: Oxford University Press, 1985); William S. Borden, *The Pacific Alliance: United States Foreign Economic Policy and Japanese Trade Recovery, 1947–1955* (Madison: University of Wisconsin Press, 1984); and Ronald L. McGlothlen, *Controlling the Waves: Dean Acheson and U.S. Foreign Policy in Asia* (New York: Norton, 1993).

44. Clearly, the history of International Relations theory precedes the era of the Cold War; see, e.g., William C. Olson and A.J.R. Groom, *International Relations Then and Now: Origins and Trends in Interpretation* (London: HarperCollins, 1991). Yet it is broadly recognized that in recent decades it has

become a discipline very much tied to U.S. policy imperatives and based on assumptions of bipolarity. See, e.g., the now classic essay by Stanley Hoffman, "An American Social Science: International Relations," *Daedalus* 106, (Summer 1977): 41–60; Steve Smith, "Paradigm Dominance in International Relations: The Development of International Relations as a Social Science," and Ekkehart Krippendorff, "The Dominance of American Approaches in International Relations," both in *The Study of International Relations,* ed. Hugh C. Dyner and Leon Mangasarian (London: Macmillan, 1989).

45. Several essays in Richard Ned Lebow and Thomas Risse-Kappen eds., *International Relations Theory and the End of the Cold War* (New York: Columbia University Press, 1995), argue that neither realism nor neorealism can explain the end of the Cold War. See as well Richard Crockatt, "Theories of Stability and the End of the Cold War," in *From Cold War to Collapse: Theory and World Politics in the 1980s,* ed. Mike Bowker and Robin Brown (New York: Cambridge University Press, 1993). Crockatt clarifies how the realist position, as exemplified in Kenneth Waltz's stress on bipolarity and system stability, has normative as well as analytic dimensions: Waltz not only anticipates continued bipolar Cold War stability but calls for it. There is thus a relationship between the normative dimension of his theory and its lack of attention to those political actors contributing to change not stability. Fraser is precisely interested in those actors promoting changes not captured by mainstream International Relations theory.

46. See Leslie Bethell and Ian Roxborough, "Latin America between the Second World War and the Cold War: Some Reflections on the 1945–8 Conjuncture," *Journal of Latin American Studies* 20 (May 1988): 167–89; Ruth Berins Collier, "Labor Politics and Regime Change: Internal Trajectories versus External Influences," and Paul W. Drake, "International Crises and Popular Movements in Latin America: Chile and Peru from the Great Depression to the Cold War," both in *Latin America in the 1940s: War and Postwar Transitions,* ed. David Rock, (Berkeley: University of California Press, 1994); and Margarita López-Maya, "The Change in the Discourse of US–Latin American Relations from the End of the Second World War to the Beginning of the Cold War," *Review of International Political Economy* 2 (Winter 1995): 135–49.

47. As Maier says in "The Politics of Productivity," 141, that politics "had necessarily to include a trade union dimension." U.S. trade unions through the AFL-CIO's international activities pursued anticommunist policies linked to the politics of productivity. See Ronald Radosh, *American Labor and United States Foreign Policy: The Cold War in the Unions from Gompers to Lovestone* (New York: Random House, 1969); Hobart A. Spalding Jr., "US Labour Intervention in Latin America: The Case of the American Institute for Free Labor Development," in *Trade Unions and the New Industrialisation of the Third World, ed. Roger Southall* (London: Zed Books, 1988); Beth Sims, *Workers of the World Undermined: American Labor's Role in U.S. Foreign Policy* (Boston: South End Press, 1992).

48. In addition to Brenda Gayle Plummer's own book, *Rising Wind: Black Americans and U.S. Foreign Affairs, 1935–1960* (Chapel Hill: University if North Carolina Press, 1996), other recent work includes Mary L. Dudziak, "Desegregation as a Cold War Imperative," *Stanford Law Review* 41 (November 1988): 61–120; Thomas Borstelmann, *The United States and Southern Africa in the Early Cold War* (New York: Oxford University Press, 1993); Penny M. Von Eschen, *Race against Empire: Black Americans and Anticolonialism, 1937–1957* (Ithaca, N.Y.: Cornell University Press, 1997); "Symposium: African Americans and U.S. Foreign Relations," *Diplomatic History* 20 (Fall 1996): 531–650.

49. See John Lewis Gaddis, "The Long Peace: Elements of Stability in the Postwar International System," *International Security* 10 (Spring 1986): 99–142, and in *The Long Postwar Peace: Contending Explanations and Projections,* ed. Charles W. Kegley Jr. (New York: HarperCollins, 1991).

50. Mary Kaldor, *The Imaginary War: Understanding the East-West Conflict* (Oxford: Basil Blackwell, 1990).

51. In addition to books and articles about anticommunist attacks on colleges and universities, see James Hershberg, *James B. Conant: Harvard to Hiroshima and the Making of the Nuclear Age* (New York: Knopf, 1993); Noam Chomsky et al., *The Cold War & the University: Toward an Intellectual History of the Postwar Years* (New York: New Press, 1997); and National Science Foundation, *Science, Technology, and Democracy in the Cold War and After: A Strategic Plan for Research in Science and Technology Studies* (Arlington, Va.: National Science Foundation, n.d.).

52. For an introduction to further work along these lines, see the special issue of *Radical History Review,* no. 63 (Fall 1995), "The Cold War and Expert Knowledge: New Essays on the History of the National Security State," edited by Michael A. Bernstein and Allen Hunter; Paul Forman, "Behind Quantum Electronics: National Security as Basis for Physical Research in the United States, 1940–1960," *Historical Studies in the Physical and Biological Sciences* 18, no. 1 (1987): 149–229; Philip Mirowski, "When Games Grow Deadly Serious: The Military Influence on the Evolution of Game Theory," in *Economics and National Security: A History of Their Interaction* (Annual Supplement to *History of Political Economy*), ed. Craufurd D. Goodwin (Durham, N.C.: Duke University Press, 1991); Stuart W. Leslie, *The Cold War and American Science: The Military-Industrial-Academic Complex at MIT and Stanford* (New York: Columbia University Press, 1993); Paul N. Edwards, *The Closed World: Computers and the Politics of Discourse in Cold War America* (Cambridge, Mass.: MIT Press, 1996).

53. See Andrew Jamison and Rod Eyerman, *Seeds of the Sixties* (Berkeley: University of California Press, 1994), for a discussion of fifteen intellectuals (including Hannah Arendt) whose work not only foreshadowed the political and cultural concerns of the 1960s but also stood as a reproach to the conformity and timidity of academic work harnessed to Cold War imperatives and disciplinary narrowness. For fuller discussions of Arendt and Williams, see Jeffrey C. Isaac, *Arendt, Camus, and Modern Rebellion* (New Haven, Conn.: Yale University Press, 1992); and Paul M. Buhle and Edward Rice-Maximin, *William Appleman Williams: The Tragedy of Empire* (New York: Routledge, 1995).

54. Nor should U.S. foreign policy have been the main objective of criticism by dissidents in communist societies, as Noam Chomsky makes clear in "The Treachery of the Intelligentsia: A French Travesty," in his *Language and Politics,* ed. C. P. Otero (Montreal: Black Rose Books, 1988).

Part I

Creating the Cold War

Chapter 1

Rethinking the Cold War and After: From Containment to Enlargement

Walter LaFeber

Since 1945, as Ruth Sivard has reminded us, a series of long and short wars has cost the world 21 million dead. Four million died during the thirty-year Vietnam conflict. Others have noted that the United States has deployed forces for combat on the average of once every eighteen months since the close of World War II. That statistic does not include U.S. military advisers, CIA covert operatives, and combat troops in such long-running conflicts as the Salvadoran civil war and the contra-versus-Sandinista struggle in Nicaragua.[1]

How this fifty-year-plus legacy is affecting the quite different world of the 1990s has been well argued in essays by Walter Russell Mead, Bruce Cumings, Stephen Van Evera, and Jessica Tuchman Matthews, among others.[2] Most of these analysts agree with Mead's observation that "the U.S. Government seems lost without something to contain. . . . At a time of diminishing national resources and power, the U.S. has not lowered its foreign policy horizons, it has universalized them." This essay agrees with that conclusion but approaches it from a different perspective, focusing on the domestic rather than the international arena and emphasizing the deeper historical roots of American policies during and after the Cold War.

Morton Halperin and Jeanne M. Woods recently observed: "The national security apparatus that was put in place to wage the Cold War is now a burgeoning bureaucracy in search of a new mission. It is busy identifying new enemies, based on an expanded definition of national security, that justify its continued existence and funding."[3] The problem, of course, is more complicated than that statement implies, but there can be no doubt that the Clinton administration's top foreign policy officials sought "a new mission" based "on an expanded definition of national security." That is, the first Democratic executive branch in the post–Cold War era demonstrated in its initial year that certain pivotal parts of its foreign policies were of a piece with those of the Cold War—and, indeed, the years going back at least to the Progressive era. Anthony Lake, assistant to the president for National Security Affairs (and supposedly the administration's primary source for new foreign policy ideas), delineated those parts in his first full-dress speech on September 21, 1993. Arguing that Americans must "not only . . . be engaged, but . . . lead," he believed that "our central purpose" could "be found in the underlying rationale for our engagement throughout this century." That central purpose arose from "dynamics" that "lay at the heart of [one of] Woodrow Wilson's most profound insights"—that is, "that our own security is shaped by the character of foreign regimes."[4]

This U.S. dependence on how other people govern themselves, Lake candidly admitted, required that Americans go beyond their post-1945 containment policy—and, apparently, back to the even more ambitious Wilsonianism of the Progressive era: "The successor to a doctrine of containment must be a strategy of enlargement—enlargement of the world's free community of market democracies." The open-door principles about which William Appleman Williams wrote so provocatively in his *Tragedy of American Diplomacy* were now to be truly universalized, especially since an opposing superpower was no longer in existence to check them. Williams, if he had lived to read Lake's words, might have borrowed a phrase from one of his favorite historical characters, Brooks Adams, and justly declared that his emphasis on the prevalence of open-door ideology in American thinking had been proved so correct that "it knocks the stuffing out of me."[5] Neither Williams nor most other revisionists, however, would have been surprised that when the Clinton administration first tried to implement this policy of "enlargement," tragedies of American diplomacy appeared in Somalia, Bosnia, and Haiti—followed in each instance by a reevaluation of the enlargement policy. Projecting Wilsonianism into the Balkans or Haiti or impoverished and warring former European colonies worked no better for Clinton that it had for Wilson in exactly these same three arenas.

The so-called revisionist historians, it can be argued, both caught the contradictions of Cold War policies and anticipated Lake's post–Cold War approach.[6] The contradictions involved imposing a Cold War economy and a resulting $4 trillion debt on Americans in order to defeat the Soviet Union, whose power (especially in the economic realm) was consistently overrated (notably by agencies such as the Central Intelligence Agency, whose budgets could be at stake) and whose society showed little ability to adapt to the post-industrial society that emerged in the 1960s and after.[7] Revisionists anticipated Lake by emphasizing two characteristics that are deeply woven into the century-old fabric of modern American policies and seemingly cannot be removed without ripping apart the garment itself. The first is the legacy of American Progressivism's intellectual and diplomatic history, which Lake's speech illustrated. The second is another Progressive era legacy, although most highly developed after 1945: presidential powers. These powers have become the iron link tying the Progressive Cold War traditions to the post-1945 national security state whose job it has become to make real "the world's free community of market democracies," for otherwise, as Lake admits, "our own security," which is shaped by the character of "foreign regimes," will be continually endangered.

Justifications for U.S. foreign policies since 1945 have run from Harry Truman's "police" action in 1950 to John Foster Dulles's 1954 announcement that "the situation [in Guatemala] is being cured by the Guatemalans themselves," to Lyndon Johnson's 1964 claim that North Vietnamese torpedo boats had without provocation attacked U.S. warships, to Ronald Reagan's declaration that the Sandinistas immediately endangered Harlingen, Texas. Those and most other justifications for the use of U.S. force since the 1940s, however, have rested on the generic policy—formed by Truman and Undersecretary of State Dean Acheson in 1947—known as the Truman Doctrine: the world is simply divided into two parts, one part based on "the will of the majority" and the other on "the will of a minority forcibly imposed on the majority." Congress and the American people, Truman argued, had to choose whether or not to follow the president when he decides that military force and large expenditures of money are necessary to defend the "majority."[8]

The Truman Doctrine is the most brilliant political device created in the history of American foreign policy since James K. Polk resurrected the forgotten Monroe Doctrine in 1845. Resembling the Monroe Doctrine in several ways, the Truman Doctrine has been defined and, when needed, redefined by the executive. It captures the political high ground by appealing to the hearts rather than the heads of the American people. Once its assumptions are granted, the use of military power can be easily justified. And like the Monroe Doctrine's appeal to a hemispheric system, the Truman Doctrine's simple division of the world into two parts bears little resemblance to reality—which is not to say that it has not created a reality of its own.

Now that the Truman Doctrine's world has been fragmented, the opposing camp is so chaotic and weakened that even Pat Buchanan is willing to follow George McGovern's advice: "Come Home, America." Yet in the years since the collapse of the Soviet's satellite empire, the United States has used massive offensive military force twice, has in addition used force to intervene for avowed humanitarian reasons, and has threatened to use force several other times. With the end of the Cold War has come a continuation, if not an acceleration, of U.S. military commitment. If the definition of the world's power balance offered by the Truman Doctrine was accurate, then, with the disintegration of the communist camp, such military commitments should have diminished. This has not occurred.

A number of reasons explain why U.S. presidents have found it imperative to use such force after the Cold War has been declared to be over. Of special importance, although the Cold War as it has been too narrowly defined since 1945—that is, the U.S. bloc versus the Soviet bloc—may have wound down, the circumstances that brought Americans to great-power status in the 1890s and led to repeated use of U.S. force over the next half-century have not disappeared. The cessation of the traditional Cold War means only a return to many of those circumstances that led Americans to exercise military force regularly before the Bolshevik Revolution. The intervention in Panama and the neck-high military involvement on the side of a reactionary Salvadoran government in the late 1980s, for example, are not the early pages of a new world order but continuing chapters of the old world order put into place by presidents from Monroe to Wilson. And like those earlier executives, presidents can, for the first time since the 1940s, now use military power in such areas as the Western Hemisphere and even East Africa without having to worry about a Soviet military response.

The root of this U.S. policy is not in anticommunism but in a Progressive quest for stability. The policy is founded not on a Johnsonian fear of another Castro but on a Theodore Rooseveltian determination to have order and order's more interesting twin—control. There is a notable double irony here. The first irony is that this determination to have order and control was necessary in American minds precisely because American and other imperial ambitions helped create the disorder in the first place. For in truth, Americans did not initially seek order between the 1890s and the Cold War; they sought opportunity—opportunity for their business, cultural, and political interests. And they refused to back down even when that search resulted in revolutionary upheavals in Nicaragua, Cuba, Hawaii, the Philippines, and Mexico before 1920, or played a lesser but nevertheless significant role in the 1911–19 Chinese upheavals. The expansion (or, as Anthony Lake would have it, the "enlargement") of U.S. market, cultural, and political principles during the Progressive era produced not stability but revolution. The presidents then stepped in to try to restore order and control by using U.S. military forces in every one of the upheavals listed above except the post-1911 Chinese revolution. The twentieth-century presidency thus had its roots in the late nineteenth- and twentieth-century American expansionism.[9] This led to the second irony: The United States became the preeminent world power at the moment the world fragmented into a series of revolutions. Seeking order and stability for their own dominant interests, Americans seldom realized how their interests and power had contributed to disorder and instability.

As in the 1890s to 1940s, so in the late 1980s and 1990s the clash between expanding U.S. market, cultural, and political interests and indigenous nationalisms has produced disorder and, as Chinese authorities well realize, threaten even more disorder. President George Bush symbolized these links between the two eras (and expressed his own admiration for Progressive era diplomacy) by taking down Calvin Coolidge's picture from a White House wall and replacing it with Theodore Roosevelt's portrait.[10] Several times Bush warned that the central problem in the world was not Communism or the Japanese economic machine but "unpredictability." That remark provided insight into Americans' transition back to the Progressive era's beliefs. Like those of the multicultural 1990s, moreover, these earlier Progressive foreign policies exalted a nationalism that was to make more cohesive an American society torn by class division, racism, new immigration, and a growing gap between rich and poor.[11]

The imperialism of the Progressive era has turned out to have been not an aberration but a seedbed of twentieth-century American diplomacy. It was also a historical laboratory that demonstrated the results when diplomacy simultaneously seeks both stability and the enlargement of U.S. market, cultural, and political forces. The idea of Wilsonian self-determination, for example, is disorderly and easily becomes revolutionary. Americans have pushed for self-determination in Latin America in recent years because it reflects what they like to think are their historic values, and because U.S. officials have believed that they can control the rate of change in the hemisphere. After three-quarters of a century, moreover, those officials have finally concluded that favoring electoral processes is preferable to the damage done by aligning the nation's interests with the D'Aubuissons, the Pinochets, and other military rulers with whom Americans have historically cohabited. And, it should be recalled, as the Progressive reformers easily distinguished between bad elections (those that produced political machine winners) and good elections (those that produced reformers), their recent descendants refused to recognize elections in El Salvador in 1982 and in Nicaragua in 1984, which produced the "wrong" winners. The twentieth-century use of self-determination in U.S. foreign policy too often resembles Edmund Morgan's description of popular sovereignty in the late eighteenth century: taken literally, he said, it is as fallacious as the divine right of kings, and though it serves often as a convenient fiction to undercut opponents, "to take the fiction literally is dangerous."[12] Bush was not foolishly consistent in this respect. The Russian republic moved through a remarkable process of self-determination to elect Boris Yeltsin its president and to become a more autonomous state within the former Soviet Union, but Bush consistently—and with a sharp understanding of what he conceived to be U.S. interests—preferred to work with Mikhail Gorbachev, who was elected to his office only by a small group of soon-to-be-discredited communist apparatchiks.

Perhaps the contradictions that arise in what Lloyd Gardner has termed the covenant with power (that is, the need to use military power to reconcile the contradictions between self-determination and stability) appeared with special clarity in the war against Iraq. The original objectives, as President Bush stated them, were acceptable to an amazing spectrum of Americans ranging from Alexander Haig to George McGovern and Jesse Jackson. Those original objectives involved protecting Saudi Arabian oil, pressuring Iraq out of Kuwait, and destroying Iraq's growing nuclear and chemical weapons capacity. It was when the president publicly aimed at getting rid of Saddam Hussein that the trouble began, for the Kurds and Shiites in Iraq took the president's words literally and began to move toward their own versions of self-determination, versions that threatened to create chaos and possibly an unwelcome balance of power in the Middle East. At that point U.S. policy appeared paralyzed; Saddam Hussein survived, and Kurds and Shiites died in large numbers. Americans discovered that a new order could be a contradiction in terms: it could not be both new and orderly—regardless of U.S. military superiority in the post–Cold War era. Bush hid the fatal contradiction at the core of his diplomacy by celebrating the initial military victories with Fourth of July triumphalism.

His predicament, however, has to be understood. Americans have used force even after the Cold War because they continue to see the use of force justified by traditional American principles, much as did their Progressive ancestors when they embarked on their own contradictory course of seeking both opportunity and stability. But another reason for this commitment to force is deeply rooted in Americans' collective mentality and their political system. For President Bush's immediate problem, both at the outset of his invasion of Panama in December

1989 and his dispatch of U.S. troops to Iraq in the late months of 1990, was to maintain the strongest possible political consensus for his decision to deploy troops. The key word is "maintain"; Americans will support the president in nearly any policy for a short time if the costs appear to be cheap. To maintain that consensus, presidents have concluded that they must exaggerate the threat. Woodrow Wilson exaggerated when he asked a joint session of Congress in 1914 for authorization to intervene in Mexico; Truman exaggerated the division of the world in 1947; and George Bush, to understate the case, exaggerated when he compared Saddem Hussein to Adolf Hitler. Once a president has unilaterally made a military commitment, however, he is politically as well as militarily exposed and must enlarge the threat to justify both his political risk and the possible loss of American lives. The root cause of this terrible problem is, of course, American acquiescence over the past century in presidential subversion of the meaning of the Constitution's commander-in-chief clause. The executive, by deploying troops around the globe with little or no formal consultation with Congress, has translated that clause into a weapon that has virtually destroyed Congress's constitutional right to "declare" war.

Bush's handling of Congress in the Gulf War was no exception to that statement. He used his commander-in-chief power not only to put the original 200,000 troops in the battle zone but in November 1990 to double the number until the only real alternatives were war or withdrawal. It was after this second deployment, carefully timed for two days after the congressional elections, that he asked Congress to support or disavow him in a formal vote on war authorization. Congress finally gave him the support he sought, but just to keep the record clear, and to avoid appearing to surrender powers assumed by earlier presidents who were determined to use military force on their own initiative, Bush explained in May 1991 that he had no doubt of his "inherent" right to use military force in the Middle East, whether or not Congress supported him. That statement was bad enough, but he then went on to quote James Madison, in a mistaken and grotesquely distorted form, to justify this spread-eagle use of presidential power in the military realm.[13]

One of William Appleman Williams's most important insights had to do with Madison's argument in *Federalist* No. 10 that the republican form of government required the United States to "extend the sphere" in which the republic operated. This meant, according to Williams, the need to extend and expand continually— especially over a continent that seemed to have a virtually limitless "frontier" into which to expand—if the republican system established in 1787 was not to stagnate and break down. (Williams's idea was vigorously attacked by Arthur Schlesinger Jr., who denied this interpretation of American expansion and argued, instead, that Madison meant only to "extend the sphere" over the then thirteen states.[14] Williams took Schlesinger's attack as the final confirmation that his own interpretation must be correct.)

The costs of that foreign policy that conquered a continent, as Williams never stopped reminding us, were incredibly high. One of his most provocative (and indeed, to some, infuriating) conclusions was that slavery was not as important in determining Lincoln's position in 1861 as was the choice Lincoln faced between maintaining a continental empire and honoring the principle of self-determination. Wherever we come down on the problems that Williams pointed out in Madison's theory, it is probable that Madison would have argued in the 1880s that his system had at least helped maintain and expand republican forms of government, that the institution of slavery had been destroyed, and that it remained possible for Americans to use their constitutional apparatus to counter the threat of political and economic consolidation. But it was here, of course, in the 1880s and 1890s, that Williams began his study of *The Tragedy of American Diplomacy,* and one key portion of the tragedy was the consolidation in the twentieth century of presidential power over the ultimate question of using military force. If U.S. foreign policy to the 1890s at least kept open the possibility of democratic controls over that ultimate question, since the 1890s the president's use of the commander-in-chief clause has systematically reduced that possibility. As U.S. power has globalized, foreign policy decision-making has centralized, and it has centralized to the point that a president can, with impunity, declare his "inherent" right to wage war as he sees fit. Bush's claim to inherent right added a whole new dimension to the recent American debate over natural law.

Since the 1890s and the Progressive era, then, we have created a system in which Americans invite the president to mislead, to exaggerate the reasons for expressing the most fundamental and far-reaching state power—the decision to use force— and in return to receive high approval ratings. Nor do Americans understand that this use of force and perversion of the Constitution's provisions has often moved directly out of their own tradition (rooted especially in the Progressive era) of expanding or enlarging their own principles of self-determination and, as Lake phrased it, "market democracies." Americans ask only that the president's war be as short and as costless to themselves as possible, a request guaranteeing that in order to escape the deadly Vietnam syndrome the president will either use force as massively as possible (as in Panama and Iraq) or, if the power has to be applied over the long run, as secretly and covertly as possible (as in Nicaragua and El Salvador). To achieve high ratings, the president usually has to blot out parts of the past, relegating to the Orwellian Memory Hole some earlier promises—to democratize Panama, stop the huge illicit drug trade that continues to move through Panama, destroy Saddam Hussein's regime—and Bush's and the CIA's cooperation with Manuel Antonio Noriega to fight the Sandinistas. Not only have presidents made a covenant with power but, since the 1890s (not merely since 1945), Americans have made a covenant with presidents to use that power. To paraphrase Randolph Bourne, military interventionism has, to an impressive extent, become the health of the presidency.

Some of the reasons why Americans have allowed presidents to use this power are understandable; some are much less so. Certainly many scholars have encouraged such use of power by accepting the so-called realist view that the international system must be studied in terms of its state components. Too often, observers have been awestruck, in Richard K. Ashley's words, by "the blinding light of the halo surrounding the state in neorealist thought."[15] That halo allowed the Reagan and Bush administrations to impose censorship and boundaries on knowledge and discussion that no self-respecting Congress would have tolerated. When Senator Jesse Helms becomes the leading advocate for the opening of State Department and other executive department documents, the political position of those in the bureaucracy, Congress, and—above all—the executive itself who oppose Helms seems to fall completely off the far right side of American politics. Moreover, presidents have the refuge of the National Security Council with its virtual immunity to consistent public scrutiny. Garry Wills put the Iran-contra debacle in perspective when he observed, "Remember, always, that the dispensers of our fate, in the Bay of Pigs and the assassination attempts on Castro and the mining of the Nicaraguan harbors, may have been a bit less loony than Oliver North (who is not?), but they prepared the way for North. They made him possible."[16] It need only be added that Wills does not start far enough back to account historically for the Oliver Norths.

The problem, then, might be phrased as follows. The 1945 to 1989 Cold War has ended, but the historic purposes that propelled U.S. foreign policy and the presidential power that guided and carried it out have not been transformed. If anything, these purposes and powers have been reinforced by the collapse of the communist empire and by what Americans accepted as the successful use of U.S. military power in Panama and Iraq, which sought both the restoration of order and the increase of presidential popularity. That popularity has for fifty years been increasingly dependent on the use of military force. The fact that U.S. military power was checked during the early Clinton administration in Somalia, Bosnia, and Haiti did not cause a rethinking but led instead, as Lake's September 21, 1993, speech illustrates, to a restatement of and commitment to the historical principles (complete with a reference to Woodrow Wilson) that helped trigger the initial uses of military power in post-1890 U.S. foreign policy. The much-debated and inevitable expansion of NATO eastward is a continuation of the application of those principles.

Meanwhile, many scholars and other responsible political observers have stood by and allowed the realists, led by Hans Morgenthau and Reinhold Niebuhr and their descendants in the 1970s and 1980s, to claim the Founders of the 1780s as their own because the Founders supposedly followed balance-of-power politics. As historians from Gordon Wood to Merrill Jensen have shown (and no one demonstrated it more clearly then did Williams), the fundamental contribution of the Founders was not so-called realist foreign policy but their assumptions that (as Madison phrased it) what renders Americans happy and prosperous at home will make them respectable abroad, and that all power must be checked in an equitable system of government. Perhaps we will know that a new order in American foreign policy is about to begin when Theodore Roosevelt's portrait in the White House is replaced with James Madison's or, better, Elbridge Gerry's.

Notes

1. Ruth Sivard's figures are footnoted and discussed in Walter LaFeber, *America, Russia, and the Cold War, 1945–1990,* 6th ed. (New York: McGraw-Hill, 1990), 321–31. Throughout this essay, "America" and "American" refer to the United States and its population; I use them for purposes of word variation.

2. Walter Russell Mead, "Germany and Japan—Dragging Their Boots," *New York Times,* February 3, 1992, E19; Bruce Cumings, "Trilateralism and the New World Order," *World Policy Journal* 8 (Spring 1991): 195–222; Steven Van Evera, "Primed for Peace: Europe After the Cold War," *International Security* 15 (Winter 1990–91): 7–57; Jessica Tuchman Matthews, "Redefining Security," *Foreign Affairs* 68 (Spring 1989): 162–77.

3. Morton Halperin and Jeanne M. Woods, "Ending the Cold War at Home," *Foreign Policy,* 81 (Winter 1990–91): 141.

4. These and the following quotations are from Anthony Lake, "From Containment to Enlargement," speech delivered September 21, 1993 (copy obtained from the National Security Council), esp. 4–5.

5. Williams's best known and most influential work on the open door is *The Tragedy of American Diplomacy,* (1959), rev. ed. (New York: Dell, 1962). His view of Brooks Adams can be found in "Brooks Adams and American Expansion," in *Behind the Throne* ed. Thomas J. McCormick and Walter LaFeber, essays in honor of Fred Harvey Harrington (Madison:University of Wisconsin Press, 1993), 21–34.

6. The term "revisionist" is overly general and misleading (most historians who significantly reinterpret the past can be termed revisionist), but the term has been usefully and more narrowly de-

fined in the sense I use by Jerald A. Combs in *American Diplomatic History: Two Centuries of Changing Interpretations* (Berkeley: University of California Press, 1983), esp. 252–57.

7. See Dietrich Fischer's review of *Essays on the Cold War* by Murray Wolfson, in *International History Review*, 15 (August 1993): 653; Peter Drucker, *Post-Capitalist Society* (New York, Harper Business, 1993).

8. Truman's speech of March 12, 1947 can be found in *The Record of American Diplomacy*, ed. Ruhl Bartlett (New York, 1964), 723–27.

9. This argument is made in detail in Walter LaFeber, *The American Search for Opportunity, 1865–1913*, in *The Cambridge History of American Foreign Relations*, ed. Warren Cohen (New York: Cambridge University Press, 1993).

10. *Washington Post*, August 24, 1990, A34.

11. A summary of the situation is Robert J. Samuelson, "The Fragmenting of America," *Washington Post*, August 7, 1991, A15.

12. Edmund Morgan, "The Great Political Fiction," *New York Review of Books*, March 9, 1978, 17–18.

13. The background for this episode, the quotation, and other points made by Bush about the Iraqi war can be found in Theodore Draper, "Presidential Wars," *New York Review of Books*, September 26, 1991, 64–74.

14. Arthur Schlesinger Jr., "America II," *Partisan Review* 4 (1970): 509.

15. Quoted in Robert Keohane, ed., *Neorealism and Its Critics* (New York: Columbia University Press, 1987), 280.

16. Garry Wills, "The Man Who Wasn't There," *New York Review of Books*, June 13, 1991, 7. The background for much of this analysis of the president and his reliance on what Lowi calls the "quick fix" of using force in foreign affairs is Theodore J. Lowi, *The Personal President: Power Invested, Promise Unfulfilled* (Ithaca, N.Y.: Cornell University Press, 1985) esp. 15–20, 168–73.

Chapter 2

Rethinking the Division of Germany

Carolyn Eisenberg

Although a divided Germany was the central front of the Cold War world, there have been surprisingly few efforts either to chronicle or to explain its emergence.[1] The scholarly vacuum reflects the longstanding tendency of commentators of diverse political persuasion to regard a partitioned Germany as part of the European landscape. Over decades the existence of East and West Germany assumed an aura of such permanence that the split began to seem less a historical creation than a fact of nature.

The sudden reunification of the country in 1989 challenged this mind-set by demonstrating how forced and artificial the partition had always been. It is perhaps more obvious now than during the intervening forty years that the line across Germany was the product of human decisions and that other outcomes were possible. Yet even recent changes in Central Europe have not yet stimulated the missing debate.

In the hope of generating such discussions, this essay engages two fundamental problems: Why was postwar Germany cut in two? How do developments in the German arena illuminate the causes and character of the Cold War itself?[2] I argue that the partition of Germany was an American decision, strongly supported by the British,[3] and bitterly opposed by the USSR. U.S. policymakers were primarily disturbed by the industrial stagnation of the Western zones, which seemed to imperil the revival and integration of the capitalist economies of Europe. By opting for schism, they pushed their conflict with the Soviets to the point of no return, thereby creating an overriding imperative for military strength. Once East-West rivalry was militarized during the course of the Berlin blockade, political movement was frozen on both sides of the line.

The Partition

For the American public, the Berlin Wall was a prime symbol of the Cold War era. It exemplified the Soviet habit of foisting communism on unwilling peoples and imprisoning them forever. If there was any curiosity about the reasons for Germany's division, the Berlin Wall—built twelve years after the establishment of the two separate states—seemed to embody the answer. As with most of the evils of the postwar world, the Russians were seen as the culpable party.

Yet in the years immediately following World War II it was the Americans and British who took the formal steps toward partition. In violation of the quadripartite framework established at Yalta and Potsdam, they opted to fuse their two zones economically (December 1946), to incorporate Western Germany in the Marshall Plan (July 1947), to implement a separate currency reform (June 1948), and to convene a Parliamentary Council for the establishment of a West German state (September 1948). In each case there was some equivalent move in the East. Yet the pattern of U.S.-British action and Soviet response was a consistent one.

As in a divorce where the partner filing papers is not necessarily the one who caused the rupture, the formal situation can easily be misleading. At the time they took these steps, the Americans and British maintained that the Soviets had created the schism through their unofficial obstruction of German unity. In subsequent years these claims nourished the impression of both publics that Germany was divided because the USSR had closed off the East.

From the beginning of its occupation in April 1945 the Soviet authorities did impose a stern regime that restricted German freedoms. When the Americans and British began their formal moves toward partition, however, the Eastern zone was still a relatively open place, certainly in comparison with what it subsequently became.[4] Predictably, the greatest latitude existed in the quadripartite city of Berlin where, under the protection of the Allied Kommandatura, people and goods were circulating freely and political parties competing fiercely for public support.

Because Berlin was inside the Soviet zone, this ferment and diversity spilled over to the surrounding areas, limiting the Russians' ability to control the sentiments and activities of the populace. Although relationships were less fluid among the four zones than in Berlin, there was substantial trade and travel with an associated transmission of books, newspapers, and ideas. Political conditions inside the Eastern zone tightened appreciably after March 1946, when the Soviets forced a merger between the Communist and Socialist Parties and granted the new Socialist Unity Party (SED) predominant power over administrative agencies. Even then, two bourgeois parties—the Christian Democrats (CDU) and the Liberal Democrats (LDP)—were allowed to operate independently, each with its own press and regular public meetings. Though sometimes harassed, these anticommunist groups participated actively in provincial elections and polled a strong vote in the fall balloting.

The same mixed pattern obtained in the economic sphere. During September 1945 the Soviets had pushed through a radical land reform measure, breaking up all estates over 100 hectares and distributing the resulting parcels into the private hands of landless settlers and poor farmers. In the industrial field, the Soviets had quickly authorized the *laender* to sequester "ownerless property" as well as the property of the German government, the Nazi organizations, and "leading members and influential followers" of the Nazi Party. Yet they were slow to transfer ownership to the state. During the summer of 1946 the Eastern provinces held referendums on the disposition of the sequestered facilities, thus paving the way for substantial socialization. Some numbers of these confiscated enterprises, however, were returned, or resold to other private individuals. In conjunction with properties that had not qualified for sequestration, this meant that much of the Eastern zone's industry was still under private ownership.

After 1947 Soviet policy accelerated in a dictatorial direction, and by the end of 1949 the ostensible commitment to political and social pluralism had given way to one-party control and state direction of economic life. The chronology remains pertinent, however, to distinguishing cause and effect. In the summer of 1947, when the Americans and British reached a clear decision to divide Germany, the presence of these trends had not yet obliterated the alternative voices, political organizations, and social institutions in the East.

Moreover, although American and British officials were disheartened by the internal trends in the Soviet zone, these were never their primary focus. Among policymakers it was widely accepted that if a satisfactory formula for reunification could be found, those trends might still be ameliorated. Unfortunately, during a succession of four-power Council of Foreign Ministers meetings—commencing in

April 1946 and culminating in November 1947—the leaders of both governments concluded that such a formula was impossible. When they referred to Soviet intransigence and obstructionism, they had chiefly in mind the USSR's conditions for amalgamating the zones.

And yet to a remarkable extent those conditions remained unchanged from the time of Yalta and fell far short of anything resembling a revolutionary agenda. It is particularly instructive to consider the USSR's negotiating position at the Moscow Council of Foreign Ministers in March–April 1947. This was the first such meeting devoted exclusively to a consideration of the German and Austrian problems, and it was by universal agreement the most important policy discussion since the end of the war.[5] Because the conclave occurred against the background of the Truman Doctrine speech and an overall deterioration of East-West relations, it would not have been surprising if the Soviets had been uncooperative.

As presented by Foreign Minister V. M. Molotov, the Russian package was designed to meet pragmatic security and material requirements. In speeches already stale with repetition, Molotov stressed the necessity for reparations and reaffirmed the figure of $10 billion, which he now insisted should come from current production rather than capital equipment. He also called for four-power control of the Ruhr and a vigorous policy of "democratization"—by which he denoted land reform, denazification, decartelization, the rapid reconstruction of trade unions, and other social reforms. In the biggest alteration of Soviet policy, he accepted the concept of a freely elected German provisional government, which he expected to be centralized along the lines of the Weimar constitution.[6]

During the official sessions the Russian spokesmen promised that if their terms were met, they would accept an upward revision of the German level of industry and would facilitate the rapid re-integration of the zones. Off the record, their representatives intimated to their Western colleagues that some of their terms might be modified if their desire for reparations could be satisfied.

Whatever the merits of the Soviet program, it did not differ substantially from that advanced by liberals in the Roosevelt administration, whose ideas had been partly embodied in the Yalta reparations clauses, the German provisions of Potsdam, and the Joint Chiefs of Staff directive JCS 1067. Such convergence was admittedly of slight comfort to the less reform-minded members of the Truman team who viewed these documents skeptically. Their displeasure notwithstanding, the USSR was still exhibiting a surface willingness to accept the norms of parliamentary democracy and to open a wider door for capitalism in the East.

Throughout the proceedings the Americans had little doubt that the Russians wanted German unification. Though some versions would clearly not be acceptable: They would not, for example, forfeit reparations claims in the East in order to reintegrate the country. Their reasons for seeking a bargain, however, were scarcely mysterious. As settled at Yalta, the Western zones of Germany included most of the country's land, people, and industrial resources. The Ruhr alone contained sufficient coal, steel, and chemicals to make West Germany an economic and political power in its own right. Should the country be split, not only would the Soviets lose access to the wealthiest portion; it was also apparent that West Germany could, in association with the Western nations, become a grave military threat.

During the two difficult years that followed the Moscow deliberations, the Americans and British never lost sight of this Soviet wish to reconnect the zones. Once the Marshall Plan was launched, with its presumption of West German participation, their policy was shaped by a fear that the desperate Soviets might offer a deal that could not be rejected. That anxiety was articulated by Ambassador Walter Bedell Smith in a frank letter to his friend Dwight Eisenhower. Writing from the London Conference of Foreign Ministers in December 1947, he reflected: "The difficulty under which we labor is that in spite of our announced position, we really do not want nor intend to accept German unification in any terms that the Russians might agree to, even though they seemed to meet most of our requirements."[7] In the wake of the Berlin blockade, Smith himself would become more receptive to unification. Yet even in the darkest days of that crisis—when the success of the airlift was in doubt, and a third world war seemed to threaten—the U.S. government was phobic about negotiations, perceiving a Soviet ambush that could forestall the German partition.

In implementing the division of the country, then, the Americans and British were not simply ratifying an already existing situation. The conditions of the Eastern zone remained unsettled, and the Soviet bargaining position showed numerous signs of flexibility. Even in the gathering momentum for a separate West German state, there was continuing evidence that unification could be achieved.

At the end of World War II, U.S. policy had faced in a quite different direction: The prevailing assumption was that the United States and the Soviet Union must work together in the supervision of a united Germany. Even in defeat, Germany was viewed as the main threat to the post-war peace. If the Allies failed to collaborate, there was a danger that it could revive as a military force.

Also on the horizon for U.S. officials was the then dimmer menace of Soviet power. Should Stalin cast aside wartime pledges and embark on a path of revolutionary expansion, American interests would be gravely imperiled. Most remained hopeful that he would eschew this course if Russian security goals were satisfied; hence, the German settlement was crucial. The Soviets expected compensation for the massive damage inflicted on their country and safeguards against the revival of German militarism. If these could be provided, the USSR would have strong incentive to moderate its behavior in other arenas.

There were many sharp differences among American leaders about the character of postwar Germany. New Deal liberals, grouped around Secretary of the Treasury Henry Morgenthau Jr., desired large reductions in the level of German heavy industry and favored substantial reparations from capital equipment. They were also committed to a drastic reform of German society, encompassing such programs as denazification, reeducation, the elimination of cartels and centralized banks, the strengthening of German labor unions and consumer groups, and the implementation of land reform.[8] More conservative elements, clustered around Secretary of War Henry Stimson and Assistant Secretary John McCloy, were emphasizing the imperatives of European reconstruction. Their goal was to revive the economies of Europe rapidly and integrate them into a new international system in which goods and capital could flow freely across national borders. In their judgment this rapid recovery could not occur unless Germany participated in the process.[9]

The position of the Stimson-McCloy group was complex. Most recognized that during the war Germany's industrial economy had been overbuilt; steel capacity, for example was far in excess of what was needed for normal peaceful trade. Thus they saw some room for the reduction of German industrial capacity and the provision of reparations to Soviet and European claimants. They also acknowledged the need for a certain amount of reform. Nazi Germany was far from a free market economy, for state controls had enabled a handful of banks and industrial firms to dictate the patterns of economic activity not only within Germany but internationally as well. The American multilateralists wanted to break the power of the fascist state, eradicate Nazism, and force German companies to submit to the discipline of the marketplace. Their reform commitment was limited by their wish to avoid measures that would interfere with the creation of a strong industrial economy or that would reduce the incentives of the German capitalist class. The ferocious internal quarrel over the character of postwar Germany did not initially disturb the consensus on cooperating with Stalin. Both American factions assumed that there was sufficient basis for accommodating the Soviet requirements, so long as the USSR was not bent on communizing the country.

But this American attitude had been dramatically transformed by the time of the Moscow Conference of Foreign Ministers in March 1947.

To the extent that commentators have noted the shift, the predominant explanation has been that U.S. policy-makers changed course when they became convinced (accurately or not) that the USSR had embraced the expansionist approach.[10] This account gains credence from the voluminous public statements of American officials who, in the period after Moscow, evoked the specter of Soviet subversion in western Germany. It is also supported by the piles of internal memoranda penned in the transitional period by people such as George Kennan, who warned of a Russian takeover of a unified Germany.

The limitation of this interpretation is that it ignores another pile of documents written by American officials in Berlin, who described a very different situation and recommended a divergent course. Until mid-1947 the prevailing impression within the U.S. military government (OMGUS) was that communism was very weak in western Germany, that the Soviets had little realistic hope of changing this state of affairs, that the Socialist Unity Party's grip on the Eastern zone was tenuous, and that the practical meaning of unification would be the extension of democratic influences beyond the Elbe. It was also their perception that the Russians were economically desperate and so fearful of West German militarism that they would pay a high price for amalgamation.[11]

In explaining the American embrace of partition, it is therefore insufficient to cite the anticommunist ethos or apprehensions about Soviet aggression. Several other circumstances seem relevant.

First, by 1947 liberals had lost all control of U.S. German policy. The American approach was being set by the Stimson-McCloy heirs, whose main desire was to rehabilitate a German capitalist economy and to reintegrate it with the rest of Europe. Although this group was initially supportive of U.S.-Soviet cooperation, its agenda provided narrower grounds for an accord than did the program of the liberal faction.

Second, after two years of vigorous effort, the economies of the Western zones had not revived. Industrial production in the U.S. zone stood at about one-third of prewar levels, and in such crucial areas as coal, productivity in the Ruhr hovered at about 40 percent. Meanwhile, the economies of Western Europe continued to languish, a condition that the Americans attributed to the paralysis in Germany.

Third, so long as each zone was operating independently, the Americans had very little ability to shape economic policies in the British or the French zone. The Americans thought this disastrous in both instances—because of the exploitive and destructive attitude of the French toward German resources, and because of the over-centralized administration of the British and their predilection for socialist experimentation.

Fourth, in the context of western Germany's economic stagnation and tensions with the other Western powers, Soviet demands became increasingly problematic. The insistence of the Russians on substantial reparations not only in capital goods but in current production, their agitation for more rigorous denazification and de-cartelization, their support of centralized and politicized trade unions, and their persistent claim to a role in the Ruhr seriously challenged the American economic program.

It was against this backdrop that Washington officials adopted the strategy of partition. By incorporating the three Western zones into a single entity and elim-inating Soviet interference, they hoped to achieve the elusive goal of rehabilitating Germany and integrating it with Western Europe. This choice had a provisional character, for in early 1947 the Americans did not rule out the possibility that once West Germany became viable and strong and West European recovery assured, the USSR might be impelled to surrender completely its position in eastern Germany.

Between the decision to divide Germany and the formal establishment of a West German state in September 1949, there were two years of intense maneuvering during which the Americans might have reconsidered their position. The process of carrying out the partition and incorporating the Western zones into the Mar-shall Plan, however, were associated with new international dynamics that rein-forced the original determination and eliminated the dissent inside OMGUS.

As of mid-1947 Soviet rhetoric and behavior became substantially more provoca-tive. Within Europe the formation of the Comintern was accompanied by a sum-mons to western Communist Parties to engage in disruption and sabotage and by mounting repression in Hungary, Romania and Poland. Inside Germany itself the Western Communist Party (KPD) was mobilizing working-class resistance to the Marshall Plan, while the Soviet military authorities were accelerating the trend to-ward one-party rule in the East. Taken in aggregate, these developments seemed to confirm the analysis of those American officials who viewed the Soviets as un-scrupulous partners whose only genuine goal was world revolution. When these transgressions were capped by a Russian decision to blockade Berlin, the brief against the USSR hardened into doctrine.

Any American disposition to reevaluate German strategy was also offset by new cleavages within the Western camp. In moving closer to the economic and politi-cal restoration of western Germany, the Americans faced a host of challenges from German and West European allies. Hardest to adjudicate was the conflict between the punitive French and the increasingly assertive politicians of western Germany. As they sought to control obstreperous partners, U.S. policymakers found the prospect of Soviet reinvolvement unappealing.

The Berlin blockade helped fix the American attitude not only for the obvious reason that it highlighted Russian malevolence but because it demonstrated the uses of Cold War polarization. Aware of fissures in the Western camp, the Soviets had begun the blockade hoping to widen them and thereby arrest the momentum toward partition. Yet with the inception of the airlift the Americans discovered, to their surprise, that the East-West confrontation was enabling them to solve previously intractable problems. Under the shadow of the blockade they were able to forge agreements on an international organization for the Ruhr, the reduction of economic controls in western Germany, and the structure and powers of the new West German state.

Although it is clear that progress toward the partition of Germany was accompanied by mounting fear of Soviet expansionism, there was a certain obtuseness in the American thinking. Especially noteworthy was the early disposition of top U.S. policymakers to accept worst-case analyses from people remote from the scene—such as George Kennan in Moscow—while ignoring more hopeful descriptions from some who were there, including General Lucius Clay and his closest associates. When Western initiatives in subsequent years were accompanied by more obnoxious Soviet behaviors, there was no willingness to consider how these developments might be connected.

Given these circumstances, it is tempting to conclude that U.S. policy was simply irrational, an unfortunate result of flawed thinking. But the core of realism in the Americans' position was their realization of a genuine clash of interest between even the minimum Soviet program for reparations and security, and their own aspiration for West European recovery and capitalist integration. Though it had initially seemed possible to reconcile the two agendas, difficulties in procuring coal, steel, and chemicals from the Ruhr and restoring the German market for West European goods had reduced that prospect. As frustration mounted, each Russian demand—for reparations deliveries, for quadripartite controls in the Ruhr, for decartelization, for denazification of management, for encouragement of labor unions—became harder to tolerate. Ultimately, it became an intellectual fine point whether these Russian claims reflected sincere anxieties about German militarism or nefarious schemes for taking over the country. What mattered to U.S. officials was Soviet interference with their plans for German rehabilitation.

Arguably, this careless ascription of motivation may have produced some irrational effects. At crucial moments it prevented U.S. officials from making hard headed assessments of opportunities. One such moment was the Moscow Conference of Foreign Ministers when General Clay urged his American colleagues to authorize a technical study of current production reparations in order to determine whether there was some level of allocations that could be harmonized with a German recovery program. This modest, sensible idea was buried by the ideologues on the U.S. delegation for whom the practical arithmetic was eclipsed by the diabolical nature of the Soviets.

A similar dynamic was at work eighteen months later when George Kennan offered Plan A as a possible solution to the Berlin Crisis.[12] By this time Kennan had drastically modified his earlier views and had become profoundly disturbed by the impending division of Europe. To arrest this development in Germany he crafted a proposal that provided for a single provisional government and for scaling back the political and military presence of the occupying authorities. Because the plan was stacked with one-sided clauses, such as the provision for a united Germany to participate in the Marshall Plan, Kennan was doubtful that the Soviets would accept it. Yet were they acquiescent; they would be surrendering their position in the East in exchange for a very limited role in the West. Remarkably, it was Kennan's superiors who were loath to explore the matter, preferring not to know whether the USSR would accept the strict conditions.

Such willed ignorance and fear were recurrent features of the American stand in Germany and formed a constant thread in the early Cold War. Though partially stimulated by the obvious benefits of polarization, this attitude also derived from a perception of Soviet vulnerability. The Americans, for all their alarms about Russian aggression, saw the Soviets as weak both economically and militarily. This perception allowed them to disregard the USSR's interests with a sense of impunity and to sacrifice potentially favorable bargains within the expectation of a complete Soviet collapse down the road.

A Divided Germany and the Origins of the Cold War

By the time it ended, the Cold War had become an undifferentiated competition between the United States and the Soviet Union in which each battlefield seemed almost as important as every other. This state of affairs yielded its most grotesque results during the Vietnam War when the American expenditure of lives and resources was so ill proportioned to the concrete interests at stake.

The habit of homogenizing situations was the product of prolonged international polarization. At the inception of the Cold War, however, individual issues were more sharply etched, and apart from nuclear weapons there was no single international question that had more direct bearing on the future of the United States and the Soviet Union than the treatment of occupied Germany. From a military standpoint, both powers were vitally concerned lest German nationalists return to the fore and, either in isolation or in association with a foreign country, undertake new aggression. From an economic standpoint, both viewed the industrial resources of the Ruhr as indispensable to their postwar plans. And from a political or ideological standpoint, both recognized that an unfriendly Germany would be a source of infection to surrounding areas.

Because these concerns were so fundamental, American and Soviet policymakers hoped to avoid the uncertainties of competition. This hope gave rise to the quadripartite experiment and kept it alive when other quarrels were gnawing at the wartime friendship. So long as the two powers were cooperating in Germany, other disputes remained side plots whose resolution was undetermined. Conversely, when the Allied project failed and it became evident that there would be two Germanies instead of one, the Americans and Soviets became mortal enemies. The struggle for Germany was of such profound interest to both sides that the adversarial involvement of each power posed a dire threat to the other. This gave a new degree of structure, permanence, and menace to their earlier antagonism.

If the German partition fanned apprehensions on both sides, it is likely that the effects on the USSR were more traumatic. As suggested by the foregoing account, the American and Russian roles in determining the German settlement were not symmetrical. Partition was essentially an American choice, which partly reflected the greater importance of the Western zones. Additionally, to the Germans the American way of life was always more congenial than that of the Soviets, a condition constantly aggravated by Russian harshness and despotism. By any criterion, the division of the country left the Soviet Union as the more vulnerable principal.

Against this background it seems a reasonable speculation that the most offensive behaviors of the Soviets in the post-1947 period—the unleashing of the West European Communist Parties, the brutal crackdown in Eastern Europe, and ultimately their buildup of military force—were direct responses to their exclusion from West Germany. It was during this period that they began accusing the Americans and British of using the Western zones as the launching pad for a new "imperialist war." And while this claim struck American policymakers as preposterous, given the Soviet experience of Nazi invasion and their own ideological view of the West, such fears may well have been genuinely felt.

In the transition to the Cold War order, the real rite of passage on the American side was the Berlin blockade. From that encounter came a renewed appreciation of the necessity for military power of both the conventional and nuclear variety. Throughout the crisis the Americans faced the skittishness of West European allies, who were alternately alarmed by Soviet bellicosity and by the dangers of

German revival. Though themselves skeptical of the uses of conventional force, the Americans realized that such strength was the price of ensuring Western Europe's cooperation in the maintenance of continental division. As for managing the Soviets, their method of choice was to brandish atomic bombs. During the blockade the implicit threat of such weapons appeared to set limits on Russian behavior. This initial foray into nuclear blackmail however, also taught them that since threats might entail use, a large and deliverable stockpile was indispensable.

In the aftermath of the blockade, the existence of two hostile rump states in the heart of Europe, possessing divergent social and economic systems and each eventually incorporated into a rival military alliance, made the relative strength of the two camps a matter of abiding anxiety. Within this framework the allegiance of individual countries became more essential, drawing increasingly remote nations into the German vortex. The result was a somewhat deranged contest over "credibility," leading American officials to fret that losses in the Third World would inspire new Russian initiatives in Berlin.

In the wake of the Vietnam war many historians concluded that the overall thrust of America's foreign policy was both grandiose and impractical.[13] They perceived an occupational inability of U.S. officials to recognize limits to American power and to adjust their ambitions accordingly. In the 1960s and 1970s, when the USSR had become a nuclear superpower and much of the Third World was engulfed in revolutionary upheaval, this indictment had particular force. But the shattering of the Soviet Union, the destruction of the Eastern bloc, and the erosion of socialism around the world opened an analytical chasm in the scholarly literature. The apparent victory of the United States in the Cold War seemed to vindicate the wisdom of earlier decisions and to make developments that once seemed tragic and threatening appear benign.[14] Such complacency was particularly marked with regard to U.S. German policy: The West German absorption of the East eliminated the incentive for critical scrutiny and helps to explain why the issue of the German partition still elicits so little scholarly interest in the United States, despite the drama of reunification.

From an academic standpoint, the conclusion of the Cold War provides an appropriate corrective to certain revisionist criticisms by reminding us how fragile the Soviet empire looked at the end of World War II. Many U.S. policymakers believed that the USSR was seriously overextended and could not overcome a firm Western strategy. Indeed, it is startling to review with hindsight the records of the American deliberations in the late 1940s and see how pervasive was the assumption that a sovereign East Germany could not survive. As we have seen, it was this sensibility that infused their approach to the German problem. At a moment when the Western zones were still heaped with rubble, when Ruhr workers were not producing, when currency was virtually worthless, and factories were at a standstill, American leaders projected an economic renaissance in which the West would exert an irresistible attraction for the East. Many also foresaw that for the short term, the Soviet response would be heightened coercion. If West Germany proved to be the magnetic force that was planned, the USSR would make herculean efforts to sever connections. Yet sooner or later these schemes would founder on the resistance of the East Germans and the probable weakness of the whole Eastern bloc.

We can now see that these predictions were not nearly so simpleminded as they once appeared, yet it remains significant that they did not come to fruition for forty years. In the intervening period extraordinary damage was done, the effects of which we can scarcely begin to reckon. These consequences will linger with us long beyond the smashing of the Berlin wall and the dissolution of the Soviet Communist Party. Whether calculated in the billions of dollars spent for weapons, the militarization of our own and Soviet societies, the eradication of personal freedom in the East, the curtailment of self-determination in the West, or the extension of fear and warfare to many remote places, the rupture in Central Europe was a profound human misfortune. A cautious reading of the evidence would suggest that American officials did far too little to avoid what still remains a tragic outcome of World War II. A less conservative rendering might tell us that these American leaders were ultimately responsible for the schism.

In either case, we are left with conclusions that are almost as unpopular now as they were at the height of the Cold War. With Soviet communism so severely discredited, there is again a temptation to lay at the feet of the USSR the blame for every international transgression. This disposition has been quite naturally strengthened by the opening of archives that offer new manifestations of Eastern bloc despotism.

Though the atmosphere is unpropitious, there is still good reason for historical accuracy. The oppressive internal policies of the USSR, which were gradually imposed upon the population of East Germany, were not the source of the postwar settlement. In the aftermath of Allied victory, what shaped that unwanted result was an ambitious American agenda imposed on a European continent that was more impoverished, strife-ridden, and unruly than anyone in Washington had envisioned. In conjunction with America's preponderance of military and economic power, this yielded high-risk policies whose most painful consequences were frequently borne by others. Enough of these elements persist in the contemporary setting to strengthen the imperative for fairness in the exploration of Cold War origins.

Notes

1. Although most surveys of the Cold War include some compressed discussion of the question, the only full-length studies to appear in the United States are Manuel Gottlieb, *The German Peace Settlement and the Berlin Crisis* (New York: Paine-Whitman, 1960); Bruce Kuklick, *American Policy and the Division of Germany: The Clash with Russia over Reparations* (Ithaca, N.Y.: Cornell University Press, 1972); and John Backer, *The Decision to Divide Germany: American Policy in Transition* (Durham, N.C.: Duke University Press, 1978).

2. This essay is based on Carolyn Eisenberg, *Drawing the Line: The American Decision to Divide Germany, 1944–49* (New York: Cambridge University Press, 1996), which relies heavily on archival materials from the United States and Britain; further documentation for my chief conclusions can be found there.

3. Some recent scholarship in Britain and Germany has argued that the United Kingdom was the prime mover in the drive for partition. See Anne Deighton, *The Impossible Peace* (Oxford: Clarendon Press, 1990); and Josef Foschepoth, "British Interest in the Division of Germany after the Second World War," *Journal of Contemporary History* 21 (1986): 391–411. But although the British played an important role, the United States was the more influential participant and (after 1946) the more consistent advocate.

4. The English-language literature on early Soviet policy in the Eastern zone, focuses on acts of repression without placing these in the context of remaining freedoms. See esp. Gregory W. Sandford, *From Hitler to Ulbrecht: The Communist Reconstruction of East Germany* (Princeton: Princeton University Press, 1983); and Henry Krisch, *German Politics under Soviet Occupation,* (New York: Columbia University Press, 1974). Two notable exceptions are J. P. Nettl, *The Eastern Zone and Soviet Policy in Germany, 1945–50* (London: Oxford University Press, 1951); and Jonathan Steele, *Inside East Germany,* (New York: Urizen Books, 1976).

5. See the discussion of the Moscow meeting in Backer, *Decision to Divide Germany,* 149–69; and critical commentary in Charles P. Kindleberger, *Marshall Plan Days* (Boston: Allen & Unwin, 1987), 189–93.

6. The Soviet negotiating position is contained in V. M. Molotov, *Speeches and Statements at the Moscow Session of the Council of Foreign Ministers* (Moscow: International Press, 1947).

7. Walter Bedell Smith to Dwight David Eisenhower, December 8, 1947, in Smith Manuscripts, Dwight David Eisenhower Library, Abilene, Kansas.

8. For a useful discussion of the liberal position, see Warren F. Kimball, *Sword or Plowshares: The Morgenthau Plan for Defeated Nazi Germany* (Philadelphia: Lippincott, 1965). Also illuminating is the *Morgenthau Diary: Germany* (Washington, D.C.: Senate Committee on the Judiciary, 1976).

9. The multilateralist view is treated in Kuklick, *American Policy and the Division of Germany,* 1–47; Gabriel Kolko, *The Politics of War* (New York: Random House, 1968), 314–43; Fred Block, *The Origins of Economic Disorder* (Berkeley: University of California Press, 1977), 1–46; Thomas J. McCormick, *America's Half-Century,* (Baltimore, Md.: Johns Hopkins University Press, 1989), 17–69.

10. Backer, *Decision to Divide Germany.* Also see John Backer, *Winds of History* (New York: Van Nostrand Reinhold, 1983), 170–77; Daniel Yergin, *Shattered Peace* (Boston: Houghton-Mifflin, 1977), 303–35; W. W. Rostow, *The Division of Europe after World War II: 1946* (Austin: University of Texas Press, 1981).

11. For Clay's perspective, see *The Papers of Lucius D. Clay,* vol. 1, ed. Jean E. Smith (Bloomington: Indiana University Press, 1974). The outlook in these documents forms a significant contrast with

the material contained in Clay's memoirs, *Decision in Germany*, (Garden City: Doubleday, 1950). Also important is Jean E. Smith, *Lucius D. Clay* (New York: Henry Holt, 1990), 356–422.

12. Memorandum, Director of Policy Planning Staff (Kennan) to Secretary of State and Undersecretary of State, August 12, 1948; Report by the Policy Planning Staff, "Position to Be Taken by the US at a CFM Meeting," November 15, 1948, *Foreign Relations of the United States*, 1948, II: 1287–97; 1320–38.

13. The notion of U.S. overextension was present in two types of revisionist studies, those that viewed U.S. foreign policy as an exaggerated response to the Soviet threat, and those that saw it as rooted in domestic political economy. For the former, see, e.g., Stephen Ambrose, *Rise to Globalism: American Foreign Policy since 1938* (New York: Penguin Books, 1971); Richard Barnet, *Roots of War* (New York: Penguin Books, 1974). For the latter, Lloyd C. Gardner, *Architects of Illusion* (Chicago: Quadrangle Press, 1970); Joyce and Gabriel Kolko, *The Limits of Power: The World and United States Foreign Policy, 1945–1954* (New York: Harper & Row, 1972).

14. The chasm is most interestingly illustrated by the change in perspective between Melvyn P. Leffler's critical essay "The American Conception of National Security and the Beginnings of the Cold War 1945–48," *American Historical Review*, April 1984, and the conclusion of his influential book *A Preponderance of Power* (Stanford, Calif.: Stanford University Press, 1992), 495–506. Whereas in the article Leffler describes U.S.-European policy as being both grandiose and counterproductive, in his book he finds it fundamentally "prudent."

Chapter 3

Revising Postrevisionism: Credibility and Hegemony in the Early Cold War

Thomas D. Lairson

An important convergence of themes in postrevisionist thinking about the early Cold War requires clarification and in some instances considerable modification. These themes involve the arguments of John Gaddis, Melvyn Leffler, and Geir Lundestad regarding the role of credibility in U.S. policy, the nature and consequences of power relationships in the international system, the differentiation of vital and peripheral interests, and the Korean War as the event that introduced global notions of containment.[1] Gaddis has seen unfounded or irrational worries over credibility, especially in relation to policy in Asia, as the factor blocking a realistic policy in the early Cold War. His approach to these matters leaves three questions largely unanswered: (1) What was the role of credibility in U.S. policy during the early Cold War? (2) When and over what issues did thinking about credibility arise? (3) How do we explain the fixation on credibility? Leffler and Lundestad, because they appreciate the importance of U.S. power advantages for shaping events in the Cold War, provide support for solving these problems, but they too have important weaknesses. Lundestad misses the key role played by credibility in defining the responsibilities of world leadership.[2] Leffler, for all his attention to power relationships, lacks a theoretical basis for an understanding of how and why all the pieces fit together.

This essay addresses these issues and develops three main points. First, the postwar U.S. approach to credibility must be understood as a syndrome of concepts, assumptions, and propositions held by U.S. officials. These include an acute sensitivity to the elements of interdependence in the international system and to the power relationships and balance of risk-taking between the Americans and the Soviets; a firm conviction that unchecked instabilities in world affairs would be amplified into much greater threats; and an extreme concern over expressions of fear and doubt by Allies and over the consequences of an adversary's doubts about U.S. resolve.

Second, this credibility syndrome originated with U.S. policy toward Europe between 1947 and 1949. At the same time, credibility worries and "realist" efforts to differentiate interests often coexisted uncomfortably during the early years of the Cold War. The combination of the Berlin crisis and Soviet atomic bomb development accentuated credibility thinking, which spilled over into Asian policy, where the effort to differentiate vital and secondary interests was the strongest and also where this failed, even before the Korean War.

Third, the essay offers a detailed explanation of the growing importance of this credibility syndrome for U.S. decisions. Gaddis would have us believe that the bipolar structure of the international system shaped the behavior of the major antagonists in the Cold War. The alternative proposed here traces credibility thinking to the U.S. position of world leadership and the political and psychological requirements of assuming and exercising this responsibility. That is, U.S. hegemony generated the opportunity and the incentives for officials to define much of foreign policy in terms of its effects on an image of reliability in supporting commitments. Further, this process tied all U.S. interests together through concerns over credibility, made officials fear the cataclysmic consequences of any failure to act, and undermined efforts to differentiate vital and peripheral interests. The test of this argument lies in a detailed engagement with the documentary evidence for the 1945–50 era.

John Gaddis and Postrevisionism

Gaddis's conception of a postrevisionist synthesis on the origins of the Cold War consists of broad propositions about a scholarly consensus, generalizations about the nature of international relations, and more specific interpretations of particular events. He argues that most scholars have come to accept the revisionist thesis about the extensive use of U.S. economic power to forward its political objectives, although the strategic purposes in containment were more important in motivating policy than were economic interests. Further, U.S actions produced a considerable empire, but this expansion arose mostly from the invitation of other states and was motivated by defensive purposes.[3]

Gaddis sees the postwar world as a bipolar one and this international structure as essentially responsible for organizing world politics and preserving peace. His arguments draw on a venerable tradition among historians and political scientists.[4] Gaddis maintains that bipolarity accurately describes the power relationship between the United States and the Soviet Union, the division of the world into two competing spheres, and reflects the way U.S. officials understood their situation. Moreover, bipolarity was a "simple system" that did not require sophisticated international leadership, since alliances were stable and defections from the two blocs tolerated. Bipolarity was not a delicately balanced arrangement of world power.[5]

In the early Cold War Gaddis sees two quite distinct stages. The first lasted until 1950 and was defined by the strategic judgment that U.S. security depended on preserving the balance of power in Europe. The Truman Doctrine and Marshall Plan of 1947 extended and reaffirmed the same calculations that brought the United States into the two world wars. All were based on fear of the consequences of domination of the Continent by a single hostile power. Moreover, Gaddis views each policy as rooted in traditional realism—meaning that the ends of policy were adjusted to the means and capabilities of the United States. This balancing of means and ends required the establishment of a clear set of priorities and sharp distinctions between vital and peripheral interests. Accepting limits on its resources, the United States drew a line around those special places whose loss might add considerably to Soviet capabilities.[6]

In the second stage, this rational and realistic course was undermined by the process of defining a policy for the rest of Asia and by designing a response to the Soviet atomic explosion in 1949. Decisions regarding Korea and Formosa produced a fragile consensus on an island defensive perimeter and a disguised pullback from Korea. The Soviet bomb led to NSC 68—National Security Council document number 68, one of a series of basic statements of the world situation and United States policy—which cast aside the balance of ends and means and the focus on vital interests and substituted a policy emphasizing U.S. credibility, perception of a delicate global power balance, military superiority, and an intense fear about the loss of any additional area to communism. The Korean War served to confirm these views and prompted not only U.S. military intervention to enhance credibility but a globalization of containment. This new version of containment was "deeply flawed," as it led to a disjunction of ends and means and an unnecessary and unwise expansion of U.S. power and commitments.[7]

Gaddis's most important contribution to postrevisionism is a coherent and reasoned interpretation of the development of the Cold War based on detailed empirical evidence. Much of this can be accepted. But the theoretical underpinnings of his argument in the concepts of bipolarity and "empire" are weak and cannot account for some of the most important aspects of the Cold War. Gaddis has difficulty reconciling his notion of a U.S. empire based on greater power than the Soviets with the equal-power arrangements of bipolarity. Moreover, bipolarity cannot make sense of the shift from realism to credibility in the development of U.S. policy.

There are two central weaknesses in bipolarity as a model of the international system during the Cold War. First, it does not conform to the realities of power in the system. Certainly bipolarity captures one central truth: namely, the division of much of the world into two competing blocs led by the two most powerful states. But bipolarity misses the even more important fact that one nation and bloc—the United States and the West—were always much stronger in political, military, and economic terms.

Second, the predictions of the bipolar model are contradicted by the most important aspects of U.S. behavior. Gaddis suggests that bipolarity is a simple system to manage: given stable alliances, and the fact that defections could not meaningfully alter the power balance between the two blocs, each side could easily tolerate the loss of some of its members.[8] But this expectation is dramatically disconfirmed by U.S. efforts to organize and solidify the Western bloc and most blatantly by the intense U.S. concern over its credibility, a hallmark of U.S. Cold War policy. If a bipolar world was so stable, how are we to explain the enormous effort to preserve and enhance U.S. credibility in Europe, Korea, Vietnam, and elsewhere?[9]

Gaddis has emphasized and criticized the effects of credibility on U.S. policy but has neither explored the relationship of bipolarity and credibility nor offered very convincing explanation for the importance of a reputation for resolve.[10] At one point he suggests that imperial states have typically found differentiating vital and peripheral interests somewhat difficult.[11] Earlier, he attributed this difficulty to a process in which the United States "had backed into" a system of credibility and overcommitment.[12] But these are ad hoc and somewhat poorly developed arguments. Why should we expect empires to behave in this fashion? What evidence do we have to support this substantial generalization?[13]

The problem in explaining credibility does not lie with Gaddis alone; rather this central element in U.S. Cold War thinking has not been effectively understood in any of the literature.[14] Perhaps if we reconsider the actual power relationships in the system and the special nature of the demands on U.S. power, we can figure it out. In what follows I develop an alternative model of the Cold War international system, use it to explain the U.S. attachment to credibility, and review the evidence to validate the argument.

Hegemony and Credibility

An effective place to begin the explanation of any international phenomenon is with the international system, since this helps us identify the key environmental factors that constrained or encouraged national choices. The model here tries to specify lines of causation between the structure of the international system and the perceptions, calculations, and actions of national leaders. It assumes that the structure is important when it produces an array of incentives and opportunities that shape the situation and choices of policymakers. Our task is to uncover the logic of the system—that is, how its incentives and opportunities directed thinking and choices—and look for traces of this process in policymakers' statements and actions.[15]

The realities of power imbalance in the postwar world have been captured best by the concept of hegemony, a term developed by scholars of international political economy to understand the U.S. role in creating an international economic order.[16] As used here, hegemony means the use of substantial power advantages to exercise global leadership in establishing a broad international order or organization of sovereign states. More specifically, hegemony is a theoretical model that combines a particular configuration of power in international affairs and a set of political logics that influence the behavior and actual policies of particular states during a particular international epoch.

Absent from most discussions of U.S. hegemony is a detailed description of the full range of actions and behaviors—military, political, strategic, and economic—that this phenomenon comprises. This narrowness led Lundestad to reject the concept of hegemony and adopt instead the notion of empire. Lundestad is right to criticize research in international political economy for ignoring crucial features of this process; scholars have paid little attention to America's leadership of the "free world" and take for granted the U.S. leadership role in defining and gaining acceptance of a common security system.[17] The result is that we lack a comprehensive sense of the process by which the United States assumed responsibility for international peace, prosperity, and security in the years 1940–50. This leadership was exercised over sovereign states with substantial political and military strength, long histories as great powers, and a tradition of fierce independence. Consequently U.S. hegemony required a subtle and complex array of political, psychological, and economic arrangements to ensure its success.

What did a hegemon need to do to operate as world leader in the mid-twentieth century? Because of its domestic political and economic traditions, U.S. hegemony had a decidedly "liberal" cast and focused more on shaping than on coercing behavior.[18] This involved two mutually reinforcing sets of political relationships: convincing allies to buy into the American vision of a liberal world order, and controlling the use of force in the system. U.S. officials sought to organize the cooperation of many states in orienting their foreign policies toward U.S.-defined objectives and accepting incorporation in a U.S.-designed economic and political system. But because many of these countries were deeply divided, with much opposition to a U.S.-based system, the United States needed to reinforce the political standing of those groups favorable to its position—usually with economic aid, though sometimes with military force. With American power and actions as the defining element of the system, the U.S. needed to convince its allies of continuing American support and determination to defend them. That is, the credibility of the United States became the "glue" holding the system together.

Creating a voluntary and cooperative world order also required a sense of security among the participants; populations and elites needed some level of confidence that they would not be subjected to attack. In Europe the fact that any war could result in devastation of the Continent lent an air of desperation to these concerns. This had two consequences: first, to be successful preparations for war needed to deter war; second, no adversary could be permitted to use actions short of war to create a climate of intimidation and insecurity and thereby provoke political dealignment. The responsibilities of leadership required the United States to go beyond the simple deterrence of specific acts to controlling the use of force in the system. That is, aggression could not become the basis for achieving political ends.

Of course, the object of these worries was the Soviet Union, since it was the only state with the ability to disrupt the system. Controlling Soviet behavior and quarantining its impact were formidable tasks and complicated the need to convince allies of U.S. support. The inherent uncertainty of such commitments, combined with the proximity of Soviet power to many very important areas and its distance from the United States, placed additional burdens on the political psychology of

U.S. leadership. It was especially critical to prevent Soviet actions from shaking confidence in and thereby encouraging challenges to U.S. leadership.

Acting as hegemon—supplying the leadership for world order—requires a foreign policy framed by what I have termed a credibility syndrome: a collection of ideas, assumptions, and conclusions about world affairs that cohere because of the logic of hegemony.[19]

First comes the acceptance of responsibility for creating and defending this order and the political, psychological, and strategic imperatives that doing so entails. Bringing a liberal global order to fruition involves defining governing principles and values and creating institutions to express those views; persuading sometimes skeptical and even hostile nations and populations of the benefits of such an order; dealing with the myriad links among the goals and issues associated with producing this order; reconciling political, economic, and even military conflicts among participants; and providing the money, markets, and sense of security needed for a smooth operation of the system.

Second is a strong interest in the many points of interdependence in global affairs. Leaders are forced to consider and deal with the complex web of relationships involved in establishing international order, including strategic, geographical, economic, and psychological connections.

Third, officials in a hegemon must formulate a strategy applying that nation's power advantages to achievement of its goals. This is likely to prompt an intense preoccupation with power balances along with more subtle worries about how the actions and risk-taking of an adversary could affect power relationships.

Fourth, the policymakers of a hegemon have strong incentives to emphasize the nation's credibility for keeping promises and carrying out threats. Credibility becomes an operating definition of power and the essential indicator of a hegemon's willingness to preserve the system. Believable promises and threats keep allies on board and adversaries at bay.

And fifth, the combination of responsibility, attention to interdependencies, concern over power and risk-taking, and emphasis on a reputation for resolve produces a policy climate in which credibility becomes attached to all interests, and officials fear that any failure will unleash doubts among allies and challenges from adversaries. Given the sensitivity to system linkages, these fears will almost surely come in the form of the amplified effects of "bandwagoning," "falling dominoes," and greater conflict.[20]

The model of the international system articulated here—hegemony faced by a significant but inferior challenger—leads us to expect the hegemon to show great concern for credibility and to wrap this into a policy syndrome composed of responsibility, superiority of power and risk-taking, systemic interdependence, and expectations of amplified and cascading consequences from its actions. Such a hegemonic state is very much interested in its allies, both as major players in the system of world order and as crucial elements in preserving a position of superiority. Fear of the challenger is based on its potential for undermining the system by prompting defection or simple neutrality of the hegemon's allies. In this context, the resolve of the hegemon is a very major issue. Will it defend all places? What effects on the world-order system might result from the loss of one area? Will the hegemon risk war to protect the system? The challenger is in a position to exploit this situation by probing for weak spots as a way of gaining space to maneuver against what it sees as the overbearing power of the hegemon.

The United States as a Hegemonic State

Do the power relationships in the early Cold War conform to those defined in the model of hegemony? Lundestad, Leffler, and others have helped us recognize the extraordinary strength of the United States in the early Cold War years. Economic advantages are the most obvious and easiest to substantiate. The U.S. economy dwarfed that of any other state or combination of states, with 40–50 percent of world GNP and four to five times the Soviet GNP. There was also a substantial technological advantage across many fields, the key role of the dollar, and U.S. capital markets as the only source of aid and loans for the world economy.[21]

The military area is more controversial, if only because of the large Soviet army and the demobilization of U.S. forces. All the disinformation about Soviet capabilities (used to justify higher U.S. spending levels and often repeating Soviet disinformation designed to conceal weakness) should not obscure one basic military fact: by only one measure, the number of troops under arms, could the Soviets match or exceed the West—and even this figure must be adjusted to reflect their paper divisions, poor or nonexistent equipment, low morale, unreliability, domestic political and economic duties, and the serious difficulties in projecting force beyond Soviet borders.[22] Beyond this, the United States held a monopoly and, after 1949, an overwhelming superiority in atomic weapons; it possessed vast air and naval superiority, an unmatched system of worldwide bases, and an immense advantage in military reach—the ability to project its military power over great distances. During the war the United States had convincingly demonstrated that it was the only state capable of fighting a sustained global war simultaneously on two fronts separated by thousands of miles.

This array of American advantages did not mean that the Soviets were helpless before the U.S. juggernaut. The Soviet Union possessed great defensive power, as demonstrated by the war with Germany and by the difficulties U.S. military planners had in developing plans for a knockout blow with atomic bombs. Further, its geographic proximity to most of the arenas of instability, from Europe to Asia, permitted much mischief-making. Its large army, the important industrial strides of the 1930s and 1940s, and a ruthless government's ability to extract resources gave it formidable military power. These capabilities, combined with atomic capability after 1949, meant that the United States could not enter into war lightly. Although it almost certainly could have won a sustained war with the Soviets, the great costs of fighting and occupation provided strong incentives for gaining U.S. objectives short of war.

These somewhat static measures of power fail to deal with the behavior and actions of hegemony. Did the United States act like a world leader? A brief catalogue would certainly indicate that it did. At the broadest level, American hegemony involved definition of the specific purposes and shape of international order, based on a vision of a liberal-capitalist world; it was ideological in the sense that it found great resonance in the American political community and served to give expression to the mythic impulses and interests of society. More specifically, hegemony meant

1. establishing and managing a stable international monetary system, with the dollar (tied to gold) as the key currency and the United States prepared to supply liquidity for the system;
2. defining as goals open markets for goods, convertibility for currencies, free capital movement, and the protection of private property, even while tolerating and sometimes encouraging discrimination against U.S. goods;
3. providing access to oil from the Middle East at stable prices via cooperation with U.S. corporations;
4. creating the United Nations, providing crucial support for the norms of international cooperation, and uniting to block aggression;
5. accepting and fostering the assumption that U.S. military power and resources were available to control the use of force in the international system, thus providing the political basis for other states to orient their foreign policies toward U.S.-defined goals;
6. defining security relations on a global scale to include NATO, the Rio Pact, intervention in Iran, Turkey, and Greece, Franco-German security, Japan-Asian security, involvement in Korea and Southeast Asia, the establishment of military bases, and the preservation of access to strategically vital resources;

7. occupying Germany and Japan and reintegrating their resources into the international system in the service of U.S. goals;

8. reshaping and supporting the governing political coalitions of Germany, France, Italy, and Japan, thereby moving them toward acceptance of U.S.-approved goals;

9. accepting and encouraging the extension of U.S. credibility to commitments large and small, so as to reinforce the political, military, security, and economic relations of international order.

These elements of hegemony were parts of a whole, bound together by their mutual impact and by the recognition across the international system of U.S. leadership and responsibility for the postwar world.

But the most difficult test of the hegemony model is whether it can organize the documentary evidence in chronological terms and, in so doing, offer answers to important interpretive questions and problems. Three demanding questions can be used to evaluate the validity of this approach to the early Cold War. (1) When and in what way did concern over credibility begin to direct policy choices? If this occured before Korea, the model of hegemony seems a better explanation; if only with Korea, the model has serious problems. (2) In what way were credibility concerns linked to a strategy relating U.S. power to the political objectives of world leadership? That is, can we uncover a coherent syndrome of responsibility, interdependence, risk-taking, superiority, and cascading consequences linked to credibility? Absent a coherent set of connections, the impact of hegemony before Korea must be seen as substantially weaker than it would otherwise appear. (3) If the process of U.S. expansion and empire-building was mainly by invitation, how are we to understand the U.S. receptivity to these calls for help? Why did the United States have so much trouble differentiating vital and peripheral interests? If this process was associated with credibility worries, the hegemony model is supported. These demanding questions will serve as a severe test of the model of hegemony.

Hegemony, Credibility, and U.S. Foreign Policy, 1947–1950

The Truman Doctrine, the Marshall Plan, and negotiations for a North Atlantic treaty—three "halves" of the same walnut—were the first major acts of U.S. hegemony. Between early 1947 and late 1948 officials also formulated the main features of the credibility syndrome as a basis for making choices. This meant piecing together the main elements of responsibility, interdependence, superiority in risk-taking, cascading consequences, and the credibility of U.S. promises and threats.[23]

The combination of a decline in the British economic position (demonstrated by an unsuccessful $3.75 billion U.S. loan), the strategic crisis created by the British decision to withdraw from Greece, and continuing weakness in the European economy prompted the United States to assume responsibility for world stabilization. It was up to the United States to solve the looming global crisis and restore world order. This meant supplying capital, creating a sense of security, promoting confidence in recovery, and resolving political and economic conflicts among several states.

The great fear motivating such a major response was the prospect of an economic and political collapse in Western Europe and the shifting of its resources to the Soviets. Such a result would create the potential for an even contest between the United States and the Soviet Union and a militarization of American society.[24] U.S. policymakers were very conscious that the "reins of world leadership" had fallen to them and that world peace and prosperity depended on American actions. President Truman said it very clearly: "If we falter in our leadership, we may endanger the peace of the world."[25] Only the United States possessed the resources and the power to deal with the crisis at hand.

Once the concrete problems of global stabilization were tackled, the connections and contradictions among the myriad issues involved in this process pushed U.S. leaders toward a new awareness of the interdependence of global affairs. That is, responsibility brought a new consciousness of how intertwined events and outcomes had become. The point is not that international affairs were necessarily more interdependent than they had been in the past (though a good case can be made for this proposition); rather, the fact that the United States was taking responsibility for world order made all matters of interdependence relevant to its decisions and focused on one set of decision-makers.

The scope and scale of U.S. world-order objectives was breathtaking; the extraordinary expansion of interests involved nothing less than reshaping the very structure of European and Japanese politics and economies. This is revealed in a memo of the State-War-Navy Coordinating Committee (SWNCC), a precursor to the National Security Council. The U.S. had vital interests in maintaining world political and economic stability, blocking Soviet power, preventing totalitarian aggression wherever it occurred, exercising leadership to promote confidence in U.S. policies, and retaining control over strategic areas and resources.[26] Officials such as George Marshall, George Kennan, Dean Acheson, William Clayton, James Forrestal, James Webb, Robert Patterson, and Charles Bonesteel concluded that the

Western sectors of Germany had to be united, revived economically, and tied closely to Europe and the United States.[27] Such an action, judged essential for restoring the economic prosperity of Europe and for preventing the strategic assets of this area from falling to the Soviets, raised serious political and security questions for many countries. The Marshall Plan, a North Atlantic treaty, and the integration of Western Europe became the mechanisms for reconciling these conflicts.

Several lines of political, strategic, and economic interdependence emerged to complicate the problem of European and Japanese recovery. A revived Germany could undermine the security of Europe, especially of France. The economies of Europe and Japan were heavily dependent on nations on the periphery for raw materials and markets, including colonial and noncolonial areas. And officials understood that any chance of creating a multilateral system of freer trade (itself a system of interdependence) required the establishment of prosperity in Europe. Soviet power also helped to bind areas together. The Soviet Union possessed the potential for military operations in Europe, the Near East, and the Far East, and its influence over local Communist Parties allowed it to exert political pressure in many of these areas. Furthermore, U.S. control of forward bases for possible air attacks on the Soviet Union and the need to defend these bases and their lines of supply combined to generate a broad framework of strategic interdependence. And finally, events carried the potential for wide ramifications due to the psychological and political conditioning of populations and elites by World War II. Wartime demonstration of the rapidity of military operations and the ability to direct military force across great distances, coupled with new and more sophisticated communications, amplified the capacity for events in one nation to influence outcomes in others.

Each of these dimensions of interdependence affected choices concerning the Truman Doctrine, the Marshall Plan, and a North Atlantic treaty;[28] taking on the totality of problems and issues involving world order intensified the connectedness of events and outcomes as policymakers struggled to find solutions to problems. The very fact that one nation was committing its power and resources to resolving instability, insecurity, and economic chaos provided even tighter bonds of interdependence. Perhaps the chief result was that U.S. officials tended to magnify the impact of one event on others. They were prone to see dominoes and bandwagons because of the responsibilities they had assumed.

The core of the credibility syndrome was the conclusion that world stability depended not only on the commitment and application of U.S. power but equally on the firm confidence that these would continue. The credibility of its promises and threats was integral to the kind of world the United States sought: a cooperative system of liberal capitalism. Such an order required several nations with divided and weakened political systems to move toward arrangements for an open and competitive capitalism and to assume the many domestic and international risks that doing so entailed.[29] Following the U.S. lead placed significant strains on governing coalitions in France, Italy, and Germany. Only with high confidence that American power and resources were unequivocally dedicated to their prosperity and security could political coalitions favorable to the United States and liberal capitalism survive. The 1947–48 period produced an intense appreciation of this situation by U.S. officials which, combined with sensitivity to the interdependencies in world order, moved concern over credibility to the center of foreign policy choices.

From the very beginning of the 1947 crisis, officials portrayed a tightly interdependent international system poised on the brink of a "catastrophic deterioration of the world situation."[30] Most concluded that a U.S. leadership failure, particularly in permitting the British or the European position to decay in the face of the Soviet challenge, would have repercussions not only for the "control of Europe" but also in the "Middle East and Far East and throughout the colonial world."[31] Kennan, deeply concerned about "Europe's pathetic weakness," believed that the United States had to make a clear and continuing indication of its determination to provide political and economic support. An unequivocal signal of U.S. commitment was essential if European leaders were to risk aligning themselves with the United States and adopting a plan that would require a series of difficult political and economic choices.[32] "If the nations of the world lose confidence in us," said General George Lincoln, "they may in effect pass under the Iron Curtain without any pressure other than the subversive pressure being put on them."[33]

The need for absolutely clear and convincing signals of U.S. commitment was repeated over and over to support additional actions by the United States for example, in 1946 General Lucius Clay, U.S. military governor in Germany, argued for persuading the Germans that they would never be "abandoned to the Communists or the Soviets" if they cooperated with the United States. Shortly afterward, Secretary of State James Byrnes reassured the German leaders and people that U.S. troops would not leave Germany.[34] In 1947, Secretary of State George Marshall underscored the significance of convincing the French that the United States would not repudiate its allies and had a long-term commitment to controlling German power.[35] And officials hoped that a variety of signals indicating a commitment to European prosperity would encourage governments in France and Italy to exclude communists from power.[36]

Concern over the effectiveness of U.S. signals of resolve and expectations of disaster should this world-order project fail made U.S. officials especially sensitive to expressions of doubt. In January 1948 representatives in France and Great Britain described a "fear psychosis" in Western Europe accompanied by a perception of the United States as erratic. French officials asserted a "strong and widespread" belief that the United States would not defend Western Europe from Soviet aggression.[37] The French peppered the Americans with a constant barrage of fears for their security, both from Germany and the Soviets; they would be satisfied with nothing less than a concrete indication of U.S. involvement in European defense from the beginning of any war. The U.S. ambassador to Great Britain reported in August the British realization that their security and economic fate was nearly "completely dependent" on the United States: "The British see the world dangerously unbalanced, in which only a few errors of policy may lead them to national devastation. In this world they are at the mercy of forces beyond their control, and must rely at every critical turn on U.S. decisions. They are therefore extremely sensitive to any U.S. action or inaction."[38] This conclusion mirrored the words of British Foreign Minister Ernest Bevin: "Our financial weakness has necessarily increased the dependence of our foreign policy on that of the only country which is able effectively to wield extensive economic influence—namely the U.S."[39] All such fears and requests placed great pressure on U.S. policy.

The Marshall Plan funds made major strides toward addressing these issues but were insufficient to support U.S. credibility in a crisis. The Czech coup in early 1948 and the Berlin blockade made clear that constant reassurance was needed to bind the Europeans to the U.S. system. These events presented the first major "test" of American leadership and thereby prompted U.S. officials to formulate the central premises of the credibility syndrome. John Hickerson, chief of the Office of European Affairs, responded to the Czech coup with a plea for a military commitment to Europe:

The existing situation in Europe contains two dangers: (1) that the Soviet Government underestimates the present temper of Congress and the American people and may accordingly push its expansionist tactics beyond the point of forceful American reaction, and (2) that too many people in the remaining free countries will be intimidated by the Soviet colossus and the absence of tangible American support to the point of losing their will to resist. Concrete evidence of American determination to resist further Communist encroachment would go far to reduce both dangers. . . . The greatest present danger lies in the Soviet Government mistakenly believing that it could take some particular action which in fact this country could not stand. An empty bluff on our part or failure to make clear the extent of this country's determination would be equally culpable and dangerous. [Soviet successes] . . . have created widespread fear and a certain bandwagon psychology. . . . A general stiffening of morale in free Europe is needed, and can only come from action by this country.[40]

Hickerson's memo helped persuade Secretary Marshall and President Truman of the need for the United States to join talks on the Atlantic security system.[41] This memo demonstrates how the concerns and fears of American leaders were embedded in the situation of U.S. world leadership and its implications for credibility.

Similar considerations defined the U.S. response to the Berlin blockade. Averell Harriman, special representative to the European Recovery Program (ERP), warned that there was constant fear of war in Europe and that "appeasement psychology . . . is not deeply buried." In a series of meetings following the restriction of Western access, there was widespread agreement with the views of Secretary Marshall that "the U.S. had the alternative of following a firm policy in Berlin or accepting the consequences of failure of the rest of our European policy." Undersecretary of State Robert Lovett believed "that any show of weakness now will be absolutely fatal."[42] President Truman and General Clay agreed with Lovett: "If we move out of Berlin we have lost everything we have been fighting for."[43] Each of these leaders was echoing the importance of U.S. credibility to world-order goals. Their views were rooted in an acceptance of responsibility for world order, a keen sense of the interdependence of political, economic, and strategic affairs, and an intense sensitivity to the believability of U.S. threats and promises.

The application of superior U.S. power went beyond the use of economic resources. Officials were very conscious of the importance of controlling the use of military force in the system, specifically the potential for war by miscalculation and Soviet risk-taking short of war. The possibility of war, though remote, terrified the French and others and undermined their willingness to participate in the U.S. system. The ability to deter, with confidence, hostile Soviet moves served as an essential psychological underpinning to a successful world-order project.

Melvyn Leffler has demonstrated, conclusively, the role of power advantages in achieving U.S. postwar goals. Officials understood the political and strategic significance of U.S. preponderance and were determined to preserve it, extend it, and use it to gain their objectives.[44] Hegemonic capabilities were essential in the commitment of resources to Europe and Asia; they provided the support necessary to make security guarantees believable, and deterrence of Soviet aggression and risk-taking possible. Perhaps the greatest certainty rested in the conclusion that U.S. power blocked any deliberate Soviet decision to begin a war. Officials did not waver in the view that the superiority of U.S. warmaking capacity, strategic air power, and monopoly on the atomic bomb meant that the Soviets would not risk actual war. The United States held the upper hand; in a crunch, the Soviets would back down.[45]

Worries persisted about risk-taking short of war: the Soviets might be led to act by doubts about a U.S. response or provoked by imprudent U.S. behavior.[46] Policymakers wanted to prevent the development of situations that might produce war. Deterring overt Soviet military attack and risk-taking, even while avoiding provocation, called for a subtle strategy. Rather than trying to spell out the circumstances in which war might occur, the United States appears to have relied on a blanket though unstated threat of retaliation for Soviet misdeeds. Officials confidently expected American superiority and risk-taking advantages to give serious pause to a wide array of possible Soviet challenges. Essential to this process was a high degree of certainty regarding the believability of U.S. promises and threats. Military superiority, control over risk-taking, and credibility were bound together by the needs of hegemony.

The combination of superior power and an image of resolve was increasingly founded on the atomic bomb. The emergence of an explicit military dimension to hegemony in the North Atlantic Treaty accentuated the need for a viable strategy linking force and political objectives. The expansion of commitments to Europe and Asia led military officials and Secretary of Defense James Forrestal to press for dramatic increases in military spending. President Truman responded instead with a sequence of decisions expanding the production of atomic weapons. War plans, overall military strategy, and the image of U.S. military supremacy became focused on the atomic arsenal.[47] The power of the bomb, coupled with the conviction that it would be used in war, provided the military backing for the commitments of 1947–49 and, consequently, for hegemony itself. In September 1948, NSC 30 called the atomic bomb the "major counterbalance" to the Soviets, an essential ingredient in West European security and economic recovery, and warned of the dangers of any "doubt" about its use in the event of war.[48]

By the end of 1948 all the main elements of the credibility syndrome were present and directing major policy choices. U.S. responsibility for world order was a foregone conclusion. Global interdependence—strategic, political, and economic—defined the terms of the problems to be solved. Officials routinely understood situations in terms of the credibility of U.S. promises and threats.

"Confidence," "morale," and "doubts" were stock terms used in evaluating immediate threats and problems. Credibility was tied to global interdependence, and any apparent weakening in U.S. resolve was expected to result in a series of negative consequences. Bolstering credibility had become a central concern of policy, both to reassure allies and to block Soviet actions that might damage world order. Superior U.S. war capabilities and monopoly on atomic weapons, combined with resolute actions in a crisis, operated to enhance credibility, control risk-taking, and build confidence in allies.

Gaddis has argued that this period was dominated by a realistic differentiation between vital and peripheral interests, a matching of resources and commitments, and a successful resistance to globalism. Instead, we should be more cognizant of the tensions created by a policy based on the logic of hegemony. Attention to interdependence combined with the political and psychological demands of credibility produced the possibility of an exponential growth of commitments. Officials were very conscious of this process and the possible strain on resources. George Kennan expressed the dilemma facing the United States in its position as world leader: Denial of the requests for support coming from many countries would be taken as a "lack of interest" and as "evidence that we had 'written them off' to the Russians." But, cautioned Kennan, there might be "no logical stopping point" in an alliance system that "circled the globe." Secretary of State Marshall echoed these sentiments, saying that "obviously the line must be drawn somewhere or the United States would be underwriting the security of the whole world."[49]

The contradictions between the logic of world leadership and the logic of traditional realism coexisted uncomfortably in U.S. thinking during these years. The effort to gain support for a U.S.-defined world system depended on confidence in the United States, which called for reassurance and commitments along many of the lines of interdependence between Europe and the world. At the same time, many U.S. leaders recognized the implications of such a strategy: a potential loss of control over policy, and an enormous continuing obligation of U.S. blood and treasure. The tension between hegemony and realism was never clearly resolved—hardly surprising, given that U.S. officials were operating in uncharted territory. Nevertheless, the impact of world leadership was demonstrated by the steady erosion of proportionality and limitations in the face of the perceived costs of failing to act in crisis situations.

Two examples of this process came at the beginning of the Marshall Plan when European recovery and long-term prosperity were thought to depend on access to Asian and African markets, resources, and investment opportunities. The decision to revive the Japanese economy, also taken in 1947–48, not only expanded the range of interests but also accentuated the role of Southeast Asia. The Japanese and European need for resources and markets raised the stakes of the French struggle in Indochina and led in 1948 to a commitment of funds to facilitate these economic relations.[50] Despite strong sentiment for "drawing the line" in Asia, and the expression of these desires in American Policy on China, the United States was pulled closer toward commitments in Asia from 1947 to 1949.[51]

The same logic of hegemony that undermined realism on the periphery also made the advent of a Soviet atomic bomb a traumatizing event. The ten months from the discovery of a Soviet atomic explosion in August 1949 to the beginning of the Korean War in June 1950 provided the context that solidified the credibility syndrome as the operative basis for foreign policy choices. The deliberations and actions associated with the development of a hydrogen bomb, the expansion of U.S. military capabilities, and intervention in the Korean civil war demonstrate conclusively that credibility calculations were central to policymaking even before Korea. It was with these three decisions that the United States took the final steps of assuming the responsibilities of hegemony.

The response to the Soviet atomic bomb was directed by considerations of military superiority and the consequent political, psychological, and strategic issues. The evidence indicates a very deep concern for preserving the tangible and psychological advantages enjoyed by the United States and a great fear of the cataclysmic consequences of failing to act. At the very heart of this thinking was the credibility syndrome, which defined the issues associated with superiority, credibility, and risk-taking.

Military officers were the first to argue that a U.S. hydrogen bomb was essential. They did so by focusing on the impact of the Soviet H-bomb on the U.S. international position through its effects on credibility. A Soviet monopoly on the "Super" would have "grave psychological and political repercussions . . . [for the] unity of spirit, confidence and determination" in the West. The Soviets would receive a "tremendous psychological boost," prompting use of the "tremendous 'blackmail' potential of the thermonuclear weapon . . . [to] alienate" Europeans from the United States. The "magnetizing effect" of the bomb could predispose Germany toward neutrality, and the "extreme vulnerability" of Great Britain would subject it to significant pressure for accommodation.[52]

The State Department was initially more circumspect but by January 1950 had accepted the same credibility-based interpretation of U.S. interests.

Aside from the obviously dangerous military position in which we and our allies would find ourselves if the Soviet Union were the exclusive possessor of such a weapon, we must take account of the disastrous disadvantage in which we would be put in the cold war. The superior war-making potential which provides the greatest part of the stiffening that keeps the whole non-Soviet world free would or would be made to appear to have evaporated. We could no longer assure the safety of any who would resist Soviet domination. Soviet communism would have achieved a triumph which would establish it in the eyes of those who hate us, doubt us, or fear us as the [wave?] of the future. There would be created a band-wagon psychology, always so important everywhere, and particularly in Southern Europe, Latin America, and Asia, which could disastrously undermine our position.[53]

Clearly, there was a common belief throughout the government that atomic superiority was linked to credibility and to the entire structure of U.S. policy.

The formal documents supporting the January 31, 1950, decision to proceed with thermonuclear development reflect this same line of analysis. Linking U.S. military power to American world leadership and international political and psychological alignments, the JCS (Joint Chiefs of Staff) and NSC reports emphasized the role of the H-bomb in preserving and even enhancing the U.S. power position. Alternatively, Soviet possession would drastically undermine the "unity" and "spirit" of the West while providing the Soviets a capability that would permit them to "risk hostilities" in achieving their objectives. These arguments "made a lot of sense" to President Truman, and he ordered that steps be taken to determine whether such a weapon could be made.[54] Truman also approved the full-scale policy review that produced NSC 68.

NSC 68 is famous for acknowledging "the responsibility of world leadership," for asserting the importance of blocking any further Soviet advance, and for a somewhat hyperbolic estimate of the Soviet threat.[55] Accompanying the deliberations was a set of assessments that were less ideological and perhaps better reflect the state of official thinking.

A broad consensus formed around the conclusion that the end of the U.S. atomic monopoly had undermined American control of the risks of war. The Soviets were expected to "feel safe in pursuing a more provocative foreign policy" against the "many weak spots . . . which the West cannot afford to lose."[56] Officials were barraged by reports of a deteriorating psychological and political climate in Europe. U.S. representatives abroad told of doubts about American firmness and worries over a deteriorating international situation. Germans, they said, were "nervous, hysterical and uncertain and had no great confidence in the coherence of Western Europe." These feelings were thought by many throughout Europe to result from an image of the West "on the defensive while the Soviets are showing more self confidence." Europeans were described as "hypersensitive" over any indication of a possible lowering of the U.S. commitment.[57]

This was the climate of opinion when the Korean War began. Korea had served as one of the focal points of the effort to limit U.S. commitments. Concerned by the proliferation of American responsibilities around the world, policy-makers had attempted to distinguish vital from peripheral interests.[58] But the responsibilities of hegemony—particularly the unceasing demands of credibility—made any such effort problematic at best. The contradiction between limiting commitments and fulfilling the credibility needs of hegemony was managed by attempting to finesse the process of withdrawal from Korea. Additional aid and the elapse of time would shift the onus for any failure to the South Korean government itself.[59] Once war broke out, however, the United States could not escape responsibility for events. The pressures of credibility obliterated any sense of traditional realism, which would have counseled restraint in a situation of intrinsically low interests.

There was near unanimity among those responsible for American foreign policy concerning the Korean War. Events there were viewed as a "test" of American commitments and the "resoluteness" and "firmness of U.S. resistance to communist expansion." This was a "clear-cut Soviet challenge" to American power and thereby constituted "a threat to our leadership of the free world."[60] The U.S. ambassador to the Soviet Union cabled Acheson that the "entire free world [is] focusing attention on [the] U.S. reaction to [the] Korean situation." Officials throughout the government predicted extreme danger to the nation's international interests and objectives in Asia and Europe and increased risks of general war. Defeat in Korea would have "calculably grave and unfavorable repercussions" around the world, be a "severe blow" to "U.S. prestige throughout Asia," and engender a growing feeling of Soviet "invincibility" with a corresponding "bandwagon effect." The Japanese would move toward neutralism and away from alignment with the United States. In Western Europe the challenge to U.S. "might and will" could "only lead to serious questioning of that might and will," especially in Germany. What was on the line in Korea was the international calculus of American power and credibility—the "shadow cast by power"—with a significant potential for nations now associated with the United States to engage in a "fundamental reconsideration of [their] position in the cold war."[61]

These views did not suddenly emerge with Korea; they were the same fears and concerns that had been expressed repeatedly over the preceding three years.

Once again, officials were barraged with reports of extreme worry and concern in Europe over the implications of a Soviet-sponsored attack and whether and how the United States would respond. On June 27 Acheson reported that "the governments of many Western European nations appeared to be in a state of near-panic, as they watched to see whether the United States would act." Cables from McCloy in Germany and Bruce in France described great fear at the boldness of the Soviet resort to overt attack and the feeling of "extreme nakedness" from being nearly defenseless.[62] The result was a forceful U.S. intervention in the conflict and an unqualified globalization of hegemony.

Conclusion

Analyzing the early Cold War in terms of U.S. credibility is not especially controversial. Rather, the main questions are whether credibility must be seen as a policy syndrome incorporating responsibility, interdependence, superiority, and risk-taking; when and whether this syndrome directed policy choices; and why credibility assumed such a large role. Can the concept of hegemony successfully organize the documentary evidence on the early Cold War and provide a convincing explanation for the role of U.S. credibility thinking in this process?

Certainly, the evidence presented here shows the decisive importance of credibility calculations long before the Korean War. Indeed, it is impossible to understand U.S. actions from 1947 to 1950 without constant reference to the credibility syndrome. The Marshall Plan, the North Atlantic Treaty, and actions in the Berlin blockade were motivated by the need to protect the assets of Europe and the pressures of providing tangible help to the area. But the analysis of the situation was framed by the importance of world order, a sense of international economic and security interdependence, and the need to send an unmistakable signal of U.S. commitment, coupled with fears of the catastrophic consequences of a failure to act. The H-bomb decision and NSC 68 served to flesh out this logic and link it more clearly to military superiority. Efforts to put a brake on the scope of commitments eventually foundered on the deeply felt concern for credibility.

This evidence, in conjunction with measures of U.S. power and the broad array of actions establishing world order, forces a rethinking of whether bipolarity or hegemony better advances our understanding of the impact of the international system on policy choices. The concept of hegemony neither requires nor implies a unipolar system. Hegemony sees a world in which one power is significantly stronger than the rest and acts to establish an international order to its liking, but such a world does not preclude a challenger. Hence, post-1945 Europe *was* bipolar but in a very limited sense and not in the terms Gaddis and others have proposed. At all points in the Cold War the Soviets were inferior to the United States, and the difference is even more pronounced when we add in the various allies. For Gaddis's notion of bipolarity to have merit, the poles need to be roughly equal. But neither the Americans nor the Soviets acted as if they saw such an equality. The United States was constantly augmenting and applying its military, economic, and political superiority; the Soviet Union was constantly backing down, shrinking from any real risk of war, and trying to catch up.

To be sure, in the power relationship after World War II the Soviets could resist and even threaten the U.S. world order. But the U.S. posture was not just that of the other (equal) pole. The United States did not act as if it were a nineteenth-century balancer. Rather, it acted as a hegemon, determined to quarantine this challenger and contain its expansion; to reorganize the domestic political economy of its major allies; to make an absolute commitment to defend the security of those allies through a multilateral system; to reorder and stabilize international economic relations; to augment its power in order to maintain superiority; and to sustain world order along the manifold lines of interdependence linking states together. Out of this posture emerged a foreign policy based extensively on establishing, marshaling, and preserving a reputation for sustaining all promises and meeting all threats to global security and prosperity. U.S. credibility became the day-to-day currency of hegemony; without it the global order wanted by the United States would have fallen apart through defections and challenges. Gaddis's sense of bipolarity cannot account for the role of credibility at any point in the Cold War.

Furthermore, a distinct strategy linking the broad political goals of world order to credibility concerns and military force emerged in the midst of the critical 1947–49 period. Its central premise was that the Soviet Union would avoid the risks of general war because of U.S. military potential and monopoly on the atomic bomb. Thus, success in achieving world stability was tied to a recognition of U.S. superiority on the part of both adversaries and allies. This permitted the United States to make credible commitments and take risks of war the Soviets dared not match. That an asymmetry of power, not an equality, provided the central dynamic of the Cold War is unmistakably revealed in documented 1949–50 decisions and deliberations.

The expansion of American power was tied closely to the effects of hegemony and credibility. Certainly, "empire by invitation" is an effective way of seeing U.S. expansion. But in addition to urging U.S. involvement, foreign leaders also expressed fears about U.S. reliability. It was the combination of pulling by the rest of the world and great U.S. apprehension about the consequences of a failure to respond that produced the proliferation of commitments. The situation did represent a "delicate balance"—not of power as traditionally conceived but of credibility, superiority, and risk-taking. The fragility of that balance as seen by U.S. officials is understandable, given the difficulties of retaining allegiance to a complex security and prosperity system, the role of confidence and commitment, the importance of superiority in capabilities and risk-taking, and the many lines of interdependence that might have unraveled.[63]

When did U.S. policy assume global proportions? Robert McMahon asserts that "the question of when Washington adopted a globalist outlook underlies most current debates about the origins and course of the Cold War."[64] But asking when globalism happened, trying to fix a particular point in time, is the wrong approach. Globalization was a process stretching over many years, perhaps 1940 to 1950. Its underlying causes were the world economic and military crisis and the ability and willingness of the United States to act as the world stabilizer. Frequently, the immediate sources of an individual act of expansion were intense worry about U.S. credibility and the ability of the Soviets to act in ways that challenged U.S. commitments. The triumph of hegemonic conceptions of policy over traditional realism was prompted by the political requirements of world leadership and the tremendous reservoir of U.S. power. Globalism may not have been the conscious purpose of any single official, but it was a predictable consequence of the demands of world leadership in the postwar era.

Notes

Acknowledgments: This essay was originally prepared for presentation at the Conference on Rethinking the Cold War, University of Wisconsin–Madison, October 18–20, 1991. I thank Melvyn Leffler and the late Edward Pessen for their comments and encouragement, and Barton Bernstein for his unflinching criticisms.

1. Combining John Lewis Gaddis, Melvyn Leffler, and Geir Lundestad in the camp of postrevisionists may raise some eyebrows. But all share at least two essential characteristics of postrevisionism: an effort to adopt a more sophisticated understanding of the economic dimensions of U.S. foreign policy, and an attempt to use power relationships to understand the Cold War.

2. Robert McMahon, "Credibility and World Power: Exploring the Psychological Dimension in Postwar American Diplomacy," *Diplomatic History,* 15 (Fall 1991): 455–71, accentuates the significance of an analysis of credibility for understanding postwar U.S. foreign policy. McMahon's arguments hint at the relationship between hegemony and credibility, considered below.

3. John Lewis Gaddis, "The Emerging Post-Revisionist Synthesis on the Origins of the Cold War," *Diplomatic History* 7 (Summer 1983): 174–75, 177, 180–182.

4. See Thomas G. Paterson, *On Every Front* (New York: Norton, 1981); Kenneth Waltz, *Theory*

of International Politics (Reading, Mass.: Addison-Wesley, 1979); John J. Mearsheimer, "Back to the Future: Instability in Europe after the Cold War," *International Security* 15 (Summer 1990): 5–56.

5. John Lewis Gaddis, "The Long Peace: Elements of Stability in the Postwar International System," in Gaddis, *The Long Peace: Inquiries into the History of the Cold War* (New York: Oxford University Press, 1987), 221–22.

6. John Lewis Gaddis, *Strategies of Containment* (New York: Oxford University Press, 1982), 23–30, 42, 58–59, 72.

7. This argument can be found in Gaddis, *The Long Peace*, 20–102; Gaddis, "Was the Truman Doctrine a Real Turning Point?" *Foreign Affairs* 52 (January 1974): 386–402; Gaddis, "NSC 68 and the Soviet Threat Reconsidered," *International Security*, 4 (Spring 1980): 164–70; Gaddis, *Strategies*, 83–126.

8. A similar version of this argument is found in Mearsheimer, "Back to the Future," 17. He sees bipolarity as a simple system, where resolve is calculated with clarity.

9. Mearsheimer (ibid., 26–27) suggests that for about fifteen years the two superpowers needed to figure out the "rules of the road," and this led to several crises based on questions of resolve. But this argument fails to explain U.S. activities in Vietnam after 1960—when resolve issues were presumably settled—and the considerable credibility concerns of the Nixon administration. For the Vietnam decisions, see Thomas D. Lairson, "Credibility Calculations and Vietnam Decisions, 1954–1965" (unpublished manuscript); and for the Nixon years, Robert Litwak, *Detente and the Nixon Doctrine* (Cambridge: Cambridge University Press, 1984). Waltz (*Theory*, 168–72, 190) also struggles unsuccessfully with the contradiction between the presumed logic of bipolarity and U.S. behavior. Another version of this criticism is found in Deborah Larson, *Origins of Containment* (Princeton, N.J.: Princeton University Press, 1985), 18–20.

10. Gaddis, "NSC 68." In this, Gaddis is joined by Burton Kaufman, *The Korean War: Challenges in Crisis, Credibility, and Command* (New York: Knopf, 1986); James Matray, *The Reluctant Crusade: American Foreign Policy in Korea, 1941–1950* (Honolulu: University of Hawaii Press, 1985); Matray, "Korea: Test Case of Containment in Asia," in *Child of Conflict*, ed. Bruce Cumings (Seattle: University of Washington Press, 1983), 169–193; and William Stueck, *The Road to Confrontation* (Chapel Hill: University of North Carolina Press, 1981).

11. Gaddis, "Emerging Post-Revisionist Synthesis," 182–83.

12. John Lewis Gaddis, "The Strategic Perspective: The Rise and Fall of the 'Defensive Perimeter' Concept, 1947–1951," in *Uncertain Years*, ed. Dorothy Borg and Waldo Heinrichs (New York: Columbia University Press, 1980), 115–18.

13. A political scientist, Jack Snyder, has recently argued that virtually all great powers have depended on bandwagon and domino metaphors to justify foreign commitments, but his evidence for this conclusion is unfortunately anecdotal rather than systematic. See his introduction and conclusion to *Dominoes and Bandwagons*, ed. Robert Jervis and Jack Snyder (New York: Oxford University Press, 1991), 3–19, 276–90. In the same volume, 112–44, Douglas J. Macdonald, "The Truman Administration and Global Responsibilities: The Birth of the Falling Domino Principle," offers a variation of the Gaddis thesis that realism in Europe was overwhelmed by credibility in Asia.

14. Robert H. Johnson, "Exaggerating America's Stakes in Third World Conflicts," *International Security* 10 (Winter 1985–86): 32–68; Jerome Slater, "Dominos in Central America: Will They Fall? Does It Matter?" *International Security* 12 (Fall 1987): 45–62; Bruce Jentleson, "America's Commitments in the Third World: Theory vs. Practice," *International Organization* 41 (Autumn 1987): 667–704. The basic argument of this group of scholars is consistent with one other explanation offered

by Gaddis: that credibility is a result of the irrationality of U.S. officials. See Gaddis, *Strategies,* 238–43; and Gaddis, "NSC 68."

15. A systemic approach need not assume that international systems are always more important than domestic systems, or that such systems must have the same effects on all states to be worthy of investigation (Waltz, *Theory,* adopts this somewhat stringent view). Nor does it necessarily try to define which consequences were inevitable. Rather, we need assume only that international systems constrain behavior in some consistent and identifiable way.

16. Robert Gilpin, *The Political Economy of International Relations* (Princeton, N.J.: Princeton University Press, 1987), 72–80; Steven Krasner, "State Power and the Structure of International Trade," *World Politics* 28 (April 1976): 317–47; and Arthur Stein, "The Hegemon's Dilemma: Great Britain, the United States, and International Economic Order," *International Organization* 38 (Spring 1984): 355–86. Robert Keohane, *After Hegemony* (Princeton: Princeton University Press, 1984), 39–41, is unusual in addressing the question of military power and hegemony. A recent review of the thinking about hegemony is David P. Rapkin, "The Contested Concept of Hegemonic Leadership," in *World Leadership and Hegemony,* ed. Rapkin (Boulder, Colo.: Lynn Rienner, 1990), 1–19.

17. Geir Lundestad, *The American "Empire"* (New York: Oxford University Press, 1990), 33–35, 181 n. 18. The work of John Ikenberry, "Rethinking the Origins of American Hegemony," *Political Science Quarterly* 104 (1989): 375–400, closes some of this gap but still concentrates on economic issues. Despite Lundestad's commentary, hegemony is theoretically much better developed in precisely these areas than is the concept of empire and—with additional discussion of its political, military, and strategic components—captures the essence of the international system and U.S. actions to a far greater extent.

18. Lundestad, *American,* 38–39.

19. Credibility is normally thought of as the believability of promises and threats. The argument here is that the responsibilities of hegemony pushed U.S. officials to expand this notion considerably.

20. A key difference between this study and others emphasizing dominoes and bandwagons is the attention to a credibility syndrome and how these matters are linked by the logic of hegemony. This approach permits us to make a distinction between a state that sees falling dominoes and one that ties credibility to all its interests and fears the domino effects of *its* failures. For a contrasting position, see Jervis and Snyder, *Dominoes.*

21. Lundestad, *American,* 39–46; Lundestad, "Empire by Invitation? The United States and Western Europe, 1945–1952," *Journal of Peace Research* 23 (September 1986): 263–76. Also see Donald W. White, "The Nature of World Power in American History: An Evaluation at the End of World War II," *Diplomatic History* 11 (Summer 1987): 181–202.

22. See Matthew A. Evangelista, "Stalin's Postwar Army Reappraised," *International Security* 7 (Winter 1982–83): 110–38.

23. Important elements of a credibility syndrome existed before 1947. World War II established U.S. power as the arbiter of peace in the world and promoted a vastly expanded definition of U.S. national security. Given the U.S. role in organizing a global coalition to fight aggression, a nascent version of credibility and interdependence concerns emerged. See Robert Dalleck, *Franklin D. Roosevelt and American Foreign Policy, 1932–1945* (Oxford: Oxford University Press, 1979), 229–30, 215–17, 145, 179; Waldo Heinrichs, *Threshold of War: Franklin D. Roosevelt and American Entry into World War II* (New York: Oxford University Press, 1988), 46–47, 80–84, 118–23, 129, 159, 163, 210–14; and Arnold Offner, *The Origins of the Second World War* (New York: Praeger, 1975), 193, 209, 232. Also see Thomas J. McCormick, *America's Half-Century* (Baltimore, Md.: Johns Hopkins University Press, 1989), 17–42.

24. This explanation of the threat is provided most completely in Melvyn P. Leffler, *A Preponderance of Power* (Stanford, Calif.: Stanford University Press, 1992).

25. Quoted in ibid., 143, 145.

26. In *Foreign Relations of the United States* (hereafter *FRUS*), 1947, III: 208–9.

27. For a description of this process, see Michael Hogan, *The Marshall Plan* (Cambridge: Cambridge University Press, 1987), 32–45; and Walter Isaacson and Evan Thomas, *The Wise Men* (New York: Simon & Schuster, 1986), 386–418. Also very useful is Scott Jackson, "Prologue to the Marshall Plan: The Origins of the American Commitment for a European Recovery Program," *Journal of American History* 65 (March 1979): 1043–68.

28. Leffler, *Preponderance,* makes the case for this point in terms of economic linkages in Europe and with much of the world (152, 162, 164), and for a long list of political and strategic connections (200, 226). Michael Schaller, *The American Occupation of Japan* (New York: Oxford University Press, 1985), shows how U.S. officials understood the linkages between the Japanese economy and Southeast Asia.

29. Leffler, *Preponderance,* repeatedly makes this point.

30. *FRUS,* 1947, III:402–3, 397–403, 43–44, 48, 216, 345–46.

31. Ibid., 327, 476.

32. This position was taken in an extraordinary but usually overlooked memo dated September 4, 1947, and found in *FRUS,* 1947, III:397–403, see also 221–23, 225, 360–61. Support for Kennan's views is found at 688–92, 694, 709–13, 718–19, 723–25, 734–36, 761–63, 766–73, 787, 475–76.

33. Statement by General George A. Lincoln of the War Department General Staff to the Senate Foreign Relations Committee, quoted in Gaddis, *The Long Peace,* 41.

34. Leffler, *Preponderance,* 119–20.

35. Ibid., 153.

36. Ibid., 143, 157, 190, 205.

37. *FRUS,* 1948, III: 617–18, 1074–75, 1109.

38. Ibid., 1113–15.

39. Taken from a January 1947 memo now located in the Public Record Office, Foreign Office 371/62420/176. A slightly different version is cited in Peter Weiler, "British Labour and the Cold War: The Foreign Policy of the Labour Governments, 1945–1951," *Journal of British Studies* 26 (January 1987): 57.

40. *FRUS,* 1948, III:40–42. Hickerson's analysis and subsequent U.S. actions were sustained by PPS (Policy Planning Staff) 27, March 3, 1948, in ibid., 61–64.

41. Ibid., 44–52, 775–82.

42. Ibid., 183–84. *The Forrestal Diaries,* ed. Walter Millis (New York: Viking, 1951), 459, 454; report of NSC meeting, July 23, 1948 in President's Secretary File (hereafter PSF), Box 220, Harry S. Truman Library, Independence, Missouri.

43. Leffler, *Preponderance,* 221.

44. Ibid.

45. Ibid., 210, 116, 149, 307. For assessments of the Soviet-American power relationship and the chances of war, see *FRUS,* 1948, I (pt. 2): 541–42, 550–57; *FRUS,* 1948, III: 283–89 (esp. 284 n. 2, 285, 287), 184–88, 300–310; Thomas Etzold and John Gaddis, *Containment: Documents on American Policy and Strategy, 1945–1950* (New York: Columbia University Press, 1978), 114–20, 162. Kennan's analysis is found in *FRUS,* 1948, I (pt. 2): 615–24.

46. Leffler, *Preponderance,* 210.

47. *FRUS,* 1948, III, 591, 566, 557–64; *FRUS,* 1948, I (pt. 2): 644–50, 652–62, 620, 629–31,

624–25; Etzold and Gaddis, *Containment,* 164–69, 315; Greg Herkin, *The Winning Weapon* (New York: Vintage Books, 1981), 261–64, 196–98, 227–44; Kenneth Condit, *The History of the Joint Chiefs of Staff* (Wilmington, Del.: Glazier, 1979), 152–53, 191; David Alan Rosenberg, "American Atomic Strategy and the Hydrogen Bomb Decision," *Journal of American History* 66 (June 1979): 66–68; David Alan Rosenberg, "The Origins of Overkill: Nuclear Weapons and American Strategy, 1945–1960," *International Security* 7 (Spring 1983), 11–12, 14.

48. NSC 30, "United States Policy on Atomic Weapons," dated September 30, 1948, can be found in Etzold and Gaddis, *Containment,* 339–43.

49. *FRUS,* 1948, III: 285–87. (Keenan), 197 (Marshall).

50. Melvyn Leffler, "The United States and Strategic Dimensions of the Marshall Plan," *Diplomatic History* 12 (Summer 1988): 302–3; Schaller, *American Occupation,* 77–97, 122–63; Michael Schaller, "Securing the Great Crescent: Occupied Japan and the Origins of Containment in Southeast Asia," *Journal of American History* 69 (September 1982): 392–414; Bruce Cumings, "The Origins and Development of the Northeast Asian Political Economy," *International Organization* 38 (Winter 1984): 1–40; Andrew J. Rotter, *The Path to Vietnam* (Ithaca, N.Y.: Cornell University Press, 1987), 103–203.

51. Very useful on this topic is Stueck, *Road to Confrontation,* 38–57.

52. See Joint Intelligence Committee 502, 1/20/50, app. B, p. 15, and app. A, p. 5, in Records of the Joint Chiefs, CCS 471.6, USSR (Section 1), RG 218, National Archives; and *FRUS,* 1949, I: 604–10.

53. Memo from Robert Hooker, of the Policy Planning Staff in the State Department, January 14, 1950, in PPS Box 50, National Archives. For the State Department position in October 1949, supporting another acceleration of atomic weapons production, see *FRUS,* 1949, I:559–64. Examples of a more diffident position are found in memos by Paul Nitze (soon to assume Kennan's position as head of the PPS) and Secretary of State Dean Acheson on December 19 and 20, 1949; see *FRUS,* 1949, I:610–17. By January, Acheson and Nitze had moved to support the H-bomb for the same reasons as Hooker.

54. *FRUS,* 1950, I:503–23.

55. The document can be found in ibid., 237–92, and in Etzold and Gaddis, *Containment,* 385–442 (quotation at 390).

56. See the PPS memo, April 14, 1950, and Bureau of European Affairs in the State Department memo, April 19, 1950, in *FRUS,* 1950, III: 858, 843. Also see *FRUS,* 1950, I:145–47; CIA, "Review of the World Situation," 2/15/50, PSF, NSC meetings, Box 207, and CIA, "The Effects of Soviet Possession of Atomic Bombs on the Security of the United States," 6/9/50, PSF, Intelligence—Central Intelligence Reports 32–58, both in the Truman Library; and memo by Paul Nitze, *FRUS,* 1950 I:145–47.

57. CIA, "The Current Western European Attitude toward the North Atlantic Treaty," 4/27/50, PSF, Intelligence—Central Intelligence Reports 18–29, Truman Library; *FRUS,* 1950, III: 639, 1360–63, 1369–71, 913–14, 883, 60, 46.

58. Gaddis, "Strategic Perspective, 61–118; Stueck, *Road to Confrontation,* 75–110, 153–71. For an unqualified statement of credibility logic applied to Formosa prior to the Korean War, see the identical memos by John Foster Dulles and Dean Rusk in *FRUS,* 1950, VI:349–51 and I:314–16.

59. Gaddis, "Strategic Perspective," 103–4; Robert McMahon, "The Cold War in Asia: Toward a New Synthesis?" *Diplomatic History* 12 (Summer 1988): 310–14. For evidence of the application of credibility thinking to Southeast Asia before the Korean War, see Gaddis, "Strategic Perspective," 93–101.

60. *FRUS,* 1950, VII:139; CIA Memo 300, June 28, 1950, and CIA Memo 302, July 8, 1950, both in PSF, Intelligence, CIA Memos, 1950–52, Truman Library.

61. Dean Acheson, *Present at the Creation* (New York: Norton, 1969), 405–6; *FRUS*, 1950, VII:182, 139–40, 149–54, 199–202; "Conversation with Truman," June 26, 1950, and "Meeting of Executive-Legislative Leaders," June 27, 1950, both in George Elsey Papers, Box 71, Truman Library.

62. *FRUS*, 1950, IV:704, and III:1384, as cited in Ernest R. May, "The American Commitment to Germany, 1949–1955," *Diplomatic History* 12 (Fall 1989): 444. Also see *FRUS*, 1950, VII:198, 175, 201. In the Truman Library, see Acheson Papers, Memos of Conversations, 1950 (May–June); Elsey Papers, Box 71, Meetings of Executive-Legislative Leaders, June 27, 1950; and memo of NSC Meeting no. 58, June 29, 1950, PSF, NSC Meetings, Box 220.

63. On the subjective reality of closing windows of opportunity in the early Cold War, see Marc Tractenberg, "A 'Wasting Asset': American Strategy and the Shifting Nuclear Balance, 1949–1954," *International Security* 13 (Winter 1988–89): 5–49.

64. McMahon, "Cold War in Asia," 318.

Part II

Decentering the Cold War:
Looking South

Chapter 4

A Requiem for the Cold War: Reviewing the History of International Relations since 1945

Cary Fraser

It is now widely accepted that the Cold War is over and that a new era of international relations is emerging. Over the 1945–90 period the study of international relations was dominated by a focus on the rivalry between the United States and the Soviet Union and the consequences of their competition in Europe and the non-European world. As a result, the bipolar paradigm became the central prism through which international affairs were analyzed. The term "Cold War" was itself coined to portray the deep-seated conflict between the two superpowers and the European alliances—NATO and the Warsaw Pact—that they led. Despite various crises, enormous military expenditures, and the unresolved tensions underlying their relationship, the protagonists were themselves never directly engaged in a major military conflict or "hot war." It is arguable, however, that almost every war—civil or interstate—after 1945 was conducted in the shadow or with the support of one or both superpowers. Their capacity to project military power on a global scale, their ability to determine the levels of military assistance extended to the warring parties, and their control over enormous arsenals of conventional and nonconventional weapons (nuclear, biological, and chemical) allowed them to define tacitly, or on occasion explicitly, the parameters of international conflict in an unprecedented fashion.

This disproportionate military influence of the United States and the Soviet Union, including their preeminence within the major alliances of the post-1945 era, was responsible in large measure for the legitimacy accorded the bipolar paradigm in the study of international relations. In addition, the novelty of nuclear weapons, their increasing sophistication and deployment from tactical through strategic levels, and the potentially catastrophic consequences of their use inevitably required the expenditure of enormous intellectual effort to make sense of the nuclear age and the role of its leading protagonists. It would not be an exaggeration to argue that the study of international relations since 1945 has been largely defined by a fear of the consequences of war.[1] The ascendancy of the "realist" school in the study of international relations and of deterrence theory in the study of military strategy has been a function of the need to understand and calibrate the exercise of power in a context in which the axiom "War has no winners" could easily be restated as "Nuclear war would leave no survivors." The prominence of the bipolar paradigm in the analysis of international relations after 1945 encouraged a tendency to equate the Cold War—which, in strict terms, denotes the period 1945–90, covering the international relations of the European state system and the major alliances (NATO and the Warsaw Pact)—with the history of international relations since 1945.[2]

Notwithstanding its value as a heuristic device for studying the Soviet-American conflict, the bipolar paradigm has consistently proved itself inadequate as an analytical tool in studying the forces of change that have reshaped the international order. It offers a partial explanation of the parameters and dynamics of the superpower relationship but has been arguably less successful in explaining the influence of longer-term historical processes and of other state actors on the operations of the international order. Conventional wisdom posits that the overwhelming disparity in military capability of the superpowers vis-à-vis other states established the basis for a bipolar international order. But the emergence of Japan and Germany as the dominant powers of the early post-1989 order, without the military endowment of either the United States or the Soviet Union, should encourage analysts to continue rethinking the role of military power and the superpowers in international affairs. Having lost the 1939–45 "hot" war, Germany and Japan enjoyed the benefits of the Soviet-American rivalry without the enormous disruption in socioeconomic terms to which the two principals were subject. Although their relative lack of military capability has constrained their ability to pursue independent military initiatives, their comparative economic strength has served as a compensatory factor in issues of foreign policy. Since 1989, as the United States and the Soviet Union's successor states have become increasingly preoccupied with domestic problems, Germany and Japan have assumed a higher profile in international affairs based largely upon their roles in international economic affairs.

This essay seeks to challenge the common assumption that the Cold War and the history of international relations since 1945 are one and the same. It joins the ongoing debate and search for analytical frameworks within which to explain both the rise and demise of the nuclear superpower era and the continuing transformation of international relations in the contemporary world. It represents a conscious effort to bridge the present and the recent past in ways that may encourage analysts to rethink the study of international relations.[3] It argues the case for developing a historiography that reaches beyond the bipolar paradigm—so far, the most important lens through which post 1945 international affairs have been examined by both historians and political scientists. It identifies several crucial historiographical issues that cannot be adequately explained within a bipolar analysis. It argues, first, that neither the end of the Cold War via the reform processes in the USSR and Eastern Europe nor the emerging realignments in the politics of the European system of states can be explained in terms of a bipolar international order; second, that the role of the European states in reestablishing the post-1945 interstate order is more significant than bipolar models, emphasizing the role of the superpowers, have conceded; third, that the states of the Third World, individually and collectively, acted to limit the ability of the superpowers to establish and consolidate a bipolar international order after 1945; and fourth, that Third World states in pursuit of their own agendas have exploited the superpower rivalries to promote the processes of change since 1945. These four issues both validate the critique of the bipolar paradigm's explanatory power and offer some useful suggestions for elaborating a revised historiography of international relations since 1945.

The Postwar Era: A Reconsideration

The rapid disintegration of the post-1945 European state system and the waning influence of the superpowers have set the stage for scholars to rethink the course of international relations since the end of World War II. The dizzying pace of the collapse of the Warsaw Pact and its constituent regimes provided indisputable evidence that the assumptions of stability in bipolar international systems were flawed. Further, the implosion of the post-1945 European state system has revealed a wider transition from a European-dominated international order to one in which the Asian states are increasingly prominent. The magnitude of this transition and all it implies for thinking about the course of international relations since 1945 makes possible a more sophisticated appreciation of the changes under way in the international system. Rather than the transition from bipolarity to multipolarity, which has achieved great currency in contemporary debate, it would perhaps be appropriate to discuss the emergence of an Asia-Pacific-centered international system.[4]

The United States, Western Europe, and the European successor republics of the former Soviet Union have been confronted by domestic and European problems that will constrain their ability to compete with the Asian states—particularly Japan, Taiwan, South Korea, Malaysia, Singapore, India, and the People's Republic of China. Increasingly, these are the states whose policies will drive the process of transformation in the international system and set the international agenda on issues as diverse as trade, security, and responses to problems of global significance. Factors such as economic performance, technological sophistication and dynamism, population endowment, and market size have increasingly shifted the center of gravity in the world economy toward Asia and away from the North Atlantic trading system that evolved over the previous two centuries. The contemporary context, defined by the growing importance of the Asia-Pacific region and the evidence of long-term change it implies, will encourage scholars to devote greater attention to events and issues after 1945 that have hitherto been obscured by the conventional focus on the superpower conflict. By examining more systematically this transformation of the role of Asia in the international system, and the catalytic impact of the Cold War and the Korean and Vietnam Wars in that process, scholars will be able to situate the unraveling of the post-1945 European state system in a wider context.

One useful way of exploring the complexity of international relations would be to look at the events that shattered the bipolar system of Europe. The series of what have come to be called "Velvet Revolutions" in the Eastern Europe of late 1989 confront the historian with the inability of the bipolar paradigm to provide a coherent explanation of the relationship between the changes in the region and the wider disintegration of the bipolar axis upon which the international system was assumed to rest after 1945.[5] The Soviet Union under Mikhail Gorbachev after 1985 embarked upon a course of reform in both domestic and foreign policy which had far-reaching implications for the other members of the Warsaw Pact. That process of reform represented both an effort to restore dynamism to the economy of the Soviet Union and a search for a new equilibrium in Soviet relations with the Western states which would reflect greater cooperation across a wider range of issues. Although these policies were initiated by the Soviet leadership in response to domestic and foreign policy concerns on the part of the Soviet Union, it was evident that the other members of the Warsaw Pact would be affected by both the scope and pace of those changes.

Moreover, events in the smaller Warsaw Pact states influenced the reform process in the Soviet Union itself. The Soviet reform process was one consequence of a transfer of power within the Party to a new generation of leadership, but the crisis of communist rule predated Gorbachev's accession to power. Popular discontent in Hungary (1956) and Czechoslovakia (1968) had necessitated Soviet-led interventions to ensure that the pro-Soviet factions of the Communist Parties in each country could reassert their control. These interventions served temporarily to stabilize communist rule in Eastern Europe, but by 1981 the collapse of Communist Party authority in Poland necessitated the imposition of martial law to forestall military intervention by Warsaw Pact forces and to secure the fiction of communist legitimacy against the rise of popular discontent.[6]

It was this conundrum of the military displacing the Communist Party as the guarantor of the socialist state that foreshadowed the subsequent bankruptcy of East European governments. When the Soviet government refused to come to the aid of the East German regime—itself the epitome of socialist orthodoxy—against increasingly open challenges from its citizens in 1989, its collapse triggered a domino effect throughout the region. It had become evident that without a Soviet military guarantee the regimes lacked the internal legitimacy to survive challenges from their disaffected populations. The turn to the military to resolve the problems of the Polish Communist Party in 1981 portended the generalized crisis of legitimacy and power that continued throughout Eastern Europe. It is possible to argue that the Polish crisis of 1981 triggered the emergence of a Soviet reform strategy, for the tenuousness of Communist Party rule in Poland forced all the socialist countries to rethink the basis of their rule—including the Soviet Union itself. Thus, even as it served as the ultimate military guarantor of Communist Party rule in Eastern Europe, the Soviet Union was itself unable to overcome the crisis of legitimacy that afflicted all the communist regimes in Europe.[7]

Further, the forces for change acting upon the European state system and the superpowers were not restricted to Eastern Europe. The changing pattern of relations in the divided Germany fundamentally altered a major premise upon which the post-1945 European system had been constructed: the division of Germany to

prevent the emergence of a European order in which Germany was the pivotal actor. The reunification of Germany followed upon the steady rise of West German
influence as a consequence of its growing economic strength and the consolidation of a Franco-German axis in European affairs. After the collapse of communist
states in Eastern Europe and the reunification of Germany—all achieved with considerable popular support in the individual countries—it became obvious that the
earlier focus on the superpowers failed to anticipate that change from below could
force them to the margins of European developments. Notwithstanding their preeminence in European affairs, the shifting relations among European states
brought an end to the era over which the superpowers had presided.[8]

A further critique of the bipolar paradigm derives from its sense that the issues
defining the international order after 1945 were unique and thus that previous historical experience had little to offer in the way of guidelines. Nuclear weapons
served to deter interstate war and helped to create the conditions for post-1945 stability. Yet the events in Eastern Europe in late 1989 pointed to the fundamental
paradox of the nuclear age: the ability to harness the forces of destruction in the
service of peace does not imply the capacity to deter political and social change.
While the superpowers were seeking to assure their respective military security in
an age of intercontinental ballistic missiles, the European societies were seeking to
acquire or maintain room for maneuver vis-à-vis their military overlords. In the
final analysis, 1989 represented the triumph of the latter process at the cost of the
diminished military and political roles of the superpowers in European affairs, as
symbolized by the Intermediate Nuclear Forces Treaty, the reunification of Germany, and the Velvet Revolutions in Eastern Europe. Events in 1989 proved once
again that European peoples and states were capable of undermining the efforts of
major powers to stabilize the continent, nuclear weapons notwithstanding. The
only novelty here was that American and Soviet policymakers were learning that
lesson a century and a half after Metternich did when confronted by the revolutions of 1848. In effect, the bipolar state system increasingly appears to have been
but another historical phase in the evolution of Europe's efforts to create a system
for the management of the continent's conflicts.[9]

The scope of change within Europe has not been restricted to the diminution of
superpower influence in the continent's affairs. As xenophobia and nationalism
spread throughout Europe in the 1980s and into the 1990s—moving from West to
East and back again, demonstrating the interrelatedness of European societies—it
became evident that the nationalist resurgence was forcing both the pace and direction of European politics in unanticipated ways. The disintegration of Yugoslavia has come to symbolize the transition from the post-1945 European order.

This was the country that represented the fundamental paradox of that order: a communist state supported by the Western alliance which jealously guarded its independence vis-à-vis both major blocs.[10] Its survival was dependent upon a bipolar European order, but the contradictions of its existence always challenged the very sustainability of that order. The transformation of European politics in 1989 changed the context of Yugoslavia's existence, and its disintegration mirrored the central question of contemporary European politics: Could the search for greater unity among West Europeans be independent of the nationalist resurgence in the East that accompanied the collapse of the Warsaw Pact and the Soviet Union? The paralysis of the Europeans in the face of the implosion of Yugoslavia lies in part in a lack of preparedness for the irredentist sentiment driving various Serbian factions.[11] Yugoslavia also epitomizes the failure of a federalist solution to problems of ethnic pluralism in Europe and raises fundamental questions about the viability of closer integration among the West European states. In addition, the efforts by Serbian nationalists to crush Muslim self-rule—whether in Kosovo or in Bosnia-Herzegovina—and the tepid response by other European states to this campaign have provoked questions about the capacity of European polities to accommodate ethnic and cultural minority groups. As demonstrated by the surge of xenophobia in Europe, none of the contemporary European states are immune to the inherent tensions between nationalism and cultural pluralism. The vision of European integration or unity has been seriously tarnished by events in the former Yugoslavia.

The inability of the superpowers, in cooperation with the major European states, to stabilize Yugoslavia attests to the frailty of assumptions of the major powers' capabilities. The "Serbian Question" of the nineteenth century has returned in the twentieth century with a vigor that has rocked the foundations of political order in the region and the wider structure of European politics. The descent of the Yugoslav civil war into "ethnic cleansing," which evokes memories of the Nazi efforts to create a New European Order, challenges the notion that Europe has transcended its history. The legitimacy accorded to nationalism and nation-states has been a fundament of European international politics since the nineteenth century, and the genie has again been released from the bottle in the Balkans with yet-to-be-determined consequences for all of Europe. Neither the establishment of a bipolar system nor the end of communist rule in Europe has proved to be the antidote to instability in the European state system. Although the superpowers effectively maintained peace among the major European states between 1945 and 1989, in longer-term perspective it is not yet evident that their influence will be of greater durability than previous arrangements among the major powers in stabilizing the international relations of Europe.

But it was not only in Europe that there was a disjuncture between the image and the reality of superpower status. In Vietnam and in Afghanistan, both the United States and the Soviet Union learned that overwhelming military capability does not imply the capacity to control political change or fashion a new political order within another society. Further, their military defeats were exacerbated by domestic repercussions as both Americans and Soviet citizens questioned the cost and purpose of these interventions.[12] In both societies, among the long-term consequences of this challenge from the citizenry was the fragmentation of political authority and a challenge to the role of the military. In essence, if the preponderance of military might accruing to the superpowers after 1945 was an index of their power, it is not immediately obvious that their military capabilities were the fundamental determinant of relations among states, or that the sustainability of their military power would be both successful and uncontested over the long term.

Rethinking the Politics of Europe after 1945

A further step in rethinking the course of international relations since 1945 would require scholars to revisit the period between 1945 and 1950. It is generally agreed that this was the time when the Soviet-American wartime alliance collapsed and set in train the pattern of rivalry and conflict that characterized the subsequent relationship between the two powers. The conflict between the Soviet Union and its wartime partners over the future of Central and Southern Europe is generally blamed for the collapse of the anti-Axis coalition. For those attracted to simplistic verities, the struggle was one between American support for the establishment of democracies in these countries and Soviet support for the establishment of Marxist-Leninist states in the region. For those reluctant to embrace this simplistic notion of ideological struggle, other explanations—the Soviet search for a zone of influence in the region; the USSR's effort to establish the strategic depth necessary to counter a possible repeat of previous foreign invasions; the American support of West European leaders wary of the threat posed by strong Communist Parties in France and Italy to the survival of liberal-democratic regimes in the region; and the desire for an American politico-military commitment on the part of Europeans fearful of a Soviet threat or a revived Germany—have all provided rationales for the conflict over the spoils of World War II.[13]

Those factors did all play a role in Soviet-American relations and in the European state system. Other forces at work within Europe helped to shape the pattern of superpower interaction, however, and for the period 1945–50 scholars should address several key issues that may reshape conventional views. First, failure to forge a common vision of Europe undermined the ability of the continent's leaders to reestablish an autonomous state system after 1945. Polarization was one consequence of the loss of autonomy by the major European states other than Britain and the Soviet Union, and for much of the period after 1945 the Warsaw Pact and NATO served as multilateral agencies through which the Soviet Union and the Anglo-American alliance managed their respective spheres of influence. The establishment of these alliances followed upon the disagreements among the European states about the management of the process of reconstruction and their inability to agree upon the role of a reconstructed or reconstituted Germany.[14]

Second, although the Soviet role in the establishment of communist regimes in Eastern Europe cannot be denied, it is also noteworthy that the Soviet model and Communist Parties enjoyed a measure of legitimacy in Eastern Europe after 1945.[15] One possible explanation for this legitimacy was that the communists and Soviet military power were able to fashion an effective system of states out of the carnage and chaos that had beset the region over the previous century. The relative stability of Eastern Europe after 1948 followed upon a century of political change that had spanned the dissolution of the Austro-Hungarian, Czarist, Ottoman, and German empires amid increasing levels of military conflict. As the recent collapse of Soviet military influence and communism within the region has shown, political stability has not been an easy achievement for these states, and the rush to join NATO by former members of the Warsaw Pact suggests that their leaders recognize the need to participate in a multilateral framework for the management of the region's problems.[16] It is one of the ironies of history that Eastern Europe, which has been shaken by periods of virulent nationalism, has enjoyed stability only within the context of imperial or great-power condominiums which have themselves fallen victim to nationalist antagonisms.

Third, the Churchill-Stalin search for understandings on Eastern and Southern Europe were one effort to design a condominium for the region in the wake of Germany's defeat.[17] But the inability of Britain in subsequent years to reestablish itself in the Balkans, the wartime devastation of Germany, and the weakness of France in Europe and the wider world all combined to limit their influence over Eastern Europe. Given the frailty of European polities in the wake of the war, it was left largely to the United States and the Soviet Union to assume the leadership required to organize the entire European continent—the bipolar system of European states that lasted until 1989–90. Both halves of Europe outside the Soviet Union and Britain had succumbed to the excesses of nationalism in the first half of the twentieth century and paid the price of having their autonomy circumscribed by the superpower condominium after 1945.

The division of Europe into American and Soviet spheres was one consequence of the instability that beset European affairs; other fundamental problems arose out of the defeat and partition of Germany in 1945. From the 1860s onward "the German problem" precipitated several of the conflicts that afflicted the European state system. The process of German reunification occasioned two wars: the Austro-Prussian in 1866 and the Franco-Prussian in 1870. Germany's ambitions and the refusal of the other European states to accommodate German preeminence in Europe led to war in 1914 and 1939. The central task facing Europeans after 1945, from the perspective of the victors, was to construct a new European order in which Germany would not be restored to its pivotal role of 1870–1940.[18] Without the United States and the Soviet Union, that task would have proved impossible for the European states to accomplish. Analysts are thus confronted with the sense that the growth of Soviet and American influence in European politics after 1945 was due in large part to European efforts to gain their support for a system in which German influence could be contained. Despite the deep-rooted conflict between them, both superpowers enforced a collaborative agenda that was dear to the heart of many Europeans—maintaining the partition of Germany. The transformation of relations among and within the European states in 1989, especially the reunification of Germany, changed the context of Soviet-American relations in Europe. Germany is again the pivot of the European state system, and both the United States and Russia (as the main successor state of the Soviet Union) have adjusted their policies to reflect the diminution of their influence in European affairs as a consequence of the German resurgence.[19] By moving the focus away from the superpower conflict or perhaps, more appropriately, locating that conflict within the perennial question of the implications of German unification for European politics, scholars can begin to explore the evolution of European affairs since 1945 within a much more complex framework of analysis.

The fragility of superpower suzerainty over Europe was visible even in the early postwar period. The Yugoslav search for independence can be cited to demonstrate the ways in which Soviet-American relations and influence in Europe were shaped and limited by an actor whose military endowment was significantly inferior to that of either of the nascent superpowers. It is now a truism that Tito's Yugoslavia had more to do with prolonging the Greek civil war through support for the communist insurgency than did the Soviet Union. It was the British inability to sustain its military involvement in Greece in the face of the Yugoslav-supported guerrillas that led to the adoption of the Truman Doctrine.[20] Yet it was Yugoslavia under the same communist leadership which, within the next year, challenged Soviet policy in Eastern Europe and demonstrated the porosity of Soviet control over the region by using Western support to counter Soviet pressures. These Yugoslav policies and actions were occurring at the same time that the bipolar world according to the conventional wisdom, was being set in place. Yugoslavia was just the first of several smaller states that would manipulate their relationship with one or both superpowers for their own advantage.[21]

Further evidence comes from Czechoslovakia. In 1948 the communists in that country used Soviet support to undermine pro-Western groups and to establish a People's Democracy, helping to consolidate the division of Europe.[22] These events were seen as both a cause and a consequence of the polarization of the politics of the European state system. Similarly, French and Italian right-wing and centrist political forces used American support to help undermine the influence of the Communist Party in those countries in the late 1940s. The internal political alignments of the European states were as instrumental as the issue of a divided Germany in shaping the contours of post-1945 politics and the role of the superpowers in Europe. The importance of the internal politics of smaller states was again emphasized by opposition movements before 1989 in Poland, Czechoslovakia, Hungary, and East Germany.[23] These movements were instrumental in undermining the existing communist regimes, and their activities foreshadowed the collapse of the Warsaw Pact and of Soviet influence in Eastern Europe in 1989–91. Notwithstanding their condominium and military power, the superpowers were unable to control either the pace or direction of events as the internal politics of several European states set in train the collapse of the post-1945 order.

Shifting Parameters of Influence in the International System

Outside of Europe, two of the world's largest states, India and the People's Republic of China, emerged during the late 1940s, and both would have an impact upon the international order. India's reluctance to have its army used in support of Anglo-Dutch efforts to restore Dutch authority against the challenge of the Indonesian nationalist movement struck a major blow against the post-1945 European efforts to reassert their empires in Asia. India had won its independence in 1947, and the British very early recognized that India's role in Asia would affect Western policies in the region. Indian endorsement of the anticolonial struggle against European empires, not only in Indonesia but also in the United Nations and within the British Commonwealth, was of extraordinary importance to the evolution of the postwar international order. India's active diplomacy on behalf of the non-European world in a variety of forums allowed it to emerge as a major actor on the international stage after 1947, despite its relatively weak independent military capability.[24]

The role of the People's Republic of China (PRC) in the international system was largely a function of the success of the communists in the civil war and its pursuit of a foreign policy supportive of revolutionary movements. With the outbreak of the Korean War, China supported Kim Il Sung's efforts to consolidate control over the entire Korean peninsula, and the later use of its own military forces against United Nations troops would be only one of several instances when the PRC would support anti-Western revolutionary forces.[25] The Chinese role in the Korean War was also a critical factor in shaping the evolution of the Soviet-American relationship after 1950. The wariness of Mao Zedong toward the Soviet Union, following the latter's lukewarm support for the communists in the Chinese civil war and its efforts to retain great influence, if not control, over Manchuria, may have been a major factor in the PRC's search for an independent foreign policy after 1949.[26] The Chinese military assistance to North Korea and active support for the Vietminh and other insurgent forces in Southeast Asia, at a time when the Soviet Union's foreign policies were largely Eurocentric, may have been adopted by the PRC as ways of demonstrating its independence from the USSR. Whatever the motive, China was also emerging as a champion of the challenge to European colonialism and Western preeminence in Asia.

It would not be an exaggeration to argue that the emergence of India and China as independent actors supportive of the challenge to European colonialism in Asia and elsewhere constituted a major impediment to the ability of the superpowers to determine the political future of Asia during the years 1945–50. China's reunification under the Communist Party redefined its role in East Asia, transforming the country from a theater of intervention by outside powers to a major player in the regional order. China's activity in Korea upset the pre-1950 status quo there and forced the United States and the Soviet Union to recognize the reality of Chinese influence on the political future of the Korean peninsula. Chinese support for the Vietminh in Indochina helped to rout the French and encouraged the British to accelerate their disengagement from empire in Southeast Asia. In an interesting reversal of their pre-1945 roles, Japan increasingly became a bastion of American strategic influence in the Pacific, while China assumed the mantle of challenger to Western influence in East Asia.

This review of events in Europe and Asia in the decade after 1945 reveals an international order in which Soviet-American relations constituted only one of the major sources of conflict in the international system. It is obvious that the efforts of less powerful states to manipulate their relations with the United States and the

Soviet Union in order to achieve their own objectives influenced the workings of the international order and the relationship between the two major powers. In effect, superpower influence was exercised through the creation of coalitions with other states in various areas. The level of fluidity in the various contexts provided opportunities for the lesser states and actors to set agendas that the superpowers followed in pursuit of their own goals. It should be seen as a period of flux and shifting coalitions among states, including the superpowers, which demonstrated little of the stability assigned to the bipolar order by adherents of that school of thought. Further, in both Europe and Asia, perception of the capacity for independent action by smaller states may have to be reconsidered.

Later in the post-1945 period, lesser states in the international system assumed greater importance in constraining the activities of the superpowers, even as the latter consolidated their military strength through the development and control of nuclear weapons. It was Gamal Abdel Nasser of Egypt who encouraged the nationalist struggle in North Africa against French, British, and American efforts to maintain Western preeminence in the region. The Pan-Arab ideology that Nasser championed in the politics of the Middle East and North Africa during the l950s provided a platform for the wider challenge to Western influence in the Arab world.[27] Nasser's decision to nationalize the Suez Canal provoked the gravest challenge to the workings of the NATO alliance, and his search for Soviet support against the Western countries brought the USSR into the Middle East as a major player in the regional stakes. His policies toward the French and the British in the mid-1950s reduced their influence in the area and transformed the Middle East into an arena for superpower competition. The Eisenhower Doctrine was directed at Egypt and that country's efforts under Nasser to construct an anti-Western, anti-Israeli coalition with support from the communist powers. The interplay of regional politics with superpower rivalries in the Middle East was a legacy of Nasser's influence in the region, which persisted until the Gulf War of 1991. As in Europe after 1945, the capacity of a regional actor to define the framework of superpower interaction was evident in Nasser's policies over the period of his rule in Egypt.

In other contexts too these lesser powers acted on behalf of the struggle by nationalist movements to bring the European colonial enterprise to an end. Yugoslavia, Egypt, and India were central in the creation of the Nonaligned Movement, which served as an umbrella for the coordination of support for nationalist movements in non-European states.[28] Their collective efforts were the outcome both of their individual limitations vis-à-vis the superpowers and of their recognition that multilateral diplomacy offered a wider range of options than individual efforts to spur the process of change in the international system. In addition, with the superpowers controlling the United Nations Security Council and effectively using their weight within the UN to set the terms of debates, the members of the Nonaligned Movement needed a forum from which their positions could be articulated without allowing the superpowers and European colonial powers to establish the parameters of their agenda. The participation of the PRC in the initial conference (1955) of the Nonaligned Movement at Bandung in Indonesia was one index of the movement's inclusiveness of those prepared to support the decolonization process under way in the non-European world.

China played a major role in supporting the Vietnamese challenge to American efforts to prevent the reunification of Vietnam under the communists after 1954. In addition, it is possible to argue that the radicalization of the PRC from the mid-1950s on resulted in its promotion of an activist foreign policy supporting non-European nationalism as part of the Sino-Soviet struggle for symbolic leadership of the national liberation struggle.[29] This activism by the PRC and its competition with the USSR in the late 1950s was partly rooted in the perception that the Soviet Union was insufficiently sympathetic to non-European nationalism because of its search for detente with the United States. It is evident that American policymakers were successful in driving a wedge in the Sino-Soviet alliance, but it is equally plausible that the PRC was successful in undermining the Soviet-American search for detente in the late 1950s and early 1960s.[30] The Great Leap Forward campaign of 1957 radicalized the foreign policy of the PRC, especially around the issue of support for national liberation movements. In Vietnam, Laos, and Cambodia the intensification of armed conflict in the late 1950s and the 1960s cannot be divorced from the increasing activism of the PRC. This was a period marked by Chinese willingness to adopt policies in conflict and competition with the Soviet Union, and the pursuit of a prorevolutionary agenda by the PRC as it sought to project its influence beyond Asia into Africa and Latin America.[31]

An issue that has been assigned little prominence is the role of the PRC in helping to provoke the Cuban missile crisis of 1962. In the context of growing divergences between the Soviet and Chinese governments over "revolutionary strategy" in the late 1950s and early 1960s, the Cuban Revolution had become a major symbol and arena for that struggle. It is highly probable that Soviet sensitivities to Chinese criticism of its lack of solidarity with non-European revolutionary forces may have led Soviet leaders to place the missiles in Cuba. The Soviet reluctance to embrace non-European revolutionaries had been evident in the lukewarm support for the Chinese communists prior to their triumph in 1949. Its modest support for other Asian revolutionary movements, especially the Vietnamese and Korean communists, did little to improve its revolutionary credentials. By the time of the Cuban Revolution, the Soviet attitude to struggles of national liberation required a major effort to refurbish its revolutionary credentials.[32]

This Sino-Soviet competition in the non-European world was paralleled in the tensions generated within the NATO alliance by the American efforts to distance the United States from its allies' struggle to recover their influence in various parts of the world. The Suez incident of 1956 marked the eruption of simmering tensions among the erstwhile partners in the Western alliance and reminds us that American policy was also shaped by the need to contain the excesses of allies who assumed that American support could be taken for granted. As the United States extended its reach outside of Europe into other parts of the world, American policy was caught between its leadership of the NATO effort to contain the influence of the communist states and its search for independence from European partners who sought to maintain their empires in the face of nationalist challenges.[33] Even after the loss of those empires, differences about policy in the non-European world continued to inform relations among NATO partners.

Third World Countries as Agents of Change

Beyond this evidence of the ways in which the agendas of lesser powers influenced the activities and policies of the superpowers, the process of decolonization—which changed both the composition and the rules of the international system in the two decades after 1945—demonstrated the ability of actors with little military power to effect major changes in the international order. For most of those two decades, both the United States and the Soviet Union were unclear about how to respond to the growth of non-European nationalism and so were swept along by the tide. The Soviet Union recognized earlier the need to accept the inevitability of the process. The United States, besides being a colonial power itself, was constrained by the fact that several of its key alliance partners—France, Great Britain, Belgium, and the Netherlands—were under challenge from nationalists seeking an end to imperial rule. It was ill-equipped to contain either that challenge or the restructuring of the international system which ensued.[34]

But decolonization was only one of the post-1945 phenomena that have largely been ignored by those scholars who have focused chiefly upon the bipolar conflict. The emergence of the Nonaligned Movement in the 1950s testified to the inability of the major alliances to set the agenda of other actors. It also marked the effort by non-European states, with varying levels of success, to restrict the bipolar conflict to its place of origin—Europe. It can be argued that the Nonaligned Movement and the existence of neutral states were indicators of the fluidity in the post-1945 international order which prevented the development and consolidation of a bipolar international order. Thus even in situations of high international tension, as was evidenced in the Korean War, states such as India were willing to serve as intermediaries to broker solutions to conflict between the major alliances.

It can also be argued that the Nonaligned Movement was another major forum of the post-1945 international order. Consisting of those states that were not members of NATO or the Warsaw Pact, it neither achieved the level of politico-military coordination nor displayed the ideological cohesiveness that defined the major European alliances. Nonetheless, it constituted a base from which challenges to the superpowers and the European alliances could be mounted, a shelter from the bipolar conflict, and a mechanism that could contain the influence of the superpowers and their alliance partners. As Yugoslavia exemplified, even with their best and most concerted efforts the superpowers were constrained in their ability to impose a bipolar international order. The limits to superpower influence provided evidence that the distribution of power and influence in the international order was always more diffuse than overwhelming military superiority would suggest.

Limitations upon superpower influence require analysts to think more deeply about the continuous diffusion of power which has become manifest in the spread of technologies of mass destruction beyond the major alliances. From the period of the American monopoly in the 1940s, the possession of nuclear capability has served as an index of power in the international order—as has the possession of long-range missiles that can be armed not only with nuclear but with chemical or biological warheads, which may be just as effective in their deterrent and destructive capabilities. It is of considerable importance to establish why states from the People's Republic of China, through France, Britain, Pakistan, India, Israel, North Korea, Brazil, Argentina, and South Africa to Iraq and Iran have sought to acquire these technologies and how that acquisition has affected their relative power status within the international system. If the role played by the spread of these technologies is considered in a more systematic fashion, then it would be possible to argue that the superpowers, despite their advantages in the variety and number of weapons of mass destruction, have been unable to translate their possession of these complex arsenals into long-term control over the international system. If the end of atomic monopoly and the later development of ICBMs changed the power relationship between the United States and the Soviet Union, then it is obvious that a similar change occurs whenever there is a new entrant into the ranks of nuclear- and missile-equipped powers. The transformation of USSR-PRC relations in the

1960s and France's strategy within NATO during Charles de Gaulle's tenure continue to be the most vivid examples of changes in power relationships which the acquisition of nuclear capability helped to institutionalize.[35] The disintegration of the Soviet Union and the spread of its nuclear technology capability, in either human or material terms, can only contribute further to this process.

The oil crisis of 1973 and the ensuing growth of influence of the OPEC states within the international order provide further testimony of the realignment of power away from the major alliances. With the seizure of control over oil pricing in tandem with a selective embargo against Western industrial nations for their support of Israel, the Arab oil producers orchestrated a massive shift in resources and influence away from the West and toward the oil producers.[36] Though some of these gains were short-lived, they magnified the overall importance of the oil producers, particularly from the perspective of Western industrial powers whose economic competitiveness depends upon oil as an energy resource. The second oil shock of 1979, in the context of the Iranian Revolution and the subsequent Soviet invasion of Afghanistan, was a forceful reminder of Western vulnerability in the Middle East. The American quest for a permanent military presence in the Persian Gulf and its search for a mediatory role in the Israeli-Palestinian conflict have been influenced in large part by the importance of Middle East oil to American economic strategy.[37]

The increasing American dependence upon oil imports and key oil producers has, at least since 1973, undercut American strategic advantages in various regional contexts as well as in the wider international system. The roles of Mexico and Venezuela in containing American efforts to prevent the Sandinistas from taking power in Nicaragua in 1979, and the subsequent Mexican diplomacy within the Contadora group which foiled American efforts to isolate and destroy the Sandinista regime, are vivid examples of the changes in inter-American relations. It is no accident that Venezuela and Mexico, as the major Latin American oil producers, were able to pursue policies at variance with those of the United States and eventually to frustrate the policies of the Reagan administration toward Nicaragua. The assertiveness of the two Latin American oil producers, especially within the Contadora group, was vivid testimony to the impact of the politics of oil upon American foreign policy in its historic sphere of influence in Central America and the Caribbean.[38]

The upward movement of oil prices after 1973 also contributed to the growing self-assurance of the Soviet Union in its dealings with the West and its capacity to project power in the middle and late 1970s. The achievement of nuclear parity with the United States was one index of enhanced Soviet strategic capabilities, but it was the increased earnings from its energy exports and its status as the largest oil producer outside of OPEC that favored the growth of Soviet influence in the international system during this period. Control over a strategic resource and the liquidity that came from oil sales provided the Soviet Union with the political maneuverability and flexibility to become more active on several fronts. Its willingness to project military power in Ethiopia, Angola, and ultimately Afghanistan within less than a decade was certainly evidence of growing confidence in its own strategic advantages and the financial capacity to pursue expansive foreign and military policies.

The shift in strategic advantage toward the Soviet Union was not restricted to its policies in the non-European world. The oil price increases of 1973 and 1979 occurred in a context of increasing political instability and war in the Middle East, together with a rise of anti-American and anti-Western sentiment in the region. As a consequence, the West European states increasingly sought to insulate themselves from the rising tensions in the region and to reduce their dependence upon energy supplies from the Middle East; there was a greater willingness to obtain energy supplies from the Soviet Union even in the face of American opposition to such a strategy.[39] The fight between the United States and Western Europe over the pipeline issue in the early 1980s—at a time when the most recent chapter of their nuclear arms race was causing considerable tension between the superpowers—revealed the changing dynamics of intra- and inter-alliance relations in Europe. The American opposition to the construction of the pipeline served only to strengthen the determination of the West European states to seek their independence on energy issues. From their perspective it was more important to restructure the politics of Europe through the interpenetration of alliances than to reenergize the Cold War—the objective of the Reagan administration. The pipeline imbroglio should be seen as a precursor of the Velvet Revolutions of 1989, the dawn of a new era in European affairs in which the search for common ground among the European states forced both superpowers to rethink their roles in and influence over Europe.

The oil shocks of the 1970s promoted the restructuring of the international economy in the 1980s which resulted in the virtual collapse of East European industrial economies, the growth of East Asia as the dominant geographical region in the international economy, the contraction of British and American industrial sectors, and the paradox of superpowers increasingly dependent upon external capital and technology to help restructure their domestic economies. Both the United States and Russia are now ill equipped to exercise decisive influence in the international system. Their relative decline was evident in the war against Iraq in

1990–91, which had to be conducted by a coalition organized through the UN Security Council. But even before the Iraqi invasion of Kuwait, events in Europe in 1989 had demonstrated the waning of their influence. For Europeans, 1989 marked the end of the post-1945 European state system—the end of the Cold War—and opened the search for a new European order with the reunified Germany playing a pivotal role. In a sense, thse events brought Europe into step with the multipolar international order that had evolved over the previous forty years in the world outside of Europe.

Conclusion

Events in Europe in 1989 ended any pretense that the bipolar paradigm had adequate explanatory power for the course and evolution of international affairs. The history of international relations since 1945 has been about more than the relationship between the superpowers and their ability to exercise influence in the international system, individually or jointly. The collapse of the bipolar order in Europe, with the superpowers' acknowledgment of their inability to control the pace or outcome of the events that surrounded that collapse, suggests why scholars need to rethink approaches to the study of international relations since 1945. If the superpowers could not control events in the region most closely identified with the Cold War and the bipolar world view, then it becomes important to rethink both the analyses of international relations and the assumptions that have hitherto underpinned those analyses. The complexity of international relations has eluded the focus on the superpower rivalry, and with the end of the Cold War there is an opportunity to recast the post-1945 historiography of international relations.

The issues raised in this essay suggest some lines of inquiry. (1) The role of military power and nuclear weapons in shaping the post-1945 order was not as unequivocally advantageous to the superpowers as has been assumed in conventional analyses. (2) The superpowers exercised leadership within that order, but their roles were contingent upon their success in building effective alliances with other players. (3) Other states have both undermined the major alliance systems and constrained the influence of the superpowers. (4) The relative autonomy of these actors, added to their ability to manipulate the superpowers, implies that the postwar order was more complex than bipolar analyses would suggest. (5) The postwar order can be considered as reflecting a fundamental dialectic: the effort by the superpowers to centralize decision-making authority in the international system, and the challenge of other states to this process. In effect, while the superpowers were attempting to secure their position of relative privilege, other states were seeking a realignment of power that would constrain those privileges.

The scholarly community is at present moving away from conceptualizing the international system in terms of a bipolar order. This welcome development should be extended to the historiography of the 1945–89 period. The study of international relations since 1945 has been compartmentalized by the intellectual canons of academic life, fragmenting the study of international affairs among disciplinary or geographical emphases. The challenge of any new scholarship will be to integrate these disparate approaches with existing knowledge and new information to capture the complexity and essential interrelatedness of international relations. Analysts may thus come to see the events of 1989–90 in Europe and elsewhere as perhaps an inevitable outcome of the post-1945 international order, rather than the disjuncture that much contemporary commentary takes it to be.

Notes

Acknowledgments: I wish to express my appreciation to John Gaddis, Lori Gronich, Allen Hunter, Richard Immerman, Catherine Kelleher, Robert O'Neill, Judith Reppy, and the 1993–94 group of visiting fellows in the Center of International Studies at Princeton University to whom this essay was presented for their insightful comments and suggestions on earlier versions. Despite their disagreement with several ideas expressed here, both their suggestions and their criticisms have helped me to think my ideas through, and I accept full responsibility for the final product. I thank CIS Director John Waterbury for the opportunity to revise this essay within a collegial and relaxed environment at the Center.

1. For a brief but interesting retrospective of the dilemmas posed by the development of nuclear weapons, by one of the early architects of nuclear strategy, see Bernard Brodie, "The Development of Nuclear Strategy," in *Strategy and Nuclear Deterrence,* ed. Steven E. Miller (Princeton, N.J.: Princeton University Press, 1984), 3–21. Other contributors to the same volume provide a range of American perspectives on the use and deployment of nuclear weapons after 1945. Thinkers in the Soviet Union were also grappling with the impact of nuclear weapons on the conduct of potential wars; see Allen Lynch, *The Soviet Study of International Relations* (New York: Cambridge University Press, 1987), 65–66. For a British perspective, see Lawrence Freedman, *The Price of Peace: Living with the Nuclear Dilemma* (New York: Henry Holt, 1986).

2. For examples of this historiographical school, see John Lewis Gaddis, *The Long Peace: Inquiries into the History of the Cold War* (New York: Oxford University Press, 1987); Paul Kennedy, *The Rise and Fall of the Great Powers* (New York: Random House, 1987); and Raymond L. Garthoff, *Detente and Confrontation* (Washington, D.C.: Brookings Institution, 1985). In their recent work, both Gaddis and Kennedy have adopted more nuanced approaches to the complexity of international issues. See Gaddis, *The United States and the End of the Cold War: Implications, Reconsiderations, Provocations* (New York: Oxford University Press, 1992); and Kennedy, *Preparing for the Twenty-First Century* (New York: Vintage Books, 1993). Garthoff's work continues to reflect the focus on the superpowers; see *The*

Great Transition: American-Soviet Relations and the End of the Cold War (Washington, D.C.: Brookings Institution, 1994).

3. An early stimulus to the development of the ideas expressed here was Yale H. Ferguson and Richard W. Mansbach, *The Elusive Quest: Theory and International Politics* (Columbia: The University of South Carolina Press, 1988), which provides a powerful critique of International Relations theory as developed by political scientists. This essay is addressed to scholars of international relations who place greater emphasis on history than on theory in the analysis of international relations since 1945; it may also be useful to those interested in rethinking the theoretical assumptions of International Relations as a subfield within political science.

4. See Saburo Okita, "Pacific Development and Its Implications for the World Economy," in *The Pacific Basin: New Challenges for the United States,* ed. James W. Morley (New York: Academy of Political Science, 1986), 23–34; and Yung Chul Park, "Macroeconomic Developments and Prospects in East Asia," in *The Pacific Economy,* ed. Mohammed Ariff (Sydney: Allen & Unwin, 1991), 93–120.

5. For a provocative analysis of the inadequacies of conventional schools of thought, see John Lewis Gaddis, "International Relations Theory and the End of the Cold War," *International Security* 17, no. 3 (1992–93): 5–58.

6. For a prescient discussion of the Polish crisis and its implications for Soviet authority, see Edwina Moreton, "The Soviet Union and Poland's Struggle for Self-Control," *International Security* 7, no. 1 (1982): 86–104. For a longer-term view of East European efforts to delegitimize Soviet control over the region, see Agnes Heller and Ferenc Feher, *From Yalta to Glasnost: The Dismantling of Stalin's Empire* (Oxford: Basil Blackwell, 1990). For the Gorbachev period in the Soviet Union, see Robert G. Kaiser, *Why Gorbachev Happened: His Triumphs and His Failure* (New York: Simon & Schuster, 1991).

7. The interpenetration of Soviet and East European politics is illustrated in Karen Dawisha, *Eastern Europe, Gorbachev, and Reform* (New York: Cambridge University Press, 1990), 9–80. The crisis of legitimacy is explored in Ernst Kux, "Revolution in Eastern Europe—Revolution in the West?" *Problems of Communism* 40, no. 3 (1991): 1–13; and Gale Stokes, "Lessons of the East European Revolutions of 1989," *Problems of Communism* 40, no. 5 (1991): 17–22.

8. For some of the implications of these changes, see W. R. Smyser, *Germany and America: New Identities, Fateful Rift?* (Boulder, Colo.: Westview Press, 1993).

9. For a review of the history of the European system of states, see Kennedy, *Rise and Fall of the Great Powers;* and David Kaiser, *Politics and War: European Conflict from Philip II to Hitler* (Cambridge, Mass.: Harvard University Press, 1990). Tentative attempts to explore the implications of 1989–90 for the future of Europe's international relations are found in John J. Mearsheimer, "Back to the Future: Instability in Europe after the Cold War," *International Security* 15, no. 1 (1990): 5–56; and Stephen Van Evera, "Primed for Peace: Europe after the Cold War," *International Security* 15, no. 3 (1990–91): 7–57.

10. For a discussion of Yugoslavia in the post-1945 European system of states, see William Zimmerman, *Open Borders, Nonalignment, and the Political Evolution of Yugoslavia* (Princeton, N.J.: Princeton University Press, 1987).

11. For an interesting view of the incoherence of the international community, see Svebor Dizdarevic, "Capitulation de la Communaute Internationale: L'Affligeante demolition de la Bosnie multiethnique," *Le Monde Diplomatique,* October 1993.

12. For the role of the Vietnam War in American politics, see Leslie H. Gelb with Richard K. Betts, *The Irony of Vietnam: The System Worked* (Washington, D.C.: Brookings Institution, 1979). For assessments of the Afghan war's effect on Soviet domestic political debates, see Coit D. Blacker, *Hostage to*

Revolution: Gorbachev and Soviet Security Policy, 1985–1991 (New York: Council on Foreign Relations, 1993), 153–71. Riaz M. Khan, Untying the Afghan Knot: Negotiating Soviet Withdrawal (Durham, N.C.: Duke University Press, 1991), 166–82; and Sarah Mendelson, "Internal Battles and External Wars: Politics, Learning, and the Soviet Withdrawal from Afghanistan," World Politics 45, no. 3 (1993): 327–60.

13. On the factors shaping the bipolar conflict in Europe after 1945, see Gaddis, The Long Peace, 20–71; Kennedy, Rise and Fall of the Great Powers, 357–72; and Vojtech Mastny, Russia's Road to the Cold War: Diplomacy, Warfare, and the Politics of Communism, 1941–1945 (New York: Columbia University Press, 1979).

14. See David Calleo, The German Problem Reconsidered: Germany and the World Order, 1870 to the Present (Cambridge: Cambridge University Press, 1978), 161–77.

15. See Jerzy Tomaszewski, The Socialist Regimes of East Central Europe: Their Establishment and Consolidation (London: Routledge, 1989).

16. On the predicament confronting the East European states after the collapse of the Warsaw Pact, see Rudolf L. Tokes, "From Visegrad to Krakow: Cooperation, Competition, and Coexistence in Central Europe," Problems of Communism 40, no. 6 (1991): 100–114.

17. On the Anglo-Soviet search for a framework for the exercise of influence in the region, see Mastny, Russia's Road to the Cold War, 205–24.

18. For a historical overview of the German impact on European politics, see Calleo, German Problem Reconsidered.

19. For a thoughtful discussion of the changing role of Germany within Europe, see Daniel Hamilton, "Germany after Unification," Problems of Communism 41, no. 3 (1992): 1–18, and for a comprehensive overview of debates in the two Germanys prior to 1989, see Anne-Marie LeGloannec, La Nation Orpheline (Paris: Calmann-Levy, 1989).

20. For Yugoslav policy toward the Greek civil war, see Lawrence S. Wittner, American Intervention in Greece, 1943–1949 (New York: Columbia University Press, 1982), 57–60. For Yugoslav-Soviet relations during this critical period, see Vojtech Mastny, "Stalin and the Militarization of the Cold War," International Security 9, no. 3 (1984–85): 109–29.

21. Since 1945 Israel, Cuba, Egypt, India, and South Africa have all demonstrated this facility for manipulation of the superpowers to their own advantage.

22. See Tomaszewski, Socialist Regimes of East Central Europe, 116–29.

23. See Andrew Nagorski, "The Intellectual Roots of Eastern Europe's Upheavals," SAIS Review 10, no 2, (1990): 89–100.

24. For an overview of India's rise to prominence after 1947, see M. S. Rajan, ed., India's Foreign Relations during the Nehru Era (New Delhi: Asia Publishing House, 1976).

25. On the PRC's role in the promotion of revolutionary challenges in the non-European world, see Donald S. Zagoria, The Sino-Soviet Conflict, 1956–1961 (Princeton, N.J.: Princeton University Press, 1962), 3–23.

26. Ibid.

27. See Rami Ginat, The Soviet Union and Egypt, 1945–1955 (London: Frank Cass, 1993), M. M. El Hussini, Soviet-Egyptian Relations, 1945–85 (London: Macmillan, 1987); and Keith Kyle, Suez (New York: St. Martin's Press, 1991).

28. For an introduction to the Nonaligned Movement, see Peter Willetts, The Non-Aligned Movement: The Origins of a Third World Alliance (London: Frances Pinter, 1978).

29. For the roots of this dispute over strategy in the non-European world, see Zagoria, Sino-Soviet Conflict, 245–76.

30. For American policy, see Gaddis, *The Long Peace,* 147–94. For an exploration of Chinese policies, see Richard Lowenthal, "Diplomacy and Revolution: The Dialectics of a Dispute," in *China under Mao,* ed. Roderick MacFarquhar (Cambridge, Mass.: MIT Press, 1966), 425–48.

31. See Bruce D. Larkin, *China and Africa, 1949–1970* (Berkeley: University of California Press, 1971); and Peter Van Ness, *Revolution and Chinese Foreign Policy* (Berkeley: University of California Press, 1970).

32. For the evolution of Soviet policy toward non-European nationalism, see S. Neil MacFarlane, *Superpower Rivalry and 3rd World Radicalism: The Idea of National Liberation* (Baltimore, Md.: Johns Hopkins University Press, 1985). For Soviet sensitivities on this issue in the context of the Cuban missile crisis, see Vladislav M. Zubok, "The Missile Crisis and the Problem of Soviet Learning," *Problems of Communism,* spec. ed. (Spring 1992): 19–23.

33. For a discussion of American-Western European relations on the decolonization of the non-European world, see Cary Fraser, *Ambivalent Anti-Colonialism* (Westport, Conn.: Greenwood Press, 1994), 9–36.

34. Ibid.

35. The attention lavished upon issues of deterrence and proliferation by analysts involved in the study of nuclear weapons has tended to emphasize the military dimensions of the search for security. It may be timely to explore the political advantages of membership in the nuclear club, the most obvious of which is that it automatically enhances the possessor state's ability to participate in the management of issues of international security. It also provides the possessor states with a veto on the construction of security regimes from which other states may seek to exclude them. The imbroglio over the North Korean nuclear program is a recent exemple of political conflict over the utility of nuclear weapons. Britain, France, India, Israel, Pakistan, and the People's Republic of China have all recognized the importance of the possession of nuclear weapons for establishing leverage in issues of international security.

36. See Daniel Yergin, *The Prize: The Epic Quest for Oil, Money, and Power* (New York: Simon & Schuster, 1991), 625–38.

37. For an assessment of American policy, see Stephen Zunes, "The U.S.-GCC Relationship: Its Rise and Potential Fall," *Middle East Policy* 2, no. 1 (1993): 103–12.

38. For background on Mexican policy toward Central America and its role in U.S.-Mexican relations, see Jorge Chabat, "The Making of Mexican Policy toward the United States"; and Claude Heller, "U.S. and Mexican Policies toward Central America," both in *Foreign Policy in U.S.-Mexican Relations,* ed. Rosario Green and Peter H. Smith (San Diego: Center for U.S.-Mexican Studies, University of California, 1989).

39. For an insider's account (from the then American ambassador to Bonn) of the tensions among NATO members over the Soviet pipeline issue, see Arthur F. Burns, *The United States and Germany* (New York: Council on Foreign Relations, 1986). A contemporary discussion of the implications of increased ties between the USSR and Western Europe on energy issues is in Thane Gustafson, "Energy and the Soviet Bloc," *International Security* 6, no. 3 (1981–82): 65–89. For an account of the American-European divergences on energy and the resolution of the conflict, see Yergin, *The Prize,* 742–44.

Chapter 5

Cold War, Capital Accumulation, and Labor Control in Latin America: The Closing of a Cycle, 1945–1990

Ian Roxborough

In considering the influence of the Cold War and anticommunism on Latin America, most people think of the intervention of U.S. troops in the Dominican Republic and Grenada; of U.S. support for military coups in Brazil, Chile, and elsewhere; of intense U.S. pressure on the Sandinista government in Nicaragua; of U.S. support for counterinsurgency efforts throughout the region; and, of course, of the unremitting U.S hostility toward the Cuban Revolution. Important though they are, however, these actual—overt or covert—interventions are but part of the story of the ways in which the Cold War influenced Latin America. Its impact was both direct, through military and political intervention, and indirect, through shaping the contours of Latin America's political economy after World War II and in defining the parameters of political conflict. Following the end of the Cold War, new political institutions and economic models are emerging.

The opening phase of the Cold War (roughly 1944–48) coincided with the adoption of import substitution industrialization (ISI) as a conscious growth strategy in many countries of Latin America: Governments deliberately fostered industrial growth by protecting domestic industry from foreign competition. The state played an active role in the economy, often being responsible for as much as half of all economic activity and tightly regulating the economy as a whole. During this period class conflict and political struggles led to the institutionalization of systems of labor relations and to a model of capital accumulation that dominated this phase of postwar growth. Externally, Latin America's growth during the postwar period was integrally related to the worldwide economic expansion based on the international financial institutions created at the end of World War II. As the world economy slowed down in the 1970s, the accumulation model in Latin America was sustained largely through foreign borrowing and collapsed with the debt crisis of 1982. During the period 1988–90 there was a generalized move to replace it with a neoliberal growth model that will undoubtedly have considerable repercussions for political alignments and coalitions in Latin America. The key features of the neoliberal model are an emphasis on deregulation of the economy, free markets, and a very limited role for the state. Neoliberalism means a dismantling of the entire set of ISI policies. It also means a complete rethinking of the political institutions and coalitions that had characterized ISI policies.

The institutional origins of the postwar Latin American growth model (ISI) were intimately linked to the emerging Cold War, and the demise of the model was associated with the end of the Cold War. The impact of the Cold War on Latin America, then, should be seen not simply in terms of United States military and political intervention, important though it was, but also in terms of the long-term structuring of the model of capital accumulation.

The Shock of the 1930s and the Impact of War

When the world depression of the 1930s arrived, Latin American societies were still dominated by agrarian and mining elites. Challenges to this oligarchic system of domination had begun in some of the larger and more developed countries in the early decades of the twentieth century, largely by an urban middle class, but with the exception of the Mexican Revolution these challenges had had little discernible effect by the time the world crisis of the 1930s erupted.

When the world crisis hit Latin America, the *ancien régime* oligarchies were increasingly coming under attack from a growing middle class, an emerging working class, and military modernizers concerned both about emerging political tensions and the need for industrialization. Challengers sought to use an expanded state apparatus as a countervailing force and, at the same time, to cement an alliance with their new middle-class and working-class supporters. This emancipation of the state from oligarchic domination in the 1930s often resulted in political systems that are usually labeled "populist" or "corporatist." These new institutional forms obeyed a political logic: They were the response of state-builders who sought first to mobilize and then to control a broad popular base from which to consolidate their challenge to the previous regimes. New institutions for class control frequently took on corporatist forms: state-sponsored organization of sections of the subordinate classes, compulsory organization of employers, and an elaborate system of conflict regulation and bureaucratic policy formulation which enmeshed all these classes tightly within the confines of an activist state.

In some countries (Mexico, Uruguay, and Brazil) such changes proceeded relatively rapidly; in many others the reformist projects were defeated or contained. In no case were the emerging institutions either fully developed or harnessed to a new model of capital accumulation. The conscious adoption of ISI would come only with the creation of a new international economic order in the immediate aftermath of World War II.

The war at first ushered in a period of relative political stability.[1] In many cases the labor movement was induced to accept no-strike pledges (especially after the German attack on the Soviet Union) as its contribution to the Allied war effort; elsewhere (as in Argentina), dictatorships maintained social peace through repression. Later, as the outcome of the war became increasingly clear, global expectations for democracy and reconstruction created a strong momentum toward change in Latin America, and challenges to oligarchic rule were accelerated or revived.

The war stimulated economic growth, industrialization, and a considerable expansion in the labor force; in some countries the industrial labor force nearly doubled. But restrictions on imports and overheating economies produced inflationary pressures which, largely as a result of the no-strike agreements, resulted in a decline in real wages in many countries. As the war approached its end, a combination of dissatisfaction and a perception of increased organizational strength produced an upsurge of rank-and-file militancy, rapid growth in union affiliation, strike waves, and in general a political turn to the left. Communist Parties throughout the region expanded their membership fivefold. The left assumed a more varied and complex character as new nationalist and populist tendencies emerged to compete with the more traditional anarchist, socialist, and communist currents.

Moreover, since the war had been a war for "democracy," in those countries where there had been dictatorships it stimulated pro-democracy movements, often led by students and the middle classes. Throughout the continent the attack on the *ancien régime*, thwarted or incompletely carried out in the 1930s and placed in suspended animation during the first phase of World War II, was resumed.

As the war drew to a close, there was considerable discussion in circles linked with the new industrial groups and the political left concerning the place Latin America might occupy in the new world order. For most conservative elites the primary goal was a return to business as normal (that is, to an agrarian vocation and a growth model based on exports of primary products), but a section of the reformist left together with some industrialists began to sketch out an alternative vision of Latin American development.

The most articulate exponent of this alternative vision was the Mexican labor leader Vicente Lombardo Toledano. In 1938, using as his base the sizable Mexican labor confederation, the Confederación de Trabajadores de México (CTM), he set up the Confederación de Trabajadores de América Latina (CTAL). The CTAL brought together the largest unions in the majority of Latin American countries; only in Brazil and Argentina, where personalist dictators Getulio Vargas and Juan Domingo Perón had their own plans for the labor movement, did organized labor remain outside the fold. The CTAL was to be Lombardo's vehicle for a new approach to Latin American development. His position was in most respects similar to that of the Communist Parties in this period: one of unity with "national" industrialists against the twin foes of "fascism" and oligarchic "reaction." Until the Cold War crystallized in the late 1940s, antiimperialist themes in Lombardo's writings were muted; this stance in favor of alliance or coexistence with the United States implied replacing the notion of irreconcilable class conflict with a long-term strategy of class compromise.

There was a powerful logic working for this position in Latin America. The nascent bourgeoisie and the working class shared a common interest in industrialization. Sheltered behind tariff barriers as ISI got under way, workers and industrialists could collaborate in a progressive developmental program that would clear away any "feudal" legacies. The state, of course, was to intervene heavily in the economy, coordinating and overseeing this class alliance. The corporatist institutions that had begun to emerge in the 1930s and the wartime no-strike pacts could be resuscitated, enabling unions to play an important political role while facilitating class compromise. Lombardo also argued for land reform and income redistribution to generate the increased domestic demand that would stimulate further industrialization. All of this amounted to a largely nationalist program that favored industrial sectors and, by supporting the peasantry and keeping food prices low, directly threatened the interests of the agrarian oligarchy. In some ways this vision of the future drew heavily on the experience of the Mexican Revolution, while anticipating arguments that would shortly be formalized by Raúl Prebisch and the UN Economic Commission for Latin America (ECLA) and providing a Third World version of Keynesian demand stimulation.

Had this political program prospered, it might have developed into a Latin American equivalent of the Social Democratic class compromises that characterized postwar Europe. It is difficult to say whether such a project could have been realized in the Latin America of the 1940s. Both the industrial bourgeoisie and the working class were still minorities within largely agrarian societies; perhaps more important, in many countries the industrialists were still linked by complex social and economic ties to an unreconstructed agrarian oligarchy whose political pre-eminence remained fundamentally intact. Unlike the situation in many other parts of the globe, the effect of World War II in Latin America was to strengthen and consolidate the position of ruling elites, at least their economic and local domination, making the postwar challenge less likely to succeed.

Nevertheless, here was a clearly articulated and far from utopian program. It had a fair measure of credibility at the time and a political base in the CTAL and the Communist Parties, together with more diffuse support among the intelligentsia, sections of the military, and some industrial interests. In retrospect, the likelihood that Lombardo's vision could have been implemented seems slight. But it is perhaps well to remember that in 1944–46 it was by no means clear that the Cold War was about to become a reality. On the contrary, there was a widespread sense not only that the left had increased in strength but also that a wide range of political possibilities had opened up.

The Political Imperatives of United States Investment

At the end of the war several of the larger Latin American countries were positioned to embark on a deliberate program of industrialization. In these countries a political coalition favoring ISI had won the internal debates. But ISI required massive injections of capital, in the form of either aid or direct investment. Latin American proposals for managed international trade and investment ran up against a general U.S. preference for international free trade. Despite insistent pressures from the Latin Americans—headed by Mexico—for protectionism, a preferential inter-American trading bloc, commodity agreements, and so on, the United States pressed for a liberal economic regime and imposed it at the Chapultepec International Conference of American States in February 1945.[2] During the next couple of years Latin American policymakers hoped that their having supported the Allied war effort would lead to their receiving the kind of aid offered by the Marshall Plan. At the Rio International Conference of American States in the summer of 1947, however, the U.S. delegation made it clear that other regions of the world had greater priority and that aid on this scale would not be forthcoming.[3]

It became increasingly obvious that Latin Americans would have either to embark on unorthodox and largely self-reliant strategies of economic growth (a leftist version of the Lombardo project) or to rely on attracting substantial inflows of private foreign investment to foster industrialization. This choice had clear implications for political alignments, and the space for the Lombardista project rapidly vanished. Given these new realities, Latin American policymakers recognized that in order to attract foreign capital they must create a favorable "climate for investment." This meant, on the one hand, stabilization policies (usually involving devaluation and a cut in real income for the working class) and, on the other hand, reorganization of the institutions of labor control and capital accumulation to ensure both predictability in labor relations and improved channels for investment.

Here the requirements of capital accumulation coincided with the political dynamics of Cold War anticommunism. To the longstanding antiradicalism of Latin American elites were added two new ingredients: an urgent need to tame labor and the left in order to create a suitable investment climate; and a set of more specifically anticommunist concerns emanating directly from the United States. At the end of the war the United States made great efforts to forge a hemispheric security sphere. This had its roots in military collaboration during the war itself, was reinforced at the Chapultepec and Rio conferences, and culminated in the Bogotá conference in 1948, which adopted a resolution committing Latin American states to the fight against communism.

Between 1946 and 1948 most Latin American governments passed anticommunist legislation, intervened in labor unions to replace radical leaders with more compliant ones, and took a hard line against strike activity, often in the name of the "defense of democracy." Some governments actively collaborated with conservative union leaders in an effort to divide and undermine left-dominated union movements. By making anticommunism a highly visible issue, Latin American governments were able to assure the United States that they too were active in the fight against communism in the hemisphere. Even Perón's Argentina, where organized labor rose to a new pinnacle of organizational strength and political preeminence, was no exception to this story. The Peronist labor movement was militantly anticommunist; by the late 1940s any traces of independence and radicalism had been extinguished, and the movement had to a large extent become an instrument of Perón's personal power.

The principal target of the early Cold War in Latin America was the labor movement. As the end of World War II came in sight, the American Federation of Labor (AFL), backed by the U.S. State Department, began a campaign to displace the left in general and the communists in particular from their dominant position in the labor movements of Latin America. U.S. security concerns about labor as a potential fifth column in a possible third world war became evident in a direct way, reinforcing a more general anxiety about communism in the hemisphere.

The immediate aim was to divide and weaken the procommunist CTAL, which claimed to control a substantial majority of organized labor.[4] Membership statistics for Latin American unions are notoriously unreliable, but a figure of 3 to 3.5 million nominal members of the CTAL (in a total unionized labor force of perhaps 4 million) was widely accepted at the time. Paper membership aside, many important unions in key countries and in strategic industries such as docks and shipping were affiliated with the CTAL.

The AFL sent Serafino Romualdi as its "roving ambassador" to Latin America to promote more "responsible" and pro-American unionism. Like Irving Brown in Europe, Romualdi met with leaders of the moderate and anticommunist factions of the union movement in several countries. At the CTAL meeting in Lima in 1948 a split was engineered by leaders of the Chilean and Peruvian labor movements who had been in touch with Romualdi. At the same time, similar splits were precipitated or exacerbated in individual countries. Non-communists left and formed their own rival groups. In Chile, Venezuela, Cuba, and Mexico the government was directly involved in the efforts to weaken the left in the labor movement. These actions, taken together with the anticommunist legislation of the period, rapidly produced divided and weakened labor movements in which the moderate factions generally enjoyed government support. By the end of the decade, often earlier, labor militancy was contained. The CTAL lingered on for several years but only as a shadow of its former self. The purge of the Lombardistas in the Mexican CTM and the capture of that organization by conservative leaders in 1948 meant that an important source of funds for the CTAL dried up. Under the control of "responsible" leaders, most labor movements in Latin America had been domesticated and ceased to pose a threat to foreign investment.[5]

Postwar Political Systems

The confluence of the economic imperatives of the new model of accumulation (ISI) and the political imperatives of the emerging Cold War provided the setting for Latin America's conservative postwar settlement. The Lombardista project—an explicit alliance of workers and domestic entrepreneurs around an industrialization program involving substantial income redistribution—had been defeated and replaced by a much more conservative version of ISI in which foreign capital played a leading role and a central concern was the control of labor. Income distribution would worsen steadily as the model of accumulation favored capital and the professional middle classes. There was to be no attack on the agrarian oligarchy, and the peasantry was to be abandoned to its fate.

Despite their victory in the struggles of the 1940s, however, Latin American elites failed to develop a widespread legitimation for the new model of capital accumulation. Latin American societies remained deeply fractured and subject to high levels of popular contention. The conservative consolidation was fragile and seemed always on the verge of collapse. The rapidity of the processes of social change and class formation posed continuing problems of political and economic management to which these weakly institutionalized polities and dependent economies were unable to respond adequately. (The academic literature of the 1950s and 1960s diagnosed this situation abstractly as a situation of underdevelopment, without any understanding of the concrete historical conjuncture.)

Continuing political turbulence and elite domination also had the effect of shifting the direction of working-class politics. The fragility of the postwar settlement meant that social democracy was generally not accepted either by the left or by the working classes; instead, they oscillated between authoritarian nationalist projects—like those embodied in Peronism and Varguism—and a commitment to revolutionary politics that at times flowed over from rhetoric to actual insurrectionary activity. Indeed, labor and the left were generally divided and at odds throughout much of the postwar period. The artificial nature of the postwar consolidation also meant that neither labor nor the left was ever thoroughly integrated into the political system. As a result, despite the conservative consolidation of the 1940s, Latin America was the site of political turbulence and permanent revolutionary threat throughout the Cold War period. To mention only the more dramatic episodes: Bolivia, in the aftermath of the 1942 revolution, lapsed into a long period of *golpista* politics; the left-reformist government of Jacobo Arbenz was toppled by a CIA-sponsored invasion in 1954; rebels seized power in Cuba in 1959; guerrilla activity dominated the region in the 1960s (and, in some countries, beyond); in 1964 in Brazil, in 1966 and 1976 in Argentina, and in 1973 in Chile and Uruguay, governments elected by popular forces were overthrown and replaced by draconian military dictatorships. And in the 1970s and 1980s Central America became the site of insurrectionary struggle. All these events drew in the United States in its role as enforcer of the Cold War settlement.

For its part, the right, both civilian and military, constantly sought to undermine the compromises embodied in the ISI model in favor of free market economics. At times this invoked a reactionary nostalgia for the pre-ISI, pre–Cold War regimes; more frequently, it involved efforts to break loose from the inefficiencies and political compromises of ISI and to develop neoliberal economic policies under authoritarian auspices. The right's profound dissatisfaction with the conservative consolidation of the early Cold War years, and its corollaries of economic inefficiency and popular mobilization, underlay Latin America's long record of military intervention in the postwar period. In the 1960s, military dictatorships in Argentina, Chile, Brazil, Uruguay, and elsewhere essayed a break with the ISI model, but only in Chile did this produce an enduring legacy.

Internal Strains and Tensions in the Growth Model

The ISI growth model that operated in most countries of Latin America during the Cold War was riven with tensions and contradictions. The inefficiencies of the accumulation model led to erratic stop-and-go growth and to a general inability of the political system to absorb the continuing challenges from popular sectors. Lacking the etatism of their Asian rivals, Latin American governments (with few exceptions) were slow to develop industrial exports. The continuation of protection resulted in continuing inefficiencies in industry. Overvalued exchange rates failed to stimulate nontraditional exports. Government subsidies and transfers to urban consumers produced numerous allocative inefficiencies. Extensive government regulation of the economy proved a disincentive to efficient growth. Many government enterprises were badly managed, and the expansion of state employment obeyed the dictates of clientelist politics instead of administrative efficiency. Bloated public administrations produced fiscal deficits and inflation without effectively implementing policy. The rapid fluctuations of the economy as countries staggered from balance-of-payments crises to inflationary episodes to draconian stabilization programs created an atmosphere of uncertainty more conducive to speculation and capital flight than to long-term productive investment.

Yet on its own terms, ISI was successful. Latin American countries did industrialize rapidly, employment expanded, in many countries real wages steadily improved, and there was technological transfer. The real growth of this period provided the underpinnings for such class compromise and consensus as could be developed, given the weak institutions and precarious legitimacy characteristic of the polities of the region.

The conservative consolidation that underpinned the ISI project also had some notable political successes. The postwar period in Latin America was characterized by intense distributive struggle (often in the guise of populism) and by explosive expansion of the political arena as rapid urbanization and industrialization stimulated phenomenal growth in an array of disparate urban political actors. The relative success in containing these forces was a triumph for the institutions set in place by the conservative consolidation of the late 1940s.

Foremost among these institutions were the corporatist systems of labor control, which worked because of their Janus-faced nature. They were not simply instruments of repression of worker demands; rather, they structured those demands, defined the limits of legitimate action, and provided incentives for continued operation within the system. The corporatist tendency to settle industrial disputes either through the system of labor courts or through the intervention of the central government stimulated the growth of a bureaucratic stratum of professional labor leaders whose interests clearly lay in the maintenance of labor peace. The secular growth in real wages, together with the experience of social mobility consequent on rural-to-urban migration, may well have served to legitimize the system for the bulk of the organized working class; in many countries labor leaders were incorporated into the political system through corruption or through access to political power. Corporatism should be seen not simply as a transmission belt whereby governments controlled labor but as a two-way street: Both workers and union leaders appeared to receive real benefits in exchange for working within the rules of the game.

Yet even where the system worked most effectively, in Brazil and Mexico, it was fraught with tension.[6] Throughout the continent the recurrent economic crises characteristic of the ISI model of capital accumulation heightened distributive conflict, and labor militancy constantly threatened to break free from corporatist control.[7] Often, recourse to military intervention seemed the only way to rescue the system from spiraling mobilization. The fundamental reason for the frequency of military intervention in Latin America during the Cold War period lies here: in the tensions generated by the model of capital accumulation, and in the tensions generated by the low level of institutionalization and precarious legitimacy of the political system.

The Debt Crisis and the Triumph of Neoliberalism

In the end the conservative ISI project proved incapable of sustaining accumulation. As Eurodollars became increasingly available on the world market, Latin American governments sought to continue growth and ameliorate distributive conflicts by recourse to foreign borrowing. After two decades of increasingly difficult and contentious economic growth, the bubble burst with the Mexican debt default of August 1982.

The debt crisis plunged Latin America into economic chaos. Growth stopped, and real wages plummeted. At first policymakers treated the crisis as yet another conjunctural problem of economic adjustment and were slow to diagnose it as a structural problem. There were hesitant gropings toward appropriate policies, and some experimentation with unorthodox solutions (particularly wage and price controls). By the time policymakers recognized the need for an institutional reordering of the Latin American accumulation model, the international context of their discussions had altered markedly. The difficulties of social democracy in Western Europe in the 1970s and 1980s and the turn to the right there in the 1980s, the collapse of state socialism in Eastern Europe and the Soviet Union in the late 1980s, and the rapid turnaround in U.S. self-confidence as it became clear that the Cold War had been won,[8] produced a situation in which the ideology of neoliberalism carried the day and all statist programs were discredited.

For the Third World this shift can be traced clearly in the annual *World Development Report* produced by the World Bank, one of the international institutions most favorable to Third World efforts to develop. The *World Development Report* devoted increasing attention to the importance of markets as an omnibus solution to Third World problems, and complemented this with a one-sided interpretation of the reasons for the success of East Asian newly industrializing countries (NICs), downplaying the etatist direction of their economies and the influence of giant industrial-financial combines in some of them. Quite rapidly a "Washington consensus" emerged around the need to stimulate markets in Latin America and reduce the role of the state in the economy. In business circles the ideas popularized by Hernan de Soto were widely diffused.[9] The ideological climate had undergone a profound sea-change.

Although key actors were ready for a new model of accumulation, the politics of its implementation were paradoxical. In the 1960s and 1970s neoliberal programs had been instituted by authoritarian regimes, usually with backing from the United States. By the late 1980s Latin America had experienced a general turn toward democracy, and in the post–Cold War era the central problem became one of how democratically elected governments could pursue policies which, at least in the short run, ran directly counter to the interests of their constituents. In 1989 and 1990 at least four presidents were elected by popular vote in the belief that they would benefit the poor (Fernando Collor de Mello in Brazil, Alberto Fujimori in Peru) or the working class (Carlos Andres Pérez in Venezuela, Carlos Menem in Argentina). Their solution turned out to be remarkably simple: With the cry "There is no alternative," these presidents immediately implemented harsh austerity measures that directly contradicted their commitments to their low-income constituencies. The result was rioting in Venezuela, Brazil, and Argentina and a major split in the Argentine labor movement. In Mexico, where Carlos Salinas de Gortari moved from the austerity measures of his predecessor to a dramatic program of economic liberalization, real wages continued their dramatic fall, and the labor movement was induced to sign an anti-inflationary social pact with business and government. In all these cases, governments that had relied heavily on the votes of the urban poor and the working class presided over economic programs that went beyond simple austerity measures to embrace structural reform of a neoliberal kind and whose immediate costs were born by the working class and the poor.

Clearly, the difficulty these presidents faced was similar to the one that had confronted their predecessors in the 1940s: how to create institutions of labor control that would underpin the new model of capital accumulation and simultaneously prevent a legitimation crisis. It would be doubly difficult in the post–Cold War context of widespread support for the consolidation of democracy.

Political Implications of the New Model

The model of accumulation emerging in Latin America in the post–Cold War era is, first and foremost, neoliberal in inspiration. This implies a recasting of the class alliances that underpinned ISI. State managers seeking mass support no longer require strong labor unions enmeshed in a system of corporatist controls; on the contrary, they are a serious inconvenience. Complex systems of state-funded transfer payments and social security need to be scaled back. The state can no longer afford the luxury of providing unproductive employment for its clientele. Local entrepreneurs can no longer expect subsidies and protection. In all these ways, the alliance that underpinned ISI is falling apart, and new alliances are being formed.

A critical factor in these processes is labor law reform. In Chile, Argentina, Brazil, and Mexico, reform of corporatist labor legislation has been high on governmental agendas. In general, the aim has been to decentralize and depoliticize collective bargaining, to move in the direction of bargaining at the enterprise level. At the same time, there have been efforts to weaken labor leaderships by controlling union funds and in some cases to weaken unions by making unionization more difficult.

The result has *not* been the massive protest on the part of the unions that might have been expected, in part because they have been weakened by deindustrialization and deep recession, as well as by internal divisions. Instead, the bulk of protest has bypassed organized labor to take the form of spontaneous rioting. In this context it is possible that the central political role played by organized labor during the Cold War period in Latin America will disappear.

Whereas in the late 1940s the attack on the unions resulted from the coincidence of Cold War political imperatives and the need to ensure "orderly" industrial relations so that labor could be a "responsible" (albeit junior) partner in the new ISI class alliance, in the 1990s the motive behind labor law reform is to eject labor from the governing alliance altogether and to stimulate the microeconomic efficiency of the labor market. The immediate reasons behind the attack on labor are different in the two conjunctures. In the 1940s a radical and relatively independent labor movement had to be domesticated and brought into the system as a junior partner in the ISI alliance. Posed as a matter of ideology and leadership (that is, anticommunism), it was really a matter of subordinating union organizations to the industrializing goals of the state. Rising real wages and expanding employment underwrote this alliance. In the 1990s labor productivity for the first time became a central issue, and labor unions were to be taught that they must deal with the employer rather than the state. The statist alliance of which they were a part has been dissolved. Now, dealing with labor is largely a political problem; elected politicians can ill afford to alienate such an important section of the electorate.

It is perhaps too early to say what style of unionism will be preferred under the new model of accumulation. Contestation and exploration are still taking place, and some ambiguity and abrupt reversals in government policy toward labor may be expected, as well as divisions and confusions within labor as it seeks to redefine its relationship with the state.

It is well to remember that the period 1944–48 saw an attack on *parts* of the labor movement and government support for a particular style of unionism. Similarly, in the present conjuncture, some sections of the labor movement are likely to be favored. Moreover, the end of the Cold War coincided with increased concern about the consolidation of democracy in Latin America. The anticommunist imperative for an attack on union militants that was present in the early Cold War is now absent.

On the other hand, the problems of economic recovery are truly staggering in their immensity and constitute a far more serious set of constraints than was the case in the 1940s. The economic imperatives will be more pressing, and governments may well feel constrained to act in ways contrary to the wishes of their political base. At the time of writing (1997), it appears that many governments are attempting to promote a new form of "flexible" industrial relations, aimed at reducing many labor market rigidities resulting from labor legislation of the ISI period. Since this both weakens and depoliticizes existing unions, there are fierce efforts to defend the union organizations that developed under ISI. Which model of industrial relations becomes dominant will depend, to a large extent, on broader political realignments. The shift from the ISI accumulation model to neoliberalism, with its redefinition of political alliances, may well usher in a period of increased political instability and volatility. As in the 1940s, the creation of adequate institutions will be critical in determining the future of political stability and democracy in the region.

Conclusion

In the conjuncture defined by the end of World War II and the crystallization of the early Cold War, the growth model prevalent in Latin America shifted from one based on the export of primary products to one based on import substitution industrialization. This shift occurred as the United States was redefining its international role: During the war it had completed the displacement of Great Britain as the hegemonic power in Latin America and was now assuming its Cold War mantle of guardian of Western capitalism. This constrained Latin American governments both directly—in their political, ideological, and military alignments—and indirectly by fostering a sequence of political conflicts that led to a very specific, conservative version of ISI. In a series of battles with organized labor the more nationalistic version of ISI, based on greater popular participation, was defeated and a conservative consolidation imposed. Given the fragile and highly contested nature of this conservative consolidation, and despite internal tensions and repeated challenges from both the left and—more important—the right, the ISI growth model did stagger on for most of the postwar period. In the aftermath of the debt crisis and with the end of the Cold War, however, the right was able to resume its longstanding attack on ISI and its political correlates. In the 1990s it looked as if the neoliberal model of accumulation had triumphed. What remained to be seen was the shape of the institutions that would structure political conflict in the future.

Notes

1. This section draws heavily on Leslie Bethell and Ian Roxborough, "Latin America between the Second World War and the Cold War," *Journal of Latin American Studies* 20 (May 1988); and Leslie Bethell and Ian Roxborough, eds., *Latin America between the Second World War and the Cold War* (Cambridge: Cambridge University Press), 1992.

2. *Foreign Relations of the United States,* 1945, IX: 49, 64–65, 68–70, 83, 96–97, 103–5, 111–14, 138.

3. Stephen Rabe, *Eisenhower and Latin America* (Chapel Hill: University of North Carolina Press, 1988), 16–18; Forrest Pogue, *George C. Marshall: Statesman, 1945–1959* (New York: Penguin Books, 1987), 380–86.

4. In addition to Bethell and Roxborough, *Latin America,* useful works on Latin American labor during the Cold War period include John Kofas, *The Struggle for Legitimacy: Latin American Labor and the United States, 1930–1960* (Tempe: Arizona State University Press, 1992); Ronald Radosh, *American Labor and United States Foreign Policy* (New York: Random House, 1969); Gary Busch, *The Political Role of International Trades Unions* (London: Macmillan, 1983).

5. There are some superficial parallels here with the "politics of productivity" in Western Europe at this time. See Charles Maier, *In Search of Stability* (Cambridge: Cambridge University Press, 1987).

6. See, e.g., Ian Roxborough, *Unions and Politics in Mexico* (Cambridge: Cambridge University Press, 1984).

7. Thomas Skidmore, "The Politics of Economic Stabilization in Postwar Latin America" in *Authoritarianism and Corporatism in Latin America,* ed. James Malloy (Pittsburgh: University of Pittsburgh Press, 1977); Guillermo O'Donnell, *El Estado Burocratico-Autoritario* (Buenos Aires: Belgrano, 1982).

8. Just a few years earlier, Americans had been anguishing over impending imperial decline, and Paul Kennedy's *The Rise and Fall of the Great Powers* (London: Unwin Hyman, 1988) became a best-seller.

9. Hernan de Soto, *The Other Path* (New York: Harper & Row, 1989).

Chapter 6

Castro in Harlem:
A Cold War Watershed

Brenda Gayle Plummer

The Cuban Revolution's significance for Latin American history is unquestioned. Historians also recognize its salience in the study of the Kennedy years and its impact on the Nonaligned Movement among emerging states. Scholars less commonly understand that the revolution represents a watershed in the Cold War's impact on U.S. society. The Cuban issue joined foreign and domestic policy considerations, helped keep U.S. race relations on the international docket, and contributed to fundamental social and political change in the American South.

This essay examines the intersection of domestic and foreign priorities at the point where U.S. policymakers confronted African American political aspirations and the Cuban challenge simultaneousiy, thus condensing several strands of Cold War history. Fidel Castro's ten-day visit to Harlem in 1960 constituted a watershed, not only because it coincided with a critical juncture in the history of U.S. race relations but also because it marked a departure in conventional ways of perceiving, and prosecuting, the Cold War. Television and print media emphasized what they perceived at the time as burlesque elements in the Cuban's sojourn. If

Castro's stay in Harlem evoked theater, it was theater on a world stage, with global celebrities enacting their politics by means of dramatic entrances and ritual processions through the city streets.

The Cold War and Race Relations

The Eisenhower administration had already realized, albeit belatedly, that it must compete with the Soviets for preponderance among nations that had "graduated" into independence from colonial mentoring systems. Emerging revolutionary states, however, born of conflict rather than tutelage, posed a novel challenge: As a third force, they delineated Cold War issues in ways that the threat of nuclear holocaust did not. Marxist ideology predicted the inevitability and righteousness of wars of liberation; these would occur as a result of historical-materialist processes and required no Soviet agency. Yet Third World civil wars and national liberation struggles seemed to enact the deferred and muted conflicts between the Western and Eastern blocs.[1]

What did this have to do with black Americans? The African American quest for full citizenship implied increased participation in all aspects of national life. Black leaders thus presented themselves as spokespersons for an ethnic constituency and sought, as did others, to influence the direction of U.S. foreign policy. The rapidly proliferating number of states joining the United Nations abetted these efforts, for international realities now dictated that the pace of desegregation in the United States not only be accelerated but be made a central focus of national policy. The presence of African and Asian states, often vocally committed to racial equality, encouraged activists to believe that the UN constituted a sympathetic forum in which to air grievances. This hope was not entirely new; African Americans had linked civil rights to human rights in the late 1940s when the National Negro Congress and the NAACP sent the UN petitions targeting human rights abuses in the United States. This brand of internationalism became discredited as the Cold War intensified and activists turned their attention to pursuing change within a purely domestic arena.[2]

Still, it was not sufficient for the United States to expedite reforms; it had also to contend with an enticing thesis that identified the black predicament with that of dominated subjects elsewhere. A "colonial model" that found increasing application in the social sciences and in popular criticism fed handily into the philosophic stream of traditional black nationalism.[3] Such black nationalist leaders as Elijah Muhammad and Malcolm X hammered on the motif of African American nationhood, the need for economic self-sufficiency, and independence from white cultural and political domination. Policymakers found this perspective difficult to neutralize, given continued resistance to change within the United States and its widespread popularity abroad. Fidel Castro reprised the same themes in the context of antiimperialist struggle during his September 26, 1960, speech to the UN General Assembly. Black Americans thus came to occupy a symbolic space in the intersection where newly independent states, constituting a third force, challenged conventional Cold War politics on anticolonial and antiracist grounds.

It is important to note here that black Americans never expressed a single, monolithic opinion on international matters, nor did foreign affairs engage their collective attention as fully as did civil rights and employment issues. A sustained preoccupation with world events has always been the province of a relative few, and African Americans are no exception. Yet this aspect of the black experience and its potential for future scholarly and practical engagement remains profoundly underestimated and discounted. Black American perceptions of foreign affairs have often hinged on domestic questions. When Ghana achieved independence in 1957, for example, civil rights reemerged not solely as an internal issue but also in the related contexts of designing an appropriate African policy and accommodating an increasingly restive black population in key electoral states. The White House needed African allies in order to cultivate African American ones. Southern black militancy after 1960 only underscored the need for change.

That U.S. sensitivity to international opinion contributed greatly to improving race relations after World War II has become almost axiomatic. Competition with the Soviets for legitimacy raised the civil rights question as a Cold War concern. Beyond this truism, however, lay the relatively uncharted terrain on which the United States had to confront the issue. How much change would U.S. society have to undergo to show the world community that it was making the transition to full democracy? Did the United States government, in distancing itself from the most egregious instances of racism, recreate its national identity, defining discrimination as a mere artifact of the South's increasingly discredited regional mores? Did state and society make enough progress after World War II to convince other nations that this was so?[4]

The Cuban Revolution became implicated in the answers to these questions. Fidel Castro rose to power just as a key transitional period in U.S. race relations was ending. The civil rights movement had made many valiant and often successful efforts to effect change over the previous twenty years yet still encountered continuing segregationist clout in Congress and resistance from northern political machines that neutralized black electoral power. All too often, extracting gains for African Americans in the North continued to engage small groups of white opinion managers, public officials, and corporate elites on one hand and an even smaller, often professional, cadre of black race relations specialists on the other.[5] By the mid-1950s that system, though not in ruins, had been significantly eroded by civil rights mass mobilization. The Montgomery bus boycott of 1955–56 had demonstrated the efficacy of popular participation and plural leadership. Direct action was replacing brokerage as the most effective way to place demands on the bargaining table in the North as well as the South. The new approach to civil rights reverberated in every aspect of American life—including foreign policy.

Harlem's black congressman, Adam Clayton Powell Jr., played a key role in introducing the new assertiveness to foreign policymakers as early as 1956. At meetings with President Eisenhower and key White House and State Department officials, Powell asked the department to inventory its black employees. Washington acknowledged that it had failed to make the Foreign Service more representative. It also realized that UN General Assembly voting on human rights issues tended to break down along the color line, with the Soviets crossing over to endorse the positions of non-European states. The United States would benefit from sending to the UN a delegation that more closely reflected its diversity. Powell suggested that the government sponsor an Asian or African summit conference and called for a more vigorous approach to selling the American viewpoint abroad.[6]

Powell's efforts were largely futile, however, and he partly attributed governmental intransigence to Secretary of State John Foster Dulles and the State Department. Dulles privileged the Cold War above all other foreign policy considerations. "Dulles's bête noire was nonalignment," one former ambassador to the United States recalled. "Everything was either black or white and the archenemy was Communism. . . . There was no getting away from it." This preoccupation blinded him to the autonomist aspirations evinced by former subject peoples, which he was likely to attribute to communist subversion. Black Republicans as well as Democrats began to resist this interpretation. They wished to uncouple communism from other issues affecting African and Asian states. They too wanted an integrated Foreign Service, greater respect for neutralism, and positive U.S. support for decolonization and racial equality worldwide.[7]

Warming to Cuba

Over the course of the 1950s, as more colonies gained independence, Dulles's policies met growing opposition at home and abroad. Dulles and Eisenhower, both ill when dictator Fulgencio Batista fled Havana on New Year's Day,

1959, offered little leadership on Cuba. Initial intelligence information suggested that communists there lacked clout among the revolutionaries, who nevertheless wanted to press forward with a program of extensive agrarian and social welfare reforms. Washington officials, aware of the considerable U.S. investment in Cuba, rejected this agenda. Castro, invited to the United States in April 1959, fielded hostile questions at a meeting of the Council on Foreign Relations but walked out of the assembly when he found he could not placate an unfriendly audience preoccupied with communist influence and possible expropriations. Castro began moving rapidly to the left as this and other experiences defined the limits of U.S. support for radical change in Cuba.[8]

U.S. assessments of Castro in 1959 took place in relatively restricted milieus such as Harvard, where the Cuban leader also made a speech, and in private settings such as the Council on Foreign Relations. As the general public had no access to such venues, its initially sanguine view of Castro underwent no sudden change. The widely distributed black magazine *Ebony* portrayed the revolution favorably in an April 1959 essay on Afro-Cuban heroes in historical perspective. The article by veteran reporter Simeon Booker, mentioned Antonio Maceo—a black general of the independence era for whom many African Americans at the turn of the century had named their children—and recounted the military exploits of Commandante Juan Almeida Bosque, implicitly linking him to the black Cuban heroic tradition. Castro's avowed intention to establish racial justice in the island republic, Booker averred, had encouraged Almeida to join the revolution.[9]

Ebony's approval had practical as well as ideological importance to Cubans: The revolution had ruined conventional tourism, but "revolutionary tourism" helped shore up the island's faltering travel industry and provided a needed public relations service for the regime. Hoping that sympathetic responses from the U.S.intelligentsia might help neutralize the mounting hostility to Castroism in government and corporate circles. Havana invited diverse intellectuals, artists, journalists, and politicians—black and white—to witness the revolutionary process. Among those who accepted in 1960 were singer Marian Anderson, historian John Henrik Clarke, writers Leroi Jones (now Amiri Baraka) and Julian Mayfield, and journalist William Worthy. Many returned to write favorable accounts of their experiences.[10] Small approving groups could not sustain an entire industry, however; luxury hotels stood deserted, and a $60 million business came to a standstill.

The Cuban office of tourism had begun advertising to African Americans as early as December 1959, touting tropical resorts that no longer practiced the Jim Crow restrictions of the Batista era. Tourism officials realized that an increasingly prosperous black American middle class had dollars and few places to spend them in the segregated U.S. travel sector. In early 1960 the Cubans negotiated an agreement with a black public relations firm in which former boxing champion Joe Louis held a partnership. Havana planned to spend $282,000 on ads in black print media—at the time, an unprecedented sum for non-corporate sponsors. Louis's firm would realize a 15 percent commission. Louis praised Cuba as a recreational site for blacks, who could now vacation there without experiencing racial discrimination.[11]

Once the summer 1960 travel season began, however, Joe Louis found himself castigated by the white press because of his Cuban associations and because his firm had registered as an agent for a foreign government. His partner defended Louis and the deal they had negotiated: "This contract is being aimed at the Negro market through the use of Negro newspapers, radio stations and magazines," Alvin Lockhart declared. He saw nothing illegal in doing business with a government that the United States fully recognized. The *Pittsburgh Courier*, a leading black newspaper, wondered why the arrangement caused so much concern, as white firms had even more lucrative contracts with Cuba but kept their officers' identities private. As for representing foreign governments, many white-controlled corporations did this, and no one condemned them for it. The conservative *Courier* viewed the unfavorable publicity as an attack on black business development. The Castro controversy raised hackles across the African American political spectrum. Most black leaders had become firm members of the liberal, anticommunist camp early in the Cold War era. Although opposing communism per se had never been as important to blacks as to whites, African Americans perceived that they could exploit East-West rivalries to advance the civil rights cause. For some individuals, however, conventional orthodoxy was breaking down in the face of the appealing unconventionality of the Cuban revolution and its seeming support of racial integration and equal opportunity.[12]

Spotlight on Harlem

The Cuban controversy formed part of a contentious atmosphere during the 1960 election year, and nowhere was this more evident than in Harlem. Longtime resident Elombe Brath and Booker Johnson, a member of the Nation of Islam, later recalled 1960 as a time of mounting politicization. It was "the peak of the street speakers in Harlem," Johnson reminisced. In Brath's recollection, a Garveyite tradition cast the soapbox oratory of racial protest in international—and antiimperialist—terms. On July 2 violence erupted in Harlem between pro- and anti-Castro contingents.[13]

Near the end of the year, then, Fidel Castro came to a Harlem ready and able to link Jim Crow to world events. The decline of colonialism was one of those events. Seventeen new states, most of them African, became independent in 1960, and the political as well as epidermal complexion of the UN General Assembly seemed permanently altered. At its fifteenth meeting, in September, scheduled speakers included many of the world's most influential leaders: U.S. President Dwight D. Eisenhower, Soviet Premier Nikita Khrushchev, President Kwame Nkrumah of Ghana, Josip Tito of Yugoslavia, President Gamal Abdel Nasser of the (then) United Arab Republic, Prime Minister Jawaharlal Nehru of India, Sukarno of Indonesia, and Cuban Premier Fidel Castro. Their presence created an epic security problem for local police and a political pageant for New York City residents.[14]

The Cuban delegation arrived in the city on September 18, 1960. Castro and the other members, some bearded and bohemian in appearance, found hospitality strained at New York's elite Shelbourne Hotel, where they had reserved rooms. Unsubstantiated press reports had them plucking chickens in their suites and otherwise dirtying the hotel, whose management rapidly grew antagonistic. The delegation, after refusing UN Secretary-General Dag Hammarskjöld's offer of other accommodations, vacated the Shelbourne and rented rooms at the Theresa Hotel in Harlem.[15]

Teresa Casuso, a delegate who later defected, claims that Castro had planned the dramatic Harlem move from the start. Other accounts vary, some attributing the idea to Richard Gibson, an African American television journalist and founding member of the Fair Play for Cuba Committee. Whatever the origin of the delegation's unconventional arrangements, once the State Department learned of them, it offered to pay the tariff for the Cubans at a downtown luxury establishment instead. They rejected this overture and moved into the Theresa on September 19, 1960.[16]

Mainstream broadcast and print media covered Castro's Harlem sojourn with amused curiosity. Though blacks might wish to stay at white hotels, in 1960 it was virtually unheard of for reputable whites to register at black ones. Further, the Cuban mission's physical appearance challenged customary Anglo-American notions of respectability. Delegation members, who resembled New York's working-class Latino population, enhanced the general amazement and drew both curiosity seekers and activists to the streets outside the Theresa. The milling crowds included supporters of embattled Congo premier Patrice Lumumba, who made common cause with Cuban antiimperialism; pro- and anti-Castroites; civil rights sympathizers, gratified that Castro had challenged Jim Crow mores. African American and Hispanic residents of Harlem turned out to see the Cubans. "To say that Harlem was flattered was to put it mildly," the *Pittsburgh Courier* reported. "She didn't give a continental as to whether the move of Castro to 'uptown' was a smashing propaganda victory for the Cubans. She was happy to know that Castro and his party were thinking of them. . . . One of the locals quipped: 'Why shouldn't we like him? He ended racial discrimination in Cuba and that's more than the United States has done in this matter. We're for him and we like him.'" Columnist James L. Hicks of the *Amsterdam News* expressed similar sentiments: "Though many Harlemites are far too smart to admit it publicly, Castro's move to the Theresa and Khrushchev's decision to visit him gave the Negroes of Harlem one of the biggest 'lifts' they have had in the cold racial war with the white man."[17]

The Cuban leader held veritable court at the Theresa. American guests included L. Joseph Overton, president of the New York NAACP; Muslim leader Malcolm X; and Robert F. Williams, the NAACP official from Monroe, North Carolina, who had traveled to Cuba in July and had shocked the national NAACP by advocating armed self-defense. Business executive and former baseball star Jackie Robinson arrived at the hotel, but it is not clear whether he had an interview with Castro. Robinson did speak to the press, however: Harlemites enjoyed the Cuban presence, he asserted, but resented being singled out. He observed that the Cuban delegation was making a pitch for African support at the UN, and it is possible that Castro's rental of the Theresa meant to evoke the housing discrimination problems that African diplomats were then experiencing in New York City.

To drive home the intended message of solidarity, the delegation sent for the Cuban army's black commander, Commandante Juan Almeida Bosque, to join Fidel and meet with African American leaders. A thousand persons enthusiastically cheered as Almeida walked Harlem's streets. Photographs show him on a Hotel Theresa balcony arm in arm with Castro.[18]

The Cuban leader also hosted a bevy of foreign dignitaries. He received Khrushchev at the Theresa on September 20; Nasser dined with him on September 25; and Nehru and Foreign Minister V. K. Krishna Menon of India followed suit two days later. The presence of such renowned personages subverted the conventional perception of Harlem as a seedy, insignificant ghetto. Nasser's visit prompted a thousand members of the Nation of Islam to mass on the south side of 124th Street while Castro met with the Arab Egyptian leader. Marshal Tito did not come to the hotel but did appear nearby in a motorcade on September 25. Crowds loudly acclaimed the European neutralist as he rolled through the 125th Street business district.[19]

Not every black New Yorker shared the public enthusiasm and festival atmosphere. Five hundred Baptist clergymen wired their vehement condemnation of Castro to New York City's Mayor Robert Wagner and Governor Nelson Rockefeller. Cuban popularity distressed other local leaders as well. They enjoyed Castro's on-site meetings with Third World leaders but became distinctly uncomfortable when he embraced Khrushchev in the Theresa's lobby. Stories by James Booker, the *Amsterdam News* reporter who covered the visit, maintained a tone that ranged from noncommittal to hostile. Most conventional African American dignitaries refused any association with the newly organized Fair Play for Cuba Committee and boycotted a planned reception for the Cubans. Those who declined invitations included Joseph Overton, who had earlier met Castro in his suite (ironically, certain prominent individuals who called on Castro personally distanced themselves from any group claiming to support him) and writer Langston Hughes.[20]

Representative Adam Clayton Powell Jr. aptly illustrated black politicians' ambivalence. Powell had vocally opposed in Congress the deposed dictatorship of Fulgencio Batista and the U.S. policy of supporting it; he even went so far as to defend the revolutionary government's right to execute political prisoners under the rules of due process. But Powell did not reap any advantages from his early support of the Castro regime; his own account of his overtures stresses the suspicion in which Havana held him, a distrust that he attributed to Cuban communist machinations. Growing official hostility toward Cuba exacerbated Powell's difficulties, and the revolution's increasing radicalism eventually forced him to distance himself from it in the interest of maintaining his own credibility and national stature as a leader. Powell, schooled in the arts of the political brokerage that was then deteriorating, also resented Castro for upstaging him on his own turf.[21]

The congressman attempted to offset Castro's dramatic impact by extending simultaneous invitations to Nasser, Nkrumah, and Sekou Touré of Guinea to visit Harlem. Powell had met Touré at an official dinner, and Nasser at the 1955 Bandung conference of nonaligned states. Nkrumah, as a merchant seaman and foreign student in the 1930s, had occasionally attended the Abyssinian Baptist Church when Powell's father was pastor. Powell denounced Castro for opportunistically appearing in Harlem after ignoring invitations that he and others had extended during the Cuban's 1959 trip. Harlem blacks were not "dupes," Powell warned, and did not welcome any communist agitation: "We Negro people have enough problems of our own without the additional burden of Dr. Castro's confusion," he averred.[22]

The equivocal responses of Jackie Robinson, Joseph Overton, and Adam Clayton

Powell to Castro compared intriguingly with the reactions of ordinary Harlem residents. Many of these resented being looked at askance by outsiders. "Some Negroes appeared extremely sensitive to the situation," UPI reported. "They turned away angrily when asked their opinion about Castro." This reaction is more understandable when one realizes that, as James Farmer remembered, "this was an era when most civil rights activists sought not to improve conditions in the ghetto but to wipe out the ghetto itself." Attentions from foreign dignitaries affirmed Harlem's positive identity during a time when only a few scholars and black nationalists appreciated its history, and the developing struggle for racial justice was still emerging from legal and political straitjackets.[23]

The Cuban government understood all this and how to exploit it. Aside from drawing invidious comparisons, Havana made opposition to racial discrimination a component of its burgeoning policy of rapprochement with developing nonaligned states. To this end, Castro's four-hour speech to the General Assembly on September 26 used the Cuban delegation's Harlem stay as the backdrop for professions of solidarity with Africa. After rhetorically establishing that the experience reflected North American racism and hypocrisy, Castro went on to position Cuba "on the side of the remaining colonial peoples in Africa and on the side of the Negroes against whom discrimination is exercised in the Union of South Africa."[24]

Castro had additional motivations, including fear of a possible U.S. attack. Marxist officials, among them Raul Castro and Ernesto "Che" Guevara, proposed a preemptive alliance with the Soviets. Others distrusted both the Soviets and the indigenous Cuban Communist Party, which had not been a vigorous early supporter of the revolution. By grouping itself with the Afro-Asian neutralist states, Cuba would find an alternative to full alignment with the Eastern bloc. It could thus embrace a wider world community within the contev of two parallel historical processes: the Cold War and decolonization. Neutralism would guarantee Cuban autonomy and preserve some freedom to resist Yankee domination. Cuba could furthermore assure its survival by distancing itself from actual insurgencies in the Western Hemisphere.[25]

Cuban foreign policy moralism championed the rights of historically oppressed communities. The Castro regime widely publicized its efforts to rid Cuba of the legacy of slavery and racial discrimination. It also depicted sovereignty as the sine qua non of liberation. "Colonies have no voice," Castro told the General Assembly. "Colonies are not recognized in the world as long as they have no opportunity to make themselves heard." Yet independence alone did not suffice: "Freedom does not consist in the possession of a flag, and a coat of arms and representation in the United Nations," for "there can be no political independence unless there is economic independence."[26]

African Americans, who had no independent state of their own to be courted, nevertheless served a useful symbolic purpose. By challenging the United States on its own ground and drawing attention to the black American struggle for social justice, Cuba put Washington on the defensive. The Cubans also claimed some solidarity with African Americans on a racial level, based on perceptions of race and color specific to Latin America. Racial solidarity understood as an essentialist biological affinity, however, formed only one part of Cuba's outreach. The Cubans also understood, on a more profound level, the ongoing cultural challenge that African Americans posed to the North American status quo. Black insurgency had a clear political objective: the elimination of all forms of segregation and civil inequality. Such large-scale reform required a revolution in attitudes and values. The old order would pass, for the United States could not improve life for blacks without fundamentally altering mainstream society. Black insurgency, political and cultural, also fed the currents of a growing discontent with the complacency of the 1950s. Even historian Arthur Schlesinger Jr. sensed a malaise and suggested that the young felt it most keenly. "The undergraduates were delighted," Schlesinger recalled, when Castro gave a speech at Harvard in 1959. "They saw in him, I think, the hipster who in the era of the Organization Man had joyfully defied the system."[27]

Poet Leroi Jones, then still part of the Beat Generation, expressed the sentiment more emphatically. "The young intellectual living in the United States inhabits an ugly void," he wrote in his essay "Cuba Libre." "He cannot use what is around him, neither can he revolt against it." The increasingly influential Jones lyrically described his 1960 trip to Cuba as a major turningpoint and depicted the Cuban uprising as a genuine cultural revolution in carnival form. "What was it, a circus? That wild mad crowd. Social ideas? Could there be that much excitement generated through all the people?" The festive rallies Jones attended during the early, celebratory phase of the revolution led him to question further the sober conformity of mainstream North American life and the separation of politics from culture.[28] Castro's visit to Harlem recapitulated the gaiety that Jones had experienced in Cuba. The cheering crowds and parade of celebrities seemed linked to the island's theater of politics, climaxed by the September 26 speech to the General Assembly.

The Cuban delegation returned to Havana on September 28. Castro had been in Harlem a scant ten days. How should his impact be assessed? Was his sojourn simply a media tour de force? Of course it made the major dailies, film, and television—yet the press, including the black press, did not fully recognize the crisis of legitimacy that the shock of raising the race question in an international context represented at the time. The African Americans who disapproved of Castro but lined up to see him never entirely comprehended the basis of their own mixed reactions. Certainly most Harlemites were not *fidelistas,* but like other African Americans they did resent continued impediments to civil rights progress and economic opportunity. Those who kept abreast of the news realized that conscious efforts at racial reform in Cuba had proceeded well ahead of any comparable U.S. agenda. Castro and the Afro-Asian states had in a sense colluded with black Americans in a symbolic disruption of the degrading political invisibility of people of color. Following adjournment of the General Assembly and the departure of Castro and other international figures from New York, U.S. politicians reaffirmed Harlem as a place that counted as both Republicans and Democrats stumped with renewed fervor for their candidates in the 1960 elections.[29]

Could Castro have captured the African American imagination outside the sophisticated New York milieu? The Cuban Revolution undoubtedly resonated among intellectuals but offered varied and complex attractions. Historian John Henrik Clarke, though an urbanite and Harlem resident, declared that what had aroused his interest was agrarian reform, a policy that he, as the son of landless Alabama sharecroppers, could readily appreciate.[30] For others, Cuban phenotypic diversity challenged the rigid bipolarity of North American ideas of race. Civil rights activist Bernice Reagon remembers that the St. Louis Cardinals maintained a farm team in her hometown of Albany, Georgia, during the 1950s and recruited new Cuban players every year. Their dark complexions barred them from association with local whites, and they functioned socially within the black community. Contrasts between conventional North American understandings of race and class and those prevalent elsewhere were troubling during an era of increasing challenge to the racial status quo. Cultural differences in racial perception, coupled with Cuba's oppositional stance, challenged taken-for-granted categories of domination.[31]

Cuba also joined the debate over civil rights militancy through Robert Williams, the NAACP official who responded to white supremacist violence in the Monroe, North Carolina, area in 1959 by advocating the right of armed self-defense. Williams also incurred NAACP disapproval for publishing favorable material on the Cuban revolution in his periodical, *The Crusader.* National NAACP leadership viewed Cuban interest in black Americans as both opportunistic and intrusive, "callous interference in a native American problem." Williams, however, "doubted the wisdom of keep[ing] this life-death struggle a family affair." He linked civil rights to a broader agenda. "Any struggle for freedom in the world today affects the stability of the whole society of man," he argued. "Why would you make our struggle an exception?"[32]

Williams's subsequent censure and dismissal by the national NAACP provoked lasting conflict within the organization, which sought to curtail protest that did not conform to nonviolent tactics. It coupled its reproof of Williams with an article in its own organ, *The Crisis*, by a black anti-Castro Cuban: Juan René Betancourt charged the *fidelistas* with suppressing Afro-Cuban culture while simultaneously touting the virtues of integration. The radical journal *Freedomways* took issue and featured an essay by another Cuban who criticized traditional black Cuban organizations as socially and politically reactionary.[33] The entry of *Freedomways* into the fray reflected the ongoing debate over militancy in the civil rights movement and the degree of linkage to other struggles that various parties deemed acceptable. The epoch that treated African Americans as an isolated people had passed, and linkages became a standard convention of movement rhetoric even when no actual networking was contemplated.

Camelot

Castro's visit to Harlem in the last weeks before a major presidential election highlighted growing public dissatisfaction with U.S. foreign and domestic policies. The electorate gave John F. Kennedy, who defeated vice-presidential incumbent Richard Nixon, an opportunity to revise many of these. Kennedy's Africa policy was linked with domestic goals during the campaign, because the candidate used Africa as a bridge to the black electorate to compensate for his demonstrably poor civil rights voting record. "Kennedy offered little in the way of concrete programs to black Americans," Richard D. Mahoney observes. "Instead, he made constant references to relations with Africa." Mahoney terms this ploy "a minor classic in political exploitation of foreign policy." Kennedy was thereby able to present himself as a liberal on racial matters without directly confronting the segregationist wing of his party.[34]

The emphasis on Africa also allowed the new president to compete with the seductive Cuban rhetoric of Third World solidarity. His administration supposedly showed greater respect for Third World neutralist predilections than had its predecessor, though in reality, Cold War preoccupations continued to prevail over concerns about freedom and development. It was more important to ensure indigenous leaders' anticommunist credentials than to uphold the right of self-determination. Washington's clash with Havana thus transcended a mere test of ideological wills. The United States, in line with a posture of continued readiness, would counter such insurgency with economic as well as military resources. The

Eisenhower administration had closed stateside ports to Cuban sugar when Cuba nationalized U.S. oil companies. It suspended relations with Cuba and instituted a travel ban in January 1961. Plans to unseat Castro, begun during the Eisenhower years, rapidly unfolded during the early months of the Kennedy presidency. Even as Washington publicized the ambitious Latin American aid program, Alliance for Progress, it covertly coordinated an amphibious attack on Cuba to begin on April 17, 1961. Cuban forces successfully repelled the Bay of Pigs invasion, mounted by Cuban exiles with Central Intelligence Agency aid.[35]

The U.S. public responded negatively to the Bay of Pigs assault, in part because it had failed. Popular criticism focused on its poor timing and preparation rather than on the wisdom of having attempted it at all. A minority that sympathized with the Cuban regime questioned the revival of retrograde "gunboat" policies just when the Kennedy administration had begun to tout the Alliance for Progress. African American radicals worried chiefly about the survival of the regime: "Following the Bay of Pigs," according to attorney Conrad Lynn, "many black militants throughout the country became alarmed over the possibility that Kennedy might stage an all-out offensive against Cuba to wipe out the revolution." Lynn, Julian Mayfield, John Henrik Clarke, William Worthy, James Boggs, and Ossie Davis threatened to "launch an armed struggle in the United States to aid our Cuban brothers and sisters" if the government made further attempts on Cuba. Veteran activist Malcolm X also linked Cuba with civil rights issues. His reputation as an extremist allowed him to pursue an interest in world affairs, free of the constraints that forced others to be circumspect. Malcolm advocated forging unity between U.S. blacks and liberation movements abroad.[36]

Leftists such as Lynn and black nationalists such as Malcolm X, though the most vocal, did not constitute the sole anti-intervention constituency among African Americans in spring 1961. Black press views of the Bay of Pigs reflected a fundamental ambivalence about the Cuban revolution. Even after official U.S. hostility became unmitigated, the press, generally liberal but hardly radical at the time, failed to climb on the bandwagon with unanimity. Some moderate newspapers opposed the invasion and linked it with government elements that they regarded as antagonistic to blacks. The *Cleveland Call and Post*, for example, labeled the Central Intelligence Agency "Dixie-dominated": CIA officials had underestimated Cubans in much the way southern whites misjudged African Americans, the Ohio paper editorialized. The *Los Angeles Herald-Dispatch* found the Bay of Pigs invasion "ridiculous and stupid." The *Norfolk* (Virginia) *Journal and Guide* opined that U.S. support for anti-Castro Cubans would undermine Washington's credibility in the American republics; it advocated seeking conflict resolution through consultation among such international agencies as the United Nations and the Organization of American States rather than resorting to unilateral force.[37]

Martin Luther King Jr., a major figure by 1961, also doubted the wisdom of the U.S. approach to Cuba. In May 1961 a correspondent asked him to comment on the U.S.-assisted landing. "I think our country has done not only a disservice to its own citizens but to the whole of humanity in dealing with the Cuban situation," King replied. "There is a revolt all over the world against colonialism, reactionary dictatorship, and systems of exploitation. Unless we as a nation join the revolution and go back to the revolutionary spirit that characterized the birth of our nation, I am afraid that we will be relegated to a second-class power in the world with no real moral voice to speak to the conscience of humanity." King added his name to a petition protesting the invasion. "I am as concerned about international affairs," he declared, "as I am about the civil rights struggle in the United States."[38]

Only ten days before King expressed these views, the Senate Internal Security Committee began hearings on Cuban influence among African Americans. It subpoenaed Joe Louis and probed his business transactions with the Cuban tourist commission. Louis, who had fallen behind on federal tax payments, was persuaded to repudiate the Cuban arrangement in a public news conference. He declared that he had no political objective other than to promote tourism; he was canceling his participation not because he thought it wrong but out of respect for public opinion and his wife's wishes. Louis went further, however, in vowing that if his associates did not follow suit by severing all Cuban connections, he would leave the firm. The Internal Security Committee published an annex to its final report, "Cuba and the American Negro," aimed at discrediting Cuban claims of success in turning black Americans against their government.[39]

The Cuba issue seemed indeed to revive earlier Cold War themes. After William Worthy, a reporter for the *Baltimore Afro-American*, had journeyed illegally to China in 1957 to file stories for CBS and the *New York Post*, the State Department revoked his passport. Worthy subsequently traveled to Cuba without papers and was arrested in Miami on his return. His conviction attracted worldwide attention, as he was the only U.S. citizen at that time to face prosecution for leaving and returning to the United States. Worthy, author James Baldwin, and civil rights organizer Bayard Rustin later worked with such prominent figures as Norman Thomas, Dorothy Day, and A. J. Muste in defying the ban on food and drug shipments to Cuba.[40]

These events occurred in an atmosphere of worsening relations with the USSR, and in view of mutual Soviet-American brinkmanship the circumstances of the Cuban missile crisis in late October 1962 made a nuclear war seem quite plausible. A last-minute resolution of the deadlock sent Soviet warships home as the United

States pledged to dismantle Turkish missile sites close to Soviet borders and to refrain from bombing Cuba. The experience turned administration attention forcefully toward tensions involving non-European states.[41]

Soviet expectation of Ghana's and Guinea's cooperation in providing refueling facilities and airspace during the Cuban missile crisis created an opportunity to check spreading radicalism in Africa. These states had become concerned with Cuba's retreat from neutralism and evidence of its internal suppression of Afro-Cuban culture. Their refusal to accommodate the Soviet air mission was a factor in the USSR's decision to abandon nuclear confrontation. Ghana and Guinea attracted considerable attention in the African American press, and the stance they took might have aided the administration's ongoing quest for an African policy that integrated regionalist and globalist concerns while reconciling both with a domestic racial reform agenda. Yet policymakers who wanted more attention paid to African affairs for both foreign and domestic reasons proved unable to build on this potential. Kennedy remained publicly identified with a friendly posture toward African powers, but Cold War considerations retained top priority. When Sekou Touré visited Washington in 1962 seeking aid after a break with the Soviets, for example, officials asked him to expel Eastern bloc technicians and refrain from discussing U.S. race relations.[42]

The missile crisis reinforced Cuba's desire to mitigate its isolation and dependence on the Soviets through activism in Africa.[43] Cuban internationalism paralleled a similar move by the black establishment in the United States, which had joined the Cold War "scramble for Africa." The American Negro Leadership Council on Africa (ANLC)—headed by Martin Luther King Jr., James Farmer, Dorothy Height, Roy Wilkins, Whitney Young, A. Philip Randolph, and others—convened for the first time in 1962 to press for a larger African American voice in shaping U.S. policy for Africa. Growing public support for civil rights also spurred the group to urge desegregation of the State Department. Its spokesmen quickly gained the ear of President Kennedy, Secretary of State Dean Rusk, and others, yet late in 1962 the ANLC discovered that Washington had increased South Africa's sugar quota to offset the loss of the prohibited Cuban product. In their protest to Secretary of Agriculture Orville Freeman, ANLC leaders carefully refrained from defending Cuba, but anti-Castroism and racial insensitivity seemed paired in official circles.[44]

The challenge facing U.S. advocates of just and coherent public policies, foreign and domestic, was to uncouple the link between firm anticommunism and tolerance of racial injustice. The Kennedy administration committed itself from its inception to a pursuit of the former but did not move beyond symbolic efforts to address the latter. Former Undersecretary of State George Ball recalls "the mood . . . at the beginning of 1961" as so complacent that "even though Montgomery and Little Rock were place names with epic connotations, those at the top reaches of the Administration showed only a shadowy appreciation of the civil rights movement and the turbulence it would create." This complacency ended abruptly in 1963 as a world audience watched film footage of police in Birmingham, Alabama, setting dogs on demonstrators and dousing marchers with high-pressure fire hoses. It viewed with horror the bombing deaths of four young black girls and other seemingly endless acts of violence.[45]

Secretary of State Rusk circularized all U.S. ambassadors to do whatever they could to restore the nation's flagging reputation on the race relations front. As federal officials hoped, most African leaders accepted as good-faith efforts the executive initiatives undertaken to affirm equal rights and protect civil rights workers in the South. Black militancy at home, however, threatened to undermine Washington's achievements. Presidential action, constrained by politics, could not effect the permanent changes that society now required; only federal legislation could institutionalize reform. An omnibus civil rights bill, hastily drafted by Kennedy's aides and nurtured in the chastened climate following his death, became law in 1964. The State Department under Rusk's leadership endorsed the Civil Rights Act of 1964 and the Voting Rights Act of 1965. In making desegregation its official policy, the nation lessened its vulnerability to negative propaganda, gained added insurance against possible UN sanctions, and bought time for reforms to bear fruit. Federal authorities distanced themselves from social and political practices that could now be labeled as local, archaic, and aberrant, freeing the United States to pursue the Cold War less encumbered than in the past by ideological contradictions.[46]

Kennedy's changed attitude toward the civil rights movement coincided with secret approaches to Castro in 1963. UN Ambassador Adlai Stevenson gave a pacificatory address on Cuba on October 7; the administration halted raids on the island by exiles and tried to assert control over the CIA. Broader detente was the order of the day as Washington also sought fresh approaches to Hanoi and Peking, and signed a test-ban treaty with Moscow in August. These changes reflected the growing cost to the United States, and to Kennedy especially, of brinkmanship. They also represented a coming-to-terms with the global pluralism that the president had previously so strongly resisted.[47]

Conclusion

Castro's Harlem sojourn constituted an opening volley in the assault on Cold War bilateralism. The Cuban leader targeted the election-year ferment in the capital of black America and helped revive a neglected paradigm that placed civil rights in international perspective. In so doing, he independently confirmed what many African Americans already understood about the global salience of the black freedom struggle. Castro, and the celebrity visitors to his hotel suite who colluded with him to this end, also served notice that neither domestic nor international politics could continue to be predicated on the invisibility of peoples of color. Harlem became, briefly, a world capital; its collective life and its relationship to the U.S. mainstream could no longer be disguised. The United States, as the leader of the Western powers, had to be morally and politically persuasive enough to offset the enticing linkages that common experiences of racial-ethnic domination constructed, and compelling enough to defeat their resulting implications for political action.

Federal officials soon understood the dimensions of this task. The United States Advisory Commission on Information (USACI) in 1963 associated the Cuban revolution with "a new phase in the cold war" and advocated intensified efforts to influence international public opinion, including funding for a larger U.S. Information Agency (USIA). Its recommendations assumed increased importance with the realization that the Castro government sought to capture African American sympathies. The influential Assistant Secretary of State for Inter-American Affairs Edwin M. Martin suggested that Cuba had planned the broadcasts "Radio Free Dixie" and "The Friendly Voice of Cuba" to "arouse racial antagonism in Negro audiences."[48]

One might view the tumultuous events of the 1960s as lashing the coasts of U.S. society in successive waves that cumulatively and permanently altered the shoreline. Or perhaps the metaphor of a land between two rivers is more provocative. When the Cuban delegation arrived at the Hotel Theresa, it ventured upon social and political terrain that the most intrepid domestic reformers had just begun to tread—between swift currents running toward the past and to the future. The more navigable latter course inaugurated profound and lasting changes that would have been inconceivable before 1960. The old order, shored up in some respects by ideological reinterpretations and practical adaptations, had nevertheless eroded. New approaches to race, culture, and politics fundamentally altered our national politics and our thinking about the state and society in ways that no one could have predicted before Castro came to Harlem.

Notes

1. Eqbal Ahmad, "Victims of the Long Peace," paper presented at "Rethinking the Cold War: A Conference in Memory of William Appleman Williams," University of Wisconsin–Madison, October 20, 1991.

2. Brenda Gayle Plummer, "Evolution of the Black Foreign Policy Constituency," *TransAfrica Forum* 6 (Spring–Summer 1989): 67–81. On the admission of new states to the United Nations, see plenary meeting, September 20, 1960, in UN, General Assembly, 15th sess., *Official Records,* 5–7.

3. Michael Omi and Howard Winant, *Racial Formation in the United States* (New York: Routledge, 1986), 47–51.

4. Bert Lockwood Jr., "The UN Charter and U.S. Civil Rights Litigation: 1946–1955," *Iowa Law Review* 5 (1984): 948; Mary L. Dudziak, "Desegregation as a Cold War Imperative," *Stanford Law Review* 41 (November 1988): 61–120.

5. Frank F. Lee, "Changing Structure of Negro Leadership," *The Crisis* 65 (April 1958): 197–200, 251; James Farmer, *Lay Bare the Heart* (New York: Arbor House, 1985), 196–97. On leaders' early ambivalence about mass participation, see F. D. Patterson, "Report on the Capahosic Conference," March 3–4, 1956, Claude Barnett and Associated Negro Press Papers, Chicago Historical Society; Charles Denby, *Indignant Heart* (Detroit: Wayne State University Press, 1989), 184–85.

6. *Congressional Record,* April 18, 1956, 6596–98.

7. Vijaya Lakshmi Pandit, *The Scope of Happiness* (New York: Crown, 1979), 250. On Dulles's statesmanship, see Townsend Hoopes, *The Devil and John Foster Dulles* (Boston: Little, Brown, 1973); Richard H. Immerman, ed., *John Foster Dulles and the Diplomacy of the Cold War* (Princeton: Princeton University Press, 1990); Congressional Record, April 18, 1956, 6596; interview in Chester Bowles memoir, Oral History Collection, Columbia University, New York; Chester Bowles, *Promises to Keep: My Years in Public Life, 1941–1969* (New York: Harper & Row, 1971), 250; Percival L. Prattis to William G. Nunn, January 20, 1956, Percival. L. Prattis Papers, Moorland-Spingarn Research Center, Howard University, Washington, D.C.

8. Richard E. Welch Jr., *Response to Revolution: The United States and the Cuban Revolution, 1959–1961* (Chapel Hill: University of North Carolina Press, 1985), 32, 197 n. 6; Stephen G. Rabe, "Latin America and Anticommunism," in Immerman, *John Foster Dulles,* 187; Laurence H. Shoup and William Minter, *The Imperial Brain Trust: The Council on Foreign Relations and United States Foreign Policy* (New York, 1977), 42–43.

9. Simeon Booker, "Negro Heroes of Cuban Revolt," *Ebony* 14 (April 1959): 51, 52. On Maceo, see J. A. Rogers, *The World's Great Men of Color* (New York: [privately published], 1947), 2:272–78; Philip S. Foner, *Antonio Maceo: The "Bronze Titan" of Cuba's Struggle for Independence* (New York: Monthly Review Press, 1977).

10. *New York Times,* September 21, 1960, sec. 17, p. 6; John Henrik Clarke, "Journey to the Sierra Maestra," *Freedomways* 1 (Spring 1961): 32–35; Julian Mayfield, "The Cuban Challenge," *Freedomways* 2 (Summer 1961): 185–89; *Time,* June 6, 1960, 36; Teresa Casuso, *Cuba and Castro* (New York, 1961), 245; Charles P. Howard, "The Afro-Cubans," *Freedomways* 4 (Summer 1964): 375–82.

11. U.S. Senate Committee on the Judiciary, Internal Security Subcommittee hearings, *Communist Threat to the United States through the Caribbean,* 86th Cong., 2d sess., 7, 437–38; *Atlanta Daily World,* May 26, 1960, and *Pittsburgh Courier,* June 17, 1960, Tuskegee Clipping File, Tuskegee Institute, Tuskegee, Alabama (hereafter TCF); *Time,* June 6, 1960, 36.

12. *Pittsburgh Courier,* June 17, 1960, TCF. On black public opinion and communism, see Alfred O. Hero Jr., *American Religious Groups View Foreign Policy* (Durham, N.C.: Duke University Press, 1973), table 6–11, 409–10.

13. Quoted in Rosemari Mealy, *Fidel and Malcolm X* (Melbourne: Ocean Press, 1993), 29; *New York Times,* July 3, 1960, Schomburg Clipping File, Schomburg Center for Research in Black Culture, New York Public Library (hereafter SCF).

14. Dwight D. Eisenhower, *Waging Peace, 1956–1961* (New York: Doubleday, 1965), 576–77.

15. Casuso, *Cuba and Castro*, 237, 240–41; Carlos Moore, *Castro, the Blacks, and Africa* (Los Angeles: Center for Afro-American Studies, 1988), 77, 78. On chickens, see John Hess to the Editor, *Columbia Journalism Review*, July–August 1991, 10.

16. Casuso, *Cuba and Castro*, 237, 240–41; Conrad Lynn, *There Is a Fountain* (Westport, Conn.: Greenwood Press, 1979), 168; Moore, *Castro, the Blacks and Africa*, 78–79.

17. *New York Times*, September 22, 1960, sec. 14, pp. 2–4; *Pittsburgh Courier*, October 1, 1960, TCF; *Amsterdam News*, September 24, 1960, 10.

18. On the problems of African diplomats, see *New York Times*, September 20, 1960, sec. 1, p. 2, and sec. 16, pp. 2–3; September 21, 1960, sec. 17, pp. 7–8; September 22, 1960, sec. 14, p. 5, *The Crisis* 68 (January 1961): 100; (October 1961): 499; Eisenhower, *Waging Peace*, 586.

19. *Black Dispatch*, September 30, 1960, TCF; *New York Times*, September 26, 1960, sec. 16, p. 2; September 28, 1960, sec. 18, p. 8; *Amsterdam News*, October 1, 1960, p. 35.

20. Senate Committee, "Cuba and the American Negro," in *Communist Threat*, 780; Welch, *Response to Revolution*, 128; *Amsterdam News*, October 1, 1960, 35; *New York Times*, August 28, 1961, sec. 4, p. 3.

21. *The Worker*, January 11, 1959, SCF; *Chicago Defender*, February 21, 1959, TCF; Welch, *Response to Revolution*, 127–28; Adam Clayton Powell, *Adam by Adam* (New York: Dial Press, 1971), 186–88, 191–98.

22. *New York Times*, September 22, 1960, sec. 14, p. 8; September 26, 1960, sec. 16, p. 4.

23. Author's conversation with Sr. Reynaldo Peñalver, Havana, Cuba, July 19, 1990; *Miami Herald*, September 23, 1960, TCF; Farmer, *Lay Bare the Heart*, 196–97.

24. Speech of Prime Minister Fidel Castro at the plenary meeting of the UN General Assembly, 15th sess., September 26, 1960, *Official Records*, 118, 132.

25. Moore, *Castro, the Blacks, and Africa*, 65, 71.

26. UN General Assembly, 15th sess., September 26, 1960, *Official Records*, 119, 132, 136.

27. Arthur Schlesinger Jr., *A Thousand Days* (Boston: Houghton Mifflin, 1965), 207.

28. Leroi Jones, "Cuba Libre," in *Home* (New York, 1963), 43, 39; Van Gosse, "The Cuban Revolution and the Origins of the New Left: Revising the History of Declension," paper presented at "Toward a History of the 1960's," conference of the State Historical Society of Wisconsin, May 1, 1993.

29. *Amsterdam News*, October 8, 1960, *passim*.

30. Clarke, "Journey to the Sierra Maestra," 32–35.

31. Bernice Reagon, "Impressions of Cuban Culture by an Afro-American Artist," *Black Scholar* 8 (Summer 1977): 51.

32. *New York Times*, September 21, 1960, sec. 17, p. 6; Robert F. Williams, *Negroes with Guns* (Chicago: Third World Press, 1962), 71.

33. Juan René Betancourt, "Castro and the Cuban Negro," *The Crisis*, 68 (May 1961), 270–274; Sixto Gaston Agüere, "The Negro and the Cuban Revolution," *Freedomways* 1 (Summer 1961), 152–57.

34. Richard D. Mahoney, *JFK: Ordeal in Africa* (New York: Oxford University Press, 1983).

35. Senate Committee, *Communist Threat*, 222; Thomas G. Paterson, "Fixation with Cuba: The Bay of Pigs, Missile Crisis, and Covert War against Castro," in *Kennedy's Quest for Victory: American Foreign Policy, 1961–1963*, ed. Thomas G. Paterson (New York: Oxford University Press, 1989), 124–27.

36. Fair Play for Cuba Committee press release, April 19, 1961, SCF; Lynn, *There Is a Fountain*,

170–71; Ruby Essien-Udom and E. U. Essien-Udom, "Malcolm X: An International Man," in *Malcolm X, the Man and His Times,* ed. John Henrik Clark (New York: Macmillan, 1969), 259–60, 265.

37. Quoted in *The Worker,* May 7, 1961, SCF.

38. Martin Luther King, quoted in Barbara Lindsay to W.E.B. Du Bois, May 16, 1961, in *The Papers of W.E.B. Du Bois* (Sanford, N.C.: Microfilm Corporation of America, 1980).

39. *New York Times,* August 28, 1961, 4:3; Senate Committee, *Communist Threat,* testimony of Joe Louis Barrow and William Rowe, June 5, 1961, 771–87, and "Cuba and the American Negro," 789–92; Arnold Rampersad, *The Life of Langston Hughes* (New York: Oxford University Press, 1988), 2: 322–23, 330–31.

40. *New York Post,* editorial, July 19, 1962; open letter from A. Philip Randolph, August 24, 1962; Carlton B. Goodlett to Randolph, August 31, 1962, *New York Times,* October 12, 1962, clipping, all in Carlton B. Goodlett Papers, State Historical Society of Wisconsin, Madison; U.S. House Committee on Un-American Activities hearings, May 6–7, and 23, 1963, 88th Cong. 2d sess., pt. 1, 319; William Worthy to author, June 20, 1988 and enclosures; *Liberation* press releases, February 3 and December 7, 1962 (advertisement on back cover), SCF.

41. On the Cuban missile crisis, see Walt Rostow to the President, November 11, 1961, Kennedy Library, Declassified Documents Reference Service (DDRS); Paterson, "Fixation with Cuba," 150–51; Richard Ned Lebow, "Domestic Politics and the Cuban Missile Crisis: The Traditional and Revisionist Interpretations Reevaluated," *Diplomatic History* 14 (Fall 1990): 471–92.

42. Moore, *Castro, the Blacks, and Africa,* 129–32; Thomas J. Noer, "New Frontiers and Old Priorities in Africa," in Paterson, *Kennedy's Quest for Victory,* 253–83.

43. Mahoney, *JFK: Ordeal in Africa,* 205, 223, 224, 180–81.

44. George M. Houser, "Freedom's Struggle Crosses Oceans and Mountains: Martin Luther King, Jr. and the Liberation Struggles in Africa and America," in *We Shall Overcome: Martin Luther King, Jr. and the Black Freedom Struggle,* ed. Peter J. Albert and Ronald Hoffman (New York: Pantheon, 1990),186–87; Carlton B. Goodlett to Theodore Brown, January 21, 1963, and Brown to conference participants, February 8, 1963, both in Goodlett Papers.

45. George Ball, *The Past Has Another Pattern* (New York: Norton, 1982), 165.

46. Bowles, *Promises to Keep,* 445–46; U.S. Department of State, "Status Report of African Reaction to Civil Rights in the United States, Week ending July 12, 1963," DDRS 1976 171 A; Rusk, *As I Saw It,* 83, 585.

47. Kirkpatrick Sale, *Power Shift: The Rise of the Southern Rim and Its Challenge to the Eastern Establishment* (New York: Random House, 1975), 128–29; Radio Free Europe, Background Reports, Country Series, Cuba, no. 957, 1960, and no. 997, 1961; Non-Target Communist Area Analysis Dept., "The High (and Rising) Cost of Castro," report, January 24, 1964, 3; Henry Wriston, *Diplomacy in a Democracy* (New York: Harper, 1956), 12–15; Richard J. Walton, *Cold War and Counterrevolution: The Foreign Policy of John F. Kennedy* (New York, 1972), 221.

48. USACI press release, January 28, 1963, in Barnett Papers; Edwin M. Martin's testimony, February 18, 1963, in U.S. Senate Committee on Foriegn Relations, Subcommittee on Inter-American Affairs hearings, *Castro-Communist Subversion in the Western Hemisphere,* 88th Cong., 2d sess., 6.

Part III

Explaining the End of the Cold War

Chapter 7

The End of the Cold War and Why We Failed to Predict It

Michael Cox

Whatever else might be said about the Cold War, the one thing it cannot be accused of is having failed to engage the interest and attention of the Western intellectual community. As a problem, it very likely generated more discussion and controversy than any other single topic in the postwar period. The reason is clear: It was a system from which none of us could escape. From the Third World to the countries of Eastern Europe, from the front line of a once divided Germany to the American Midwest, the Cold War constantly made its presence felt. In the process it inserted itself into the economies of the two protagonists, shaped people's political choices, and led to the deaths of millions. It also made some individuals and states rich and powerful, others poor and miserable, and for the better part of forty years it threatened to destroy us all—which according to recent research it might have done more easily than most opponents of nuclear weapons ever believed possible.[1] Little wonder that the Cold War was studied in such minute detail. In many ways it was the most important relationship in our lives.

All this leads, however, to a simple but crucial question: If the Cold War was analyzed in such detail, why were we, the so-called experts, unable to anticipate its conclusion in the late 1980s? Here after all was a phenomenon dissected to the nth degree. But when that same phenomenon first showed signs of fatigue, then wilted visibly, and finally passed away altogether, the intellectual and policy-making community was left shell-shocked. Naturally, it later attempted to explain why the conflict had come to an end, but this couldn't hide the fact that at the end of the day nearly all of us were (in the words of the song) "bewitched, bothered, and bewildered" by the passing of the old order. One of the most crucial developments of the twentieth century caught us all by surprise. Those who made policy, those whose job was to comment on it, insiders and outsiders alike: all were dumfounded.[2]

This collective failure to prepare for the unexpected has of course provoked considerable comment. Some have simply dismissed the charge of failure. The task of the social scientist, they maintain, is to explain, not predict; hence it is unfair (and beside the point) to accuse commentators of not foreseeing the great international earthquake of the 1980s. It just wasn't their job. Others have been a good deal less defensive. John Gaddis, for example, accepts that there is a charge to be answered. He points the finger, however, not at the intellectual community as a whole but at the theoretical pretensions of international relations as a subject. Indeed, according to Gaddis, the discipline's failure to anticipate the end of the Cold War proves (if proof were needed) that all so-called scientific attempts to understand the human condition are bound to come to grief. In his work Allen Lynch takes an altogether different tack: Indeed, in his opinion there is nothing to apologize for at all, because the Cold War had actually come to an end almost two decades before. Thus why bother to apologize for our inability to predict the end of something that had already passed away?[3]

However interesting these observations may be, they still do not explain why most of us thought the Cold War would endure. But there is an answer—a rather obvious one, I would submit. In effect, most of us assumed continuity in world politics because we viewed the antagonism as the expression of a profound and irreconcilable opposition between well-established social systems. The idea that either of them would actually fail seemed beyond the bounds of possibility, a mere fantasy indulged in by utopians but not to be taken seriously by mature commentators. Yet the USSR did implode, and as a result the Cold War came to an end, suddenly and without much warning. But who anticipated this? Hardly anybody—certainly not those whose professional job it was to explain how the Soviet system functioned. Sovietologists in particular failed to come up with the intellectual goods. In fact, not only did the Kremlinologists not foresee the possibility that a specifically "Soviet" history would come to an end, but their ways of understanding the USSR (and there was clearly more than one) virtually precluded them from doing so.

Consider what academic Soviet Studies overlooked. First, many of the discipline's more conservative practitioners did not think it possible for someone like Mikhail Gorbachev to come to power in the first place. Many were then slow to understand the full implications of his radically new agenda; a few even regarded his talk about *glasnost* and the like as a trick designed to undermine the West. A large number also assumed (quite wrongly) that he would soon be overthrown and the old order restored. Others believed (again incorrectly) that he would succeed in his endeavors and actually revitalize the USSR. But nobody expected the USSR to withdraw from Eastern Europe in 1989 and collapse two years later.[4]

Naturally, there were exceptions to this general rule. Some brave souls even got it right. But in the main, those who had had the temerity to suggest that the USSR was historically doomed—as opposed to being merely weak or insecure—were peripheral, almost "dissident" figures in the academic world. The odd emigré, some neoconservatives (Richard Pipes), and one or two Marxists (Hillel Ticktin, editor of *Critique*) came close to the truth—but they were hardly mainstream figures in Soviet Studies.[5]

This essay therefore tries to understand what can best, and only, be described as the collective failure of a discipline: a failure to foresee the implosion of an entity whose structures, leaders, and policies it had been studying in minute detail for more than forty years. There is not just one dimension to this failure, but many; not just one ex-Sovietologist with egg on his or her face but several. I look first, however, not at Soviet Studies as such but at the position of the academic in the modern university. It is here that the cause of Sovietology's (and the Western intellectual community's) present discomfort has to be sought.

The Academic Dilemma

It can be argued (and I would certainly want to argue the point here) that academics teaching in highly specialized disciplines in Western universities are either discouraged from asking or not inclined to ask big questions. They are deterred from doing so in all sorts of ways: by a doctoral system that emphasizes the footnote over the idea; by the subdivision of knowledge that finds its organized expression in the departmental system; and finally by career opportunities that are at risk for those who stray outside the narrow channel. Universities, moreover, reward their members for the ability to publish detailed monographs in increasingly specialized journals. Indeed, there are few journals (except the less prestigious ones on the margins of academia) that actually publish nonspecialist material.

Modern academics—including those within Soviet Studies—are thus caught (and have been for a long time) on the horns of a dilemma. To succeed, they must specialize and do "useful" or "practical" research—on interest groups, party structures, electoral systems, and the like—that is recognized and rewarded by the university. But once involved in what is effectively a web of professional dependency, they find it increasingly difficult to examine larger issues; in fact, they may be thought decidedly odd if they do. In this way, large-scale problems about the dynamics or contradictions of this or that social system (including, I submit, the former USSR's) are simply pushed off the agenda.

This leads to a second general observation, not about the structural constraints imposed upon the academic in the modern university but about the intellectual ones. To put it bluntly, the very nature of conventional social sciences would have made it extraordinarily difficult for the student of the USSR to foresee its decline and final breakup. The reason, quite simply, was and remains the dominance of empiricism in the academy and its most important consequence: those so influenced simply avoided theorizing about systems in general. Indeed, they were literally invoked not to by the "greats" of social sciences, in particular by the antitheoretical Karl Popper. The result of this persistent and, in the end, effective attack upon "grand intellectual designs" was to render most academics incapable of examining the large picture historically; the large picture was precisely what they were trained not to look at. The proper object of study was the very specific and the highly detailed: parts of the whole but not the whole itself. Large issues—such as why systems rise, mature, and finally wither away—were ignored or left to the speculator or journalist. Or, it might be added, to a Toynbee or a Marx—neither of whom would have felt very much at home in an academic department in the postwar period.

The final constraint was less methodological than institutional and professional. For over forty years careers had been made, journals produced, books written, budgets justified, and international conferences organized on the assumption that something would continue to exist: the Soviet Union. It would be no exaggeration to say that the USSR became a way of life for a very large number of people—not just in universities but in Western intelligence services, military establishments, major industries, diplomatic missions, and alliances abroad—who were all directly dependent upon the Soviet Union. The object of their distrust had, ironically, become the reason for their being. The idea that one day it might no longer be there was virtually inconceivable—as one academic discovered when he asked a group of leading American officials in 1985 whether or not we should be "looking ahead to the possibility that the Cold War might someday end." According to the academic in question, John L. Gaddis, the "embarrassed silence [that] ensued" was finally broken by a highly respected senior diplomat: "Oh, it hadn't occurred to any of us that it ever would end."[6]

Soviet Studies and the Cold War

This brings us to the field of Soviet Studies itself. Here we need to ask a simple but important question: Why was the Soviet Union so great a subject of Western interest? For what purpose was it analyzed? There is no one answer to this, yet it would be somewhat disingenuous to abstract the discipline of Soviet Studies from its context, and that context was the Cold War. This, I would argue, profoundly influenced the assumptions of many Sovietologists. To understand why, we must briefly look at the development of the subject after the war.

The exponential growth of Soviet Studies as a discipline coincided with the emergence of the Soviet Union and the United States as the most important actors on the world stage after 1945. Understanding the USSR—which Churchill once characterized as this "riddle wrapped in a mystery inside an enigma"—became something of a preoccupation in Washington for two very good reasons. First, it was the only power capable of challenging or at least placing a limit on American power. Second, the world was in turmoil, and it was feared that the USSR would benefit from this fact. The United States thus had to develop an assessment of the Soviet Union's capabilities and intentions. This it did rather effectively. Indeed, if one now reads through much of the American intelligence on the subject before 1950 at least, one is forcibly struck by its many insights. The Soviet Union was of course a problem, but as the influential George F. Kennan pointed out in both his "Long Telegram" of 1946 and the "X" article a year later, Russia was "by far the weaker party." The United States therefore had little to worry about; it could do what it had to do in the certain knowledge that Moscow would be unable to upset its plans for restoring world order.

As the Cold War unfolded, however, this more or less balanced approach was replaced by one that increasingly emphasized the seriousness of the Soviet threat. The reasons for this transition were complex. In part it had to do with Soviet actions over Berlin in 1948 and 1949. The detonation of the first Soviet A-bomb and the revolution in China in 1949 further upset U.S. calculations. A year later the

North Korean attack on South Korea also did a great deal to confirm the danger-ous character of the USSR to U.S. policymakers. Finally, as the wily (but engag-ingly honest) Dean Acheson understood only too well, stressing the threat helped mobilize a reluctant people behind the new American empire. Whether or not he actually believed his own propaganda, the fact remains that in public at least he tended to emphasize Soviet power and understate its known weaknesses on the as-sumption that doing so made for an effective American foreign policy.[7]

Exaggerating the Soviet Union's strengths while underestimating its flaws had obvious consquences, the most important one being that people in general came to regard the USSR as having far greater capabilities than it really possessed. Hence the constant scares, the bomber and missile "gaps," and the "windows of vulnera-bility" that dotted the history of the Cold War. These were all part and parcel of a particular mind-set, an almost instinctive perception of the USSR which no amount of information to the contrary seemed able to dislodge. No wonder so many were taken by surprise when this apparently impregnable (and oh so dan-gerous) edifice came tumbling down—it simply wasn't in the script.

Nor, quite obviously, was the Soviet decision to disengage from the struggle with the West in the later 1980s. Again there was a good reason for the intellectual fail-ure to anticipate this, for one of the central props of the Cold War was the as-sumption that the USSR was bound by its very nature to expand. The thesis was not entirely unreasonable, given that the USSR was formally wedded to an anti-capitalist ideology; it had natural allies in the Third World; and to survive in a hos-tile setting it had to win friends and influence people abroad. All this was obvious. The problem was that those who stressed Soviet expansion appeared oblivious to other facts: that the Soviet reach was never great; that Moscow frequently exercised great caution; that it sometimes retreated voluntarily; and perhaps most impor-tant, that for an inefficient and uncompetitive system like the Soviet Union, ex-pansion was an extraordinary burden and one likely to grow as the economy be-gan to slow down. Yet hardly anybody anticipated that the USSR might one day do what all other declining powers have been impelled to do in history: that is, retreat from an empire it could neither afford to support nor hope to control over the longer term.[8]

The assumption that the USSR could never withdraw from entrenched posi-tions also helps explain why Soviet Studies failed to predict the most important strategic development of all in the postwar period: Soviet disengagement from Eastern Europe in 1989.[9] All strands of Sovietological opinion had assumed that the USSR would stay where it was—for apparently good reasons. First, according to the strategic wisdom, the USSR would remain where it was because doing so both placed pressure on the West and reduced Western pressure on itself. Second, it limited German ambitions by guaranteeing Germany's continued division; indeed, if there had been no other reason for the USSR to remain in Eastern Europe, the desire to keep Germany divided would have been enough. But there was more. The USSR needed Eastern Europe (or so it was argued) both for economic purposes and for the conduct of its foreign policy, because without the support of its Warsaw Pact allies it would not have been able to project its influence so effectively. And finally, to withdraw from the region would have threatened the integrity of the USSR itself. For all these reasons, it was believed, the USSR could not possibly do what it finally did in 1989: disengage and return to home base.[10]

In considering the impact of the Cold War upon Soviet Studies, one must also look at the dominant paradigm of the Cold War: totalitarianism. Deployed initially as a term to describe fascist Italy in the 1920s, and subsequently applied by analysts to understand Nazi Germany and Soviet Russia in the 1930s, it became increasingly popular after the war as a means of characterizing the USSR. The postwar influence of the concept is readily explainable: It was simple; it seemed to describe the peculiarities of the Soviet system rather well; it was politically correct by the conservative standards of the time; and it provided a moral justification for Western policy in the Cold War by equating the Soviet Union with Nazi Germany.

In fact, precisely because it looked like an ideological device designed to legitimize (and perpetuate) the Cold War, the idea of totalitarianism later came to be opposed by many within the Soviet Studies profession.[11] Yet despite the backlash, the totalitarian thesis continued to exert a tremendous influence on Soviet Studies—with the important consequence that those who still supported the idea (and there were many) tended to assume the persistence of the Soviet regime not because it was legitimate but because it could deploy an enormous battery of controls to prevent latent discontent from becoming overt. These controls, such observers pointed out, had guaranteed the system after the Bolsheviks seized power in 1917, had been perfected under Stalin, and—whatever their modifications after his death—remained in being until the 1980s. The people might mutter and the intellectuals moan, but given the power of the secret police and the atomized character of the population, there was no possibility that society's contradictions could ever express themselves. In fact, according to emigré writer Alexander Zinoviev (whose work exercised a great deal of influence in the West following the publication of *The Yawning Heights* in 1976), "Homo Sovieticus" was so traumatized that he (and presumably she) preferred the order guaranteed by Soviet communism to the likely disorder that would follow its demise. The system therefore was secure, strong not only in its own right but in having actually implicated the ordinary Soviet citizen in his or her own subordination to this perfected form of the Leviathan state.[12]

The Social Sciences

The Cold War shaped the contours of Soviet Studies for nearly two decades. In the 1960s and 1970s, however, there was a serious and determined drive both to modernize the subject and to integrate it more completely with the broader social sciences.[13] The effort proved very effective, and by the early 1980s the discipline had changed beyond recognition. Yet despite this methodological invasion of what had once been a rather isolated academic preserve inhabited by the emigré, the government official, and the conservative, the new wave proved no more successful in predicting the upheavals of the late 1980s than their more or-thodox predecessors. Carrying neither the intellectual nor the political baggage of the "totalitarians," the second generation of Sovietologists failed as completely as their less liberal opponents in anticipating the collapse of the Soviet system. Why?

One part of the answer, ironically, has to be sought in the new cohort's rejection of the original totalitarian model.[14] Supporters of that model, recall, believed that the USSR would remain in being not because the system was popular or inherently stable but because the Soviet state was extraordinarily repressive.[15] According to a number of social scientists who rose to intellectual prominence in the 1970s and 1980s, this view was profoundly misleading: It not only overemphasized the role of force in maintaining the Soviet regime but seriously underestimated the reserves upon which the regime could draw to reproduce itself. That the system was not democratic in the Western sense did not mean that it was without support. On the contrary, it had deep roots in the Soviet population. Some even spoke of a "social contract" between rulers and the ruled in which the former fulfilled their part of the bargain by guaranteeing the latter full employment and minimal welfare. Moreover, it was argued, the Soviet people were proud of their country's achieve-ments; they had been given far more educational opportunities than their parents or grandparents had had, and their children, crucially, had the chance of an even better life. So why should they want to destroy or undermine the system?[16]

But it was not merely sociological factors that challenged the totalitarian myth of a system held together only by terror. The fact that the post-Stalin elite permit-ted some degree of group involvement and popular participation in the political process also suggested that the Soviet system was less unstable than some conser-vatives maintained. In fact, according to one leading American political scientist, the Soviet Union was nearly as open (if not more so) than the liberal democracies of the West.[17] Moreover, although Soviet elections may have been a facade, it would be wrong to conclude that they were meaningless. If nothing else, they allowed yet one more access point for the ordinary citizen to be involved in, or at least bring pressure to bear upon, the deliberations of government—further proof, if proof were needed, that the USSR was a long way away from the totalitarian nightmare portrayed in the popular literature by George Orwell and in the academic field by such notables as Carl Friedrich and Zbigniew Brzezinski.[18]

The new writing had a profound impact upon the way the USSR was perceived in the West. First, it made the Soviet system look decidedly less unpleasant than it had before; second, by implication, it led many who analyzed the USSR to the not illogical conclusion that the system was relatively stable. In fact, how could such an order—one that guaranteed jobs for life to an upwardly mobile, patriotic people who were not excluded from the political process—be on the verge of disintegration? That was beyond the bounds of possibility, a mere fantasy, entertained by extremists but not supported by the facts.

This conclusion was endorsed (in part) by another innovation introduced by the social sciences into the study of the Soviet system: that of political culture. Again trying to move beyond the limits of a totalitarian model whose residual influence probably had "less to do with its scholarly merits than with its ideological attractions," a number of leading scholars (political scientists in particular) sought to use the concept of political culture as a way of "allowing a greater degree of attention to be paid to the historical and national specificity of Soviet politics, as well as to the similarities it shares with other political systems."[19] The results, though not devoid of merit, nevertheless tended to reinforce the view of the USSR being a good deal more stable than it actually was. After all, according to the "culturalists," the system had been particularly successful in shaping Soviet beliefs and attitudes. Moreover, in their view the regime had acquired legitimacy by doing things, especially in the socioeconomic sphere, that fulfilled popular needs and demands. David Lane, for one, thought that the study of Soviet political culture not only revealed a previously unknown degree of "congruity between the attitudes" of the political elite and the people but showed that the political system itself was perceived positively because it was "carrying out many desirable policies." It was reasonable to conclude, therefore, that the elite (or more precisely, "political elites") had some level of "support among the population" as a whole.[20]

Finally, the argument that the regime may have been more successful than the totalitarians had assumed was implicit in much (though not all) of the new writing on the national question.[21] Here, once again, traditional views came under attack from a group of social scientists who neither sympathized with nationalist aspirations nor believed that nationalism was as potentially dangerous to the system as had previously been supposed. Implicitly, and in some cases explicitly, attacking the thesis that the USSR was a "prison house of nations," a modern generation of analysts arrived at some decidedly revisionist conclusions about the ethnic question in the USSR.

The first and perhaps least controversial was that in spite of the great wrongs historically done to many nationalities, the policy of the center after Stalin's death had been culturally tolerant, politically fair, and, by and large, economically equitable. Thus there was little reason to assume that so-called captive nations were straining at the leash to escape their now relatively benign captors. Nor did it follow that there was an inherent conflict between being a member of one of the various nations and a citizen of the wider Soviet Union. As one writer put it, ethnic consciousness "did not necessarily signify a lack of loyalty to the Soviet regime."[22] In fact, according to another analyst, it could be channeled to make it "integrative" rather than disintegrative of the state.[23] There was, in other words, no prima facie case for thinking that nationalism presented the system "with an impossible or even a potentially disturbing future."[24] As another commentator noted in a popular and widely used textbook published in 1986, "For the foreseeable future, most communist states, certainly the more legitimate ones [such as the Soviet Union], should be able to cope with," though "not fully solve the problems of nationalism and ethnic conflict."[25]

The Soviet Economy

Thus far it has been argued that the real cause of the failure to anticipate the end of the Cold War lay in a collective failure to recognize the USSR for what it was: a weak and flawed system in terminal decline. Nowhere was this failure more pronounced than in the study of the Soviet economy. Of course, most Western economists agreed that planning was inferior to the market; they also acknowledged in the 1980s that the Soviet economy was in difficulties. But few believed that the country's great (and growing) economic problems would actually bring about its disintegration.[26] The consensus was that although the economic system was in trouble, it had enough reserves to get by. This was certainly the view of the CIA, which in a well-publicized report of 1982 concluded that the Soviet leadership would be able muddle along almost indefinitely.[27] Significantly, it was also the opinion of influential American economist Ed Hewett, who went on to become Bush's principal adviser on Soviet affairs. As late as March 1989, Hewett warned the West not to overestimate Gorbachev's economic problems. The Soviet economy faced challenges, but it would be foolish to think it was "teetering on the brink of collapse." That line had been peddled before, he said, but should not be repeated; there was too much at stake.[28]

Why did so many Western experts fail to detect the fact that the Soviet economy was in terminal decline? One reason (we now know) was technical. Using Soviet figures, as most of them did, Western economists were bound to arrive at overly optimistic conclusions about the USSR's potential, for these figures both hid the degree of the Soviet slowdown and seriously overestimated the actual capacity of the economy. In fact, according to figures released by Moscow *after* 1989, the Soviet economy was not merely smaller than that of the United States but only one-third its size. Previous Western estimates of Soviet per capita income and productivity turned out to be even further off the mark. In other words, the Soviet economic system was not merely inefficient (that, we had always known) but far, far weaker than could have been imagined.[29]

There was, however, a second and more political reason why some underestimated the Soviet economic malaise. Throughout the 1980s there had been fierce infighting between those in the United States who promoted a strategy of confrontation and others who simply wanted to manage the Soviet Union in a stable bipolar environment. The former, naturally enough, sought to justify their approach by stressing the critical condition of the Soviet economy.[30] The latter, not surprisingly, tended to point to the system's enduring qualities. Indeed, so opposed were those in the second group to the policy of squeezing the USSR that they were inclined to seize any means to undercut the neoconservative case, and the simplest and most effective one was to pour cold water on the right-wing thesis that the USSR was in dire trouble and could be forced onto the ash heap of history. The result was to lead a large section of the American establishment—effectively its liberal or "realist" wing—to the incorrect conclusion that the Soviet economy had more vitality than it really did.

Finally, the debate about the Soviet economy necessarily became intertwined with the wider discusssion about economic change. The majority of analysts (economists in particular) believed in the possibility of economic reform. That profound obstacles stood in the way of restructuring was self-evident, but there was no reason in principle to conclude that improvements could not be made. There might even possibly be some "third way" between the Scylla of the command system and the Charybdis of the free market. This is where Gorbachev enters the picture. Assuming, or at least hoping, that he would directly address some of the difficulties facing the USSR, economists and others helped reinforce the belief (very widespread before the Gorbachev strategy began to implode) that the system would persist not because the economy was working well (it obviously was not) but because it was susceptible to improvement from above.[31]

The Gorbachev Factor

From the perspective of the 1990s Gorbachev looks like a transitional, quasi-tragic figure who failed in nearly everything he attempted to do. In 1985, re-member, he set out to revitalize the Soviet economy, yet in the end he managed only to accelerate—some would insist, cause—its collapse. He sought to transform the USSR into a more dynamic and attractive superpower; however, by the time he was forced from office in 1991 the Soviet Union was no longer a major force in world politics. And he tried to construct a new relationship between the peoples of the So-viet Union, but his ambiguous policies in this vital area only led to the empire's frag-mentation. History, one suspects, may not deal Gorbachev a particularly good hand.

But to most professional students of the USSR at the time, the early Gorbachev years appeared to be a golden age dominated by an energetic reformist leader—the modern combination of Peter the Great and Stalin, according to one noted com-mentator.[32] Indeed, how could one not be impressed by the man—especially since he was providing Soviet Studies with the biggest boost the field had received in over twenty years? Here perhaps is the key to understanding the "Gorbymania" that swept Soviet Studies for a short while: For the first time in many years the world as a whole was intensely interested in the Soviet Union, and who was on hand to provide instant, in-depth analysis about the latest developments in the Kremlin? None other than the long-ignored Sovietological experts. Many an academic ca-reer was given a sudden shot in the arm by Mikhail Gorbachev.

To say that the vast majority of those in Soviet Studies were supportive of Gor-bachev would be an understatement. Until the end of 1989 at least, he assumed an almost heroic status in the eyes of most Western experts, so much so that those who were less than enthusiastic about him were regarded as either unreconstructed reactionaries who only wanted to return to the good old days of the Cold War, or ultra-left fanatics. For a while it was not de rigueur to be negative about Gorbachev or his policies.

Besides boosting the sales of books on the USSR, this temporary cult of Gorbachev had dual consequences for Soviet Studies. One, of course, was to make a number of well-known Western scholars virtual cheerleaders for *perestroika* abroad. The other was to obscure from view what was actually taking place in the USSR. The common wisdom was that Gorbachev was renovating the Soviet Union; in reality, the combination of changes he was implementing accelerated its decline and fragmentation. Yet few seemed to appreciate the fact; certainly not many talked about it; and when more finally did, it was too late. Momentarily buoyed up by the new man in the Kremlin, most seemed to feel (until it became clear in 1990 that the system was falling apart) that Gorbachev was breathing new life into the Soviet Union. Consequently, observers ignored or failed to see what was really occurring: that behind the facade of superpower summits and the new entente cordiale between East and West, the country and its economy were imploding. It took the coup of August 1991 for many to find out just how far the process had gone.

Socialists and Stalinism

It would be easy to leave the discussion at this juncture, to point the finger at either shortsighted policymakers or those within the corridors of academic power. But this would be both intellectually one-sided and politically misleading. The left also bears a responsibility. After all, it had spent a good deal of time debating the "Russian question" and reflecting upon East-West relations; those two issues indeed seemed to preoccupy the left. In the end, however, radicals (with one or two notable exceptions) were no more capable of understanding the peculiar downward dynamics of the USSR than their more mainstream colleagues.[33] As a result, they were as astounded as nearly everybody else when Stalinism collapsed and the Cold War came to an end in the late 1980s. The interesting question is, why?

One reason, clearly, is that many on the left either identified with, were sympathetic to, or had residual faith in the Soviet project. Accordingly, they believed (or hoped) that the USSR would prosper and survive. This is hardly surprising, given their general understanding of the system. Critical of the Soviet Union's political arrangements, many socialists nevertheless saw the system as economically and socially superior to Western capitalism. Whatever its flaws, these had to be set against the USSR's many past achievements and its continuing deep reservoir of support among its people. Moreover, under Gorbachev's leadership there was a good chance that its problems could be resolved, through a process either of economic adaptation or political reform or a combination of the two. Anyway, the USSR had confronted hard times before and won, and it would do so again. Soviet socialism had been created against the odds in the 1930s and 1940s. There was no reason to believe it could not be "remade" in the 1980s and 1990s.[34]

More critical voices on the left took a somewhat less sanguine approach. According to the Trotskyists, the USSR was a species of degenerated workers' state that could be regenerated only after the workers themselves had taken political power. But even the most orthodox of Trotskyists did not believe the entire system would disintegrate. How could they? The USSR, though truly socialist in their view, still retained its planned character; by definition, therefore, it was economically more dynamic than Western capitalism. Furthermore, its noncapitalist character had to guarantee full employment to the workers and thus, despite its deformed nature, was bound to retain their loyalty. The USSR may have been in crisis, as Ernest Mandel admitted, but it would continue to function—and once the proletariat assumed the helm and recreated the conditions for socialist democracy, it would do so even more effectively.[35]

The idea that the USSR would continue was upheld even by socialists who had no illusions about the system at all: namely, those who supported the politically virtuous but theoretically idiosyncratic view that the Soviet system was a species of state capitalism. Adherents of this particular school of thought traveled a theoretical route different from that of their rivals on the left, yet in the end they arrived at the same destination. The reason they did so was implicit in their original argument: If, as they maintained, the Soviet system was another form of capitalism, then it followed that the Soviet economy was no more (or less) likely to grind to a halt than the economies of the West. And as those economies were not on the verge of collapse, it seemed reasonable to conclude that the Soviet system would not break down either. Indeed, one exponent of the state capitalist theory went to some length in 1987 to remonstrate with those who conjectured that the Soviet economic system was in decay. It was very wasteful, he agreed, but the level of waste—and by implication the degree of contradiction—was no greater than in Western systems. Indeed, according to Mike Haynes, the USSR had quite a respectable economic record. All talk of collapse therefore was nonsense. The USSR would persist.[36]

Conclusion

I have advanced the thesis that the failure to anticipate the end of the Cold War was the result of a generally flawed understanding of the Soviet Union. To demonstrate my point I have concentrated on the body of work popularly known as Sovietology, Kremlinology, or, more plainly, Soviet Studies. Some may think that my critique is overly harsh, that at least some students of the USSR did anticipate the final demise of the Soviet system. I accept this; however, we need reminding that those who made such a prediction were really quite peripheral to the mainstream debate—whether that debate was taking place in the universites, in the wider foreign policy community, or on the broad left. This is not to suggest that those involved in analyzing the USSR were unaware of its defects, or to imply that they were blind to the fact that the system was in crisis. But what the vast majority of commentators would not accept and did not foresee was that these defects and problems would finally lead to the end of Soviet power. Nor were they likely to draw this conclusion, given their own intellectual conceptions. Their ways of seeing Soviet reality in effect precluded their anticipating Soviet collapse.

It might then be objected that the Cold War came to an end for all sorts of other reasons, so that by focusing on the demise of the Soviet Union I present a singularly one-dimensional, almost monocausal explanation of why the international system was turned upside down after 1985. Perhaps so, but reviewing all the other reasons that have been advanced to explain the end of the Cold War—from American decline to the purported part played by the peace movement in eroding the bloc system in Europe—one is ineluctably and irresistibly drawn back to the argument that the Cold War assumed two opposing social systems, that it was bound to continue in one form or another as long as the two systems endured, and that the collapse of one of them inevitably brought the antagonism to a conclusion. Of course, this line of analysis tells us little or nothing about why the Soviet system failed, or what role (if any) the United States played in undermining it. It does assume, however, that once the Soviet Union crumbled, world politics as it had been practiced since 1947 was transformed.

But even if historians failed to anticipate the end of one era and the opening of another, but they can still take heart. For now that the Cold War has passed away, they are perhaps in a much better position than ever before to understand it. In part, this has to do with the opening of archives that were previously closed. But I would want to suggest another, equally important reason: namely, that while the Cold War persisted, we were all, in our own different ways, forced to take sides. Though this may have made for an exciting life, it frequently led to bad history. But now that the dust has settled, we can begin the job (perhaps for the first time) of seriously uncovering our recent past. For this, at least, we should all be eternally grateful.

Notes

1. See Bruce G. Blair, *The Logic of Accidental Nuclear War* (Washington D.C.: Brookings Institution, 1993).

2. Perhaps the most dumfounded commentator of all would have been former President Richard Nixon. In his book *1999—Victory without War* (New York: Simon & Schuster, 1989)—

published just as the Berlin Wall was coming down—he called upon the United States to "create peaceful rules of engagement for a [superpower] conflict that [would] last until 1999 and well into the next century."

3. See John Lewis Gaddis, "International Relations Theory and the End of the Cold War," *International Security* 17(Winter 1992–93): 5–58; and Allen Lynch, *The Cold War Is Over—Again* (Boulder, Colo.: Westview Press, 1992). Gaddis observes that the inability of those in International Relations to foresee the end of the Cold War must raise big "questions about the methods" they previously employed (6). That is precisely my argument about Soviet Studies.

4. Mary McAuley, *Soviet Politics: 1917–1991* (New York: Oxford University Press, 1992), 9.

5. See Richard Pipes, *Survival Is Not Enough: Soviet Realities and America's Future* (New York: Simon & Schuster, 1984); and Hillel Ticktin, *Origins of the Crisis in the USSR: Essays on the Political Economy of a Disintegrating System* (New York: M. E. Sharpe, 1992).

6. Quoted in John Lewis Gaddis, *The United States and the End of the Cold War: Implications, Reconsiderations, Provocations* (New York: Oxford University Press, 1992), vi.

7. The problem of effectiveness in U.S. foreign policy is explored in Richard A. Melanson, *Reconstructing Consensus: American Foreign Policy since the Vietnam War* (New York: St. Martin's Press, 1991).

8. Interestingly, one of the few serious commentators to suggest that the USSR might be impelled to retreat from empire because of "relative economic decline" was not a Sovietologist but a historian of comparative civilizations: See Paul Kennedy, *The Rise and Fall of the Great Powers: Economic Change and Military Conflict from 1500 to 2000* (London: Fontana Press, 1989).

9. Naturally, it was assumed that *perestroika* in the USSR would bring about what one commentator called "fundamental changes in the ways" East European societies were "organized and run." What was not foreseen was that the Soviet Union would finally disengage from the region. See David S. Mason, "Glasnost, Perestroika, and Eastern Europe," *International Affairs* 64 (Summer 1988): 431–48.

10. Typical examples of views on Soviet–East European relations before Soviet disengagement in 1989: In early 1986 one noted writer believed that Gorbachev "recognized" certain "limits that he himself cannot overstep"; see Vladimir V. Kusin, "Gorbachev and Eastern Europe," *Problems of Communism* 35 (January—February 1986): 53. The following summer another commentator emphasized, "No one can doubt that the region continues to provide a vital security guarantee that Moscow is unlikely to abandon"; see A. James McAdams, "New Deal for Eastern Europe," *The Nation,* June 13, 1987, 800. At about the same time, Charles Gati speculated that the most likely outcome of change in Eastern Europe would be to undermine *glasnost* in the USSR itself; see his "Gorbachev and Eastern Europe," *Foreign Affairs* 67 (Summer 1987): 958–75. As late as June 1989 another expert could still write that the states of Eastern Europe would "survive, albeit greatly changed"; see Valerie Bunce, "Eastern Europe: Is the Party Over?" *Political Science & Politics,* June 1989, 238–39.

11. One of the most influential early critiques of the totalitarian model was H. Gordon Skilling, "Interest Groups and Communist Politics," *World Politics* 18 (April 1966): 435–51. For a useful and less critical discussion, see Archie Brown, *Soviet Politics and Political Science* (London: Macmillan, 1974), esp. 30–41. Rather oddly, once the applicability of the concept of totalitarianism to the post-Stalin period had been questioned, a number of writers began to challenge its relevance to the 1930s as well! This attempt to rethink Stalinism (or, some would argue, provide an apologia for it) was led by Arch Getty in his *Origins of the Great Purges: The Soviet Communist Party Reconsidered, 1933–1938* (Cambridge: Cambridge University Press, 1985).

12. See Alexander Zinoviev, *The Reality Of Communism* (London: Paladin Books, 1984).

13. According to Robert S. Sharlet, "Concept Formation in Political Science and Communist Studies: Conceptualizing Political Participation," *Canadian Slavic Studies* 1 (Winter 1967): 641, the problems facing Soviet Studies in the late 1960s stemmed from its "isolation . . . from the best of systematic and comparative political science." Because of this, it had "grown up methodologically impoverished."

14. For a brief but fairly scathing attack on the notion of totalitarianism by one of the new cohort of social science scholars, see David Lane's highly influential *Politics and Society in the USSR* (London: Weidenfeld & Nicholson, 1970), 188–90.

15. See Leonard Schapiro, *Totalitarianism* (London: Macmillan, 1972).

16. For a sample of the new literature on Soviet stability, see David Lane, *The End of Inequality? Stratification under State Socialism* (Harmondsworth, Eng.: Penguin Books, 1971); Timothy J. Colton, *The Dilemma of Reform in the Soviet Union* (New York: Council on Foreign Relations, 1984); and Seweryn Bialer, *The Soviet Paradox: External Expansion—Internal Decline* (New York: Vintage Books, 1986).

17. This is certainly implied by Jerry Hough in his controversial rewrite of Merle Fainsod's classic, *How the Soviet Union Is Governed* (Cambridge, Mass.: Harvard University Press, 1979), 276. It is also suggested in his *Soviet Leadership in Transition* (Washington, D.C.: Brookings Institution, 1980), 15.

18. For an early attempt to demonstrate how certain groups exploited their access to the policy-making process, see Joel J. Schwartz and William R. Keech, "Group Influence and the Policy Process in the Soviet Union," *American Political Science Review* 62 (1968): 840–51.

19. Stephen White, *Political Culture and Soviet Politics* (London: Macmillan, 1979), 4, ix.

20. David Lane, *The Socialist Industrial State: Towards a Political Sociology of State Socialism* (London: Allen & Unwin, 1976), 91.

21. For a more "traditional" (some believed, at the time, apocalyptic) treatment of the national question in the USSR, see Hélène Carrere d'Encausse, *Decline of an Empire: The Soviet Socialist Republics in Revolt* (New York: Newsweek Books, 1979).

22. Brian Silver, "Social Mobilization and the Russification of Soviet Nationalities," *American Political Science Review* 68, (1974): 66.

23. Peter Rutland, "Nationalism and the Soviet State: A Functionalist Account," (paper presented to the annual conference of the National Association of Soviet and East European Studies, Cambridge, England, March 1982), 1.

24. Mary McAuley, "In Search of Nationalism in the USSR" (paper presented to the annual conference of the National Association of Soviet and East European Studies, Cambridge, England, March 1982), 2.

25. Leslie Holmes, *Politics in the Communist World* (Oxford: Clarendon Press, 1986), 353.

26. Marshall I. Goldman, *Gorbachev's Challenge: Ecnomic Reform in the Age of High Technology* (New York: Norton, 1978), 262, expressed the dominant Western view in 1987. Having surveyed the prospects for reform he concluded that "short of some unexpected catastrophe, the Soviet economy is unlikely to come close to collapse. . . . In the end, Gorbachev, like his predecessors, will probably have to settle for an economy that has to rely more on its natural riches than on its creative potential."

27. The CIA concluded in 1982 that although there had been a marked "slowdown" in Soviet growth since the 1970s, the Soviet economy was "not going to collapse." Indeed, the agency expected "GNP to continue to grow, although slowly." For the full text, see Henry Rowen, "Central Intelligence

Briefing on the Soviet Economy" (December 1, 1982), reprinted in *The Soviet Policy in the Modern Era,* ed. Erik P. Hoffmann and Robbin F. Laird (New York: Aldine, 1984), 417–46.

28. Ed. A. Hewett, "An Idle U.S. Debate about Gorbachev," *New York Times,* March 30, 1989, warned against overestimating Soviet weakness—"something we have done in the past"—because there were still "strengths and reserves" left in the system. These included "a huge defense industry producing many world-class products; a formidable, hitherto underutilized scientific establishment; enormously rich natural reserves; a modest international debt, and a well-educated workforce."

29. See Michael Wines, "C.I.A. Accused of Overestimating Soviet Economy," *New York Times,* July 23, 1990; and Colin Hughes, "CIA Is Accused of Crying Wolf on Soviet Economy," *The Independent,* July 25, 1990. For a defense of the CIA's record, see Richard J. Kerr (acting director), "C.I.A.'s Track Record Stands Up to Scrutiny," *New York Times,* October 24, 1991.

30. President Reagan's views on the "crisis" of Soviet "totalitarianism" were unambiguously expressed in his speech to the British Parliament on June 8, 1982. See "Promoting Democracy and Peace," in *Realism, Strength, Negotiation: Key Foreign Policy Statements of the Reagan Administration* (Washington, D.C.: U.S. Department of State, 1984), 77–81.

31. Moreover, as Anders Aslund pointed out in *Gorbachev's Struggle for Economic Reform* (London: Pinter, 1989), 195, "the world" was "likely to be a safer place if the Soviet reforms" succeeded.

32. Phillip Hanson, "The Soviet Twelfth Five-Year Plan," in *The Soviet Economy: A New Course?* (Brussels: NATO, 1987), 10.

33. One of the few Marxists (apart from Ticktin) who saw the USSR tending toward absolute stagnation was Pavel Campeneau; see *The Syncretic Society* (New York: M. E. Sharpe, 1980), published under his pseudonym, Felipe Garcia Casals.

34. This was certainly the message conveyed in Jon Bloomfield ed., *The Soviet Revolution: Perestroika and the Remaking of Socialism* (London: Lawrence & Wishart, 1989).

35. For an orthodox Trotskyist assessment of the USSR under Gorbachev, see Ernest Mandel, *Beyond Perestroika: The Future of Gorbachev's USSR* (London: Verso, 1989). For a less orthodox, Trotskyist perspective on the Soviet Union in the late 1980s, see Tariq Ali, *Revolution from Above: Where Is the Soviet Union Going?* (London: Hutchinson, 1988). One of the two people Tariq Ali dedicated his book to (the other being Boris Kagarlitsky) was Boris Yeltsin!

36. See Mike Haynes, "Understanding the Soviet Crisis," *International Socialism,* no. 34 (1987): 4–5.

Chapter 8

Mythmaking about the Character of the Cold War

Charles W. Kegley Jr. and Shannon Lindsey Blanton

The Cold War has only recently vanished from the international scene, yet many observers look back on it with unabashed nostalgia. Most center their attention on the fact that for nearly fifty years the great powers managed to contain their protracted conflict without a single instance of war among them. To them, the Cold War was really a "long peace";[1] with its death, war among the great powers is likely to reemerge.

To prevent future great-power disputes from becoming violent, it is important to uncover the true character of the Cold War. By becoming more reflective in our ways of thinking about and remembering the Cold War, we will be better able to extract accurate lessons that can be applied to the management of great-power conflict. Consequently, it is necessary to understand the factors that prevented the Cold War from turning hot. If peace is to endure into the twenty-first century, it will largely depend on our ability to understand correctly how it has been achieved in the recent past.

This essay takes issue with a number of prominent explanations for the attributes and causes of the long Cold War peace. Discourse has not produced consensus; indeed, varied and contradictory explanatory propositions abound. Among these has emerged a body of mainstream and hard-line realist explanations of the Cold War which, upon close examination, can be seen to lack empirical substantiation. Yet they are still voiced reflexively and at times used to undergird future policy thinking. Such explanations may be seen as providing more ideological comfort than analytical clarity. The end of the Cold War offers an opportunity for critical reflection on the state of knowledge about the sources of great-power peace, but mainstream and hard-line realist mythmakers unknowingly threaten such an endeavor. Their myths, having helped set and legitimate policy during the Cold War itself, counterproductively mask the unnecessary costs of the Cold War and exaggerate the purported benefits of a militant U.S. foreign policy.

We assess a number of the unwarranted causal inferences that have gained currency among those who subscribe to realpolitik, and suggest that such Cold War "myths" are based on unsubstantiated assumptions about the world.[2] By working within the same paradigms accepted by their "perpetrators," we offer an internal critique of these unfounded suppositions, which have been used to justify a hard-line U.S. policy. A safer and saner world is dependent on rejection of conventional wisdoms that are more conventional than wise.

Myths about "Facts"

The period extending from the birth of the modern world system in 1945 to the present is considered remarkable in that it constitutes the longest period of great-power peace ever. In the aftermath of the Congress of Vienna (1815–48) and of the Franco-Prussian War (1871–1914), comparable state systems managed for protracted periods to persist without a major war between European powers, but neither peace endured as long as the present one. In historical perspective the durable post–World War II peace is truly remarkable, for across the span of nearly a half-century of turbulent change in world politics "there have been no wars among the 48 wealthiest countries in all that time."[3] This continuity, against a backdrop of dramatic changes, calls for consideration of a number of unorthodox questions. The answers, however, invite possible misunderstanding if the empirical character of the Cold War peace is itself misunderstood. Among mistakenly ascribed attributes are the contentions that the period was (1) peaceful, (2) stable, and (3) permanently institutionalized. It has been none of these.

The Cold War peace was not peaceful. When we speak of the "Cold War peace," we employ a great misnomer and misrepresent reality, for since 1945 only the great powers have avoided war against one another. If the entire international system, and not just the subsystem of great-power interactions, is made the object of observation, the Cold War peace appears more accurately to have been a "long war."[4] A stable great-power tier emerged alongside a highly unstable Third World one, so that from the perspective of most countries the "end of war" was a fantasy. In fact, the internationalization of civil wars through great-power military intervention made war a defining feature of the developing world, where since 1945 "there have been 149 wars and 23.1 million war-related deaths."[5]

The disappearance of large-scale warfare concomitant with the ascendance of small-scale warfare produced two systems, a stable "central" system and an unstable "peripheral" one. Thus, while developed countries, which can be visualized as the core of the international system, virtually remained at peace with other states in the core, developing countries occupying a peripheral position in the global hierarchy of power experienced not only chronic domestic conflict but also active aggression between states within the periphery and across the core-periphery boundary.

The persistence of war since 1945 is supported by Herbert K. Tillema's study of military intervention. His findings depict a world experiencing great levels of armed conflict and the frequent use of military force, not one characterized by peace.[6] To the discouragement of those who envision the obsolescence of war, evidence of recurrent postwar violence amid great-power peace is a sobering fact of life that underscores the need to refrain from characterizing the Cold War system as peaceful.

The Cold War peace was not stable. It was, rather, fraught with tension and continual crises threatening to escalate to war. Just consider, for example, the Cuban missile crisis, which brought the United States and the Soviet Union to the brink of war, or the Iranian hostage crisis, during which the United States and Iran nearly came to blows. Evidence gathered by Michael Brecher documents the extent to which the tense postwar era continually wavered between peace and war.[7] Although since 1945 the capacity of the great powers to manage crises may have strengthened through experience, crisis management may be but a dangerous illusion if the pressures for confrontation become powerful and persistent. The disturbingly recurrent incidence of situations at the brink of war does not inspire confidence that non-great-power states with unstable governments will develop crisis management skills commensurate with their growing warmaking capabilities. It would be a mistake to dismiss war resulting from mismanaged crises as an aberration—as the Persian Gulf War, Operation "Just Cause," and the wars in and between countries of the former Yugoslavia attest.

Equally disturbing are the empirical and conceptual flaws embedded in the notion of a Cold War peace. As Brecher and Wilkenfeld show, "266 international crises erupted from June 1945 to the end of 1988." A narrow perspective of peace "excludes proxy wars and 'near-miss' direct superpower military hostilities" and fails to recognize the Cold War's chronic instability, in which fully 25 percent of the 266 crises escalated to full-scale war.[8]

The Cold War peace is not permanent. Many observers treat trend as destiny and mistakenly assume that long-perpetuated conditions are likely to persist. The prolonged peace between great powers is one trend that evokes a false sense of continuity; extrapolating, some assume that the Cold War past is prologue, and therefore the great-power peace has become so entrenched and customary that it presages the obsolescence of war.[9] History suggests that this kind of persistence forecasting is naive: for one thing change is endemic; for another, cycles of war have in the past repetitiously followed periods of peace. Hence, from the perspective of a sufficiently elongated observation period, it is doubtful that the Cold War peace could have survived indefinitely, for the foundations upon which that peace rested were inherently fragile, and the pillars upon which it precariously sat were institutionally weak and insufficiently strong to assure long-term survival.

Many believe that the Cold War provided clear guidelines that are applicable to the post–Cold War world, yet the most prominent ideas about the underpinnings of sustained peace fail to supply conclusive answers. By bringing this disagreement about the postulated causes of the Cold War peace to the surface, we can better appreciate the variety of contending interpretations and the obstacles to discovery of more adequate explanations. Questions raised about the choices among alternative paths to peace reveal the danger of relying on reassuringly simple solutions. These, on closer inspection, may prove fallacious and the policies they rationalize counterproductive.

The Roots of Cold War Peace

To separate sense from nonsense, we must critically confront a series of frequently advanced propositions about the reasons for the preservation of great-power peace during the Cold War. Among them, the following are perhaps the most frequently and enthusiastically advanced: (1) Bloodshed was avoided because of bipolar competition; (2) containment worked; (3) preparations for war preserved peace; (4) Western alliances kept the Soviet Union at bay; (5) nuclear deterrence kept the peace; and (6) the United States maintained the peace. What logic underlies these questionable propositions?

Bipolarity kept the peace? This especially dubious proposition suggests that the forty-five year great-power peace during the Cold War was a product of a stable bipolar division of the world into two opposed blocs. John J. Mearsheimer's celebrated structural realist model even predicted that "the prospects for major crises and war . . . are likely to increase markedly if the Cold War ends [because] the distribution and character of military power are the root causes of war and peace."[10]

Central to an assessment of the validity of characterizing the bipolar world as stable is the way "stability" is defined. Does stability mean merely the absence of major war or, as others maintain, something broader, including systemic equilibrium which—despite shocks—preserves the international system's essential properties within stable boundaries?[11] Unfortunately, discourse about polarity configurations has not adhered to a consistent definition. In defining stability narrowly as the avoidance of great-power war, Mearsheimer and his structural realist colleagues fail to capture the turbulence and recurrent threats to global peace that were self-evidently salient characteristics of the bipolar Cold War system.[12] Moreover, their restrictive conception of stability as the absence of war risks making their arguments tautological.

To describe as stable the Cold War division of the globe into antagonistic blocs is to ignore the fact that bipolarity by its very nature created conditions conducive to a struggle for dominance: "The leaders of each bloc [tried] to destroy and revolutionize their rivals [and sought] to wear down the other [by] using force to maintain and expand their blocs."[13] Further, bipolarity embodied zero-sum politics that promoted pure conflict between the superpowers. The pregnant fear of aggression and hegemonic domination diminished the perceived security among the great powers and exacerbated their perception of threats. In an almost self-fulfilling manner, bipolarity also fed the arms race and contributed to the mutual security dilemma. The undeniable result: The ostensible Cold War "stability" was endemically unstable. As Hans J. Morgenthau grimly but accurately described it, the threatening bipolar landscape reduced the international system to "the primitive spectacle of two giants eyeing each other with watchful suspicion. They [bent] every effort to increase their military potential to the utmost, since this is all they [had] to count on. Both [prepared] to strike the first decisive blow, for if one [did] not strike it the other might. Thus, contain or be contained, conquer or be conquered, destroy or be destroyed, [became] the watchwords of Cold War diplomacy."[14]

If we take cognizance of the dangers and tensions intrinsic to the Cold War's essential duopoly of power, it appears illusory to portray this competition as stable, and therefore unwarranted to dread its disintegration. Given the ubiquity of threats to international peace during the Cold War, the phrase "bipolar stability" seems an oxymoron. The stability of bipolar distributions of power relative to their tri- and multipolar counterparts remains a longstanding theoretical and empirical issue that has occupied the attention of scholars for many years. It is instructive that their efforts have not converged in a consistent set of research findings or culminated in consensus over whether multipolar systems, comprising several leading powers, or bipolar systems, comprising only two, are more stable. Because "there is no real consensus on whether systems with a certain number of poles are more war prone than others,"[15] it would be prudent to await the results of further investigations before accepting the theory that bipolarity in itself breeds stability.

In general, then, a direct relationship between multipolar systems and the probability of war cannot be safely drawn. *Ceteris paribus,* multipolarity may be more turbulent than bipolarity but not necessarily more prone to culminate in war. Indeed, substantial evidence indicates that "bipolarity can, at times, be just as destabilizing as multipolarity."[16] Among examples of unstable bipolar systems are the rivalries between ancient Athens and Sparta, between Hapsburg and Valois in the sixteenth century, between England and the Netherlands a century later, and between England and France in the eighteenth century.

Containment kept the peace? Ever since its advent as a doctrine, containment's meaning has been reinterpreted in response to changes in global conditions. We witnessed in the early 1990s the making of a new containment myth—or, more accurately, the reaffirmation of the premises regarded by George F. Kennan as mythical, which were embraced in the late 1940s with the enunciation of the Truman Doctrine.[17]

Many hard-line realists interpreted Mikhail Gorbachev's alleged surrender as proof of their theory that American superiority in the arms race and its confrontational strategy accounted for the Soviet acceptance of the implosion of its external empire. Indeed, most neoconservative realists reached premature conclusions about what drove the Soviets to abandon the communist experiment: They believed the West successfully "spent" the USSR into submission. By engaging the Soviet Union in a prohibitively costly arms race, the United States supposedly forced the Soviets into an economic competition that they could not sustain and that subsequently exhausted their capacity to continue the struggle. This position, frequently voiced by Secretary of Defense Caspar Weinberger,[18] was predicated on the dubious premise that, as Richard J. Barnet phrased it, "a willingness to spend enough and deploy enough produces the right sort of perception in the minds of Soviet leaders. Anything less might cause them to become dangerously confused."[19] The estimated price of this spending contest—$10 trillion (inflation-adjusted)[20]—is claimed to have been modest, given the substantial return on the investment in the form of Soviet bankruptcy and retreat. Against this, of course, is the possibility that the spending binge has left the United States so debt-ridden that its victory is pyrrhic.

This dominant interpretation overlooks the rival theory that militant, confrontational containment may have exacerbated and prolonged the Cold War rather than bringing it to an end. We need to ask whether, if "Kennan's [original] view and his recommendations had prevailed," the world might have moved "beyond containment . . . sooner and at less expense."[21] If this plausible position has merit, then containment did not work—it was never tried. For the United States rejected Kennan's definition of containment, which recommended waiting for "the internal weakness of Soviet power, combined with frustration in the external field, to moderate Soviet ambitions and behavior" rather than encircling the Soviet Union and threatening it with massive destruction.[22] Arguably, the strategy of military intimidation hardened Soviet resistance and prolonged the Cold War.

Preparing for war kept the peace? According to this proposition, America's (and NATO's) expanding military capabilities challenged the Soviet Union with an unmatchable arsenal and forced it to accept imperial devolution. President George Bush embraced this belief when he stated, "There are few lessons so clear in history as this: only the combination of conventional forces and nuclear forces have ensured this long peace in Europe."[23] Similarly, Richard Perle has maintained that "the collapse of the Soviet empire in Eastern Europe is in large measure a result of the [West's] postwar strength. . . . Those who argued for nuclear deterrence and serious conventional military capabilities contributed mightily to the position of strength that eventually led the Soviet leadership to choose a less bellicose, less menacing approach to international politics. . . . We're witnessing the rewards of the Reagan policy of firmness."[24]

At first brush, this thesis is disarmingly attractive, because it must be acknowledged that the Cold War peace did unfold alongside the vertical and horizontal proliferation of weapons, a massive worldwide arms race, and the global dispersion of military capabilities through the mounting arms trade. From this, a direct correlation appears to exist and a corollary is deduced: namely, that the militarization of the globe has been medicinal. Persons of this persuasion are easily convinced of the validity of their prior belief in the sacred axiom worshiped by military planners: "If you want peace, prepare for war." To true believers in this core tenet of realpolitik, the conclusion that preparations for war have prevented war is unassailable.

Yet this intuitive conviction cannot be supported logically or empirically. The capacity of armaments to prevent war is highly debatable. For example, examining the impact of U.S. military preparations, Robert Johansen discerns no evidence for faith in the conventional belief that weapons of mass destruction contributed to the Cold War peace; rather, he contends that arms competition diminished the actual security of nations.[25] If this is so, then a rival image appears more realistic than does the orthodox view about the pacifying effects of weapons: "From the paradox that defenselessness decreases the probability of attack [comes] the corresponding wisdom that defensive measures only breed more dangerous countermeasures to nullify them."[26]

Preparations for war, in short, may have been counterproductive in that they raised tensions as much as they preserved peace.[27] In accordance with this proposition is Johansen's contention that "it strains credibility to claim that today's security system is substantially less war-prone than ever before. War may be somewhat less rational than ever, but that does not make war significantly less likely—especially when national security managers emphasize that the key to preventing war is to be willing to fight it, and to express that willingness even though to do so appears to be irrational."[28] It follows that "the mere passage of [five] decades since 1945 without direct combat between major powers provides little assurance of permanent peace."[29]

Furthermore, it is a faulty argument to assert that "peace through strength" produced Soviet retreat in Europe, Afghanistan, and elsewhere, since it can be cogently demonstrated that rapprochement with the West "was only achievable *after* the leadership change in the Soviet Union."[30] It is likely that Gorbachev's rise to power was as responsible (if not more so) for the decline of Soviet international aggression as tough bargaining strategies and a massive arms buildup on the part of the United States.

Alliances kept the peace? From the 1950s on, NATO in particular and Cold War alliances in general were advocated as a viable means of keeping the peace and preventing Soviet expansionism. Yet the postwar record provides little support for the direct role often ascribed to Cold War coalitions in fostering extended deterrence. Instead, the impact of those alliances was indirect and contingent upon the nature of the commitment. Some postwar alliances such as NATO provided focal points around which tacit ground rules for the coordination of expectations developed and eased the transition from a Cold War to a post–Cold War world.[31] Other alliances, however, entailed commitments that exceeded the capabilities of the parties involved or drew third parties into conflicts in which their vital interests were not at stake. This conflict-expansion syndrome was often the case with superpower involvement in the Third World. Yet despite the entanglements encouraged by some Cold War alliances, great-power peace was preserved.

On balance, alliances probably made only a modest contribution to the preservation of the Cold War peace. Although fluid alliance systems existed alongside stable great-power relations, full credit for the absence of great-power war cannot be assigned to the impact of alliance structures. Among the many enthusiasts and policymakers who often argue that it can President Bush claimed that "containment worked . . . because our alliances were and are strong."[32] Yet though it is true that there has been no world war since the North Atlantic Treaty was signed, and also true that NATO was created in part to deter such a conflict, it does not necessarily follow that it was NATO that prevented it. No war occurred in the tense 1945–49 period before NATO was formed, either, and what deterred the Soviet Union from launching a preemptive strike after NATO's creation could have been the fear of a "conventional" war on a scale as great as or greater than that of World War II.[33] The widespread belief that the Soviet Union was deterred from expansionism by the Atlantic alliance cannot be proved.[34] If the Soviet Union never seriously craved territorial conquest, there is no basis for concluding that the Atlantic alliance was responsible for Soviet restraint; an alliance cannot be given credit for preventing something that was not sought in the first place. As Robert Johansen argues, "The post–Cold War opening of Soviet archives . . . provides no evidence of the Soviet intention to attack Western Europe or the United States at any time since 1945."[35]

Moreover, it cannot be conclusively demonstrated that the Atlantic alliance was an altogether constructive force in postwar world politics. Perhaps, at enormous expenditure of resources, the Atlantic alliance instead institutionalized East-West discord and inhibited accommodation. It is quite possible that the Soviet Union, confronted by a group of hostile states united behind a common cause, hardened its resolve and that the Cold War was consequently prolonged.[36]

Nuclear deterrence kept the peace? Many feel intuitively that nuclear deterrence helped guarantee peace for nearly fifty years.[37] The conventional statement of this widespread conviction was captured in Winston Churchill's well-known speculation that in a nuclear armed world "safety will be the sturdy child of terror, and survival the twin brother of annihilation."

It does seem clear that "any assessment of deterrence will be hard-put not to acknowledge that in a world of widespread nuclear knowledge and at least six nuclear powers, deterrence has been a significant factor in preventing the use of nuclear weapons."[38] In other words, there are powerful reasons to infer that the terror of nuclear devastation, and the deterrence strategies that relied on that terror, prevented the use of nuclear weapons and thereby preserved great-power peace.

Yet as intuitively attractive as this simple "counterfactual" explanation is, its validity is nonetheless suspect. We cannot know for sure whether it was nuclear weapons or the interactive effects of other factors that kept the peace. "There is no *direct* evidence for or against the contention that peace has been preserved with threats of nuclear retaliation, [and to accept this hypothesis on faith] is to believe in magic."[39] Hence, it can be argued with equal cogency that, as we said above of NATO, nuclear weapons exacerbated tensions that otherwise would not have existed, and that the awesome military capabilities of *both* superpowers "helped to prolong the Cold War by at least 15 years and to impede disarmament and the demilitarization of international relations."[40]

It is quite possible that strategies predicated on the theory of nuclear deterrence may not serve as a reliable method for keeping the peace but may instead create the very outcome they seek to prevent. Deterrence requires a causal inference that also depends on counterfactual analysis, because, as Joseph Nye explains, although it "seems to have worked for [over] forty years . . . pro-deterrence strategists make too much and the antinuclear critics make too little of the absence of any war between the superpowers for the past [five] decades. The . . . pronuclear argument . . . begs the question of why the future should resemble the past. For those who believe that catastrophic failure is inevitable, it is no answer to say simply that deterrence has worked in the past."[41]

John Vasquez contends that nuclear deterrence and mutual assured destruction may be interpreted as cures in search of a disease, a set of mythical assumptions constituting little more than folklore.[42] It cannot be cogently shown that deterrence through nuclear weapons and strategic targeting kept the Cold War peace. The image of the superpower rivals restrained from the impulse to attack each other at the first sign of weakness by the terror of nuclear annihilation is flawed because neither superpower ever directly threatened to attack the other's territory, and nuclear weapons were primarily developed for defensive purposes.

It may be that the prospect of war (even one fought with conventional arms) more potently deterred a superpower confrontation than did the singular nuclear threat of massive destruction—because the threat of war was more credible. Hence, the prevailing axiom, which posits that nuclear deterrence strategies raised the cost of conflict by promising mutual destruction and in turn prevented destruction by discouraging direct superpower war, is suspect. Merely because five decades of peace coincided with five decades of nuclear arsenals does not establish that the latter caused the former. Once again, correlation is not causation. Hence, the relationship of nuclear deterrence to Cold War peace must be evaluated more carefully if the necessary and sufficient conditions for war prevention are to be discerned.

The United States kept the peace? Besides crediting certain characteristics of the interstate system with keeping the peace, many realists, somewhat inconsistently, also point to U.S. policies as preventing a general war. Emerging dominant in the global arena after World War II, the United States set out, in Harry S Truman's words, "to take the lead in running the world in the way that the world ought to be run."[43] As hegemon during this unipolar "moment" in history, the United States made and enforced the system's rules. Acting as a global policeman, it engineered a Pax Americana to bring about what Henry Luce in 1941 proclaimed to be the advent of "the American century."[44]

America's global rule was largely an exercise in economic imperialism and dollar diplomacy. It stopped short of a serious effort to control the world by force. Given its superordinate military power, the United States acted internationally with considerable constraint (in comparison with previous hegemonic leaders) and did not, in its hope to make American ideals and institutions universal, pursue territorial conquest. And in the five decades since the conclusion of the last struggle for global supremacy in 1945, we observe not a single war between America and any other great power. Of course, many of America's excessive efforts to maintain order and the balance of power brought destruction (not peace, prosperity, or democracy) to those countries that became the targets of U.S. intervention. In propping up friendly tyrants and waging wars in remote places for obscure purposes, America's globalist management was not very constructive or altogether medicinal, despite the best of intentions.

Even more dubious is the related proposition that the globalist, anticommunist posture characterizing U.S. foreign policy in the five decades since the last great war was responsible for great-power peace. This hypothesis greatly exaggerates the extent of American ability to manage world order, while grossly underestimating the contribution to peace made by the conciliatory reactions of others to assertive American intitiatives. For example, just as Mikhail Gorbachev's vision kept the East-West conflict from escalating in the 1980s when the United States labeled his state an "evil empire" and pledged its defeat, so too the Cold War peace may have persisted in large measure on account of many other countries' leadership and pacific responses to explosive global situations. To assert that the United States alone kept the peace would be to write fiction.

Partly as a result of their global ambitions and presence, both the United States and the Soviet Union experienced rapid decline relative to such powers as Japan, Germany, and China.[45] What consequences may result from these great powers' decay of power? The past five centuries of world politics suggest that when the hegemonic status of a world leader was stable, a fragile status quo materialized; but when the position of the world leader eroded and power become dispersed among rival contenders for hegemony, a spasm of instability and carnage followed.

Theories of long cycles[46] and hegemonic stability[47] suggest that hegemonic decline unaccompanied by war is improbable, for the economic and military decline of hegemons has historically presaged a new wave of global war. If this pattern holds, we have reason to fear the decline of great powers, even while we have reason to pray that Cold War antagonisms do not resume.

Facts about "Myths"

Many of the "causal stories" that have emerged from speculation about the reasons for Cold War peace are logically inconsistent. All such analyses necessarily rest on assumptions about particular factors that potently influence international conduct. If these assumptions are warranted, then reasonable conclusions can be derived. But misguided assumptions can easily lead to very mistaken conclusions that not only misinform; worse, they can cause great damage. When accepted on blind faith, "myths" can rationalize decisions that, despite the best of intentions, produce the worst of effects.

"Causal stories" based on a purely speculative causal script mask its partisan purposes. Neither logical analysis nor empirical investigation sustains the claims considered above about the character of the Cold War; consequently, it can be inferred that interpretations of the Cold War peace based on these claims are infested with mere conjecture. Such a flawed approach to explaining the Cold War peace is inadmissible because intuition and common sense recognize no scientific liabilities, and common sense has repeatedly demonstrated itself to be a deficient basis for knowledge (as somebody once said, "Common sense is that which tells us the world is flat"). Throughout history such means of discovery have commonly led to mistaken claims. Thus, polemics are not sufficient to trace causation or to ground causal speculations empirically.

There is danger in accepting prevalent claims about the character of the Cold War's peace: If these are embraced without greater confirming evidence, it is unlikely that adequate preparations will be made for preserving peace in the post–Cold War era. Security strategies built on fallacious Cold War convictions will *not* provide useful guidelines to deal with the ethnic and low-scale internal rebellions throughout the globe that have undermined international security in the 1990s. What is needed is a post–Cold War strategy for a post–Cold War world, not an anachronistic application of dubious Cold War practices for an altogether nonanalogous global system of the twenty-first century.[48] For a new vision, correct inferences about the causes of great-power peace are the sine qua non.

Toward the Future

On October 15, 1993, President Bill Clinton reflected, "We look back to that era now, and we long for a—I even made a crack the other day, I said, 'Gosh, I miss the Cold War.'"[49]

That nostalgia may be for a remembered past that never existed. True, the main axis of world politics was self-evident. And true, the world survived that global cleavage without a general war. But the Cold War was *not* peaceful, stable, or even simple. It tottered on the brink of annihilation. And the means of escaping the insecurities that went with that danger were *never* self-evident: "There was certainly none of the unanimity that nostalgics now pretend there was."[50] Throughout the Cold War's half-century evolution, policymakers and academic specialists were divided at every turn about the safest ways of preventing it from turning hot. Nothing could be more misleading or misguided than to now pretend that a Cold War consensus existed, and to extrapolate from its imagined clear and simple lessons to the uncertain geostrategic landscape that we now face. Wistful recollections of what seemed to work in the past will not prepare us for the kinds of conflicts that are likely to erupt in the post–Cold War future.

To the extent that untested beliefs about the Cold War remain entrenched dogma, there is a risk that false historical lessons will be embraced and that policymakers will blindly incorporate simplistic and seductive convictions into their decisions without considering alternative paths to lasting peace. The now fashionable belief that confrontational containment worked prescribes policy choices that are likely to inhibit the search for cooperative multilateral strategies through which worldwide peace might better be institutionalized. By conditioning Western political leaders to seek ceaselessly for advantage, these prevailing myths could tempt policymakers to concoct new rationales for old policies. Perhaps an awareness of this danger was behind U.S. Secretary of State Warren Christopher's warning that "we cannot engage in a neo-containment of Russia."[51]

We have attempted to show that hard-line realist positions may be more adept at disseminating ideology than providing insight and thus do not constitute the best guide for future policy. Even though we do not have a basis for proving their claims are completely false, the evidence needed to accept them as true, or even as leading hypotheses, is lacking. What is required is a more elaborate set of hypotheses about the causes of the Cold War peace, superior to the propositions questioned here. This is a research priority that those working in the field of international relations and diplomatic history need to confront,[52] because "we are still hobbled by our Cold War ways of looking at the world."[53]

If the causes and character of the Cold War are not understood, its consequences for the future are likely to be misunderstood, and such misunderstandings bode ill for future policymaking. If ideologists cling to mistaken beliefs, a historic opportunity for cementing global rapprochement may be lost, and we will have to live for the forseeable future under the cursed shadow of the Cold War and bear the extraordinary costs that the resumption of great-power conflict will extract.

Notes

Acknowledgments: The authors thank Allen Hunter for his insightful and helpful comments on an earlier draft of this essay.

1. See John Lewis Gaddis, "The Long Peace: Elements of Instability in the Postwar International System," *International Security* 10 (Spring 1986): 92–142; John J. Mearsheimer, "Back to the Future: Instability in Europe after the Cold War," *International Security* 15 (Summer 1990): 5–56; Charles W. Kegley, Jr., ed., *The Long Postwar Peace: Contending Explanations and Projections* (New York: Harper-Collins, 1991).

2. None of our work is meant to exclude left-wing positions from scrutiny; however, such interpretations are not treated here because radical explanations of the Cold War and its end are not as salient as centrist-conservative ones, do not resonate in the broader U.S. political culture, and provide few prescriptions for policymaking in the post–Cold War world.

3. John Mueller, "Dropping Out of the War System," *Los Angeles Times*, September 12, 1988, 5. See also Peter Wallensteen and Margareta Sollenberg, "The End of International War? Armed Conflict 1989–1995," *Journal of Peace Research* 33 (August 1996): 353–70.

4. Such an assertion can also be made with regard to the long peace of the nineteenth century, because that period represented the high point of European colonization and involved considerable military violence.

5. Ruth L. Sivard, *World Military and Social Expenditures 1993* (Washington, D.C.: World Priorities, 1993), 20.

6. Herbert K. Tillema, *Contemporary Military Intervention* (Columbia: University of South Carolina Press, 1998). See also Alpo Rusi, *A Dangerous Peace* (Boulder, Colo.: Westview Press, 1997).

7. Michael Brecher, *Crises in World Politics* (Oxford: Pergamon, 1993).

8. Ibid., 576.

9. E.g., John Mueller, *Retreat from Doomsday* (New York: Basic Books, 1989).

10. Mearsheimer, "Back to the Future," pp. 6, 7; see also John J. Mearsheimer, "Why We Will Soon Miss the Cold War," *Atlantic Monthly* 266 (August 1990): 35–50.

11. Kenneth Waltz, "The Emerging Structure of International Politics," *International Security* 18 (Fall 1993): 47.

12. E.g., Alvin M. Saperstein, "The 'Long Peace'—Result of a Bipolar Competitive World?" *Journal of Conflict Resolution* 35 (March 1991): 68–79.

13. Stephen Pelz, "Changing International Systems, the World Balance of Power, and the United States, 1776–1976," *Diplomatic History* 15 (Winter 1991): 74–75.

14. Hans J. Morgenthau, *Politics among Nations: The Struggle for Power and Peace*, 6th ed., rev. Kenneth W. Thompson (New York: Knopf, 1985), 379.

15. Bruce Russett and Harvey Starr, *World Politics: The Menu for Choice*, 3d ed. (New York: W. H. Freeman, 1989), 112. For a review of this debate, see Charles W. Kegley Jr. and Gregory A. Raymond, *A Multipolar Peace? Great-Power Politics in the Twenty-first Century* (New York: St. Martin's Press, 1994).

16. William R. Thompson, *On Global War: Historical-Structural Approaches to World Politics* (Columbia: University of South Carolina Press, 1988), 220.

17. See George F. Kennan, *Memoirs* (Boston: Little, Brown, 1967), 361; see also Charles W. Kegley Jr., "The New Containment Myth," *Ethics and International Affairs* 5 (1991): 99–114.

18. Caspar Weinberger, *Fighting for Peace* (New York: Warner Books, 1990).

19. Richard J. Barnet, "Reflections," *New Yorker*, March 9, 1987, esp. 78.

20. Carl Sagan, "Between Enemies," *Bulletin of the Atomic Scientists* 48 (May 1992): 25.

21. Strobe Talbott, "Rethinking the Red Menace," *Time*, January 1, 1990, 70.

22. Kennan, *Memoirs*, p. 364.

23. Roy W. Apple Jr., "Navigating the Future: A New Europe Comes into Focus for George Bush," *New York Times*, May 6, 1990, 1; George Bush, "Transcript, Second Presidential Debate," *New York Times*, October 15, 1988, A11.

24. Richard Perle, "Military Power and the Passing Cold War," in *After the Cold War: Questioning the Morality of Nuclear Deterrence*, ed. Charles W. Kegley Jr. and Kenneth L. Schwab (Boulder, Colo: Westview Press, 1991), 33–38.

25. Robert C. Johansen, "Do Preparations for War Increase or Decrease International Security?" in Kegley, *The Long Postwar Peace*, 224–44.

26. Arron Wildavsky, "Serious Talk about the Nuclear Era," *Wall Street Journal*, March 16, 1989, A16.

27. Michael D. Ward, "Differential Paths to Parity: A Study of the Contemporary Arms Race," *American Political Science Review* 78 (June 1984): 297–317.

28. Robert C. Johansen, "Global Security without Nuclear Deterrence," in *The Nuclear Reader: Strategy, Weapons, War*, 2d ed. Charles W. Kegley Jr. and E. R. Wittkopf (New York: St. Martin's Press, 1989), 72, 74–75.

29. Ibid., 74.

30. Thomas Risse-Kappen, "Did 'Peace through Strength' End the Cold War?" *International Security* 16 (Summer 1991): 163.

31. Charles W. Kegley Jr. and Gregory A. Raymond, "Networks of Intrigue? Realpolitik, Alliances, and International Security," in *Reconstructing Realpolitik*, ed. Paul Diehl and Frank Wayman (Ann Arbor: University of Michigan Press, 1994), 185–203.

32. Bush, "Transcript."

33. Mueller, *Retreat from Doomsday*.

34. Though we are skeptical of the extent of NATO's influence, U.S. conservative scholars and policymakers are not alone in regarding it as an important factor in preserving peace; many Soviet and East European dissidents also believe that NATO performed a pacifying influence in postwar politics.

35. Robert C. Johansen, "Swords into Plowshares," in *Controversies in International Relations Theory*, ed. Charles W. Kegley (New York: St. Martin's Press, 1995), 259.

36. See, e.g., Charles W. Kegley Jr., "How Did the Cold War Die? Principles for an Autopsy," *Mershon International Studies Review* 38 (supp.) (March 1994): 11–41.

37. E.g., Kenneth N. Waltz, "Nuclear Myths and Political Realities," in *American Political Science Review* 84 (September 1990): 731–45.

38. National Conference of Catholic Bishops, "Nuclear Strategy and the Challenge of Peace: The Moral Evaluation of Deterrence in Light of Policy Developments, 1983–1988," in Kegley and Wittkopf, *The Nuclear Reader*, 69.

39. J. Kugler, "Terror Without Deterrence: Reassessing the Role of Nuclear Weapons," *Journal of Conflict Resolution* 28 (September 1984): 472, 501. For discussions of counterfactual arguments, see Philip E. Tetlock and Arron Belkin, eds., *Counterfactual Thought Experiments in World Politics: Logical, Methodological, and Psychological Perspectives* (Princeton, N.J.: Princeton University Press, 1996).

40. Georgy Arbatov, "Spending Too Much on the Military," *World Press Review* 37 (April 1990), 50.

41. Joseph S. Nye Jr., "The Long-Term Future of Deterrence," in Kegley and Wittkoph, *The Nuclear Reader*, 81–82.

42. John Vasquez, "The Deterrence Myth: Nuclear Weapons and the Prevention of Nuclear War," in Kegley, *The Long Postwar Peace* 205–23.

43. Quoted in Charles W. Kegley and Eugene R. Wittkopf, eds., *American Foreign Policy: Patterns and Process* (New York: St. Martin's Press, 1991), 40.

44. See Robert E. Herzstein, *Henry R. Luce: A Political Portrait of the Man Who Created the American Century* (New York: Scribner, 1994).

45. Paul Kennedy, *The Rise and Fall of the Great Powers* (New York: Random House, 1987). See also Richard Ned Lebow and Janice Gross Stein, *We All Lost the Cold War* (Princeton, N.J.: Princeton University Press, 1994).

46. See, e.g., George Modelski, "The Long Cycle of Global Politics and the Nation-State," *Comparative Studies in Society and History* 20 (April 1978): 214–235; Joshua S. Goldstein, *Long Cycles: Prosperity and War in the Modern Age* (New Haven, Conn.: Yale University Press, 1988).

47. See, e.g., Robert Gilpin, *War and Change in World Politics* (Cambridge: Cambridge University Press, 1981); Robert O. Keohane, *International Institutions and State Power: Essays in International Relations Theory* (Boulder, Colo.: Westview Press, 1989); George Modelski and William R. Thompson, *Leading Sectors and World Politics: The Coevolution of Global Economics and Politics* (Columbia: University of South Carolina Press, 1994).

48. An example is provided by U.S. strategy in the mid-1990s, which, based on Cold War logic, continued to abide by the assumption that nuclear weapons are needed to keep the peace, even though the aggressor to be deterred was uncertain. As the *Defense Monitor* 22, no. 10 (1993): 2, lamented, "The United States will spend $31 billion in 1994 and more than $300 billion over the next ten years to prepare for nuclear war." Furthermore, despite pleas for defense conversion to redirect budgets from armaments to internal develoment, U.S. defense spending in 1993 exceeded the *combined* military expenditures of Russia, China, France, Japan, and Germany (U.S. Arms Control and Disarmament Agency, *World Military Expenditures and Arms Transfers, 1993–1994* [Washington, D.C.: U.S. Government Printing Office, 1994], 4, 5).

49. Quoted in Charles Krauthammer, "The Greatest Cold War Myth of All," *Time,* November 29, 1993, 86.

50. Ibid.

51. Quoted in James Hoagland, "Christopher's Approach Subdued, but Policy Is Hardening," *Washington Post,* November 30, 1993, A14. The legacy of Cold War approaches on U.S. policy is illustrted by the fact that Christopher's advice was not heeded; America's NATO policy in 1997 was based on the dubious "notion that Russia is the rival of a Western bloc under increasingly hegemonic American influence," despite the evidence that "since 1989 Russia has tried to become fully included in the international system of the democracies" (William Pfaff, "Russia: Made an Outsider Again by America's NATO Policy," *International Herald Tribune,* March 24, 1997, 8).

52. For some suggestions about how this challenge might best be met, see Kegley, "How Did the Cold War Die?"

53. Ronald Steel, *Temptations of a Superpower* (Cambridge, Mass.: Harvard University Press, 1995), 5.

Chapter 9

Nations and Blocs: Toward a Theory of the Political Economy of the Interstate Model in Europe

Mary Kaldor

One way of explaining the Cold War is in terms of the emergence of new state forms in the aftermath of World War II. The bloc system can be said to have prefigured new methods of political organization which arose because of the limitations of the nation-state.

The postwar period is often considered the apogee of the nation-state. It was only after 1945 that the entire globe was parceled off into separate nation-states. Yet from the early twentieth century the nation-state was becoming inadequate to cope with growing social, economic, and military pressures in advanced industrial countries. In the early nineteenth century its proponents, such as Giuseppe Mazzini and Friedrich List, did not regard it as a final goal, an immutable creation. Rather, they had a functional view of the nation-state as a viable political unit for the development of democracy and industrialization—a stage in the progress from local to national and eventually global society.

The early nationalists envisaged the construction and spread of a national language, for ease of communication, alongside local and regional dialects. It was only later, when the nation was homogenized under the impact of a national language which was stabilized by administrative support, that the concept of the nation-state became tied to a notion of national culture and viewed not as a political artifact but as the natural political unit for a historically established community.[1]

I suggest that the nineteenth-century nation-state was and is a temporary phenomenon, even though there remains a very powerful attachment to the idea, especially in Eastern Europe and the Third World. The Cold War was a way of reconciling the attachment to the nation-state with the need for larger forms of political organization. Most explanations of the Cold War, which derive from the prevailing ways of thinking about international relations, are rooted in nineteenth-century assumptions about the nation-state and consequently have become part of a discourse that legitimizes the Cold War. It is extremely important to question these explanations in order to understand the current international conjuncture and possible historical directions for the post–Cold War period.

This essay is divided into three parts. The first part compares the characteristics of nations and blocs; the second analyzes competing explanations of the Cold War; the last part examines implications for the post–Cold War period.

Characteristics of Nations and Blocs

The nation-state is a particular form of state power that came into being in the nineteenth century with a quantitative increase in the scale of administration. Evolving from what has been called a night watchman state hardly impinging on most people's lives, the nation-state became a far-reaching institution that individuals encounter in one form or another in most everyday activities.

The typical characteristics of the nation-state are these:

Territoriality. Borders become fixed instead of shifting and indistinct, and
   sovereignty is based on territory instead of kinship or religion. In other
   words, the political reach of the state extends to all inhabitants of a particular territory, rather than to all Catholics, say, or to all who are related to or
   owe allegiance to a particular dynastic family.
Recognition of multiplicity. The existence of stable borders implies the existence of other states, which mutually recognize one another's sovereignty.

The nation-state is part of a collectivity—a nation-state system, in contrast to earlier empires.

Cultural homogeneity. In earlier societies horizontal high cultures, generally independent of the state and linked to religion, coexisted with a wide variety of vertical low cultures based on vernacular language, customs, and so on. Within this relatively stable social stratification, cultural diversity was an essential element.[2] The nation-state takes responsibility for cultural production and, in particular, the construction and spread of a national language, which gradually eliminates other languages, dialects, and cultures.[3]

Unified currency. The minting of money was generally a royal prerogative, although many princes and noblemen had the right to create money as well: In fifteenth-century Germany there were some 600 coinage authorities. The development of a centralized coinage controlled by central banks instead of kings was an essential element in the rise of the nation-state.

A monopoly on violence. Max Weber's definition of the state as "a compulsory political association with continuous organization" which "successfully upholds a claim to the *monopoly* of the *legitimate* use of physical force in the enforcement of its order" actually applies only to the nation-state.[4] Feudal states, for example, tolerated private armies, whereas the nation-state eliminated private armies in favor of regular armed forces commanded by professional staff. It also distinguished between internal (police) and external forces (the military), and reduced internal violence: for example, violent forms of punishment, the use of physical force in the exploitation of labor, and the like.[5]

Together these five characteristics can be said to constitute a legitimizing principle. The nation-state derives its legitimacy from the fact that it is the only organization (given its monopoly on violence) capable of defending the borders (territoriality) and the economy (currency) of the nation (defined in terms of cultural homogeneity) from other nation-states (multiplicity).

But these are characteristics, not explanations, of the nation-state. Most analysts emphasize the importance of industrialization—Ernest Gellner says that it was nations, not classes, that were the outcome of industrialization.[6] It would be excessively functionalist to argue that nation-states were established because of the requirements of industrialization. One can say, however, that earlier state forms were inadequate to cope with the demands of industrialization: a mobile work force whose members can communicate with one another; infrastructure; standard regulations that require a common language; a unified currency and banking system.

One can also argue that the nation-state succeeded, at least for a while, because it provided a viable framework for industrialization.

This does not mean that no other state framework could have succeeded in doing so, or that this was *the* reason why the nation-state came about. Two other factors are of great importance. One is the emergence of what Benedict Anderson calls an "imagined community," in which people who are not related by family ties or even acquainted can feel themselves part of a common endeavor. Such communities were made possible by the development of print technology and the transformation of vernacular languages into widespread written languages. Anderson sees the novel and the newspaper as key ingredients.[7] The second factor is war. Charles Tilly argues that the nation-state was formed through war.[8] Borders were established by war; the requirements of war greatly expanded the administrative reach of the state; in wartime, taxation was regularized and extended, and thereafter levels of public spending never returned to prewar levels.[9] Successful wars also established the legitimacy principle of the nation-state.

If the nation-state provided a framework for at least the early stages of industrialization, it also had many shortcomings, which became increasingly evident in the twentieth century. In different ways, it was both too large and too small. It was too large to protect cultures: Cultural homogeneity involved the elimination of lesser cultures. Some were absorbed relatively painlessly; others resisted and displayed separatist tendencies. It was also too large for efficient democratic decision-making. Even though the spread of the nation-state was linked to self-determination and the establishment of democratic institutions, widened suffrage and majority rule nevertheless meant that real participation in decision-making was very difficult and that these democracies were very vulnerable to the appeal to irrational prejudices for the purpose of winning votes.

More important, the nation-state was too small to regulate what was becoming a global economy. This task, undertaken by Britain in the nineteenth century, was no longer possible in the twentieth century, especially after the introduction of mass production and mass consumption. Likewise, the nation-state was too small to prevent wars, and this became critically important during the twentieth century when industrialization so enormously increased their destructiveness. The very fact that the legitimizing principle of nation-states was based on territory and nation meant that cooperation either to regulate the economy or to prevent wars was very difficult.

The basic elements of the bloc system came into being as a result of alliances that were formed during World War II, then reproduced and somewhat realigned by the Cold War. The bloc system was a form of partial integration; in effect, it insulated

the industrialized part of the world. The Western bloc comprised all those countries linked to the United States through institutionalized alliances: Western Europe, Japan, Canada, and Australasia. (Alliances with less developed regions such
as Latin America and Southeast Asia did not have the same permanent, institutionalized character.) The Soviet bloc comprised all those countries in which
Soviet-style political and economic systems had been introduced and in which the
ruling parties were directly subservient to Moscow. The bloc system was associated
with further administrative expansion: increased state interventionism through
warfare and welfare states in the West, totalitarian control in the East.

These are the characteristics of blocs:

Ideology, not territory, as a basis for organization. Membership in the bloc is
  based on loyalty to an idea that is linked to the social system: during the
  Cold War, democracy and capitalism in the West, socialism in the East.
  Blocs can acquire new members converted to the idea (e.g., as the Eastern
  bloc acquired Cuba), and bloc borders are not necessarily fixed.
Cohesion of states rather than multiplicity. Members of the bloc stick together. Unlike nation-states, which are separate and thus inherently limited, the bloc is, in principle, universal and limited only by the refusal of
  other states or individuals to accept its informing idea. In both Cold War
  blocs there was, of course, a dominant nation. In the case of the West it is
  probably correct to say that cohesion was based on consent: that is, acceptance of the idea that those parts of the world characterized by democracy
  and market economy constitute a common community. In the East, however, the idea of a socialist community was, by and large, imposed by force.
  Hence, a question arises as to whether the Eastern bloc was a new state
  form or a re-creation of the great Asian empires—a "suzerain states system," to use Martin Wight's term, in which an empire is surrounded by
  vassal states.[10]
Cultural homogeneity among elites. Each Cold War bloc created a new
  transnational set of horizontal structures among both security and business
  elites in which one language was spoken—English and Russian, respectively. Interestingly, certain elite discourses developed, having to do in the
  West with the language of nuclear strategy and of economic management,
  and in the East with the language of Marxism-Leninism.
Hegemonic money. The need for international money became apparent at an
  early stage of industrialization. In the nineteenth century, sterling functioned as international currency, alongside the gold and silver standards.

The postwar monetary system outside the Soviet bloc was essentially a dollar system, although the dollar was not delinked from gold until 1971. The Soviet bloc operated, in theory, on a ruble system, but intra-bloc trade was in practice a kind of barter system: rubles served as a standard of value, supplemented by world prices, but not as a means of exchange or a store of value.

Reduction of national control over the means of violence, except in the case of the dominant powers, the United States and the Soviet Union. Perhaps the most important feature of the Cold War bloc system was the integration of national armed forces into an integrated command system. Aside from Britain and France, other members of the blocs were not capable of waging separate national wars; hence, what had been viewed as an important element of national sovereignty was abrogated.

In short, the blocs prefigured new state forms in that they were not simply new coalitions of nation-states. In the notion of an ideological community rather than a territorially or culturally based community, in the a priori if not de facto universalism of the bloc, in the construction of new horizontal cultural structures, and above all in the limitations on national armed forces, the bloc system marked a decisive break with the system of nation-states. These characteristics gave rise to a new legitimizing principle that supplemented, if it did not displace, the national legitimizing principle: that the bloc defends ideas (freedom or socialism) against alien ideas (totalitarianism or imperialism). On the other hand, it could also be argued that the blocs were reversions to earlier empires, particularly in the East. In the West, the hegemonic role of the United States within the bloc and its imperial role elsewhere were critical to the cohesion of the bloc.[11]

If the nation-state provided a framework for the early stages of industrialization, then the bloc system provided a framework for the spread of the so-called Fordist stage. The bloc system succeeded in overcoming the shortcomings that arose from the fact that the nation-state was too small. In the West, it enabled an expansion of the market, a new system of financial regulation based on the dollar, and the spread of Fordist technology. In the East, for good and for ill, rapid industrialization on the Soviet model became possible. (Perhaps because the Soviet Union skipped the first phase of industrialization, the continuity of the bloc system with a pre-nation-state type of imperial absolutism was more evident.) Furthermore, the bloc system suppressed (although not entirely) national wars and through the concept of deterrence was able to retain the idea of war as a legitimizing principle while avoiding its destructiveness. I use the term "imaginary war" to denote this legitimizing principle.[12]

But the bloc system still exhibited many of the limitations of the nation-state. It was a kind of transitional state form, a halfway house. It could not satisfy cultural or democratic demands, and the military burden especially for the Soviet Union, was crippling. Moreover, the dominance of two great powers imparted an inflexibility to the system. One advantage often touted for nation-states in contrast to earlier empires is flexibility: hegemony can pass from one nation to another while the system remains intact. By comparison, the bloc system was more like earlier empires—a characteristic which, at least in the Soviet case, proved fatal. Finally (for reasons touched on the last section), the bloc framework proved inadequate to cope with the demands for speed, interdependence, and diversity that are associated with the emergence of what is sometimes known as a post-Fordist stage of industrialization, based on electronics and information technology.

Explaining the Cold War

The bloc system emerged out of the experience of World War II and resulted in the ongoing confrontation known as the Cold War. The Cold War established horizontal organizational structures such as NATO and the Warsaw Pact, which provided an umbrella for and legitimized other horizontal structures: the European Community (EC), Council for Mutual Economic Assistance (COMECON), International Monetary Fund (IMF), inter-Party networks within the Eastern bloc, and so on.

How does an explanation of the Cold War based on the requirement for new state forms differ from other prevailing explanations? I want to distinguish five types of explanation for the Cold War: three "from above"—that is, they are to be found in the statements of politicians and others close to government—and two "from below": that is, they emerge out of analyses provided by opposition movements.

The first explanation is the orthodox Western one: The Cold War was a struggle between democracy (represented by Western governments and the Western military alliance) and totalitarianism (represented by the Soviet state and the Warsaw Pact).

The second explanation is the orthodox Soviet one, which has now virtually disappeared: The Cold War was a struggle between capitalism (with Western governments serving as the mouthpieces of the capitalist class) and socialism (identified with the Soviet Union and its satellites).

Both these explanations derive evidence from the history of the early stages of the Cold War. The first argues that once the Soviet Union had imposed control over Eastern Europe, the West had to prevent further territorial expansion of communism; hence, NATO was a response to the Soviet threat. The orthodox Soviet explanation holds that the formation of NATO was an indication of the Western determination to roll back communism and to impose a capitalist system on the East. Hence the Soviet Union, and later the Warsaw Pact, had to defend itself against the Western threat.

The third explanation, to be found in both Western and Eastern official circles especially during the latter part of the Cold War, is that the Cold War was simply a traditional form of great-power rivalry. A great power always has to ensure against the risk of expansion by another great power; therefore, the existence of military capabilities on one side implies the need for an equivalent military buildup on the other.

These first three explanations are based on the premise of interstate rivalry similar to traditional nation-state rivalry. All three consider military power essential to protect territory (in the first two cases, systemic expansion is elided with territorial expansion), and all three place considerable importance on the concept of balance of power. Unlike the eighteenth- and nineteenth- century view that the balance of power was primarily a way of preventing the dominance of any one power, however, the Cold War concept is identified with deterrence: that is, a way of preventing war.

The explanations to be found among opposition circles also view the Cold War as a systemic conflict, but systemic conflict is not necessarily the same as interstate conflict. The fourth is the revisionist explanation, which has several variants and some elements in common with the official Soviet (second) explanation. It posits that the Western bloc was formed because of the need, demonstrated in the interwar depression, to increase the scale of government, to fund new mechanisms for preventing destructive international economic warfare, and to minimize the influence of the Socialist and Communist Parties. Still, the revisionist explanation is not entirely economistic. Alan Wolfe explains the Cold War as the chosen solution to these economic requirements in terms of domestic American politics, the need to renew the wartime bipartisan consensus.[13] A number of European writers emphasize the importance of domestic European political factors and the need to find a compromise between left-leaning European governments and right-wing tendencies in the United States. But the primary explanation, according to revisionists, is to be found in the expansionary nature of capitalism. The revisionists do not generally explain the origins of the Soviet bloc; it is often assumed to be a consequence of the formation of NATO: the imposition of communist regimes in Eastern Europe followed the decision to confine Marshall Plan aid to the West (or rather to offer it to the East on unacceptable terms) and to create a West German state. Even so, some variants of the revisionist explanation are not inconsistent with the view that the separate development of the Soviet bloc legitimized the formation of NATO.

The fifth explanation, which was to be found in dissident circles in the East, does concern the formation of the Soviet bloc and the determination of the Soviet regime to hold on to the territory acquired during World War II. In this view, the explanation for the imperial nature of the Soviet Union stemmed from its totalizing and militaristic characteristics. With a whole system built on the notion of threats both internal and external, mobilization for war was the only way of mobilizing the economy. All-pervading fear was what made such mobilization possible—fear of the external threat, fear of repression, and, above all, fear that past crimes would be revealed. The system worked by incorporating everyone so that every individual became both victim and accomplice. Thus, paranoic fear that any opening up in Eastern Europe or the Soviet Union would lead to questioning and could undermine the whole system led inexorably to a tightening Soviet grip over Eastern Europe and at home.[14]

This fifth explanation, which is also to be found in orthodox Western accounts (for example, that of Zbigniew Brzezinski),[15] does not explain the origins of the Western bloc. It is generally viewed as a response to the formation of the Eastern bloc, a way of preventing the further spread of the Soviet empire. Some dissident writers such as George Konrad, however, view the formation of NATO as an independent development that legitimized the permanence of the Soviet bloc.

My own explanation is a combination of the fourth and fifth. It is true that the Cold War offered a solution to domestic political and economic problems in capitalist countries, but it could not have done so without the image of an "other" that had some real substance (nor was it the only possible solution). The West needed a Soviet threat to legitimize the construction of the Western bloc. The Soviet system did represent an undesirable alternative, even though few people at that time viewed it as a territorial threat. Likewise, the Soviet system, founded as it was on fear, needed the image of a Western threat to substantiate at least some of that fear. Deterrence, then, became a way of imagining war, of playing out a pretend war day after day, using real soldiers, weapons, military planners, and the like. The point of this imaginary war was to keep alive the idea of interstate conflict so as to legitimize the blocs, to apply nation-state assumptions to the new situation. Yet precisely because the blocs were based on support for ideas about how to organize political and social systems, rather than on territory, neither territorial expansion nor wars of conquest were relevant to bloc expansion. Moreover, the two sets of ideologies were not so much competitive as complementary, each requiring the other for explanation. The elision of systemic and territorial expansion actually served as part of the legitimizing discourse of the imaginary war.

In what sense can this explanation be described as a political economy approach? As a matter of fact, "political economy" was the term used by nineteenth-century economists to denote economics. Today, however, the term tends to refer to a more political approach to economics or, alternatively, to emphasis on the influence of economic factors in political analysis. My explanation thus involves political economy in the modern sense.

First, like economics, it focuses on how or why institutions are reproduced rather than on how they originated. In economics, however, the concern is with the production and reproduction of material goods; here, the concern is with the production and reproduction of power. Most explanations of the Cold War focus on its origins, on who started it. If one assumes that the method of reproduction takes the form of an interstate conflict along traditional lines, then the origins are relevant. But if one questions the assumption of a traditional interstate conflict and hypothesizes an alternative explanation based on conflict as spectacle rather than coercion, then the origins are less relevant. It is more important to ask why the appearance of conflict was sustained, why each side was able to justify behavior in terms of the behavior of the other side—why, in short, the Cold War continued for so long without either erupting in war or fading away. The revisionist explanation of the Cold War in the West argues that the conflict was economically functional; even if it originated in a political constellation that was specific to the late 1940's, the bloc system provided the underpinning for post-war prosperity and was able to sustain political support for postwar governments. The dissident explanation for the Cold War in the East argues that the bloc system was politically functional, justifying a sustained mobilization based on fear.

Second, my approach emphasizes both the influence of economic factors on political change and the influence of political factors on economic change. I would argue that economic factors are predominant in some periods of history and political factors predominant in others, depending on the methods of reproduction. In capitalist economic systems economic change is continuous and rapid, while political democracies tend to be rather slow to change. The Eastern political systems were virtually immune to change, since economics was subordinated to politics, and there were no established mechanisms for political change. By and large, the more militarized systems change more slowly than less militarized systems, and the Eastern systems were highly militarized. Hence the direction of influence depends on the relative pace of change. The tendency is for periods of economic transition (when economic change is rapid) to alternate with periods of political transition.

The 1950's and 1960's were decades of rapid economic change. As postwar prosperity began to falter, the bloc system came under strain. The various phases of detente and renewed Cold War can be interpreted as responses to that strain. Even though the West was able to respond more flexibly than the East, the rigidity of the bloc system became an obstacle to renewed prosperity in both. The 1989 revolutions ushered in a period of political transition—involving a search for or a process of experimentation with new forms of state organization—much like the period that ended in the late 1940s with the onset of the Cold War.

To recap, the nation-state system came into being because of the inadequacies of earlier forms of state organization to cope with the demands of industrialization, though the specific character of the nation-state has to be explained by political factors, especially wars. The establishment of nation-states in turn profoundly influenced the pattern of industrialization. Likewise, the bloc system came into being because of the inadequacy of the nation-state system to cope with the demands of the twentieth-century world economy, though the specific character of the bloc system was the outcome of a set of political factors in both East and West, including the experience of the Second World War. And the bloc system in turn influenced the pattern of industrialization, allowing the spread of what has become known as Fordism in the West and the Soviet model of industrialization in the East.

After the Blocs?

During the 1970s and 1980s a revolution occurred in what is generally known as information technology—the consequence of the combination of large-scale data processing (made possible by the use of microelectronics) and enormous improvements in telecommunications (both because of the use of microelectronics for switching and because of new forms of transmission such as fiber optics and satellites). This revolution has had and is having so profound an impact on all aspects of economic, social, and political life that its results are sometimes described as postindustrialism or, at least, as a phase of industrialization so entirely new as to compare in importance with the original industrial revolution.

In particular, the new technology seems both to speed up the global integration of economies and, at the same time, to make possible greater decentralization of both production and consumption. On the one hand, the ability of nation-states to influence national economies continues to be eroded by the globalization of production, trade, and finance. On the other hand, mass production and mass consumption in a physical sense have become less important: Instead of the production of standardized products on huge assembly lines, reprogrammable standardized machines can cater to a much wider variety of tastes and produce in much smaller quantities, so that products and production processes can be organized around local skills and local markets.

I do not wish to suggest that political institutions are determined by technology. Technology itself is a consequence of wider economic, social, and political trends: the capitalist drive for ever increasing productivity; the need to save space, energy and raw materials and to find new market niches; the particular form of skill stratification in Japan which first integrated the new technologies into production processes; the military quest for accuracy, and so on. The point is rather that the bloc system turned out to be unable to adjust to the changes wrought by the new phase of industrialization: dramatic shifts in the patterns of production without corresponding shifts in the pattern of demand, resulting in the reemergence of large-scale unemployment; the shift in the pole of accumulation from the United States to Japan and Western Europe and the loss of cohesion in the Western bloc; changes in social composition, particularly the decline in the traditional working classes; the increase of educated white-collar workers, and a new underclass of immigrant and female workers not reflected in political representation; the emergence of new horizontal cultural networks making use of new technologies—especially telecommunications—that go beyond and in some cases challenge the horizontal elite networks; pervasive new electoral techniques, based on the use of opinion polls and advertising, that erode channels of influence between the political realm and society; the rapid speedup of international monetary transactions and the loss of hegemonic control over money creation; fundamental changes in military technology and the loss of credibility of the imaginary war scenario.

I want to outline two possible models for the future. One is a combination of blocs and nations. The other is a new set of horizontal international state structures—prefigured by the blocs but not based on the imaginary war legitimizing principle—combined with vertical, territorially based, relatively small national units. It should be stressed that these are *models:* ideal types or examples of what might happen, depending on what kind of political choices are made now. In a sense Model A is based on current elite thinking—an attempt to reestablish the partial integration of the Cold War model on a new basis. Model B arises out of the thinking of the peace movement and the dissident movement. Reality is likely to be quite different from either model; they are intended to assist our thinking about reality.

Model A. In Model A, the Western bloc recreates itself with a stronger European Community, possibly including some East European countries such as Hungary, Poland, the Czech Republic, perhaps Slovenia. Its key features are a coalition of advanced industrial countries based on a military alliance or a set of military treaties, and the integration of (Western) Europe as a European nation-state, with a European currency and a European army, rather than as a new state form. The reformed bloc would have these characteristics:

> Membership based on ideology: that is, commitment to democracy and market economy rather than territory.
> The cohesion of advanced industrial states.
> A unifying materialist culture on the Americo-Japanese model, gradually eliminating other cultures.
> Competing blocs of currencies: the yen, the ECU (European Common Currency), and the dollar.
> The integration of armed forces so that only the European Community and the United States have the capacity to wage war.

Such a bloc would be more like the nation-state than the previous ones, in that the EC would be more a nation-state and less a loose structure and that globalized consumer culture would become more pervasive. Because the model requires a legitimizing principle, especially given the scale of the units and the difficulty of influencing decision-making, it is associated with an increasing tendency toward opinion poll democracy in which a citizen becomes a consumer, choosing candidates on the basis of image. The Gulf War represents a kind of preview of this approach. Although it was a real war, it was experienced in Europe and America as spectacle. The principle was democracy versus fundamentalism (religious fundamentalism in this case, but it could also be exclusive nationalism as it is emerging in Eastern Europe). The tool was flashy new technology—never mind whether it actually worked; it was the appearance that mattered. It is interesting to note that research and development budgets have not declined as much as military budgets; the present phase could turn out to be military restructuring rather than disarmament.

In this model the bloc system is exclusive. Outside the blocs the nation-state remains. But given economic inequalities and exclusion from Europe, the tendency is for exclusive, culturally based nationalism to thrive, accompanied by growing populist authoritarianism and the spread of violence on the Yugoslav model—or, alternatively, for the spread of Islamic fundamentalism. These tendencies actually provide the "other" required by the bloc.

Model B. In Model B, new horizontal state forms come into being. These are prefigured by already existing structures—NATO, the EC, IMF, COMECON, the Organization for Security and Cooperation in Europe (OSCE), the General Agreement on Trade and Tariffs (GATT), the Commonwealth, and so on—but they acquire new forms of supranational accountability. In other words, the new horizontal organizations are more than just inter-governmental institutions because they can override national sovereignty, but they are not new nation-states. Moreover, their power derives not from a new hegemon, or from cohesion in response to an external menace, but from popular consent. They regulate relations among smaller local and national territorially based units. These are the characteristics of such structures:

Concerned with particular issues—human rights, security, the environment, economic and financial management—rather than territory. Their territorial reach varies and is open to addition through voluntary membership. Thus, the membership of the CSCE covers the whole of Europe plus North America; the EC might cover Western and Central Europe with a separate Soviet economic community, and so on.

Membership representing coalitions of cooperating states or even cooperating groups of citizens.

A horizontal political culture based on a commitment to solve certain shared global problems—ecology, peace, development, human rights—combined with the multiple and diverse popular cultures of relatively small local and national territorial units.

National or bloc currencies linked to a genuine form of international money guaranteed by international financial institutions that are democratically accountable.

Severe curtailment of the national capacity to wage war by means of a series of interlocking security arrangements, including multinational units responsible for peacekeeping and a complex mutual inspection framework arising from arms control agreements. National armed forces more or less become cultural relics (Scottish bagpipers, Croatians in Austro-Hungarian uniforms).

The key feature of this model is its basis in a different kind of legitimizing principle: consent. The imaginary war could be described as ideological coercion and, in that sense, was preferable to real war: that is, physical coercion. But to be consensual requires, first, that as many decisions as possible are taken by the smallest political units; in EC jargon this is known as the principle of subsidiarity. Second, it requires horizontal organizations that are open and accountable to public opinion, not just intergovernmental bodies that take decisions behind closed doors and override democratically reached decisions, as has been the case up to now with both NATO and the EC. This means either direct elections to separate international parliaments (with real control) or perhaps assemblies of local territorial units. Third, it requires a change in the process of governance. These new organizations are not simply democratic in their own internal structures. They have the capacity to enhance local democracy by solving problems that cannot be solved at a national level *and* by guaranteeing local autonomy; hence, their role is enabling rather than interventionist. In other words, they act through local alliances with local or territorial units or nongovernmantal organizations.

The small territorial units become primarily repositories of culture—using the term "culture" in the broad sense to include types of education, the protection of languages(s), the pattern of ownership, the type of healthcare provision, and so on—determined according to local demands and restrained only by common international standards (guaranteed by the larger horizontal communities) concerning human rights, the environment, international economic relations, and security.

In principle, Model B is much more suited to the new phase of industrialization than Model A, which would recreate the Cold War model with all its shortcomings: Consumption remains focused on military and private consumption; some redistribution takes place among three main competing blocs; there are no mechanisms for local decision-making or for local diversity. Model A would likely involve a combination of authoritarianism within the bloc system and chaos beyond. In contrast, Model B would involve a shift in patterns of demand with much greater emphasis on global redistribution and the application of new technologies to environmental and social purposes.

In practice, the choice between Model A and Model B depends on politics. That Model B is more compatible with the new phase of industrialization does not mean that it is more likely to be introduced. Model B requires that the construction of the post–Cold War order be regarded as a common global endeavor, not just a Western endeavor. Eastern Europe and, indeed, the Third World must be brought into the international system. This involves responsibilities on both sides. A Western world view that excludes Eastern Europe and the Third World would exacerbate (it has already done so) exclusivist, violent tendencies within those countries. By the same token, exclusivist, violent tendencies in Eastern Europe and the Third World would provide an argument for exclusion. An exclusive Western bloc would feed on nationalism and religious fundamentalism and vice versa, just as NATO fed on Soviet totalitarianism and vice versa. So far, the tendencies are not hopeful. Although East European countries are allowed to join the IMF, the Organization for Economic Cooperation and Development (OECD), and the World Bank, and there is talk of membership in the European Union (EU) when they can meet the criteria for membership (which may take a long time), the OSCE is still very weak in comparison to NATO, and readiness to solve the vast environmental and economic problems has not been great.

So long as people stick to nation-state conceptions, Model A is a much more likely outcome. Model B would involve a break with the dominant political assumptions of the past. In particular, explanations of the Cold War that sustain the myth of traditional territorial conflict have to be challenged. For example, the view prevalent in Western official circles that NATO's military strength, especially the deployment of cruise missiles, actually brought about the Soviet collapse presupposes the first explanation of the Cold War: that of a territorially based conflict between democracy and totalitarianism. In fact, for thirty years NATO's military strength sustained the Soviet system. In an imaginary war situation only domestic political pressure can really influence institutions, but domestic political pressure is always squeezed by war or imaginary war. It was only in the context of detente that nonviolent revolution could succeed. The failure to challenge this assumption means that the same approach is tried out against Iraq or any other fundamentalist enemy (say Serbia); it is the kind of thinking that sustains fundamentalism.

An alternative way of thinking that seeks a consensual approach to international institutions can arise only out of a transnational political culture that can create transnational public opinion. To some extent such a culture does already exist, although it is not very visible. One interesting feature of the new social movements that emerged in the 1970s and 1980s is their transnational character, in contrast to earlier emancipatory movements—say, the liberal and labor movements—which aimed at access to national politics. These new movements have not been very successful in transforming themselves into political parties; indeed, they have often adopted an anti-party stance. Groups like Amnesty International and Greenpeace, however, have been very successful in developing transnational constituencies. The Helsinki Citizens Assembly, a coalition of individuals and civic initiatives in East and West, is a deliberate attempt to create a new horizontal nongovernmental structure.

A key feature of the political thinking of such movements is the commitment to influence ideas as a way of influencing rather than capturing power. The argument is that honest debate is very difficult in party political forums because electoral considerations there influence expressed opinion. In the era of opinion polls and advertisements this problem is all the more serious. Vàclav Havel's concept of anti-politics or "living with truth" was an attempt to introduce serious, honest debate into politics. A transnational debating forum designed to widen the scope of debates about public affairs is absolutely necessary if democracy is to be deepened and if we are to move away from both war as war and war as spectacle.

The two models can be illustrated in terms of responses to the war in Bosnia. Had the EU acted as a Model B horizontal institution, it would have had to recognize that there was no future for the former Yugoslavia as *either* a unitary state or a collection of new ethnically based nation-states. Any future political organization for the area would have had to be integrated into European and global arrangements and to be much more democratic at a local level. Second, it would have had to operate closely with those groups in society that have this conception of the future, be they nongovernmental groups such as those concerned with peace and human rights or political institutions such as municipalities. Third, it should have intervened not on one side or another but in such a way as to provide civic and political space in which this kind of conception of the future could develop. This was the idea behind the notion, favored by local peace and human rights groups, of an international protectorate for Bosnia-Herzegovina. The role of the international community was seen as an enabling one. But to act in this way, the institution would have needed alternative sources of legitimacy and hence alternative mechanisms of accountability not based on nation-states.

In practice, the behavior of the international community was quite different. The dominant approaches were drawn from Cold War and pre–Cold War thinking. On the one hand, the Americans perceived the war as a conflict between democracy and totalitarianism in which Serbia represented the remnants of totalitarianism to be "deterred" by the threat of air strikes and economic sanctions. On the other hand, the Europeans conceived of the war as a traditional national war in which all sides were responsible. Both were territory-based approaches. The (final?) outcome at Dayton was a dirty compromise between the two approaches which awarded territory to "ethnic gangsters" in a way that cannot be sustained in the long run.

There was a third approach, adopted under pressure from the global media and citizens' group in Bosnia and across Europe and the United States, which conceived of the war neither as an ideological conflict nor as a national war but as a massive violation of international principles. Security Council resolutions establishing safe havens, humanitarian corridors, and the war crimes tribunal, if seriously implemented, could have added up to a new form of humanitarian intervention which might have been able to underpin a new kind of issue-based legitimacy for international institutions. Unfortunately, this approach was largely cosmetic: Safe havens were not defended; humanitarian corridors were not enforced; war criminals were never captured. The end result is a Bosnian black hole in which violence, poverty, exclusivism, and criminality are rife and which sucks the rest of the Balkans into an anarchic mire. The signs are already evident in Albania, Macedonia, Serbia, and Bulgaria. The whole of the Balkans plus territory farther east is beginning to be treated as a new "other" that can legitimize a Model A future.

The problem with the Model A approach is that it does not seem to work. The international failure in Bosnia, and in other places such as Rwanda and Somalia, seems to be linked to a pervasive loss of political legitimacy throughout the advanced industrial world. It is very difficult to insulate the Western world from the troubles of the East and South, as can be seen in the West European nervousness about refugees from Bosnia or Albania. Yet the leap of political imagination needed for Model B has not yet taken place.

Notes

1. See Eric Hobsbawm, *Nations and Nationalism since 1780: Programme, Myth, Reality* (Cambridge: Cambridge University Press, 1990), esp. chapter 2. Mazzini, for example, did not support the independence of Ireland because he thought that Ireland was not viable as a nation-state.

2. See Ernest Geller, *Nations and Nationalism* (Oxford: Basil Blackwell, 1983).

3. At the time of Italian unification, only 2.5 percent of the inhabitants of Italy spoke Italian. According to Massimo d'Azeglio, "We have made Italy, now we have to make Italians" (quoted in Hobsbawm, *Nations and Nationalism since 1780*, 44).

4. Quoted in Robert Dahl, "Power as the Control of Behavior," in *Power*, ed. Steven Lukes (Oxford: Basil Blackwell, 1986), 39.

5. See Anthony Giddens, "The Nation-State and Violence," in Giddens, *A Contemporary Critique of Historical Materialism*, vol. 2 (Oxford: Polity, 1985).

6. Gellner, *Nations and Nationalism*.

7. Benedict Anderson, *Imagined Communities* (London: Verso, 1991).

8. Charles Tilly, "Reflections on the History of European State-making" in *The Formation of Nation States in Western Europe*, ed. Charles Tilly (Princeton, N.J.: Princeton University Press, 1975).

9. Ibid., 75: "Recently, we find a chain of causation running from (1) change or expansion in land armies to (2) new efforts to extract resources from subject populations to (3) the development of new bureaucracies and administrative innovation to (4) resistance from the subject population to (5) renewed coercion to (6) durable increases in the bulk or extractiveness of the state."

10. Martin Wight, *The System of States* (Leicester: Leicester University Press, 1977).

11. For an analysis of the Soviet bloc as imperial and the Western bloc as hegemonic, see Giangiacomo Migone, "The Decline of the Bipolar System and a Second Look at the History of the Cold War," in *The New Detente: Rethinking East-West Relations,* ed. Mary Kaldor, G. Holden, and R. Falk (London: Verso, 1989).

12. See Mary Kaldor, *The Imaginary War* (Oxford: Basil Blackwell, 1990).

13. Alan Wolfe, "American Domestic Politics and the Alliance," in Kaldor, Holden, and Falk, *The New Detente.*

14. George Kennan makes this point in relation to Poland in his *Memoirs 1925–50* (London: Hutchinson, 1968), 203: "What was bothering Stalin was not, as many people assumed, just the desire to have a 'friendly government' on the other side of the Polish frontier. What was bothering him was the need for collaboration of any future Polish political authority in repressing evidences and memories of actions by Soviet police authorities in the period 1939–41, for which no adequate and respectable excuse could be found. It was clear that a Polish authority that could be depended on could never be other than a Communist one under Soviet control." The revelations of the early 1990s about Soviet massacres of Polish officers in the Katyn Forest in 1944 seemed to bear out this point.

15. Zbigniew Brzezinski, *The Soviet Bloc: Unity and Conflict* (Cambridge, Mass.: Harvard University Press, 1967).

Chapter 10

Warsaw Pact Socialism: Detente and the Disintegration of the Soviet Bloc

Harriet Friedmann

In this essay I argue that tensions within the Soviet bloc became fatal because of the disintegrative effects of trade and debt relations with the West. Bloc cohesion was undermined in the 1970s and 1980s when the USSR and East European countries entered capitalist markets in money, energy, and grain. The courageous popular movements that toppled one ruling Communist Party after another took advantage of political spaces opened by economic realignments between the Soviet Union and East European countries, including internal use of Western currencies, as the bloc adjusted to ties to the West. The permeability of Soviet bloc boundaries compounded the economic burden of the arms race, and was more corrosive than earlier containment by the West. My argument, therefore, shifts attention away from the contrast between abstractly defined social systems and toward the relationships between actually existing socialism and capitalism, as they evolved throughout the Cold War and detente.[1]

The collapse of Soviet socialism was bound up with the bloc character it assumed within the framework of the Cold War. It is illuminating to identify and analyze what I call Warsaw Pact Socialism (WPS). The economic space of actually existing socialism in Europe was The Council for Mutual Economic Assistance (CMEA) established in 1949 as an alternative to U.S. Marshall Plan aid, which was rejected by Eastern Europe under Soviet pressure. Although the match was not fixed or perfect, the boundaries of the CMEA were enforced by membership in the Warsaw Treaty Organization. The Warsaw Pact formalized in 1955 the political-military basis of the bloc, which was constructed under Soviet occupation after World War II.[2] Beneath the formal equality of Warsaw Pact allies was the real hierarchy of ruling Communist Parties, with the Soviet Party at the pinnacle. The hierarchy of states ruled by unequal Communist Parties was the institutional framework for economic planning in the CMEA.

The argument falls into the following sections: (1) the chronic tension between national planning and bloc-wide integration in WPS; (2) the dilemma posed by the capitalist energy crisis for CMEA trade and prices; (3) the scissors effect for Eastern Europe of declining terms of trade with both the USSR and the West, which was met by borrowing in Western money markets; (4) a loss of confidence by Western banks and the debt crisis that was the context for political mobilization, beginning with Polish Solidarity; (5) the use of Soviet hard currency to buy feed grains, which led to a grain trap parallel to Eastern Europe's debt trap; and (6) the stake of Western capitalists in economic relations with WPS, and the worsening of capitalist economic instability as the ties with the socialist bloc unfolded.

Warsaw Pact Socialism

National versus bloc-wide economic growth strategies were a persistent tension within Warsaw Pact Socialism. This tension reflected the contradictory legacy left by Stalinist autarky and by post-Stalinist attempts to construct a bloc-wide division of labor based on national specialization and trade. Because of the autarkic pull, the reorientation of Eastern European economies to the CMEA was never fully effected. With liberalization after Stalin, the USSR was less able to prevent national developments in Eastern Europe, including renewed ties with the West.

Stalin's policy of "socialism in one country" was based on the drive to build a powerful state and industrial economy by expropriating landlords and then squeezing the peasants beyond past practices. The state-building project continued the long history of what Charles Tilly calls the "coercion-intensive path" of state formation. In contrast to West European state-builders, who found ways to benefit from the private accumulation of capital, East European rulers had "squeezed military force from landlords and peasants without raising large amounts of cash."[3] The Bolsheviks' first act (together with withdrawing from World War I and repudiating foreign debts) was to get rid of the landlords. The response of the capitalist West was to lay seige to the revolutionary government, first in alliance with counter-revolutionaries during the Russian civil war, and then in isolating it from world commerce and politics.

Expropriation of land enhanced the powers of the former Russian state and left only the peasants to squeeze. International isolation and domestic repression favored Stalin's harsh and rapid path of forced collectivization. An alternative was proposed by the now celebrated A. V. Chayanov, who was murdered and his work suppressed; he advocated a policy of incentives and infrastructure to encourage peasants to modernize through cooperation and extension into agro-industrial production.[4] Absent investment in agriculture, collectivization based on force was necessary to ensure appropriation of food for state-building and industrialization. Thus, in addition to repressive Party rule, the Soviet economic legacies to WPS were national autarky and forced collectivization of agriculture in the service of rapid industrialization.

Warsaw Pact Socialism originated in the shift from socialism in one country to socialism in one bloc, from a socialist state under siege to a socialist bloc competing for world power, from a "union of republics" ruled by the Communist Party of the Soviet Union (CPSU) to a hierarchy of formally independent states integrated through the domination of the CPSU over the ruling parties in Eastern Europe. According to Fernando Claudin, a member of the Spanish Communist Party until his expulsion in 1965 and a trenchant analyst of communism as a historical movement, Stalin's retrenchment from international revolution to Soviet national interest became the defining feature of the bloc created by Soviet occupation.[5]

The ideology of Soviet rule combined exaltation of the USSR as a model and enforcement of allegiance to Party doctrine, with each national Party taking its lead from the Soviet Party. Every aspect of economic policy became intimately bound up with the politics of the bloc. National independence, construed as disloyalty to the Soviet Union and therefore to socialism, merged with repression of national policies alternative to those imposed by the Soviet Party. Thus, opposition to forced collectivization of agriculture within the East European countries, notably Poland and Hungary, was denounced as "Titoism."[6] Not surprisingly, Yugoslavia did combine independence with alternative agricultural policies. Soviet doctrine defined the "construction of socialism" as the mimicking of Soviet experience by each party ruling national within WPS, down to the specific rate of growth of each national sector specified in each Five-Year Plan.[7]

Autarkic reconstruction was particularly wrenching in light of Eastern Europe's historic economic relations with Western Europe. Although some argue that Nazi Germany's coercive integration of Eastern Europe was the model for postwar Soviet policy in the region,[8] in reality the Soviets enforced imitation rather than complementarity. The East European countries had only recently been formed out of the dissolution of the Hapsburg and Ottoman Empires. Although they had erected especially high protective barriers during the depression of the 1930s, these were combined with trade with Western Europe.[9] In the Nazi period, Germany had compensated for the lack of an overseas empire (whose raw materials supported metropolitan industry in France and England) by creating in Eastern Europe a contiguous empire.[10]

Stalin's goal was rapid industrial development in the "Peoples' Democracies" so that they would not need imports from capitalist countries, and it was obvious to him that they would prefer trade with the Soviet Union.[11] After 1945 countries such as Hungary were refused investment credits by Western banks, and Western Europe offered few prospects for trade.[12] When, under Soviet pressure, they refused Marshall Plan aid and then Yugoslavia distanced itself from Soviet control, CMEA was formed and Stalinist economic policies were imposed.[13] Between 1937 and 1953 the share of East European exports to the West dropped from 59 to 19 percent, while intra–East European trade more than doubled (to 30 percent) and exports to the USSR rose from 1 to 39 percent.[14] A combination of Soviet policy and Western isolation created an economic dam between Atlantic and Soviet blocs.[15]

In 1962, drawing on the reference in CMEA's founding statement to the "possibility" of economic "cooperation," Khrushchev enunciated the principle of a "socialist international division of labor." Supranational planning was more logically coherent than replicating central planning in each small economy, and more practical than slavish imitations of Soviet central planning in widely varying national circumstances. It was also more strategic in encouraging an economic base for bloc military unity. But it was too late to extend central planning to the bloc as a whole. The principle foundered on the contradictory requirements of bloc unity and national autarky. It succumbed to the violent opposition of Romania, which feared that planned specialization throughout the bloc would force it to abandon industry in favor of modernizing its agriculture.[16] The Romanian Party stuck to the Stalinist program of industry and autarky. This occurred against the backdrop of the Sino-Soviet split of 1961, and the withdrawal or expulsion of China and Albania, also reflecting national pressures on bloc unity.

With the defeat of Khrushchev's proposal for integrating the CMEA, space was left for the development of alternative projects. Hungary and Poland early proposed more flexible ways to coordinate national plans through market mechanisms, involving domestic reforms unacceptable to other ruling parties.[17] These built on practical experiences which had led to distinct national paths to agricultural development for more than a decade. The Hungarian and Polish ruling parties had found specific compromises between Soviet power and national interests.[18]

Thus "socialist internationalism" and "national sovereignty" remained unreconciled principles of the CMEA. By the 1960s each of the WPS economies had reached the limits of extensive development of industry.[19] Trade within WPS had very limited economic potential, given the replication of national economies. Soviet ideology pointed to the solution of deeper integration through coordinated planning, parallel to international restructuring of production in the capitalist world. But bloc-wide planning succumbed to national opposition, which found its material basis in the autarky originally dictated by Stalinist economic policy. Without a solution to economic stagnation, Party rule was vulnerable, since its ideological claims lay not only in social justice but also in economic superiority.

The Soviet Dilemma: Hard Currency versus Bloc Unity

In retrospect one can see that in 1970, WPS faced the choice between deeper economic integration of the bloc and reorientation of each country to the West. The crucial choice about the bloc was overshadowed by more visible choices about national planning: between market reforms of the sort introduced with Soviet acquiescence in Hungary in 1968 and other ways to improve central planning in each country. Of course, national choices were framed within the rules and relations of CMEA trade—rules and relations that changed when member states began to trade with and borrow from the West.

In general, trade within the "socialist division of labor" was based on Soviet oil and other raw materials in exchange for East European manufactured goods. The extensive industrialization of East European economies during the 1960s depended on a cheap, reliable source of energy in countries that for the most part lacked an adequate resource base. The USSR sold them oil, which was not readily salable in the West before 1973 and in return guaranteed them a market for manufactured goods that might not have been able to compete with higher-quality goods in the West. For its part, the Soviet Union acquired goods that it did not produce domestically in sufficient quantities. At the same time it got access to the Western technologies incorporated into East European goods, which were either produced under license or imported as components.[20]

De-Stalinization reversed the subsidy initially imposed on East European satellites after World War II.[21] With the normalization of bloc economic negotiations, the intra-bloc prices set in practice for each five-year planning period were based on the (capitalist) world price at the time the plan was established: 1961–65 prices were based on 1958, 1966–70 prices on average 1960–64 world prices. Since the terms of trade had moved in favor of manufactured goods as against raw materials in the West, CMEA price policy favored East European manufactured exports over Soviet energy exports. Soviet planners had long been complaining when the OPEC oil crisis struck in 1973–74.[22] In 1974 the CMEA began to revise prices annually, still with reference to the world price, but since world oil prices had tripled in 1973–74, the balance shifted toward Soviet exports relative to those of Eastern Europe.

The oil crisis created new opportunities for the USSR to earn hard currency through energy exports, which doubled during the 1970s.[23] Although Soviet petroleum exports to Western Europe had generally tended to increase during the 1950s and 1960s, Cold War restrictions had led to unstable trade and often sales at cut-rate prices. Embargoes also led to delays in construction of pipelines to transport oil to Western Europe.[24] Between 1966 and 1972, however, the various West European countries created joint commissions with the USSR to negotiate trade on a commodity-by-commodity basis, creating the framework for enhanced energy trade when the OPEC crisis struck.[25]

WPS planners hoped to use selective economic relations with the West to renew and deepen bloc planning. The Bucharest Program of 1971 had announced the "necessity" of economic integration among CMEA members. First Ostpolitik and then detente opened trade dramatically—in time, it seemed, for WPS to benefit. The Soviet Union could improve its access to Western goods and technology by trading oil for them directly, rather than getting them in a partial, ad hoc way via East European manufactures. With the price of oil at three times its former level, it seemed possible to balance subsidies within WPS by means of foreign exchange from trade with the West.[26]

There is evidence that even at the time of the second oil shock at the end of the decade, the Soviet Union continued to subsidize the economies of Eastern Europe by selling its exports at rates fixed well below what it would have earned through sale on capitalist markets.[27] Between 1974 and 1979 the average price of Soviet exports to the bloc rose by 80 percent, compared to a rise of only 50 percent for its imports from the bloc, yet in 1979 Soviet oil was still selling at about a 20 percent discount relative to the world price.[28] Michael Marrese and Jan Vanous estimate these implicit trade subsidies totaled about $87 billion (in 1980 dollars) between 1960 and 1980, of which approximately $75.5 billion was transferred in the 1970s.[29]

Through this implicit trade subsidy, combined with explicit credits totaling $4.5 billion in the 1970s, the USSR paid "the economic cost of the political cohesion of the bloc."[30] The strategic nature of the subsidies is clear from the pattern within WPS. The greatest Soviet subsidies went to the German Democratic Republic (GDR), Czechoslovakia, and Poland. East Germany was at once the most militarily exposed of the WPS states and the major source of the USSR's high technology imports. It was also the most loyal Soviet ally, formally leading the denunciations of Czechoslovakia in 1968 and Poland in 1980–81. Czechoslovakia, the second major recipient of Soviet trade subsidies, was another major supplier of consumer goods (including those with Western technology) and an important exporter of goods (including arms) to the West. After the Warsaw Pact military occupation of Czechoslovakia in 1968, repression there was combined with the attempt, supported by Soviet trade subsidies, to increase legitimacy through improved consumption. Poland, the third major recipient and long a source of political tension within the bloc, was a strategic asset whose economic crises prompted frequent challenges to Party rule. Massive infusions of Western credits in the 1970s created extra space for the Solidarity movement. When a military coup replaced Party rule in 1981, Western credits were suspended but Soviet aid increased.[31]

Yet the bloc strategy for WPS foundered on the volatility of Western prices and currencies, which were incorporated into CMEA planning. Even before the energy and money crises, bloc accounting was shifting from rubles to hard currency. In 1970 a bank established to facilitate CMEA trade operated almost from the beginning in hard currencies. Even before 1973 these accounted for more than 70 percent of its transactions; after 1973 they rose to 90 percent. The bank borrowed on Eurocurrency markets and lent to WPS members, in addition to borrowing directly from Western banks. The main WPS project financed by collective CMEA borrowing was the Orenburg pipeline to transport Soviet natural gas to Eastern Europe, and all members except Romania participated. The financial arrangements consisted of a combination of hard-currency loans and barter, in which the outcome for the East European borrowers depended on two factors they could not control: the rate of interest on hard currency, and the barter terms of Soviet oil. Increasingly, Hungarian economists in particular complained that the advantage was going to creditors.[32]

The Fatal Solution in Eastern Europe: The Debt Trap

Despite Soviet subsidies to bloc unity, East European economies were caught in the scissors of deteriorating terms of trade with both the USSR and the West. One blade of the scissors was declining terms of trade with the USSR after 1975. Although it never ceased to subsidize Eastern Europe through a combination of discounted energy prices and guaranteed purchase of goods that were uncompetitive on Western markets, the terms of trade were increasingly advantageous for Soviet energy exports. Hungary was one of the less strategic and less subsidized of the bloc partners. One Hungarian commentator translated the barter arrangements in the following ratio: the number of Hungarian buses that had to be sold to buy a million tons of Soviet oil rose from 800 in 1974 to 2,300 in 1981 and was still rising.[33] The other blade of the scissors was lowered Western demand for East European exports—because of recession in the wake of the oil and monetary crises—which limited hard-currency earnings.

The search for national routes to economic growth led the East European states to redirect trade away from WPS allies and to seek more economic ties with the West, particularly to obtain technologies that would allow their industrial exports to compete in capitalist markets. While the USSR was balancing its hard-currency earnings against the costs of buying off discontent within WPS, the East European countries—in a radical departure from Cold War practices—borrowed the funds made available by Western banks in the 1970s. It was difficult for the Soviets to insist on bloc loyalty, or even to define it, when the USSR was making its own deals with the West. These new relations of trade and borrowing made the boundary between WPS and capitalism more permeable and undermined the material basis of bloc unity.

The monetary and oil crises together created a surplus of petrodollars in the West, which were channeled into official debt. The energy crisis brought about recession in the advanced capitalist countries by shifting revenues from profits of developed country industries to rents of oil-rich states. At the same time, however, it intensified the growth of dollars and thus inflation. Windfall profits from oil exports were deposited in Western banks, making available a mass of investment capital just when recession limited normal investment opportunities in First World industry.

As one innovative strategy for dealing with this situation, Western banks began lending to states—not only in the Third World but also in the Soviet bloc—in excess of any reasonable likelihood of repayment. Western bankers eager to dispose of excess money lent over $12 billion to the six East European members of CMEA between 1974, when petrodollar lending began, and 1979, when the Solidarity crisis erupted in Poland. During the same period combined loans to CMEA banks and the USSR, which could count on hard currency earnings from energy exports to repay, totaled only $5.5 billion. Poland, Hungary, and the GDR each borrowed almost a quarter of the total; Bulgaria, Czechoslovakia, and Romania more or less equally shared the remainder.[34] Until 1979, then, differences among WPS borrowers were less significant than the watershed of massive financial dependency of WPS states on capitalist banks.

Decades of Cold War antagonism made Eurocurrency loans to Eastern Europe more remarkable than comparable loans to Third World states. Western banks justified CMEA loans with the "umbrella theory" of WPS, which expressed a belief that the USSR would cover its satellites and not allow them to default on Western loans. The belief had some basis, as we have seen, in the Soviet use of scarce hard-currency earnings to mollify popular demands in strategic WPS states, particularly Poland. Yet in financial terms, it was not realistic to imagine a Soviet umbrella able to expand indefinitely to cover WPS debt. Without modernization and increasing sales in Western markets, WPS borrowers would not be able to repay principal, which would simply accumulate, as would interest. Inefficient East European economies were unlikely to change rapidly enough to make products competitive in Western markets. Most East European exports were within the ruble market and generated no hard currency. The recession of Western capitalism, which created the loan funds in the first place, limited the ability of Eastern debtors to find buyers in the West.[35] The umbrella theory was abandoned with the Polish Solidarity crisis, which was the first moment in the collapse of the hierarchy of Communist Party–ruled states.

The 1980s: Political Crisis and Debt Crisis in WPS

The collapse of WPS was the culmination of a decade of economic realignments that helped undermine the political institutions of the Soviet bloc. The economic crises following the opening to the West count among the sources of the popular mobilizations that broke the chain of Party rule in WPS. Popular movements grew up in the turbulent conditions created by the merger of internal reforms with external debt in contracting export markets. Western and Soviet responses to debt and political mobilizations sent WPS states onto different paths, but each contributed to the economic and political instability of the bloc.

Official borrowing by most states in the WPS bloc became highly erratic in the

1980s. In the early years of the decade it was absent or virtually so in Poland, Romania, Bulgaria, and Czechoslovakia.[36] The Solidarity crisis in Poland and the technical default of Poland and Romania made it increasingly clear that the USSR would not "extend its financial 'umbrella' to help its allies maintain payments on their debts in order to assure [CMEA] solvency and credibility and to attract further Western credits."[37] Even before the Mexican default initiated the capitalist debt crisis in 1982, Western banks lost confidence in East European debtors, even countries with excellent records such as East Germany and Hungary.[38] The unreliability and then disappearance of Western credits after several years of accumulated debt was disastrous. The responses of Poland and Hungary were opposite but had similar effects on bloc unity.

In the Polish crisis, credits became part of the competitive strategies of both blocs and prefigured the end of economic competition between them. By 1980 Poland was receiving massive credits from East and West alike. In that year the foreign trade bank of the Soviet Union led a consortium of international banks to lend Poland $1.1 billion. In total that year, Poland received $2.5 billion in credits from the USSR alone.[39] Far from stabilizing the Polish economy, however, credits coming from opposite directions contributed to economic instability. Borrowed funds in Poland led to distributional struggles and competitive sectoral alliances between workers and enterprise managers, at the expense of investment.[40] Far from satisfying popular demands for increased consumer goods, credits led to an unsustainable compromise: WPS loyalty was ensured at the expense of its defining feature, Party rule, when a military coup suppressed the Solidarity movement and for the first time removed a ruling Communist Party from power. The military coup d'état in Poland simultaneously challenged the West. Western banks cut off further loans for most of the 1980s and for five years (until 1986) refused Poland's bid to join the International Monetary Fund. Yet weighed against the political motivation to sanction the military regime in Poland, was the economic interest in securing WPS loans.

The longer-term Western strategy was "deployment of the credit gun," beginning in Hungary.[41] In 1981, with barely a ripple of amazement that the USSR would allow a Warsaw Pact ally to accept the discipline of Western creditors, Hungary (and later Romania) joined the International Monetary Fund.[42] Hungary was the only state to receive new loans consistently during the 1980s. The level of lending rose from about $600 million per year between 1980 and 1983 to between $1 billion and $2 billion between 1984 and 1989.[43] In contrast, Romania borrowed virtually nothing during the decade and undertook the unprecedented task of complete repayment of its Western debt, at staggering cost to its economy and the welfare of its people.[44] Whereas Romania avoided the Western credit gun by shooting itself, Hungary accepted the representatives and policies of the IMF as a condition of continuing Western credits.

Peter Bihari argues that the change of political power in Hungary in 1990 was only apparent, since by then those who lost and won power shared a commitment to markets that had already dominated Hungarian politics for a decade. In the early 1980s, he argues, given the constraint of the debt trap, the 1960s and 1970s commitment to reform socialism through markets took a decisive turn toward commitment to profits and other capitalist principles. The reforms that began in 1968 had attempted to combine efficiency with economic democracy, and to compensate by increased social allowances for the losses of security and income which attended market reforms. These attempts did not prevent the stagnation of real incomes, however, and Hungary began to borrow heavily when Western banks made cheap money available in the mid-1970s. By 1979 it was clear that Hungary would not be able to generate the resources to service its debt, and new credits would have to go to debt service rather than to restructuring the economy. Creditors lent just enough from 1980 onwards to prevent collapse.[45]

Beginning in 1981, according to Bihari, creditors gained a direct voice in Hungarian politics: the IMF's representative in Hungary was a leading economic policy official in the Hungarian government and a member of the Central Committee of the Hungarian Communist Party. Further credits were made conditional on a variety of policy, personnel, and institutional changes.[46] Hungary adopted some practices that later came to be associated with IMF and World Bank austerity measures, such as reduction or elimination of consumer subsidies.[47] It permitted private banking, private incorporation of companies, regulations for exchange of stocks and securities, bankruptcy, provisions for unemployment, and other institutions of a capitalist economy. Thus, before the official change of government in 1990, which precipitated the privatization of state enterprises, Hungarian response to its debt dependence was to change political ideology in favor of efficiency and profits, and to exacerbate social distress by extracting social resources to pay foreign creditors. Not surprisingly, the legitimacy of its rulers plummeted.[48]

Although the 1981 coup d'état in Poland had been planned well in advance, two days before the imposition of martial law the Solidarity movement called for a referendum on Warsaw Pact membership and on having multiple political parties in Poland, and it addressed support for free trade unions to other members of WPS—thus confirming Soviet fears of the "Polish disease."[49] At stake was the military alliance and the viability of Party rule in each state. By the end of the decade political discontent culminated in the fall of the Berlin Wall in 1989, followed by the formal dismantling of bloc economic and military institutions, and struggles leading to the abolition of Communist Party rule in Eastern Europe and ultimately in the Soviet Union itself. It is time to inquire why the USSR did not look for economic or military strategies to limit the crisis in the bloc.

The Fatal Solution in the USSR: Trading Oil for Food

The Soviet Union had the advantage, in the peculiar WPS language of the 1970s, with respect to "hard goods"—those that could generate hard currency. While its allies were experiencing economic and political troubles, after 1974 the USSR had the opportunity to use its hard-currency earnings to restructure its domestic economy. Had it done so, it might have been better able to shape reform in Eastern Europe and to realize the anticipated benefits of bloc unity.[50] But not until the beginning of *perestroika* in 1984 was too little attempted too late. Instead, the USSR made fatal decisions to use its hard currency to increase consumption rather than to modernize production. In addition to its inability to counter the centrifugal pulls on bloc allies, the USSR became dependent on imports from the West, most significantly on grain and soybeans for animal feeds.

Under Leonid Brezhnev the Soviet state made a fatal choice to use oil revenues to finance increased consumption. At one level, larger imports of Western consumer goods sold in special shops increased the numbers of those with the special privileges of the ruling elite, which may have corroded the legitimacy of a regime proclaiming egalitarian principles.[51] At the same time, imports of feedstuffs were used to mollify popular demands for greater consumption of meat.

Stemming from the Soviet Union's history as a major grain exporter, one of its CMEA obligations was to supply grain to Eastern Europe. Although the USSR was a net importer of agricultural products within WPS, those imports consisted of fruits and vegetables (mainly from Bulgaria), meat (from Hungary), and wine (from both), while it was obliged to export grain. Even though food prices were fixed lower than oil prices, in hard-currency terms this was a further subsidy to the bloc.[52] To compound the problem, when the USSR had shortfalls in domestic grain production, it used hard currency imports to meet WPS deliveries.[53]

With both domestic and bloc obligations, the USSR was caught in the vise between stagnant domestic productivity and hard-currency imports. Even though the individual state and collective farms had more success than is sometimes recognized, Stalinist collectivization left a legacy of chronic agricultural stagnation.[54] Agriculture's role under Stalin had been to supply resources for rapid industrialization without receiving investment, technical support, or incentives to increase productivity. Khrushchev had attempted to change the situation through a combination of opening new lands, allowing private production (which worked to some extent), and improving the technical conditions of production (which did not work very well). Subsequent regimes continued to prioritize agriculture, but never corrected its deep problems.[55]

It is conceivable that agriculture could have been improved, as it was in Hungary in the 1970s. There the agrarian lobby successfully pressed for foreign exchange to import machinery and chemicals in order to reconstruct agriculture along U.S. technical lines. In a virtuous circle, agricultural exports became "hard goods," generating foreign exchange to pay for inputs to increase productivity. Hungary achieved a completely new and highly successful social structure in the rural cooperatives, which combined private and public ownership and large- and small-scale production units.[56] Although that success was not extended to industry, the reform of Hungarian agriculture and the example of its food supply might usefully have informed Soviet policy.

By importing feedstuffs, the USSR fell into a grain trap parallel to the East European debt trap.[57] The extraordinary grain deals that were part of detente between the United States and the Soviet Union coincided with the first year of the energy crisis. In 1972 the USSR increased its grain and soy imports from 8.3 to 22.8 million tons. In 1975 the United States and the Soviet Union entered into the first of several long-term agreements that kept trade high in the 1970s and 1980s.[58] When energy prices collapsed in the 1980s however, just as soaring interest rates were closing in on WPS debtors, Soviet hard-currency earnings plummeted.[59] For its own reasons, the United States was compelled to sustain exports to the collapsed Soviet market, which had become the second largest in the world. It did so through credit guarantees and export subsidies originally designed as food aid to Third World countries.[60] Until its collapse in 1991, and even afterward, the former Soviet Union was simultaneously a military superpower and a recipient of food aid from the West.

Pyrrhic Victory: Socialist Collapse and Capitalist Instability

If capitalist energy and monetary crises contributed to socialist economic instability, the Soviet Union returned the favor by precipitating a capitalist food crisis. The Soviet-American grain deals threw world food markets into a confusion from which they have never recovered. Soviet purchases removed so much grain from world commerce that the chronic surpluses—which had weighed on farmers and governments for decades—suddenly disappeared, and skyrocketing prices threatened the world's poor with starvation. Although the scarcity was temporary, food markets remained chaotic. The return of surpluses simply meant more intense export competition, verging on trade wars, in the 1980s. The conflicts that emerged between the United States and the European Community, and the United States and Japan, continued to be played out until the prolonged Uruguay Round of the General Agreement on Tariffs and Trade (GATT) was finally concluded in December 1993. There is reason to doubt that deregulation of national agricultural policies agreed to in the GATT will stabilize the world food economy, even with the progressive lowering of trade barriers under the new World Trade Organization.[61]

There was also a connection between Western monetary crises and the bloc structure of the postwar order. The Bretton Woods monetary rules, which were in effect until 1968, fixed the ratio of the U.S. dollar to gold and the ratio of other currencies to the dollar. In the absence of a central world bank and world currency, the dollar became world currency and the U.S. Federal Reserve the de facto central bank. This created a tension between America's national interest and its responsibility as regulator of the international currency. As long as the U.S. balance of payments was positive, based on its relative economic strength, this tension was not a problem. But during the 1960s the U.S. trade balance deteriorated, and during the same period trade between Western Europe and Eastern Europe tripled—culminating in the West German policy of Ostpolitik, or opening to the East. In 1969 the United States changed its laws prohibiting trade with communist countries, responding to and opening the way for a policy of economic and political detente.[62]

In 1971 the United States unilaterally suspended gold convertibility. A crisis of the dollar, marked by inflation and by the reluctance of the West German government in particular to support the dollar, precipitated this dramatic change in the rules and cooperative practices of international monetary relations.[63] Although specific U.S. policies exacerbated the situation, the problem lay in the unregulated European market in dollars which had mushroomed in the 1960s.

Ironically, the origins of the Eurodollar market were the dollars owned by the USSR and China and deposited in West European banks during the late 1940s and 1950s because of fear that deposits in U.S. banks would be confiscated. The shortage of dollars in Europe encouraged bankers to accept the deposits, and London bankers created Eurodollars as the first offshore currency. Regulation was understandably confused, as there was little precedent for how states might regulate their currencies outside their territories.[64]

The series of oil crises that began in 1972 diverted a jolting proportion of the capitalist world's liquidity toward the oil exporting states—including the Soviet Union. The OPEC countries "recycled" their oil earnings through U.S. and European banks. The net result was a shift of investment capital away from industry and into banks. Thus, at the same moment that the dollar ceased to function according to the old rules, the normal outlets for bank capital shrank with the oil-induced recession. Eurocurrency markets exploded. Banks sought borrowers wherever they could find them—including Eastern Europe.

The search by Western capitalists for markets, energy, and official borrowers in WPS ultimately increased the instability of the capitalist economy. Energy prices continued to be volatile, and the politics of oil continued to be a source of international conflict. The debt crisis, which was officially inaugurated by the default of the Mexican government in 1982, had been preceded by a game of mirrors surrounding Western bankers' perceptions of the solvency of debtor states in Eastern Europe. A new caution overtook Western financial institutions in the 1980s, along with a deepened awareness of the political basis of official debt. The imposition of capitalist banking criteria led to a drop in both East European and Third World manufactured imports from the West.[65]

The stake of Western capitalists in economic openings to the East was reinforced by competitive rifts within the Atlantic alliance. Economic ties across blocs in the 1970s and 1980s, therefore, expressed the relative economic decline of *both* superpowers, the United States no less than the Soviet Union. For all their shared obsession with industrial might, both superpowers intensified their exports of raw materials as a response to national economic difficulties. The United States pursued "Green Power" through agricultural exports,[66] and the Soviet Union sought foreign exchange through energy exports. The export imperative in both cases overrode the superpower interest in bloc unity. Trade in energy and agriculture became major links across blocs—and major sources of tension within blocs.[67]

Conclusion

Existing socialism, I have argued, foundered when the tension between national and bloc organization shifted because of irreversible ties to Western money, energy, and food markets. The Communist Party of the Soviet Union compromised its responsibility to the bloc in favor of its national interest in hard-currency earnings. The Communist Party of each of the Eastern European countries struck out on its own in Western capital markets. The bloc could not hold, and neither could the economies and ruling parties within it.

Parallel tensions can be said to have existed in actually existing capitalism. In the late 1960s the United States compromised its role as de facto regulator of the international economy when the Bretton Woods rules ceased working to the United States national advantage. The United States refused its obligations as linchpin of the system rather than negotiate new monetary rules. For its part, the European Community allowed private bank lending to Eastern Europe and turned to the Soviet Union for cheap, reliable sources of energy. The United States then played its next trump card in Atlantic economic competition through aggressive food export policies. Energy, money, and food provided the motivation and the means for competitive U.S. and European overtures to the East.

The blocs also differed in the weights between national states and bloc unity. I agree with Kaldor's argument (Chapter 9 in this volume) that antagonistic military blocs mutually defined the spaces of capitalism and socialism. The economic integration of the capitalist bloc was considerably greater than that of the socialist bloc; however, whereas Stalinist autarky never succumbed to attempts at bloc-wide planning in WPS, integration of North American and European economies proceeded very far through sectoral reorganization by private transnational corporations.[68]

The collapse of Warsaw Pact Socialism, then, marked the end of Atlantic capitalism, a particular phase of capitalist history, which was organized not only by U.S. hegemony but also by the bloc structure of the Cold War. I hope in this essay to have shown how the logic of the bloc system fatally played itself out in the East. Rivalries in the Atlantic bloc have so far been contained by deep economic integration, but as Kaldor says, the political disintegration of Eastern Europe cautions against complacency.

Notes

Acknowledgment: I thank Robert Albritton, Barry O'Neill, and participants at a seminar in the Department of Political Science, Yale University, for helpful suggestions in revising an earlier draft. Allen Hunter's editorial assistance was invaluable in clarifying and restructuring the essay. Yildiz Atasoy provided research assistance.

1. For the methodological approach, see Philip McMichael, "Incorporated Comparison within a World-Historical Perspective: An Alternative Comparative Method," *American Sociological Review* 55 (June 1990): 385–97.

2. The practice shifted from unilateral Soviet intervention in Hungary in 1956 in the name of "socialist internationalism," to Warsaw Pact intervention in Czechoslovakia in 1968 under the rubric

of the "Brezhnev Doctrine," to encouragement of the national military coup in Poland in 1981. See Charles Gati, *The Bloc That Failed: Soviet-East European Relations in Transition* (Bloomington: Indiana University Press, 1990), 39–55.

3. Charles Tilly, *Coercion, Capital and European States, AD 990–1990* (Cambridge, Mass.: Basil Blackwell, 1990), 187.

4. A. V. Chayanov, *The Theory of Peasant Economy* (Homewood, Ill.: American Economic Association, 1966).

5. Fernando Claudin, *The Communist Movement: From Comintern to Cominform* (Harmondsworth, Eng: Penguin Books, 1975).

6. Joan Sokolovsky, *Peasants and Power* (Boulder, Colo.: Westview Press, 1990).

7. Ivan Berend, "The Problem of Eastern European Economic Integration in a Historical Perspective," in *Foreign Trade in a Planned Economy*, ed. Imre Vajda and Mihaly Simai (Cambridge: Cambridge University Press, 1971), 18.

8. Andrzej Korbonski, foreword to Michael Marrese and Jan Vanous, *Soviet Subsidization of Trade with Eastern Europe* (Berkeley: University of California Institute of International Studies, 1983), xii–xiii.

9. United Nations *Economic Bulletin for Europe* 37 (1985): 3.4.

10. Albert O. Hirschman, *National Power and the Structure of Foreign Trade* (Berkeley: University of California Press, 1945).

11. Cited in Claudin, *Communist Movement,* 596.

12. Berend, "Problem of Eastern European Economic Integration," 9.

13. Ibid., 15.

14. United Nations *Economic Bulletin for Europe* 37 (1985): 3.5.

15. Fred Halliday, *The Making of the Second Cold War* (London: Verso, 1986), 5.

16. Françoise Lemoine, *Le COMECON* (Paris: Presses Universitaires de France, 1982), 31.

17. Wlodzimierz Brus, "Evolution of the Communist Economic System: Scope and Limits," in *Remaking the Economic Institutions of Socialism,* ed. Victor Nee and David Stark (Stanford, Calif.: Stanford University Press, 1989).

18. Sokolovsky, *Peasants and Power.*

19. David Stark and Victor Nee, "Toward an Institutional Analysis of State Socialism," and Ivan Szelenyi, "Eastern Europe in an Epoch of Transition: Toward a Socialist Mixed Economy?" both in Nee and Stark, *Remaking the Economic Institutions of Socialism,* 9–13, 211–13.

20. Walter D. Connor, "Imperial Dilemmas: Soviet Interests and Economic Reform," in Nee and Stark, *Remaking the Economic Institutions of Socialism,* 308–9.

21. Korbonski, foreword, xiii.

22. Lemoine, *Le COMECON,* 46–50.

23. Gati, *Bloc That Failed,* 119.

24. John van Oudenaren, *Detente in Europe: The Soviet Union and the West since 1953* (Durham, N.C.: Duke University Press, 1991), 260–61.

25. Ibid., 264–66.

26. Charles Zorgbibe, *Le Monde depuis 1945* (Paris: Presses Universitaires de France, 1982), 122–26; Lemoine, *Le COMECON.*

27. Marrese and Vanous, *Soviet Subsidization of Trade.* The criticisms of Marrese and Vanous's findings are not about the fact of the subsidy but about the degree and the interpretation. See Gati, *The Bloc That Failed,* 119–24.

28. Lemoine, *Le COMECON*, 46–50.

29. Marrese and Vanous, *Soviet Subsidization of Trade*, 3.

30. Lemoine, *Le COMECON*, 55.

31. Marrese and Vanous, *Soviet Subsidization of Trade;* Korbonski, foreword, xix–xxii.

32. Lemoine, *Le COMECON*, 94.

33. Cited in Connor, "Imperial Dilemmas," 323.

34. Organization for Economic Cooperation and Development (OECD), *Financial Market Trends* 45 (February 1990): 32.

35. Peter Bihari, "Reflections on Hungary's Social Revolution," in *Communist Regimes: The Aftermath, Socialist Register 1991*, ed. Ralph Miliband and Leo Panitch, (London: Merlin Press, 1991), 284.

36. OECD, *Financial Market Trends* 45, (February 1990): 32.

37. Korbonski, foreword, xxv.

38. Ibid., xxv.

39. Lemoine, *Le COMECON*, 97.

40. Charles Sabel and David Stark, "Planning, Politics, and Shop-Floor Power: Hidden Forms of Bargaining in Soviet-Imposed State-Socialist Societies," *Politics and Society* 11, no. 4 (1982): 468–73.

41. These are the words of Bihari, "Reflections," 284.

42. Joyce Kolko, *Restructuring the World Economy* (New York: Pantheon Books, 1988), 281.

43. OECD, *Financial Market Trends* 45 (February 1990): 32.

44. Gati, *Bloc That Failed*, 112–13.

45. Bihari, "Reflections" 283–84. See also Kolko, *Restructuring*, 286–89.

46. Bihari, "Reflections," 284–85, 299 n. 5.

47. Kolko, Restructuring, 285.

48. Bihari, "Reflections," 294–85, 299, n. 5.

49. Gati, *Bloc That Failed*, 50–51.

50. A Hungarian colleague asked me rhetorically in 1984, "Would you rather analyze data on an IBM or a Soviet computer?"

51. Halliday, *Making of the Second Cold War*, 134–71, calls the changes during this period an "involution." The Soviet waste and corruption due to oil revenues bear comparison to those in some Third World countries, such as Nigeria. See Gunilla Andrae and Bjorn Beckman, *The Wheat Trap: Bread and Underdevelopment in Nigeria* (London: Zed Books, 1985), 90–91.

52. Lemoine, *Le COMECON*, 49.

53. Ibid., 66.

54. Zhores A. Medvedev, *Soviet Agriculture* (New York: Norton, 1987), 384: "Soviet industry certainly has many problems, but they are neither as deep nor as serious as the problems in agriculture." For comprehensive, objective evaluations of most countries, see the chapters in "Pathways from Collectivism: Reform and Revolution in the Socialist and Post-Communist Agrarian Systems," ed. Ivan Szelenyi (manuscript).

55. Karl-Eugen Wadekin, *Communist Agriculture: Farming in the Soviet Union and Eastern Europe* (London: Routledge, 1990).

56. Nigel Swain, *Collective Farms Which Work?* (Cambridge: Cambridge University Press, 1985).

57. Cf. Andrae and Beckman, *The Wheat Trap*.

58. Medvedev, *Soviet Agriculture*, 391.

59. Van Oudenaren, *Detente in Europe*, 273.

60. Harriet Friedmann, "The Political Economy of Food: A Global Crisis," *New Left Review* 197 (January–February 1993): 42.

61. The "food crisis" created a huge literature and much political activity during the mid-1970s. Soviet purchases were usually included in a list of conjunctural factors such as weather and the failure of the Peruvian anchovy harvest. The idea of crisis lost currency when surpluses returned in the late 1970s; however, the structures that had underpinned the world food economy in the 1950s and 1960s were never rebuilt or replaced. See Friedmann, "Political Economy of Food."

62. Kees van der Pijl, *The Making of an Atlantic Ruling Class* (London: Verso, 1984), 256.

63. Ibid.

64. Jeffry A. Frieden, *Banking on the World: The Politics of International Finance* (Oxford: Basil Blackwell, 1989), 81.

65. Gati, *Bloc That Failed,* 117.

66. Alain Revel and Christophe Riboud, *American Green Power* (Baltimore, Md.: Johns Hopkins University Press, 1986).

67. Friedmann, "Political Economy of Food."

68. My understanding of Atlantic capitalism is largely based on van der Pijl, *Making of an Atlantic Ruling Class.*

Chapter 11

After the Cold War: International Relations in the Period of the Latest "New World Order"

Ronen Palan

The conclusion of the Cold War was instantly proclaimed as a great historical event. The image of the dawning of a "new world order," promulgated by Mikhail Gorbachev and eagerly adopted by George Bush, appeared to have captured the new direction of American foreign policy. To some, such as Francis Fukuyama, the collapse of the Soviet Union seemed to have removed the last serious obstacle to a universal liberal peace. Others, however, point to some alarming trends that may destroy this great vision of world peace and prosperity. Ironically, as the debate on the new world order progressed, it became apparent that some crucial dynamics of the Pax Americana era, important for the emergence of a new global order, were not defined by the bipolar politics of the Cold War. Indeed, if anything, the relaxation in the military sphere that was brought about by the collapse of the Soviet Union merely served to reveal some longstanding underlying tensions among the three capitalist centers: the United States, the European Community

(EC), and Japan. For those who thought that the military and ideological battle be-tween the United States and the Soviet Union was the central feature of the post-war international political order, these tensions appear to pose a new and danger-ous threat to world stability. But there is nothing new to these tensions, nor is there evidence that the end of the Cold War has in any way dramatically exacerbated their impact.

In this essay, therefore, I shift focus from the Cold War to other features of the postwar interstate system that are shaping the international arena. I take a differ-ent view from that of theorists who stress the system-destabilizing effects of the end of the Cold War. On the one hand, certain destabilizing tendencies were intrinsic to the Pax Americana itself, even without the Soviet withdrawal from the Cold War and the dissolution of the USSR. On the other hand, the power vacuum created by the USSR's collapse may even be an incentive for accommodations between major capitalist states.

My theoretical approach to the post–World War II era decenters the Cold War because I focus on the interactions between politics and economics in the inter-national system, whereas most theories of the Cold War tend to focus on poli-tics. From the perspective of International Political Economy, the Cold War may be understood not as the core of a system but as part of a larger set of structures and dynamics. However important the nuclear arms race, in the end it was the combination of economic and political crises in the Soviet system that led to the close of the Cold War and the creation of the political and ideological space in which discussions of a new world order have taken place. The history of the Cold War bears a different relationship to the post–Cold War era from this perspec-tive than it does in a view of the Cold War as the defining variable of the past half-century.

Like Mary Kaldor in this volume, I place the stress not on U.S. foreign policy but on the problematic of order in the context of modern capitalism. The Pax Ameri-cana was successful, I argue, because it represented a historically specific configu-ration by which the United States was able to integrate the world market within a system of states. But although the United States clearly played a significant role in this order, it was less its foreign policies than what Susan Strange has called its "structural power," its structural position in the world system and the world econ-omy, that produced what I would describe as centripetal tendencies at the capital-ist core.[1] The current main sources of instability are structural changes within the United States itself. In context of the Pax Americana, domestic restructuring amounts, in effect, to a restructuring of the entire world economy. Here, I would, argue, lies the key to the new world order.

Theories of Transnational Order

Analyses and predictions of the fate of the newest of all world orders, like those of any other social event, are grounded in historical analysis. Two opposing opinions, each boasting left and right variants, dominated the debate in the early 1990s.

First, the realist theory of international relations describes international politics as the struggle for power among selfish states. It views the Cold War as a repetition of the age-old pattern of great powers in competition, and sees the collapse of the Soviet Union as creating a dangerous power vacuum that may well lead to a period of instability. Indeed, strategists and international relations theorists alike have already depicted the Cold War as the golden age of social and political stability. The nostalgic yearning for a return to its perilous stability indicates a genuine fear of an imminent breakdown in the capitalist core and an era of political instability that may ultimately result in the breakdown of the world market. The left version of this argument is represented by the Leninist thesis about the inevitability of conflict among the key capitalist states. This critique doubts that any capitalist accommodation is possible in a new world order.

The second and contrary theory holds that the age-old pattern described above has been superseded through the agency of the Pax Americana. Globalization of the markets and the attendant growing interdependence among nations, so the argument goes, have rendered a new Cold War involving Europe, Japan, and the United States highly unlikely simply because it would be an irrational and uneconomical form of behavior. Trade frictions apart, there is no particular reason for the Western allies to break ranks. The new world order signifies, therefore, a new institutional arrangement among core capitalist countries. Oddly enough, a similar thesis was proposed seventy years ago by Karl Kautsky and Nicholai Bukharin, who believed that the globalization of capital would lead toward the establishment of supranational agencies of coercion, a system they termed "superimperialism." Perhaps it pushes the point, but the new world order may be understood as the flagship concept for such an entente.

Both opinions, however, are essentialist: Each is predicated upon a separation between politics and economics. The realist and interdependence theories depict international politics as an autonomous system whose dynamics evolve irrespective of socioeconomic forces. Any fundamental disagreements between the two schools concern the critical aspects of politics. For realists, short-term calculations are the ultimate cause of political action; hence, they argue, stability is attainable only under the auspices of a strong dominant power. For the interdependence school, self-interest is the key to politics, and since it is in the self-interest of states to maintain cooperation, they will likely abide by the rules of the new world order. Similarly, the imperialism versus superimperialism debate collapses into one of politics versus economics. Essentially, the debate is whether the requirements of an ever transnationalizing capital for a spatially overlapping political superstructure override the egotistic tendencies of capitalists.

Elsewhere I have argued that a relatively new approach, which I call "neostructuralism," offers a more sophisticated line of analysis.[2] From a neostructuralist perspective it is perfectly acceptable to represent a given historical situation as if it were patterned and ordered. But such patterns, which I call "transnational orders," are conceived essentially as emerging orders—totalizing but never a totality, to use Sartrean language. Such orders can be thought of as "systems" because they come into being through the interrelation of a number of social components—institutions, organizations, norms, and values—which form a "whole" that is different from the sum of its parts. It is sometimes described as the system of "embedded liberalism," or the Pax Americana. But contrary to common systemic social science theories, I would argue that such "wholes," or transnational orders, are rooted in alliances of identifiable material interests: that is, they represent constellations of interests.[3]

This kind of systemic perception has a number of implications. First, although transnational orders represent material interests, they are founded in an interrelationship between social institutions, values, power, and interests. They are therefore "relatively autonomous," to use Nicos Poulantzas's notion: not tied to any one institution or value. I argue, therefore, that the Pax Americana is relatively autonomous; it cannot be simply reduced to the activities of the American state.

Second, since transnational orders reflect alliances of interests, they are by definition conflict-ridden, and tension is intrinsic to them. Tensions and contradictions may be harmful, but they generate energy and vitality in the system; they are important positive forces of change. In discussing the latest phase of the Pax Americana, therefore, I would try to broaden, the agenda beyond the immediate concern with social, political, or economic collapse and to discuss the nature of change as it is produced in a transnational context.

Tensions and conflicts in a *pax*, or imposed peace, may take a variety of forms. The conflict may appear to be taking place outside the system—say, between capitalism and communism, as during the Cold War. But historically, intra-*pax* contradictions have expressed themselves in a variety of ways. H. R. Trevor-Roper, who described the Habsburg empires as the Pax Hispanica, interprets the Dutch revolt in the sixteenth century as an instance of trans-European class struggle between the old landed gentry, represented by the Hapsburg Crown, and an emergent bourgeoisie. Not surprisingly, these tensions exploded into open conflict where trading and manufacturing were in advanced stage.[4]

Violence, conflict, and political tensions may therefore be indicative of deeper disagreements and contradictions. But there is no necessary immediate correlation between the form a conflict takes and its underlying causes. Quite often the form of the tension is subsumed in ideological representations that serve certain purposes within the bounds of each of these orders. All this is to argue that one needs to examine critically events as they unfold and perhaps question the true significance of what appears to many to be growing conflict within the emerging triad of the United States (North American Free Trade Agreement or, NAFTA), the European Union and East Asia.

The third implication of such a systemic approach is that international organizations are forms whereby alliances of interests institutionalize their gains in bilateral and multilateral international arrangements. But once in place, the forces represented in a given transnational order experience great difficulties when they wish to transcend or discard the alliance's arrangements; they cannot simply use the institutions of the state, the United Nations, or the International Monetary Fund (IMF) in a cynical and unimpeded way for their own parochial goals (though not for want of trying). The institutions themselves take on a life of their own and become another "relatively autonomous" aspect of a given order.

To make sense of such complicated and ever changing relationships, it is useful to think of a transnational order as a nexus of centripetal and centrifugal tendencies. Centripetal tendencies are broadly conceived in support of the order; centrifugal tendencies are broadly representative of opposing interests. The centripetal tendencies are held together primarily by material interests; in the case of the Pax Americana, the spectacular growth of international trade and foreign direct investment represent a considerable vested interest in the current order. But a transnational order is also supported by a hegemonic project, a universalizing ideology that links its disparate components.[5]

The Pax Americana as a Set of Interrelating Processes

By the end of World War II the United States was uniquely positioned in world affairs. It was the richest country on earth: its gross national product soared above half of gross world production; its currency, the dollar, had become the accepted global currency; it had the sole possession of nuclear weapons; and its two former adversaries, Germany and Japan, were under its direct control. Simultaneously, the war resolved, if only temporarily, the ongoing contest in the United States between a constellation of socioeconomic interests commonly labeled isolationist, and another constellation which is designated (in the American context) universalist. Resolution in favor of the latter, plus wealth, conferred upon the United States the ability to pursue an active and effective foreign policy designed to recast the entire globe in its own image.

The Roosevelt and Truman administrations appear to have achieved a measure of cohesion in their vision of the goals of American postwar foreign policy: expand the world market under a free trade regime, and peace and prosperity would follow; conversely, if free trade should fail and the system of blocs persist, the world would be bound to descend into another and possibly greater calamity. As Cordell Hull once expressed it, "To me unhampered trade dovetailed with peace; high tariffs, trade barriers, and unfair economic competition, with war."[6] These assumptions forged a potentially powerful link between economic foreign policy, strategy, and ethics. The world market was good for American business, no doubt, but the world market was a prerequisite for peace and stability as well; hence, U.S. foreign policy goals were equated with the well-being of the entire world. With the establishment of a global market as their ultimate goal, American policymakers strove to create an international institutional structure predisposed toward business interests. Significantly aided by their allies, they proved successful in implementing their broad vision of a liberal international order. This transnational order, the "whole" whose basics were laid down in laborious negotiations at San Francisco and Bretton Woods, turned out to possess three distinctive characteristics.

First, it was grounded in the principles of free trade. The lowering of tariffs and the progressive removal of restrictions on trade, investment, and capital stimulated the globalization of the world economy and led gradually to a blurring of the distinction between the national and the world economy. Free trade implied, therefore, a commitment by the key capitalist states to the transnationalization of their own and other societies' economies, possibly with the eventual outcome of subordinating national economies to the world market. These principles were written into the Bretton Woods agreement and the General Agreement on Tariffs and Trade (GATT) and also into the charter of NATO.

Second, for historical as well as practical reasons, the transnationalization of the economy had to be accommodated by the existing system of states. Indeed, the system itself seems to have gained a new lease on life with the commitment, written into the UN charter, to sovereignty, equality and the right to self-determination.

Third, the underlying "corporatist-liberal" social bargain, as Kees van der Pijl called it, which underpinned America's commitment and that of its allies placed heavy stress on the state as the regulator of social and economic activity.[7] Thus, the Pax Americana brought about a widespread and massive increase in state intervention. As a result, the transnationalization of the world economy took place hand in hand with the expansion of national planning.

Whether alternative and better solutions were feasible or attainable at the time is a contentious question, but the solution arrived at was conflictual because it asserted the responsibility of each nation to the "community of nations" and yet affirmed the primacy of domestic interests. This paradox is seen nowhere better than in the Bretton Woods accord itself. As Richard Cooper notes, (though without, it seems to me, following his argument to its conclusion), "The Bretton Woods agreement asserted the primacy of domestic economic policy aimed at the maintenance of full employment and at the same time established the responsibility of each nation to the community of nations in the realm of international financial policy."[8] Given such a contradiction, conflict could be averted only if states were willing to exercise a considerable degree of what Henry Aubrey calls "discipline"—something, he suggests, they either lacked or, alternatively, hotly debated the exact meaning of.[9] Not surprisingly, "the discussion [at Bretton Woods] revolved around the degree of autonomy countries should be permitted in pursuit of domestic economic policy."[10] The accord required a delicate balancing act, as governments were supposed to adopt policies promoting welfare and growth and yet subordinate these, when necessary, to the broader principles of the Bretton Woods system.

The inherent contradictions in the Bretton Woods agreement merely reflected the broader theme of the disjunction between politics and economics. The architects of the postwar order were naturally cognizant of these difficulties. They were aware that a transnational economy required a concomitant, overlapping transnational politico-juridical system so that contracts would be honored, trade routes protected, foreign investment secured, and so on. They were also keenly aware of the potentially disruptive influence of states that would try to gain "unfair" advantages from the system. Hence, they devised measures, some more formal than others, to establish an operative, coherent, globally encompassing political superstructure.

First, although it is very difficult to prove the point, it appears that the key capitalist states went ahead with the implicit understanding that the transnationalization of the economy was destined to generate worldwide socioeconomic forces (that is, social classes) in support of free trade, and the "invisible hand" of the world market would generate positive effects in the new global arrangement.

The World Bank, the IMF and later on a variety of aid programs were intended to integrate Third World states into the world economy by furnishing them with adequate means for "development," which inevitably would take the form of the evolution of social classes and political interests favoring their countries' integration into the world economy.

Second, it was understood from the outset that the key capitalist countries were to undertake concerted measures to circumvent the worst excesses of a potentially anarchic international system of states. In an entente among the wartime allies, the Soviet Union, Britain, and the United States were supposed to share, through the UN, the burden of running the capitalist world economy. The UN was viewed from the outset as a club, a meeting place of states that shared certain "ideals." The UN, particularly the Security Council, was supposed to be the linchpin of a complex and intricate system of rituals by which capitalist countries sought to create a globally encompassing political superstructure. Thus, the concepts of sovereignty and self-determination were viewed as relative values, their precise definitions to be determined by the play of forces in international politics.

Third, the United States took upon itself the role of guardian of the emerging *pax*. It is important to appreciate that U.S. foreign policy was founded on a clear distinction between acceptable and unacceptable uses of violence. American commentators understand very well when (and why) the United States resorted to policies potentially damaging to its allies. Under the rubrics of "competition" and "restructuring," however, such policies had to be carried out peacefully, to remain in the realm of economic competition and not spill over into a military show of force. The enormous firepower of the United States was reserved for what American policymakers deemed to be "universal" goals: to guard and maintain trade routes, strategic raw materials, and regimes that were friendly to the trading system. America's military might was not used, therefore, simply to project and enhance America's "national interests" wherever such interests were thought to be under threat (as opposed to the covert activities of the CIA, which apparently were employed more liberally). Nor did U.S. military power evolve simply in response to a real or imagined Soviet threat. On the contrary, the Soviet threat was perceived as one of many challenges to the liberal trading system. The different between "core" and "periphery" thus ceased to be an abstraction. Although violence had become an unacceptable instrument for settling disputes among the key capitalist countries, force was liberally applied in the Third World in the name of the "free world." This fine distinction still holds today.

To summarize, the Pax Americana as a form of transnational order had an integral logic. There was a certain homology in the construction of centripetal tendencies that held the order together on a number of levels: international, national, and institutional. A growing world market was supposed to create transnational class structures in support of the system; the system of states was the primary vehicle for maintaining order; and American military and economic power was deployed to provide discreet but critical backing to the system. In retrospect, it appears that the system replicated its contradictions at each and every level and was, as a result, riddled with tension.

Contradictions of the Pax Americana

The Contradictions of American Hegemony. Conventional wisdom holds that a state's foreign policy either springs from its geopolitical position—that is, from its so-called national interest—or is guided by class or group interests. Furthermore, whatever the ultimate origins of a given policy, its successful application is contingent on the power and capabilities of the state in question. Yet the role of the United States in the formation and maintenance of the Pax Americana cannot be reduced to either of these alternatives.

Revisionists such as William Appleman Williams and Joyce and Gabriel Kolko have demonstrated the extent to which American commitment to the Pax Americana was tentative from the outset.[11] They have shown that far from responding to some abstract national interest, that commitment was grounded in a specific alliance of universalists with global interests that were challenged, off and on, by isolationists with more parochial or nationally based interests. This is significant on several accounts.

To begin with, there is a tendency, particularly in Marxist writings, to identify American foreign policy with the broader requirements of "capitalism" in its imperialist phase. This identification is accurate only up to a point. Countless detailed studies of American foreign policy have shown that the United States never achieved, nor was it ever capable of achieving, the singularity of purpose that commonly characterizes "imperial" states. As Bertram Gross puts it, "If this [the American state] be empire, it is very different from . . . any previous empire," for "U.S. imperial control is exercised not by American government and colonists, but by less direct methods." Moreover, "the local capitalists have [often] supplanted the old landowning oligarchies in trying to cooperate with, rather than break with, foreign capital. Instead of 'ugly Americans' and Europeans meddling in their affairs, many Third World regimes are increasingly manned by Americanized Brazilians,

Anglicized Indians and Nigerians, and Westernized Saudi Arabians and Egyptians.
. . . In fact, external controls are now internalized in domestic institutions, and the
new infrastructure may be more powerful than any previous colonial apparatus."[12]

But even though informal external controls operating via the world capitalist
market were internalized, it is equally significant that formal policies of control
were often incoherent. U.S. foreign policy, while preaching the gospel of universalism, was caught up in an internal struggle among various interests, making policy coherence hard to maintain and resulting in periodic flirtations with parochial-
ism. This created the perception of decline among America's allies, causing
instability in the world order. But much of the instability, as David Calleo has
demonstrated, was due to the fact that in the American political system, narrow
economic interests can considerably affect foreign policy formulation.[13] The internal battles that plagued successive administrations produced inconsistent, if not
outright contradictory, domestic and foreign policies that attempted to strengthen
and deepen the institutions of Bretton Woods and the NATO alliance, and yet tried
at the same time to shield itself from the very transnational structure they were
aiming to strengthen. The contradictions of U.S. policy were at the root of the collapse of the Bretton Woods system in 1971 and the subsequent growing suspicion
of American intentions among other member governments of the Organization
for Economic Cooperation and Development (OECD).

Because domestic instability and policy incoherence are mistaken for decline, an
attendant misperception represents a golden age when the United States was at the
height of its power and supposedly able to impose its will upon its allies—whereas
in fact a growing International Political Economy revisionist literature questions
the success of American foreign policy in the narrow economic field even in the
1950s and 1960s. David Wightman, for instance, maintains that because of American provincialism, American academics rarely bothered with European documents and as a result tended to exaggerate U.S. foreign policy successes.[14] Susan
Strange has pointed out the extent of European and Japanese resistance to American demands.[15] Kendall Stiles argues convincingly that U.S. goals were consistently compromised by GATT and in other international arenas.[16] Both the hegemony and the stability of the United States, let alone the "hegemonic stability" that
it was supposed to confer on the international system, are open to serious debate.

Given the hesitant nature of the American commitment to the Pax Americana,
the transnational liberal order has been seriously challenged from the very core,
from the American state. The challenge has taken two forms. First and predomi-
nantly, unilateral and yet inconsistent policies pursued by the American state have
increased instability and generated suspicion among its allies. Second, it is not

inconceivable, although at present rather unlikely, that the United States may withdraw altogether its support for the transnational arm of the Pax Americana.

The Contradictions of Sovereignty. In focusing solely on policy processes within the ambit of the American state, one risks losing sight of wider constraining factors. In pursuing contradictory aims the United States behaved rather like many other states that were trying to come to grips with the global market. Indeed, the founding of the Pax Americana led to a series of unavoidable contradictions which, to a considerable extent, U.S. policies expressed and which most critiques of American foreign and domestic policies, correct as they may be, tend to overlook.

Like every other social phenomenon, sovereignty is a multifaceted concept and serves several, sometimes conflicting, purposes concomitantly. As a political method of social control, sovereignty is not and never has been absolute. By the middle of the twentieth century it was clear that empires were becoming too expensive to maintain, and that the function of preserving "order" was better delegated to local elites. Decolonization, therefore, did not signify the withdrawal of Western powers from what was later described as the Third World so much as it indicated the development of a new form of globally encompassing political order. This globally encompassing order modified the relationships both within the capitalist core and between the capitalist core and the Third World.

With the establishment of a global liberal order, the concept of sovereignty became the cornerstone of modern political theory. International law views states as legal subjects possessing rights and duties. Since most commentators in international relations focus on rights, it may be interesting to explore briefly the tacit notion of duty in international politics. Under the facade of sovereignty and self-determination, the reality is that states are viewed today as part and parcel of a global order. How else is one to understand the assertion that when fighting erupts in any one corner of the world, the major powers—as members of the UN Security Council or the Group of Seven—are supposed to formulate policies that attempt to restore peace and stability? It is only in the past fifty years that the powers have taken such roles upon themselves.

Furthermore, as sovereign powers, states have a duty to guarantee that contracts once agreed upon are carried out. In one of the most controversial aspects of this duty, the sovereign rights of Third World states mean, in practice, their assuming responsibility for debts undertaken by their nationals, even if a great amount of this money never reached their shores.[17] The implicit understanding is that each individual state is the custodian of its territory in the eyes of the "world community." Each state must take care of its territory to ensure that peace is maintained, contracts are fulfilled, and the world market continues to function properly. States that fail to do so inevitably attract intervention by foreign powers.

It is therefore more than likely that the system of states will remain in the foreseeable future the optimal political structure in an expanding world market. I am not at all convinced of the argument that a conflict exists between economic globalization and the continued prominence of nation-states. Nonetheless, centrifugal tendencies inherent in the elevation of sovereignty and sovereign equality have created a series of contradictions in the system.

To begin with, although the world market has generated certain homogenizing effects worldwide with the result that nearly all societies are now fully committed to it, political divisions have functioned to delimit and, to a certain extent, isolate domestic political processes. Thus, until a certain point is reached—namely, when things go horribly wrong—each society has been permitted to develop socially and politically in relative isolation. Sovereign equality therefore produced a system that was in certain respects extremely violent. Thus, ironically, over the past fifty years an unprecedented expansion of the world market has been coupled with intensified political strife between and within states.

In short, by sustaining the fiction of sovereign equality and national self-determination, the Pax Americana established a system that was prone to conflict. This had adverse effects on the potential for growth not only in the United States but, much more important, in the world market as well, for the intensification of political strife especially in the Third World led to a significant diversion of resources from production to armaments. By the early 1980s military spending worldwide surpassed, if only for a few years, any other item of consumption such as food or shelter. It is not accidental that the collapse of the international armaments market in 1982 coincided with the so-called Third World debt. Although some countries or companies did well under these circumstances, the net effect was a diversion of resources to the production of defense hardware.

Consequently, the system of states that was supposed to provide a foundation for peace and stability produced neither. On the contrary, the contradictions of the Pax Americana were simply reproduced and left to battle it out within each state.

Sovereignty and Capitalism. Implicit in the Pax Americana were economic growth and the expansion of the world market: A growing world economy produces an international division of labor and therefore interdependence among states; the international division of labor, in turn, patterns the socioeconomic structures of societies, encouraging the formation and strengthening of social classes that are likely to lend their support to the institutional structures of the world economy. The world market creates, in other words, vested interests that favor the status quo. Nonetheless, as discussed above, the Pax Americana was perilously balanced from the outset: Whereas the growth of the world market did indeed release centripetal energies, it also generated opposing centrifugal tendencies, which found expression in the system of states. What are the origins of these centrifugal tendencies?

For the answer, one must go back to the underlying cause of the international division of labor: namely, competition. Competition in the international arena is about beating the average, or raising one's rate of return above market—an unavoidable component of the capitalist world economy. Since states are constellations of interests, capitalist competition naturally translates into competition among states. As societies seek to improve their standing vis-à-vis the international division of labor, they are under intense pressure to subvert the rules of the game of the capitalist world economy to gain an advantage. This odd interplay between the system of states and the world economy produces tensions that are rooted not in clear-cut conflicting interests but in conjunctural developments that cause incremental centrifugal tendencies. All the actors in the game are broadly in support of the multilateral trading system, but as each seeks to improve its own competitive position, they are often led into conflicting paths. Thus, competition, the very engine of capitalist growth, sabotages the political superstructure that is put in place to further capitalist accumulation.

International Relations in the Era of the New World Order

The Pax Americana originated as a historically specific configuration wherein the United States was able to integrate the world market with a system of states. It worked as an articulation of three separate levels: the world market, which was supposed to generate transnational class alliances in support of the *pax;* the system of states, which became the primary vehicle for maintaining order and stability; and American military and economic power, which, deployed to provide discreet but critical backing to the system, can be seen as the hegemonic articulation of power that held together the two other levels. Even though the interrelation of these components generated both centripetal and centrifugal tendencies, and the Pax Americana was perilously balanced from the outset, there is no evidence to suggest that the system is inherently fragmentary.

The question increasingly dominating the agenda is whether the departure of the USSR from the scene has tilted the balance in favor of centrifugal tendencies. As the Soviet "threat" has receded, Japan, Germany, and other OECD members, so the argument goes, have greater room for maneuver. But why would Japan or Germany wish to pursue policies that might endanger the Pax Americana and the world market? After all, they have done rather well under such a system. Even the American state, the least committed of the three to internationalization, still trades roughly 20 percent of its GDP (gross domestic product) to the world market. With annual exports of some $500 billion a year, the American state is ill prepared for a breakdown of the world economy.

How then, are centrifugal and centripetal tendencies reflected in Japan, Europe, and the United States?

Japan. Though it lies beyond the scope of this essay to chart the various maneuvers undertaken by the United States as it tried to manipulate the world market to suit its needs, one needs to bear in mind that the international division of labor was an American division of labor. The Japanese economy was largely structured to complement the American economy. The United States emerged naturally as the center of the world economy, the so-called capitalist core; this was the essence of its "structural power." But throughout the postwar era the United States has been losing its competitive edge in manufacturing and productivity, while Japan and (less so) Europe have been gaining. A point has now been reached when the United States is required to undergo an urgent and painful "restructuring" in an effort to revitalize its flagging economy. In the context of the Pax Americana, however, a "domestic" restructuring program undertaken by any of the key states, and in particular the United States, amounts in effect to a restructuring of the entire world economy and the international division of labor. Globalization may be integrated as a manifestation of this restructuring.[18]

How has Japan reacted to these developments? The key to its response lies, in my view, not with the Japanese decision-makers but in the structure of Japanese society. The Japanese social formation effects a tentative alliance among big industries, the petty bourgeoisie (small shopkeepers, small business) in the city, and peasants in the countryside.[19] These three combined elements form the backbone of the ruling Liberal Democratic Party. The Japanese economy is geared toward export markets but maintains restriction on imports and, not surprisingly, foodstuffs and the goods sold by the retail chains. Many years ago, sharp analysis revealed that once Japan had reached a certain maturity, this socioeconomic structure would lead to a profound conflict with the American international division of labor.

For Japan, therefore, export orientation is a structural feature not only of its economy but of its society. U.S. attempts to transform the international division of labor are perceived by Japan as a direct attack on its social stability. If those attempts succeed, Japanese postwar stability will be in tatters, a price too high to ask of any society—or is it? A plausible argument can be made to the effect that the Japanese domestic entente may no longer serve the dominant interests in the country, namely, the *zabaitsus*. Because the Japanese domestic entente is essentially protectionist, it inevitably creates conflict with other trading nations and high labor costs. It is, of course, politically wise to use the foreigner bogeyman to put across the message of the necessity of an internal restructuring program. I would argue, therefore, that Japan currently poses no threat to American hegemony, not because it is unable or unwilling to do so but because American hegemony is very useful, perhaps more than ever, in the current Japanese context.

Possibly the most significant early move in the restructuring of the Japanese society occurred with the establishment in 1984 of the Joint Japan-U.S. Ad Hoc Group for the finance ministry. Its report, "Present Status of the Prospects for the Deregulation of Finance and Internationalization of the Yen," issued in May 1984, served to accelerate financial liberalization and promote the expansion of short-term financial markets. Subsequent critical developments included domestic sale of overseas certificates of deposit, the creation of a yen-denominated banks' acceptance market, the introduction of unsecured call money transactions, and the establishment of discount short-term government bonds, culminating in 1986 in the establishment of the Tokyo International Banking Facility. These developments were at the root of massive expansion in easy credit, which in turn led to the bubble economy of the late 1980s. Easy credit translated in the Japanese context to a spectacular property and stock market boom.

Nonetheless, despite this uninvited Anglo-Saxon-style boom-and-bust cycle, which naturally raised significant but ultimately over-represented opposing voices (Japan can say no), Japanese business on the whole took advantage of its higher capitalization and began borrowing heavily in the Euromarket to finance expansion of manufacturing sites in East Asia (it is estimated that half of that expansion was financed by such borrowing). This expansion drive accidentally interlinked with the massive growth of China and the attendant economies of Hong Kong, Taiwan, and (perhaps) Singapore to generate what appears at the moment as self-sustaining economic growth in the Far East. This "core" may not need the U.S. market as much as it did before, but it does require a distant United States to negotiate its own bubbling internal conflicts: between Japan and China, China and its neighbors, Japan and other East Asian countries. It is debatable whether the East Asian growth is even sustainable in the long term without the soothing leadership posture to which the United States is so attached. In this way, trade disputes with the United States gave Japanese multinationals the perfect excuse to begin to invest abroad and effectively undermined the very fabric of the developmental state model. The United States threat was used, in other words, as an instrument of change by certain Japanese interests.

American hegemony has been of use lately in other ways as well. The new methods by which Japanese companies began financing their operation in the mid-1980s is significant. The nature of the Japanese industrial landscape is constraining for average Japanese companies: They are often members of groups centered on main banks, which have unusual control over their activities.[20] Although the average Japanese company proved more successful than its Western counterpart, the Japanese manager was more constrained than his or her Western colleagues. But in the late 1980s, as the Japanese expanded the horizons of their financial operations, this industrial control structure began to unravel, and as a result Japanese managers have gained a new and cherished measure of independence.

It appears to me, therefore, that though the changes introduced under American pressures may negatively affect the Japanese economy, they nonetheless conform to the more parochial interests of maturing Japanese business. For all these reasons, the likelihood of serious conflict between the United States and Japan seems remote. United States hegemony plays a significant functional role within Japan and East Asia. Current conjunctural tendencies are tilting in centripetal directions.

The European Challenge. As the Japanese export drive was beginning to create political difficulties in the United States, Japanese companies began to switch to the European Community, or at least add it as a potential target market for their goods. Predictably, areas of particular strength in Japanese industry, such as cars and electronics, were highly successful in this ambition. European industries lost competitiveness in their traditional areas of strength (German cameras, British motorcycles), proved incapable of reaching competitiveness in stereos, VCRs, pocket calculators, video cameras, and the like, and were left behind at the dawn of new information technologies and biotechnologies—the so-called third industrial revolution. To make things worse, it appeared that American-Japanese competition was taking place in the European common market. By the mid-1980s, in response, a constellation of interests had emerged in Europe—not surprisingly spearheaded by automotive and electronics interests—to try to defend the common market from both Japanese and American infiltration. These interests form the true social force behind the 1992 process.[21]

The 1992 process, an aggressive move by the European Community to join the race for the lucrative value-adding technologies and capital accumulation, begat a more dramatic ambition. It was rumored that a close group in the François Mitterand network (Jacques Attali, Jacques Delors) sought to ally with a resurgent Germany and transform the European Community into an alternative power center that could one day replace the Pax Americana. Such ambitions would have led to the creation of a European superstate, a centralized structure possessing a coherent foreign policy, and, of course, a common currency, the ECU. Whether these rumors were correct or not, the American response was swift. The British government, which has acted as a Trojan Horse in the European context, promoted a plan which, although it appears rather muddled, reflects what I see as a transitory alliance of British, American, and Japanese interests in Europe. In contrast to the aims of the European Union, the British champion the idea of a territorial expansion of the European Community in its current form—which, if successful, would almost certainly impede the more ambitious plans some unionists may entertain. The British plan therefore suits not only the political economy of the British state but also American and Japanese interests.

The true Achilles heel of the European challenge, however, is European foreign policy. In response to the surprise Franco-German announcement of plans for a European army (April 1992), President Bush arrived in Europe within the week, summoned a special meeting of NATO, and presented the Europeans with a stark choice: Either cease plans for a European army, or the United States will withdraw its protective troops immediately from Europe. The plan for a European army was shelved.

But the decisive act happened elsewhere—in Yugoslavia, a case that shows both the clear limits of American power and the intricacies of foreign policy today. The United States played an important role in Yugoslavian politics in the period immediately prior to Yugoslav disintegration. While the newly elected government officials of Eastern Europe were lining up in Bonn with their hands open, the Croatian Ante Markovi, then president of Yugoslavia, visited Washington and obtained from President Bush a solemn promise of American aid to the tune of $1 billion. The money was supposed to help put the Yugoslavian banking system on a sound footing. Had this reform of the banking system under the auspices of the United States succeeded, it would have cut, so to speak, the Gordian knot of communist corruption at its most vulnerable point, the banking system, and broken the traditional communist power brokers' hold on the republics.[22] Their immediate response, however, was to accelerate the disintegration of Yugoslavia: communist elites sought to preempt their impending fall from power by dissolving the federation.

The Slovenian plebiscite and the subsequent announcements by Slovenia and

Croatia of their intention to secede from the Yugoslav republic were greeted by the EC countries and the United States with trepidation. Jacques Delors, who happened to be visiting the White House on the day of Slovenia's formal announcement, issued a communiqué with President Bush condemning Slovenian and Croatian intentions. In the same week Italian Foreign Minister De Michelis, visiting Belgrade with the foreign ministers of Luxembourg and the Netherlands, declared that independent Slovenia and Croatia would not be recognized by any of the EC countries for the "next fifty years."[23] By mid-April 1991 all EC foreign ministers had ceased direct dealings with any of the Yugoslavian republics and were communicating only with the central government.

But while the European Commission and the American government were working together to halt Yugoslav disintegration, behind the scenes Germany and Austria were urging Slovenia and Croatia to secede. Slovenia declared its intended secession following three days of intense consultations in Vienna between the Slovenian and Austrian governments.[24] German policies and aims are more obscure. Following the secession of Slovenia and Croatia and the subsequent attack on them by the Yugoslav army, Germany managed to secure European recognition for these republics as well as for Bosnia-Herzegovina and Macedonia. But later reports seeping through suggest that the German Foreign Minister Hans Genscher played a significant earlier role behind the scenes urging both republics to secede and promising financial and diplomatic support. Similar rumors circulated concerning Czechoslovakia, where Germany may have pursued a similar "divide and rule" policy.

Interestingly enough, Hans Genscher resigned from his post soon after these dramatic events, but suspicion of German resurgent and expansionist tendencies lie deep. The French and British, resentful of German policy in the Balkans, resisted calls for any intervention beyond a purely humanitarian role. This fundamental split in the European "Union" revealed the fallacy behind the grand vision of a Pax Europanica. The Yugoslav affair was exploited by the United States and its ally, Great Britain. As a result, the EU is no longer considered a serious challenge to the Pax Americana.

The U.S. Experience. Clearly, the U.S. experience has been immense and varied. As argued above, internal rivalries have produced competing and sometimes conflicting policies, domestic and international, and have generated instability in international politics. The atmosphere of growing suspicion and mistrust among the key advanced countries led to the collapse of the Bretton Woods system and has cast a thick shadow over the Pax Americana ever since. One attempted solution to the problem is represented by the Trilateral Commission, established in 1972, a shining beacon of rationality in a world apparently gone mad. But though the Trilateral Commission may be the preferred "elite" solution to an impending political crisis, the likelihood of its achieving its purported aims are slim. Such solutions can work if the conflict is indeed state-based, requiring coordination of state policies through the patient application of informal diplomacy. But the immediate challenges to the Pax Americana, as I have tried to show, are not rooted in the states but only find reflection in them. American, European, and Japanese vested interest that feel threatened by developments within the United States have already demonstrated that they are prepared to tolerate, to a certain extent, the increasingly unilateralist posture of American foreign policy as long as the globalist vision is sustained in the United States.

It appears to me that the more serious challenge to the Pax Americana emanates from the very core, from the American state. The internal challenge is represented primarily by two groups, neither of which is going to be impressed by the trilateral solution. There are, first, protectionist voices emanating from the less competitive industries. As noted above, such protectionist sentiments, as well as the political form in which they find expression, are structurally embedded in the Pax Americana. But in addition, danger is emerging in response to the disorienting effects of globalization, accelerated cultural changes, growing polarization, and social upheaval: The disorienting effects of the global market are responsible, at least in part, for the rise of fundamentalism and nationalism of all sorts and descriptions—Christian, Moslem, Hindu, Jewish. The common theme in these isms is a hankering after a world gone by, a world of real or imagined slower social change and stable social environment (in Britain, a return to "Victorian values"). The potential link between the two may currently pose the main threat to the Pax Americana. The Pat Buchanan campaign in the last presidential elections clearly aimed at forging precisely such an alliance. The media-hyped conflict between Western civilization and Islamic fundamentalism, which serves as a useful proxy in the battle against all other fundamentalism (including, if not chiefly, the one at home), is in my view one of those instances in which real battles are masked in ideological garb.

The internal cohesion of the "globalist" hegemony is in danger if the two tendencies achieve a political pact. Ironically, it was the Reagan administration that showed how essentially nonglobalist sentiments can be turned around, how "unilateralist" and frankly chauvinistic foreign policy behavior can do wonders in incorporating the conservative silent majority into an essentially globalist vision. Reagan's unilateralist attitude helped secure, in the broad alliance that he represented, the support of an important section of the population which would subsequently bear the brunt of his administration's policies. Similarly, by raising to specter of Islamic fundamentalism,

both President Bush and Clinton, were able to secure the support of their own fun-
damentalists—many of whom may objectively belong to the "isolationist" camp. I
would therefore interpret a number of foreign policy initiatives undertaken by the
United States—particularly in the Gulf War, Somalia, and, in a more complicated
way, the former Yugoslavia—not as evidence of reassertion of American power and
imperialism but rather as an almost desperate attempt to maintain the hegemony of
the globalist vision at home. But because of growing, if confused, internal dissent, I
believe that the United States will continue to pursue unilateralist and therefore destabilizing policies—with potentially serious consequences to the Pax Americana.

Conclusion

The fear of an impending split among the core capitalist states is overstated, not
because the danger does not exist but because such tensions are intrinsic to the Pax
Americana itself. Current tensions in world politics among the members of the
center have little to do with geopolitical interests of the sort identified by realists.
The departure of the Soviet Union from direct competition with the United States
did perhaps create a power vacuum in world politics, but that is not the source of
any serious problems; it simply allows tensions that have been brewing for a long
while to surface. In fact, the power vacuum may actually create an incentive—
among the key capitalist states to try and reach an accommodation, especially since
the benefits would certainly outweigh the costs.

The current tension in world politics also has little to do with any notion of
American imperialism; if anything, it stems from the failure of American imperialism. Possibly the most critical aspect of the end of the Cold War is that it happened at an inopportune moment when the whole world economy was verging
upon a severe recession. Furthermore, this recession came at the end of a long period of crisis—with the following net effects:

1. Though the system required the full commitment of the American state to
   the Pax Americana, the United States is no longer capable of discharging its
   hegemonic role.
2. The system was founded upon a consensus among the leading states, but
   despite the rhetoric, no state was capable of opening up its markets to the
   extent required by the liberal trading regime. Indeed, the core capitalist
   states were in danger of disrupting the world market.
3. The system relied on the continuous success and economic growth of a

world system that should have generated the sociopolitical interests of its "supports." But no account was taken of the cyclical nature of capitalist development: For example, when capitalism goes into a downturn, common interests in the global market diminish markedly.

There is no evidence, however, of serious change in the balance of forces from centripetal to centrifugal policies. The Pax Americana has certainly a few more years to go.

Notes

Acknowledgments: I thank Jason Abbott, Brook Blair, Babek Ganghi, Allen Hunter, and Anthony Payne for their critical comments and support in revising this essay.

1. Susan Strange, *States and Markets: An Introduction to International Political Economy* (London: Pinter, 1988).

2. Ronen Palan and Barry K. Gillis, eds., *Transcending the State-Global Divide: The Neo-Structuralist Agenda in International Relations* (Boulder: Colo.: Lynne Rienner, 1994).

3. See Henk Overbeek and Kees van der Pijl, "Restructuring Capital and Restructuring Hegemony," in *Restructuring Hegemony in the Global Political Economy: The Rise of Transnational Neo-Liberalism in the 1980s,* ed. Henk Overbeek (London: Routledge, 1993).

4. H. R. Trevor-Roper, "Spain and Europe, 1598–1621," in *The New Cambridge Modern History,* vol. 4 (Cambridge: Cambridge University Press, 1970).

5. See Stephen Gill, *American Hegemony and the Trilateral Commission* (New York: Cambridge University Press, 1990); and Overbeek, *Restructuring Hegemony.*

6. Quoted in Wilfried Loth, *The Division of the World, 1941–1955* (London: Routledge, 1988), 22.

7. Kees van der Pijl, *The Making of an Atlantic Ruling Class* (London: Verso, 1984).

8. Richard N. Cooper, "Prolegomena to the Choice of an International Monetary System," *International Organizations* 29 (Winter, 1975): 85.

9. Henry G. Aubrey, "The Political Economy of International Monetary Reform," *Social Research* 33 (Summer 1966): 218–54.

10. Cooper, "Prolegomena."

11. Joyce and Gabriel Kolko, *The Limits of Power: The World and United States Foreign Policy, 1945–1954* (New York: Harper & Row, 1972); William Appleman Williams, *The Tragedy of American Diplomacy* (1959; New York: Delta Books, 1972).

12. Bertram Gross, *Friendly Fascism: The New Face of Power in America* (Montreal: Black Horse Books, 1980), 37.

13. David Calleo, *The Imperious Economy* (Cambridge, Mass.: Harvard University Press, 1982).

14. David Wightman, "American Academics and the Rationalisation of American Power," Occasional Paper no. 8, Institute for Advanced Research in the Humanities, University of Birmingham.

15. Susan Strange, "The Persistent Myth of the Loss of Hegemony," *International Organizations* 41 (Autumn, 1987).

16. Kendall W. Stiles, "The Inhibited Hegemon: The President, Congress, and the British at the GATT, 1946–1954," paper presented to the International Studies Association (ISA) conference, Acapulco, April 1993.

17. R. T. Naylor, *Hot Money and the Politics of Debt* (London: Unwin Hyman, 1987).

18. Four renewal strategies are currently debated in the United States. These are not mutually exclusive, although there is great potential for friction and contradiction among them. The first pins its hope on the development of a U.S. competitive industrial strategy. The second places the onus on American industry and managerial culture as opposed to the American state. The third was consummated through the North American Free Trade Agreement (NAFTA). The fourth, possibly dominating right now, is the trilateralist option, which seeks to replace the Pax Americana with a trilateral vision of world affairs.

19. Albert M. Craig and Edwin O. Reischauer, *Japan: Tradition and Transformation* (London: Allen & Unwin, 1989).

20. This paragraph draws on the ideas of John Groenewegen, "A Changing Japanese Market for Corporate Control," paper presented to the European Association for Evolutionary Political Economy (EAEPE) conference, Barcelona, October 1993.

21. See Lawrence Franko, "The Impact of Global Corporate Competition and Multinational Corporate Strategy," in *The Technical Challenges and Opportunities of a United Europe,* ed. Michael S. Steinberg (London: Pinter, 1990).

22. I have discussed the Yugoslav situation in Ronen Palan, "Misguided Nationalism: The Causes and Prospects for Slovenian Independence." *Contemporary Review,* September 1991.

23. Quoted in *Politika: The International Weekly,* no. 56 (1991).

24. Austria's support certainly had little to do with its professed sympathy for the national aspirations of the Slovenian people; on the contrary, it was part of a larger plan to establish a trading community on the lines of the old Austro-Hungarian Empire (which included Austria, Czechoslovakia, Hungary, Croatia, and Slovenia), with Vienna as its financial and commercial center.

Part IV

Disciplined Knowledge and Alternative Visions

Chapter 12

Academic Research Protocols and the Pax Americana: American Economics during the Cold War Era

Michael A. Bernstein

> Whatever its benefits or rewards, empire is expensive. It costs a very great deal of money. It kills a large number of human beings. It confines and progressively throttles spontaneity and imagination. It substitutes paranoid togetherness for community. It limits the play of the mind. And even at the rudimentary marketplace level it becomes self-defeating.[1]

Any evaluation of the extent to which the end of the Cold War may change the nature of American society and politics necessarily depends upon our impressions of the domestic as well as the global impact of the era of superpower confrontation. We need to know how the Cold War affected not only political parties and major political actors but also economic development and competitiveness, political discourse, racial and ethnic strife, gender relations, and more. Just how deeply the

Cold War made its way into the interstices of American life may in large part determine the potential for contemporary change.

William Appleman Williams once said that empire was and is a "way of life." The variegated and complicated ways in which this was and is true should preoccupy newer scholarship on the Cold War. And in light of those new approaches, reassessments of the Cold War era in terms of the historical evolution and maturation of professional disciplines and groups seems called for. As integral parts of the nation's intellectual and cultural (not to mention social) superstructure, professional elites provide a venue for investigations of the historical impact of major political and economic events such as the post–World War II confrontation of the superpowers. A particularly striking example is the case of the American economics profession. The trajectory of theoretical development in the field was decisively affected by the pressures, constraints, and opportunities afforded by the Cold War preoccupations of the federal government, colleges and universities, and private foundations and "think tanks."

It is the burden of the following argument that during the 1940s the needs of the War Department and related government agencies for guidance in resource allocation led to the stimulation of economics research on what came to be known as activity analysis and linear programming, which had a decisive impact on the theoretical trajectory of the discipline in this century. From such work, for example, algorithms were developed to aid the U.S. Navy in the scheduling and sequencing of supply shipments throughout the Pacific theater of operations. These advances in decision-making science, prompted by the wartime needs of the state, ultimately affected the course of research and teaching in microeconomics at colleges and universities across the country. Moreover, during the ensuing Cold War the continuing needs of government for assistance in directing military buildups and overseas troop and materiel deployment called forth further research efforts in strategic defense economics, economic intelligence analysis, development economics and the like. Thus, state-inspired activities profoundly affected research protocols and pedagogical agendas in the economics discipline as a whole.

The Cold War's enduring impact on American economics, however, resulted from the impetus it gave to the refinement of game theory and mathematical approaches to the problem of duopoly and oligopoly simulations. The formal approximation of contests between two or more actors, undertaken by mathematical economists with the support of the Department of Defense, the Office of Naval Research, and other federal agencies, linked up directly with strategic concerns about the nuclear duopoly between the United States and the Soviet Union during the 1950s, and with the potential for bilateral or multilateral conflict in the postwar world. Economists, therefore, not only had a major role in the articulation of American Cold War military and diplomatic strategies but were themselves especially privileged and influenced by the growing interest of the federal government in their strategically important work. The ultimate meanings of this mutual interaction between economists and the appurtenances of the national security state, and its implications for the postwar evolution of American economic thinking, suggest an array of ironic and ambiguous outcomes in the domestic history and dynamics of the Cold War.

* * *

It was of course during World War II that the groundwork was laid for the participation of the American economics profession in the Cold War itself. The usefulness of the economics discipline to the American war effort was demonstrated in two broad areas of endeavor: mobilization and allocation, and strategic decision-making. Economists quickly became integral parts of the government agencies established to meet the various needs and challenges thrown up by American entry into the war: the Board of Economic Warfare, the Combined Production and Resources Board, the Defense Plant Corporation, the Foreign Economic Administration, the Office for Coordination of National Defense Purchases.[2]

To be sure, the entire wartime experience of American economists played a major role in the postwar academic evolution of the discipline. From input-output analysis to statistical estimation techniques, to national income account conventions, to international financial and commodity flow tabulations, the 1940s were an extremely innovative decade in the field's history. And these intellectual developments had of course taken place within the context of a grand crusade against fascism and totalitarianism. In this sense, World War II "imparted to a community of humanist and social scientific scholars a concrete sense of the embeddedness of their ideas—and themselves—in history, which they brought back with them to their universities" and, it should be added, sought to communicate to their respective disciplines.[3]

It was in matters of resource allocation and decision-making, however, that economists made perhaps their most significant contributions, and with which they (collectively as a profession) had their most significant experience during the war. Even before the Japanese attack at Pearl Harbor, conversion to defense production had created virtually intractable problems of resource scarcity and waste for government officials. How to choose efficiently the timing and distribution of various productive activities necessary for a war effort was a major concern and, with American entry into the war, became only more intense.

Not surprisingly, the American armed services and the government agencies associated with them were particularly eager to develop allocative techniques for wartime production, transportation, and distribution that would minimize costs and waste and that would have, as their corollary, the maximization of some objective such as output, frequency, or endurance. Tjalling C. Koopmans, a Dutch physicist who came to the United States in 1940, was prominent in relevant research that in the short run stimulated a wide variety of research on related programming problems, and in the long run had a tremendous impact on the future course of research in mathematical economics in particular and economic theory in general.[4] Serving on the Combined Shipping Adjustment Board, a joint American-British effort to utilize the merchant fleets of the allied nations most efficiently, Koopmans developed a mathematical model that would aid decision-makers in the establishment of transport routes, schedules, and tonnage for the war effort around the world. His work became a linchpin in the articulation of a wide array of applications that were the foundation of the evolution of operations research and microeconomic theory in the 1950s and 1960s. By 1949 the work of Koopmans and of many investigators in mathematics and economic theory had reached sufficient maturity under the stimulus of the war years that a conference was convened at the Cowles Commission for Research in Economics in Chicago with the support of the RAND Corporation. The meeting generated information and publications that were dramatic in their impact and significance.

The Cowles conference grew essentially out of Koopmans's conviction that there was a connection between much of the allocation and operations research studies done during World War II and economic theory more generally. As one eminent participant remembered, Koopmans was "like a man on fire," and the collaboration that the conference sustained brought "instant respectability to the field" of linear programming and operations research in the eyes of many economic theorists. By "mechanizing" the problem of maximization subject to constraints, the work of the conference participants served to unify, at least in the formal constructs of mathematics, an array of problems in economics having to do with such things as the maximization of profits, the maximization of utility, and the minimization of costs.[5]

Ever since the "marginalist revolution" in economic theory at the turn of the century, American economists especially had become involved in the redefinition of economics itself. No longer the study of "the nature and causes of the wealth of nations" (as Adam Smith had claimed), or "a critical analysis of capitalist production" (as Karl Marx suggested), the discipline had become the formal study of "the adaptation of scarce means to given ends."[6] What the development of linear programming and operations research served to do was to legitimize this transformation in the object of economics research in ways that seemed entirely scientific, objective, and formal.[7] Although such an intellectual transformation had given the field an internal momentum of its own, the wartime and immediate postwar stimulus and concrete support afforded to this evolution by the needs of the state were profound.

The authority and legitimacy of the new work in economic theory that had been, in large measure, an outgrowth of the war years carried over to the postwar era and the years of the Cold War. Economic analysis came to play a significant role in activities related to the defense establishment and the new global responsibilities of the United States. From cost minimization to budgeting objectives, to the scheduling of transportation and logistical support activities, to estimations of the amounts of materials needed for military-industrial production and deployment, the research of the World War II years began to pay off. Even in the private corporate economy, not to mention the civilian activities of government, operationally useful techniques developed by economists came of age. And with these successes the prestige of those engaged in such research, along with governmental and private support for such research activity, was powerfully enhanced.[8]

It was in the development of game theory, however, that the intellectual evolution of American economics and the concerns of a burgeoning national security state truly melded. On a strictly mathematical level, the development of both linear programming and game theory depended on advances in the understanding of linear inequalities in constrained maximization or minimization problems. In this sense, the mathematical techniques used in both areas were the same. But game theory had an even more powerful appeal for strategic analysis because of its focus on *conflict* and decision-making.[9] Not surprisingly, the theory of games had been greatly stimulated by the World War II years, but it did not achieve full prestige until the coming of the Cold War.

The 1940s work of John von Neumann and Oskar Morgenstern signaled the emergence of game theory as a major part of economic analysis.[10] Their demonstration that it was possible to derive definite results from mathematical simulations of complicated scenarios of conflict and uncertainty was revolutionary. They showed that under certain conditions and assumptions, game participants could implement strategies that would secure at least certain minimum gains (or, as a corollary, at most certain maximum losses). Although it was immediately clear that their findings would be useful in microeconomic theory—especially the thorny problem of deriving determinate outcomes for oligopolistic market pricing behavior—over time it also became obvious that their work would be applicable to strategic choice problems and national defense planning.[11]

Albert Wohlstetter of the RAND Corporation was a major figure in the application of game theory to defense concerns. His work in the late 1950s focused on nuclear deterrence and what had come to be called the "balance of terror."[12] Approximations and simulations of two-person conflicts seemed appropriate scenarios in which to investigate the implications of the nuclear duopoly of the Cold War years. It was no idle exercise for Wohlstetter and his colleagues at RAND to relax over games of "Kriegspiel" and "Liar's Poker" while taking a break from their investigations of strategic choices and conflictive outcomes.[13]

The dramatic intellectual impact of the work of von Neumann and Morgenstern among academic economists was paralleled by the willingness of the state to support this particular line of inquiry. Research funding—distributed by the Department of Defense and affiliated agencies such as the Office of Naval Research and subordinate service arms—was rapidly made available to those economic theorists, especially mathematical economists, whose work in game theory and linear programming seemed to have potential value to the missions of the national defense and security establishment. Interestingly enough, the navy and the air force proved most eager to lend support to the work of game theorists and operations research specialists. The navy in particular supported much of the work in mathematical economics—in large part done by Kenneth Arrow and Gerard Debreu (both future Nobel laureates)—through its Office of Naval Research.

Crucial support, both financial and logistic, was also provided by the RAND Corporation during the 1950s. What had been Project RAND (an acronym for Research and Development) under air force supervision and had then become the nonprofit RAND Corporation of today underwrote much of the work on linear and dynamic programming that had been so decisively stimulated by the Cowles conference in Chicago. It was at RAND that George Dantzig further refined his crucial contributions of the late 1940s (with the enormously important cooperation of mathematician Richard Bellman). RAND scientists also began the application of game theory principles to war gaming and simulation.

As one of RAND's historians has noted, economists played an increasingly important role in the work of the corporation itself. In contrast to the World War II era, in which government (and associated nonprofit research institutes) deployed the expertise of physical scientists in large numbers, the Cold War years saw an increasing emphasis on the work of social scientists—in large measure, it appears, because "economists could act as the generalists and integraters in analyses of general war." The major challenges facing government officials in times of conflict, such as the "allocation of resources among expensive competing weapons systems ... [and] bargaining with a single opponent in a two-sided matrix, and so on ... were well-suited to treatment by traditional economic concepts."[14]

Under the auspices of RAND, continued research in game theory and linear and dynamic programming flourished during the late 1950s and 1960s. The corporation funded "Defense Policy Seminars" at (among other places) UCLA, the University of Chicago, Columbia, Dartmouth, Johns Hopkins, MIT, Ohio State, Princeton, and Wisconsin. By 1965 RAND had created a graduate fellowship program to support training in a variety of fields not only in the physical sciences but also economics and international relations. In that year eight such fellowships were distributed among Berkeley, Chicago, Columbia, Harvard (which got two), Princeton, Stanford, and Yale.[15] Not infrequently, talented graduate students and young postdoctoral investigators received major support from RAND for work in economics that touched upon matters of strategic decision-making. One such individual for whom this was true, and whose career as a Cold Warrior would take many twists and turns, was Daniel Ellsberg—a major figure in the 1971 Pentagon Papers scandal. His research at Harvard University and at RAND dealt primarily with strategic choice under risk and uncertainty, and in this regard his work was quite representative of the new trends in economic theory that dovetailed so nicely with the concerns of the American government during the Cold War.[16]

The increasing self-confidence expressed by the economics profession during the 1950s represented the coming of age of a powerful new field that was, in at least the formal sense of collegiate and university organization, less than a half-century old. Task forces of the American Economic Association sought to homogenize undergraduate and graduate training programs across the country; association committees to "focus informed opinion" were formed not only among members but also in the public at large with respect to major public policy questions; and the introduction of defense economics curriculums was undertaken at the major armed service academies under the direction of association members. American economists also played increasingly significant roles in the reconstruction of foreign faculties in the wake of the dislocations occasioned by World War II. These efforts involved not only the vetting of individuals for appointment to resurgent foreign institutions of higher learning but also the articulation of new programs of instruction, even reading lists. New subfields of the discipline, such as growth and development theory, garnered attention and resources, thanks to the interest of the government in fostering decentralized market growth in developing nations as a means to further U.S. foreign policy interests and forestall Soviet and Chinese initiatives around the world. American economics thus assumed greater visibility on a global scale, in addition to the discipline's growing respectability and authority at home.[17]

The establishment of a Council of Economic Advisers within the executive office of the president during the Truman era had, of course, already created high expectations for the status and importance of economics within the political realm. Not surprisingly, then, the council quickly became involved with the Cold War workings of the national security state. Council members made frequent visits to the military service academies and to such institutions as the War College of the Air Force and the Industrial College of the Armed Forces in order to discuss (and participate in conferences on) such matters as "mobilization of the national economy in the face of atomic attack," "economic stabilization after attack," "the economics of national security," and "economic preparedness."[18] The Office of Defense Mobilization, for example, requested the Council of Economic Advisers late in 1954 to initiate a series of wide-ranging discussions on the matter of "emergency economic stabilization" in the event of a nuclear exchange. Edward Phelps, assistant director for stabilization in the Office of Defense Mobilization, suggested to Director Arthur Fleming that following a nuclear attack Civil Defense authorities should be given the power to set wages, prices, and rents—as well as to ration goods and services. Since plans for such a contingency, to be effective, would need to be set up in advance, he thought the council and other government economists should begin articulating such emergency arrangements. In imagery that could not have been lost on his Cold War audience, Phelps said of his idea, "I do not envisage someone crawling out of the rubble waving a price regulation but I do suggest that certain minimum and simple rules of economic behavior may properly supplement other survival rules when it is time to move beyond the first instinctive or pre-arranged measures."[19]

It is important to remember, of course, that even while mainstream trends in American economics research were being nurtured and sustained by the interests of the state, there was actual suppression of certain tendencies in economic analysis that were regarded as dangerous, wrongheaded, or even treasonous (McCarthyism's impact on academia has received impressive attention from historical scholars).[20] If the Cold War years privileged certain kinds of academic research with funding, prestige, and government approval, they also witnessed the enfeeblement of other intellectual traditions both by the passive means of deprivation of support and encouragement, and by the active efforts of university and government authorities to deny employment and advancement to those deemed to be outside the mainstream.[21]

It would be disingenuous at best to ignore the fact that much of the preceding argument has embedded within it a rather challenging counterfactual question. In the absence of the Cold War preoccupations and commitments of the national government, would the American economics profession have evolved differently? Although any history of a non-event is an exceedingly risky enterprise, some speculative responses to this query may be ventured. There can be no doubt that the emergence of such potent subfields as linear programming and game theory was linked with irresistible forces of internal intellectual development. Most mainstream historians of economic thought can in fact trace a virtually uninterrupted line of theoretical maturation from the earliest contributions of the marginalist theorists at the turn of the century to more contemporary representations of economic theory in the hands of operations research analysts and game theorists. That is as it should be, given the purposes and roles of narrative histories of doctrinal development in any field.[22]

What matters here is not *whether* a given train of development would have taken place in the history of American economics, but *how* that particular road was chosen. Far from being products of dispassionate inquiry, some of the major advances in modern economic theory were the direct result of the wartime concerns of government and the national security agenda of the Cold War years. In the development of mathematical economics in general, it is striking that the 1940s were apparently watershed years, the start of a tremendous expansion in the publication of mathematical economics articles in leading journals such as *Econometrica* and the *Review of Economic Studies*. In the flagship publication, the *American Economic Review,* less than 3 percent of the 30th volume—published in 1940, included mathematics as a means of exposition. By contrast, the eightieth volume (1990) devoted over 40 percent of its pages to articles that utilized "mathematics of a more elaborate type."[23] The mathematization of graduate training, along with the evaluation of faculty on the basis of mathematical skills and accomplishments, similarly took off after World War II. That such transformations in the content and protocols of American economics research can in large part be traced to the 1940s is surely no coincidence, and the subsequent Cold War era served to accelerate the trend.[24]

By way of conclusion, two further points should be made. The first concerns the American economics profession in particular; the second, some general themes regarding the Cold War that bring us back to the words of William Williams with which this essay began. This is an ambiguous and ironic history that I have tried to sketch. It is possible to construe the American economics profession as an agent of or complicit with the Cold War ideology of postwar America, and at the same time to view the profession (if not its individual members) as in some way victims of the Cold War. One's particular view might depend on whether one's vantage point is inside or outside the mainstream of the present-day profession. Beneficiaries of the government's interest in the development of mathematical economics—whether individual research scholars or their students and others their work inspired—could see this history as a demonstration of the usefulness and relevance of their field. Those whose work was marginalized by the rapid explosion of interest in linear programming and game theory, especially those who may have lost jobs, advancement, or research funding during the postwar era, might well take a dimmer view. But all such impressions would border on assumptions of a fairly personal sort.

The point here is not to level accusations or deliver blandishments but rather to portray a structure of political and social events that generated within a historical context particular intellectual and policy-oriented results. What matters, then, is that past choices, which might have been made differently and which were made for a host of unconscious as well as conscious reasons, powerfully circumscribe present conditions. And yet it *appears* that the present state of affairs is not only a logical but also a necessary product of the past.

Without historical awareness, however, it would seem appropriate to conclude that the evolution of professional expertise has derived from forces inherent in the discipline itself. Events, individuals, and institutions become merely a background against which the logic of a scientific enterprise may be arrayed. In that context, what has happened within a profession in the past is either part of a continuum of advancement or an unfortunate and wasteful diversion—not an array of political and social relationships, involving power and status, between people.

Iconography has its virtues, not the least of which is the building of morale, but critical awareness is certainly not one of them. An approach to the history of the American economics profession which poses questions like mine affords a deeper appreciation both of where the profession came from and of what it has come to be. It also makes for greater sensitivity to critics, iconoclasts, and those who would have moved the vocation in other directions. Characteristics of the modern profession that we take for granted emerge as far more complicated outcomes, as well as more ambivalent (and even arbitrary) ones, than a teleological framework would suggest. As one major figure in the developments I have chronicled mentioned in another context, the "mathematization [of economics] has given rise to discordant assessments of its effects.... The quality of assessments of the phase [of mathematization] that economic theory underwent and the effectiveness of attempts to alter the course of its evolution will gain from a detailed analysis of the processes that led to its present state."[25]

At the Cold War's end, the United States is indeed now in a position to rethink its relationship with the rest of the world and to ponder the costs of empire in more systematic ways. And this rethinking of the Cold War and its meaning cannot be completely successful if exclusive focus is maintained on matters of diplomacy, security affairs, or government budgets. The Cold War affected every facet of the nation's life—even the rather esoteric and specific aspects of a profession's discourse, as I have tried to show here. Reassessments of the Cold War therefore involve reconsiderations of an enormous variety of political and social details, not simply the relations between nation-states. Hindsight contemplation of the Cold War involves a wholesale retrospection of American society. This, and much more. It involves not only remembering who we were but also judging who we are and speculating as to who we will yet become.

Notes

Acknowledgments: This essay was originally prepared for "Rethinking the Cold War: A Conference in Memory of William Appleman Williams," held at the University of Wisconsin–Madison in October 1991. I am indebted to the conference organizers, in particular Allen Hunter, for their support and encouragement. For helpful comments on a previous draft I am also grateful to my friends and colleagues Michael Cox, Michael Dennis, G. Allen Greb, Steve Hahn, Mark Kleinman, Mel Leffler, Michael Meranze, Terry Odendahl, Steve Platzer, Chris Simpson, and David Weiman.

1. William Appleman Williams, *Empire As a Way of Life: An Essay on the Causes and Character of America's Present Predicament along with a Few Thoughts about an Alternative* (New York: Oxford University Press, 1982), 221.

2. See, e.g., Bureau of the Budget, War Records Section; *The United States at War: Development and Administration of the War Program by the Federal Government* (Washington, D.C.: U.S. Government Printing Office, n.d.).

3. Barry Katz, *Foreign Intelligence: Research and Analysis in the Office of Strategic Services, 1942–1945* (Cambridge, Mass.: Harvard University Press, 1989), 198.

4. See E. Roy Weintraub, *General Equilibrium Analysis: Studies in Appraisal* (New York: Cambridge University Press, 1985), 90.

5. Interview with George B. Dantzig (a conference participant, now of the Department of Operations Research at Stanford University), May 3, 1989. Dantzig was a central figure in the development of linear programming, work he had undertaken in the late 1940s for the U.S. Air Force. His classic essay "Maximization of a Linear Function of Variables Subject to Linear Inequalities" was a central piece of the conference volume: Tjalling C. Koopmans, ed., *Activity Analysis of Production and Allocation: Proceedings of a Conference* (New York: Wiley, 1951), 339–47.

6. See Lionel Robbins, *An Essay on the Nature and Significance of Economic Science* (London: St. Martin's Press, 1969); and Robert Dorfman, Paul A. Samuelson, and Robert M. Solow, *Linear Programming and Economic Analysis* (London: McGraw-Hill, 1958), chaps. 1–3. Of course, more heterodox economists in this century have seen the very emergence of such a scientist definition of the field

in different terms. In 1955 Joan Robinson wrote: "Economic analysis, serving for two centuries to win an understanding of the Nature and Causes of the Wealth of Nations, has been fobbed off with another bride—a Theory of Value." She allowed that there was "a purely technical, intellectual reason" for this shift in emphasis but insisted as well that there were "no doubt deep-seated political reasons for the substitution" (*The Accumulation of Capital* [London: St. Martin's Press, 1969], v).

7. Although the work of the marginalist theorists had gained increasing respectability after the 1870s, earlier (and quite famous) works in this tradition had had a distinctly polemical, usually anti-Marxist quality. That tone was sharply distinguished from the apparently objective, apolitical, and elegant formulations of mid-twentieth-century mathematical economic theorists. See, e.g., Eugen von Bohm-Bawerk, *Karl Marx and the Close of His System*, ed. P. M. Sweezy (London: Merlin Press, 1975); and John B. Clark, *The Distribution of Wealth: A Theory of Wages, Income, and Profits* (New York: Kelley, 1967).

8. See, e.g., David Novick, *Efficiency and Economy in Government through New Budgeting and Accounting Procedures* (RAND Corporation Report R-254, February 1, 1954); Tibor Scitovsky, Edward S. Shaw, and Lorie Tarshis, *Mobilizing Resources for War* (New York: McGraw-Hill, 1951); S. Enke, "An Economist Looks at Air Force Logistics," *Review of Economics and Statistics* 40 (August 1958): 230–39; Charles J. Hitch, "Economics and Military Operations Research," *Review of Economics and Statistics* 40 (August 1958): 199–209; L. J. Sterling, "Decision Making in Weapons Development," *Harvard Business Review* 38 (January–February 1958): 127–36; Horst Mendershausen, "Economic Problems in Air Force Logistics," *American Economic Review* 48 (September 1958): 632–48; Charles J. Hitch and Roland N. McKean, *The Economics of Defense in the Nuclear Age* (Cambridge, Mass.: Harvard University Press, 1961); Abraham Charnes, William W. Cooper, and B. Mellon, "Blending Aviation Gasolines: A Study in Programming Interdependent Activities in an Integrated Oil Company," *Econometrica* 20 (April 1952): 135–59; H. C. Levinson, "Experiences in Commercial Operations Research," *Journal of the Operations Research Society of America* 2 (August 1953): 220–39; and M. S. Feldstein, "Economic Analysis, Operational Research, and the National Health Service," *Oxford Economic Papers*, n.s. 15 (March 1963): 19–31.

9. Dorfman, Samuelson, and Solow summarize the essential ideas of game theory in *Linear Programming and Economic Analysis*, 2: "the theory of games rests on the notion that there is a close analogy between parlor games of skill, on the one hand, and conflict situations in economic, political, and military life, on the other. In any of these situations there are a number of participants with incompatible objectives, and the extent to which each participant attains his [or her] objective depends upon what all the participants do. The problem faced by each participant is to lay his plans so as to take account of the actions of his opponents, each of whom, of course, is laying his own plans so as to take account of the first participant's actions. Thus each participant must surmise what each of his opponents will expect him to do and how these opponents will react to these expectations."

10. See John von Neumann and Oskar Morgenstern's classic work, *Theory of Games and Economic Behavior* (Princeton, N.J.: Princeton University Press, 1947). Also see R. Duncan Luce and Howard Raiffa, *Games and Decisions* (New York: Wiley, 1958). Introductions to game theory and economics for the more general reader may be found in William Poundstone, *Prisoner's Dilemma: John von Neumann, Game Theory, and the Puzzle of the Bomb* (New York: Doubleday, 1992); Morton D. Davis, *Game Theory: A Nontechnical Introduction* (New York: Basic Books, 1970); Anatol Rapoport, *Two Person Game Theory: The Essential Ideas* (Ann Arbor: University of Michigan Press, 1966); Michael Bacharach, *Economics and the Theory of Games* (London: Macmillan, 1976); and Eric Rasmusen, *Games and Information: An Introduction to Game Theory* (New York: Oxford University Press, 1989).

11. Again, see Dorfman, Samuelson, and Solow, *Linear Programming and Economic Analysis*, 2.

12. See Albert Wohlstetter, "The Delicate Balance of Terror," *Foreign Affairs* 39 (January 1959): 211–34.

13. Author's interview with Herbert Scarf (who worked at RAND 1954–57 and is now professor emeritus of economics at Yale University), May 15, 1989.

14. From Bruce L. R. Smith, *The Rand Corporation: Case Study of a Non-Profit Advisory Corporation* (Cambridge: Harvard University Press, 1969), 12–13.

15. Ibid., 16. Smith also notes that as a paid RAND consultant Thomas Schelling wrote another classic text in game theory and economic analysis, *The Strategy of Conflict* (Cambridge, Mass.: Harvard University Press, 1960). Also see Schellings's "Bargaining, Communication, and Limited War," *Journal of Conflict Resolution* 1 (March 1957): 19–36.

16. See, e.g., Daniel Ellsberg, "The Crude Analysis of Strategic Choices," *American Economic Review* 51 (May 1961): 472–78, on work he did at RAND: the U.S.-Soviet postwar confrontation is described as a 2×2 gaming matrix giving each superpower two choices—"wait" or "strike." Also see Ellsberg, "Risk, Ambiguity, and the Savage Axioms," *Quarterly Journal of Economics* 75 (1961): 643–69, on some of his work as a graduate student in economics at Harvard.

17. See Michael A. Bernstein, "American Economic Expertise from the Great War to the Cold War: Some Initial Observations," *Journal of Economic History* 50 (June 1990): 407–16. The role of the American economics profession in the reconstitution of postwar foreign faculties is the focus of another research effort on my part, currently in progress: Bernstein, "Academic Reconstruction and the 'Pax Americana': Notes on Imperial Legitimation after World War II." On the matter of development economics and growth theory, there is perhaps no better example of the resonances between that field and the Cold War concerns of the American government than Walt W. Rostow, *The Stages of Economic Growth: A Non-Communist Manifesto* (New York: Cambridge University Press, 1971).

18. See, e.g., Raymond J. Saulnier (chair, Council of Economic Advisers) to Maj. Gen. Richard H. Carmichael (commandant of the War College of the Air University, Maxwell Air Force Base, Alabama), March 1, 1960, in "Chron[ological File]" box 24, January–March 1960, Records of the Office of the Council of Economic Advisers, 1953–61, Dwight D. Eisenhower Library, Abilene, Kansas (hereafter CEA Records). Also see Saulnier to Maj. Gen. R. P. Hollis (commandant of the Industrial College of the Armed Forces, Washington, D.C.), May 6, 1957, box 25 January–June, 1957; Saulnier to Col. Robert F. McDermott (dean of faculty, U.S. Air Force Academy), October 9, 1956, and McDermott to Arthur F. Burns (chair, Council of Economic Advisers), October 2, 1956, box 25, July–December 1956; Saulnier to the Publications Division of the Industrial College of the Armed Forces, August 10, 1955, box 26, July–December 1955; and Neil H. Jacoby (member, Council of Economic Advisers) to Rear Adm. W. McL. Hague (commandant, Industrial College of the Armed Forces), May 18, 1954, box 26 January–June 1954, all in "Chron[ological File]", CEA Records.

19. Memorandum, "Stabilization Program," Phelps to Fleming, December 20, 1954, "Stabilization Policy Committee File," Box 15, CEA Records, 1953–61.

20. In this regard, see Ellen W. Schrecker, *No Ivory Tower: McCarthyism and the Universities* (New York: Oxford University Press, 1986); and J. E. King, *Economic Exiles* (New York: St. Martin's Press, 1988).

21. See Lawrence Lifschultz, "Could Karl Marx Teach Economics in the United States?" (originally published in *Ramparts*), in *How Harvard Rules: Reason in the Service of Empire*, ed. John Trumpbour (Boston: South End Press, 1989), 279–86.

22. In fact, many historians of thought point to the apparent intellectual convergence of eco-

nomic theory in Western and Soviet settings as evidence of an internalist evolution of ideas in the discipline. When Tjalling Koopmans won the Nobel Memorial Prize in Economic Science in 1975, for example, he shared the honor with Leonid V. Kantorovich of the Academy of Sciences of the Soviet Union; both men had made crucial contributions to the development of linear programming. Of course, it is also possible to understand the coincidence of their work in terms of the historical processes outlined here. The Soviet Union, like the United States, faced exceptional problems of military mobilization and planning both during and after World War II, though the Soviet state had the added stimulus of needing techniques for centralized economic planning. Interestingly enough, Joan Robinson often suggested in her critiques of mainstream (Western) economics that orthodox theory had more applicability in a planned than in a decentralized market setting; see, e.g., "Consumer's Sovereignty in a Planned Economy," in Robinson, *Collected Economic Papers* (Oxford: Basil Blackwell, 1975), 3:70–81.

23. From Gerard Debreu, "The Mathematization of Economic Theory," *American Economic Review* 81 (March 1991): 1–7. This essay was the Nobel laureate's presidential address to the 103d meeting of the American Economic Association.

24. I am aware that this essay does more to demonstrate the influence of World War II and the Cold War on certain emergent tendencies within the field of economics than to assess the difference these historical events made in broader contexts. That is to say, that the systematic portrayal of how World War II and the Cold War affected the manner in which economists selected particular topics for study, and of whether these actions generated cumulative political and ideological impact, must await further research and exegesis.

25. Again from Gerard Debreu, "Mathematization of Economic Theory," 6.

Chapter 13

Hannah Arendt as Dissenting Intellectual

Jeffrey C. Isaac

Hannah Arendt is an enigmatic figure. As one of the principal shapers of postwar academic political philosophy she is known primarily as a classical thinker whose conception of politics is drawn from the ancient Greeks and Romans. Yet she was wholly a creature of the twentieth century, preoccupied with the problems of totalitarianism, revolution, and mass politics.[1] Intellectual historians of the Cold War have properly situated Arendt amidst those "New York intellectuals" who journeyed from anti-Stalinist radicalism to liberal anticommunism after World War II. The consensus among these historians is that Arendt's books "became the canonic texts of American exceptionalism and a new liberal anti-communist reaction," that "Arendt's arguments became the philosophical cement which firmly set this new view of political realities."[2] Even Alan Wald, who acknowledges that Arendt was a "maverick thinker of considerable creativity," writes that her *Origins of Totalitarianism* "may have performed a conservatizing role" by likening Nazi

Germany and communist Soviet Union, thus dissolving "the difference between revolutionary anti-Stalinism and simple anticommunism."[3]

Arendt herself abjured all such political labels. Once asked what her "position" was on contemporary politics, she replied: "I really don't know and I've never known. And I suppose I never had any such position. You know the left think that I am conservative, and the conservatives sometimes think that I am left or I am a maverick or God knows what. And I must say I couldn't care less. I don't think that the real questions of this century will get any kind of illumination by this kind of thing."[4] One of the tragedies of the Cold War was that it rendered such sentiments difficult to sustain. Albert Camus once wrote that "nothing is true that compels us to make it exclusive."[5] During the Cold War, anticommunist liberalism and antiliberal Communism claimed just such exclusivity. As Irving Howe wrote in 1954: "The Zeitgeist presses down upon us with a greater insistence than at any other moment of the century. . . . Established power and dominant intellectual tendencies have come together in a harmony [that] makes the temptations of conformism all the more acute."[6]

As a consequence, iconoclastic perspectives were either incorporated into reigning molds, marginalized, or ignored altogether. Some of Arendt's insights about totalitarianism were appropriated by liberals without any attention to the place of these insights in her broader understanding of modern politics. But the end of the Cold War has made possible a truer appreciation of critical potentialities submerged by Cold War orthodoxy. Hannah Arendt was a radical political thinker who rejected the terms of the Cold War. Like others of her generation—Albert Camus and Dwight Macdonald spring to mind—she was an independent thinker with anarchist leanings, one who had seen totalitarianism firsthand and hoped that the resistance to it might presage a new, more humane and democratic politics.[7] She was averse to all totalizing ideological visions, including liberal anticommunism.

And yet neither did she fit easily into the mold of a "dissenting intellectual." Unlike the *Monthly Review* circle, C. Wright Mills, or even "revisionist" historians such as William Appleman Williams, she resisted the attraction of an antiimperialist politics whose legitimate criticism of American imperium often obscured the dangers of revolutionary authoritarianism.[8] Unlike the social democratic writers associated with *Dissent,* she was attached to no programmatic politics, anchored to no labor movement or political party, or even to any determinate historical tradition.[9]

Arendt was a strange radical indeed, inspired by Nietzsche and Heidegger as well as Jefferson and Kant, a passionate critic of Marxism who nonetheless declared that the revolutionary workers' movements represented the primary agencies of free-

dom in the modern world. An iconoclast, she argued with liberals, social democrats, and New Left radicals, yet she abjured these labels and refused these secure
identities. Her elusiveness is frustrating to the theorist and the activist. But as we
confront a world in which existing ideological commitments seem increasingly
hollow, it is also a source of much richness and vitality. Arendt's refusal of settled
forms of political thought, her brazen defiance of any forms of political correct-
ness, make her, I suggest, an appropriate model for the dissenting intellectual in
our times. I hasten to add that I say "*an* appropriate" rather than "*the* appropriate
model" quite deliberately. For Arendt was not the virtuous if misunderstood "true"
dissident of our times; her attitude toward the nitty-gritty realities of politics was
often disturbingly aloof. In some cases, most notoriously her criticism of school
desegregation in Little Rock, Arkansas, her thinking was encumbered by unwieldy
and untenable philosophical distinctions—such as "the social" versus "the political"—that clouded her judgment, whatever their intention or merit.[10] Yet even
here her thinking is instructive, for it courageously defied conventional wisdoms,
going against fashionable intellectual currents that leaned toward liberal integra-
tionism and presciently discerning limits to this liberal strategy.[11] It is above all this
brave effort to clear a new path for thinking about politics that needs to be retrieved
in our post–Cold War age, in which the political energies mobilized by liberal anticommunism have abated, and the ideological simplicities of that era have been
replaced by new and equally disturbing forms of thoughtlessness.

Totalitarianism and Modernity

It is widely held that the idea of totalitarianism was a weapon in the arsenal of Cold War liberalism.[12] The fact that Arendt's *The Origins of Totalitarianism,*
published in 1951, was the most influential study of totalitarianism has thus been
an important source of evidence for the Arendt-as-Cold-War-liberal view. There
is no denying that in the 1950s the discourse of "totalitarianism versus Western
freedom" served the ends of U.S. foreign policy and of liberalism more generally.
Yet it is a historical error to associate the idea of totalitarianism with the Cold War
era in which it was conscripted to serve purposes of state.[13]

The idea emerged not in the 1950s but in the *1930s,* when a traumatic series of
rapid-fire events—the rise of Hitler, the defeat of the Spanish Republic, the
Moscow trials, and the onset of another world war—provoked radical rethinking
across the political spectrum. Liberals such as Hans Kohn, Elie Halevy, and Raymond Aron, Marxists such as Victor Serge and Rudolph Hilferding, and independent

leftists such as George Orwell, Arthur Koestler, and Ignazio Silone all converged in the belief that Nazi Germany and Stalin's Soviet Union were both "totalitarian" states based upon unprecedented brutality and ideological indoctrination. Far from being "establishment" intellectuals, most of these writers were pariahs, exiles, their lives thrown into disarray by the rise of totalitarianism.[14] Leon Trotsky himself—hardly a Cold Warrior—suggested in his 1939 essay "The USSR in War" that the coming war, if it did not lead to world revolution, would lead to the triumph of "a totalitarian regime" in which "a new minimum program would be required—for the defense of the interests of the slaves of the totalitarian bureaucratic society."[15]

Arendt's *Origins* emerged from this context. Though published in 1951, it comprises materials written throughout the 1940s and primarily concerned with Nazism and the extermination of the Jewish people.[16] Its thesis is not the identity but the *essential similarity* of Soviet communism under Stalin and Nazism: the totalism of their power and the nihilistic manner in which it was exercised to commit bureaucratic mass murder. The book does not offer predictions either about the future of totalitarianism or about world politics, nor does it offer apocalyptic warnings about the need for "Western" vigilance. Indeed, the language of "West" versus "East" is entirely absent from the text, which is concerned primarily with the potential for destruction and evil latent in modernity.

The book is above all a critique of the "superfluousness of modern man" engendered by massifying economic and political forces, and of the "decline of the nation-state and the end of the rights of man" produced by national sovereignty in an age of imperialism. Arendt's 1951 preface to the first edition is hardly a celebration of American imperium. Traumatized by two world wars and horrified by the potential for future devastation and suffering presented by the postwar situation, Arendt observes: "Under the most diverse conditions and disparate circumstances, we watch the development of the same phenomena—homelessness on an unprecedented scale, rootlessness to an unprecedented depth. . . . Never has our future been more unpredictable, never have we depended so much on political forces that cannot be trusted to follow the rules of common sense and self-interest. . . . the essential structure of all civilizations is at the breaking point."[17] The themes sounded here—the death of hope, the dreadful unpredictability of the future, the anticipation of world war, the inadequacy of *all* political ideologies—are not inconsistent with the "hard liberalism" expounded by such writers as Arthur Schlesinger Jr. and Reinhold Niebuhr, but they are not compensated for by the faith in liberal reform, "modernization," and "postindustrial" technology so often articulated by postwar liberals.[18]

Any doubts about the distance separating the *Origins* from postwar liberal orthodoxy can be dispelled by a perusal of Arendt's 1953 essay "Ideology and Terror: A New Form of Government," later published as the final chapter of the 1958 edition of the *Origins*. There Arendt writes:

> If it is true that the elements of totalitarianism can be found by retracing the history and analyzing the political implications of what we usually call the crisis of our century, then the conclusion is unavoidable that this crisis is no mere threat from the outside, no mere result of some aggressive foreign policy of either Germany or Russia, and that it will no more disappear with the death of Stalin than it disappeared with the fall of Nazi Germany. It may even be that the true predicaments of our time will assume their authentic form—though not necessarily the cruelest—only when totalitarianism has become a thing of the past.[19]

Arendt makes two crucial points in this passage. The first is that totalitarianism is a product of "the crisis of our century" and is not explicable in terms of the machinations of subversives in league with an "evil empire." Indeed, she is quite clear that the emergence of the Soviet empire was a consequence rather than a cause of this crisis. Only the last third of the *Origins* actually discusses totalitarianism. The first part discusses anti-Semitism and its ties to the political economy of the modern nation-state; the second discusses European imperialism and the decline of parliaments and of the bourgeois public sphere in general, culminating in the catastrophic explosion of 1914, which "seems to have touched off a chain reaction in which we have been caught ever since." As Arendt writes: "Before totalitarian politics consciously attacked and partially destroyed the very structure of European civilization, the explosion of 1914 and its severe consequences of instability had sufficiently shattered the facade of Europe's political system to lay bare its hidden frame. Such visible exposures were the sufferings of more and more groups of people to whom suddenly the rules of the world around them had ceased to apply."[20] A long history of corruption and indifference to hidden suffering thus laid the basis for totalitarianism. Arendt makes clear that the issues she raises go much deeper than anticommunism; her 1966 Preface warns that "we have inherited from the cold-war period an official 'counter-ideology,' anti-Communism, which also tends to become global in aspiration and tempts us into constructing a fiction of our own."[21]

Her second point follows from this: The soil from which totalitarianism sprang, the political terrain that we in many ways still occupy, poses problems that are no less disturbing because they are less atrocious than totalitarianism itself. Particularly troubling to her is "the decline of the nation-state and the end of the rights of man." A main subtext of the *Origins* is that state sovereignty is incapable of handling the problems of dislocation and degradation characteristic of our world. As she puts it, in the contemporary age "the very phrase 'human rights' became for all concerned—victims, persecutors, and onlookers alike—the evidence of hopeless idealism or fumbling feeble-minded hypocrisy." She concludes that any adequate response to the horrors of totalitarianism must include a new conception of human justice and solidarity, that "human dignity needs a new guarantee which can be found only in a new political principle, in a new law on earth, whose validity this time must comprehend the whole of humanity while its power must remain strictly limited, rooted in and controlled by newly defined territorial entities."[22] The implication is clear: Far from justifying a new American imperium, the experience of totalitarianism calls for a fundamental rethinking of the institutions of national sovereignty and a promotion of human dignity more vigorous, and more innovative, than the practices engendered by even the most liberal system of nation-states.

Beyond the Cold War

If Arendt had been a supporter of Cold War liberalism then one would expect her to have held what were at the time predictably liberal views with respect to the major issues of the Cold War: loud denunciation of communism and barely audible criticism of the persecutory ethos that eventuated in McCarthyism, enthusiastic support for NATO, and backing for U.S. counterinsurgency in the Third World. But on each score, her views were unfashionable.

Arendt clearly opposed communism both as a form of politics as it was practiced in the Soviet Union, China, and Eastern Europe and as an ideology that sought to transform the world according to a conception of an end to History. And yet she numbered Marx among the greatest of modern thinkers. Far from considering Marxist ideas anathema, or treating them as incipient rationales for communist despotism, she engaged Marxism thought in a serious dialogue from which she gained much insight and freely acknowledged her debt.[23] Indeed, it is hard to think of any contemporary American philosopher of her stature who during this period so freely cited such Marxist notables as V.I. Lenin, Rudolph Hilferding, and Rosa Luxemburg. It is clear from her political and her theoretical writings that Arendt strongly criticized Marxism in all its forms, yet she refused to join the ever louder anti-Marxist chorus to which so many of her academic and literary colleagues had been recruited.

This refusal was more than a methodological commitment to intellectual openness, for it was linked to her equally unorthodox opposition to McCarthyism and the anticommunist hysteria more generally. Her private correspondence of the 1950s testifies to a growing fear that "Americanism" might become a new quasi-totalitarian ideology.[24] She articulated these fears publicly in her 1953 *Commonweal* essay "The Ex-Communists," which proceeds from a critique of Whittaker Chambers to a scathing portrait of the "ex-communist" whose anticommunism is governed by the same Manichean logic as the communism he once supported and now denounces. The ex-communists, she insists, are not simply former communists; they are "Communists turned upside down." For them as for communists, there are only Saints and Heretics. They exhibit the same contempt for allies as well as opponents, and the same faith in History. "Since they have divided the world into two, they can account for the disturbing variety and plurality of the world we all live in only by either discounting it as irrelevant altogether or by stating that it is due to lack of consistency and character." Revolted by this mentality, Arendt offers a vigorous defense of civil liberties and American constitutional government against American reactionaries such as Chambers and Joseph McCarthy, whose anticommunism threatened the very freedom it purported to defend.[25] Paralleling the arguments of Henry Steele Commager, the premier American intellectual to speak out in defense of civil liberties during this period, Arendt concludes:

> America, this republic, the democracy in which we are, is a living thing which cannot be contemplated or categorized, like the image of a thing which I can make; it cannot be fabricated. It is not and never will be perfect because the standard of perfection does not apply here. Dissent belongs to this living matter as much as consent does. . . . If you try to "make America more American" or a model of a democracy according to any preconceived idea, you can only destroy it. Your methods, finally, are the justified methods of the police, and only of the police.[26]

Arendt, a refugee from Hitler, was frightened by the nativist spirit of McCarthyism. Deeply touched by the plight of stateless people, she was particularly disturbed by the McCarran-Walters Act, which threatened to exclude or deport general categories of "alien subversives." Elisabeth Young-Bruehl has commented on the discrepancy between Arendt's "careful, reasonable public statements" about McCarthyism and the more passionate indignation expressed in her private correspondence, attributing this in part to her fear of repercussions for her unnaturalized ex-communist husband. Yet during this period Arendt supported the National Committee for an Effective Congress, an anti-McCarthy group, and was part of an abortive effort to found a civil liberties journal called *Critic.*[27]

Arendt was a lukewarm supporter of an active American role in Europe. She believed that massive U.S. economic assistance was necessary for European reconstruction and to support the containment of Soviet hegemony in Europe, yet her support was mixed with despair about the Allied reconstruction effort in Germany, which in her view failed in the task of denazification. Unlike many theorists of totalitarianism, Arendt never overlooked the fact that Germany, its NATO membership notwithstanding, had been the site of the most barbarous totalitarian regime. Her 1950 essay "The Aftermath of Nazi Rule" offers a somber portrait of postwar German politics and society. At the time it was published West Germany was the front line of the heightening Cold War.[28] Yet while many Western liberals were celebrating its "freedom," Arendt bemoaned its conformity, regretting that a militarized Germany was being established instead of the "federated Europe" which alone might aid in the reconstruction of European politics as well as economics.[29]

For Arendt the pressing concerns of human freedom and indeed human survival were best served by detaching them from the dualistic framework of Cold War thinking. She criticized European anti-Americanism for failing to recognize the advantages of such programs as the Marshall Plan, but she was equally critical of "certain current 'Americanistic' attitudes and ideologies in the United States," which sought to force everything into the terms of Cold War discourse.[30] Though critical of communist and fellow-traveling leftists such as Maurice Merleau-Ponty and Jean-Paul Sartre, whose anticapitalism blinded them to the dangers of Soviet communism, Arendt resisted that frame of mind which read any criticism of either capitalism or the United States as a form of "extremism."[31] Though she criticized those who laid all the blame for the emerging arms race on the United States, she was horrified by the atomic bomb. Like her mentor Karl Jaspers, she maintained that these weapons could never be used, and that the appearance of atomic weapons meant nothing less than that "the whole political and moral vocabulary in which we are accustomed to discuss" war and peace had become "for all practical purposes meaningless." Atomic weapons threatened humankind and human posterity, presented a problem for civilization as a whole, and implied an "intimate connection between modern warfare and a technicalized society." She criticized only one viewpoint more sharply than "anti-Americanism," and that was "the conviction that it is better to be dead than to be a slave."[32]

Finally, Arendt opposed all forms of imperialism. This is most clearly articulated in her contribution to a *Partisan Review* exchange titled "The Cold War and the West." Asked by the editors to assess "the position of the West in the Cold War" and to discuss whether the United States should support the forces of radical change or of conservatism throughout the world, Arendt offers a critique of the Cold War itself.

First, she insists that the conditions of modern warfare have rendered wars "politically, though not yet biologically, a matter of life and death. . . . Only if we succeed in ruling out war from politics altogether can we hope to achieve that minimum of stability and permanence without which no political life and no political change are possible."[33] Second, she holds that the nuclear age discloses even further dangers, our awareness of which is foreclosed by the prevailing terms of a political debate that presents only two choices, communism and anticommunism. No plausible answer can be decided "within the closed circle of this preposterous alternative," for within it both sides display a "reckless optimism": "on one side, the readiness to count the losses in the tens and hundreds of millions, . . . on the other side, the readiness to forget the concentration—and extermination—camps and with them the terrible prospect of freedom vanishing from the earth forever."[34] She rejects the cynical dialectic that would force her to choose between hanging and the firing squad, for both choices take refuge in a doctrine, foreclosing our own agency and responsibility. Arendt prefers to stake her faith on the creativity of human beings.

This leads to her most important point, that the futile superpower confrontation diverted our attention from the more politically significant phenomenon of contemporary revolution. Arendt chastises both Marxism and liberalism for their "conspicuous inability to comprehend the revolutionary spirit." Likening the 1956 Soviet suppression of the Hungarian uprising to the American Bay of Pigs fiasco in Cuba, Arendt criticizes the counterrevolutionary character of American foreign policy. "We have not understood," she insists, "what it means when a poverty-stricken people in a backward country where corruption has been rampant for a very long time is suddenly released from the obscurity of their farms and houses, permitted to show their misery and invited into the streets of the country's capital they never saw before."[35] If we did understand this, she suggests, we would recognize that in the Third World the only alternative to Bolshevik-style revolution is republican revolution, supported by a vigorous American policy of political and economic assistance. For Arendt, such revolutions represent moments of freedom to be prized and nurtured rather than suppressed or manipulated—a far cry from the doctrine of "counterinsurgency" soon to become popular among American liberals.

On Revolution

The main arguments of Arendt's book *On Revolution* are discernible in her *Partisan Review* essay: an endorsement of political rather than social revolution, and of the American rather than the Jacobin/Bolshevik model of revolutionary politics. *On Revolution* is a peculiar book. Because of its loud banishment of "the social question" from politics, and because its praise of a distinctively American politics seems to echo the postwar liberal doctrine of American exceptionalism, many commentators have seen it as the epitome of Arendt's Cold War liberalism. Yet this view is deeply mistaken.

Arendt's rejection of revolutionary Marxism rests on incisive criticisms of Marxism's reliance upon an untenable narrative of historical progress, its devaluation of problems of political judgment, and its utopian synthesis of utilitarianism and romantic individualism. Similar objections can be found in the writings of people as diverse as Dwight Macdonald, Albert Camus, Theodor Adorno, and Max Horkheimer. Far from criticizing Marxism in the name of "the vital center," Arendt is motivated by a fear that "the whole radical movement of our time was destroyed through identification with and usurpation by the Russian Revolution."[36] In short, she seeks to retrieve an authentically radical tradition, a "lost treasure" that had been submerged by Marxist ideology and liberal counterideology. In this effort at retrieval she draws on many sources beyond the American experience: the libertarian Marxism of Rosa Luxemburg, the anarcho-syndicalism of Russian and East European workers, and the resistance to totalitarianism in France, Denmark, and Hungary. Ironically, while writers like Daniel Boorstin was arguing that "the genius of American politics" was precisely its distinctively antitheoretical character, Arendt was retrieving the American revolutionary experience precisely because of the lucidity and cogency with which its protagonists self-consciously reflected upon and theorized about the creative possibilities of political action.[37] The writings of the American revolutionaries—Thomas Jefferson, James Wilson, even, strangely enough, John Adams—presented for her a vision of a vibrant, contentious, open, revisable, democratic politics.

Arendt's way of thinking, to be sure, represents a sharp rupture with conventional "left" or "progressive" thinking on politics. Traumatized by the experience of the Weimar Republic, in *On Revolution* she is highly critical of parliamentary institutions and of political parties in general. She acknowledges that representative government, in comparison with revolutionary Leninist party dictatorships, offers some personal security and civil liberty. But Arendt is suspicious of any political projects that seek state power, especially those based upon mass mobilization, and for this reason she is harshly critical of electoral politics even in constitutional democracies. Believing mass politics to be inherently disempowering and corrupt, she favors a robust civil society of voluntary associations that spring to life as the occasion arises, offering space for vigorous political participation but presenting no ideological vision or programmatic, globalizing policy.[38]

This radical republican vision is hardly complacent about contemporary American politics. Arendt argues that the statist institutions established by the Constitution have eviscerated vibrant experiments in participatory citizenship. In her writings of the 1960s, many of which are collected in *Crises of the Republic,* Arendt's social criticism becomes more pointed. "Lying in Politics," a review of *The Pentagon Papers,* disparages the national security managers responsible for American foreign policy: Capable of calculation but possessing no common sense, these bureaucrats deceived themselves and the American public, all in the name of an unjust and unwise war in Southeast Asia. Arendt also criticizes the more visionary "ideologists of the Cold War" whose "comprehensive ideology" was responsible for a situation where "sheer ignorance of all pertinent facts and deliberate neglect of postwar developments became the hallmark of established doctrine within the establishment."[39] She sees the Vietnam debacle as epitomizing the lack of judgment and moderation characteristic of contemporary politics.

These themes are also sounded in "On Violence," a blistering attack on the celebration of revolutionary violence found in the writings of Jean-Paul Sartre and Frantz Fanon. Arendt has sympathy for revolutionaries struggling against colonial oppression, but she refuses to lionize Third World revolutionaries. Criticizing Sartre's pronouncements likening national liberation movements to Marx's missionary proletariat, Arendt insists: "To think . . . that there is such a thing as a 'Unity of the Third World,' to which one could address the new slogan in the era of decolonization 'Natives of all underdeveloped countries unite!' (Sartre) is to repeat Marx's worst illusions on a greatly enlarged scale and with considerably less justification. The Third World is not a reality but an ideology."[40] Arendt of course would not deny that there is a Third World, if by that we mean a set of countries sharing a common set of postcolonial problems. But she rejects the effort to ideologize this reality, to offer a grand historical scheme in terms of which all postcolonial struggles make sense and all political agents can be deemed "progressive" or "reactionary." Like any grand ideology, she says, Third Worldism grossly oversimplifies political reality and offers its proponents a false comfort about their own righteousness. The connection between such righteousness and an authoritarian attitude toward dissent and disagreement is not accidental.[41]

But if Arendt criticizes the glorification of revolutionary violence, she is equally harsh toward the perhaps more subtle deployment of violence in liberal democracies. Her essay begins by calling attention to "the obvious insanity" of a nuclear balance of terror. Citing Noam Chomsky, she delivers a sweeping indictment of the "military-industrial-labor complex" dominating postwar American society and placing military definitions of reality at the center of political life.[42] She proceeds to defend student radicals for their courage in opposing such a system, though here too her comments are nuanced: She praises the students' "astounding will to action, and . . . no less astounding confidence in the possibility of change," yet also criticizes their theatricality, arguing that their enthusiasm is often unsupported by a sound analysis or convincing proposals.[43] The essays in *Crises* make clear Arendt's belief that the Cold War had laid the foundations for nothing less than a "constitutional crisis" of liberal politics, marginalizing dissent and closing off "all institutions that permitted the citizens' actual participation."[44]

Arendtian Politics

These criticisms of American politics were consistent with the dissenting space that Arendt had fashioned for herself since the end of World War II, in order to challenge the closed-mindedness and hypocrisy of Cold War liberalism. Underlying this dissenting posture was a coherent vision of politics. For Arendt, the human condition is inescapably a condition of natality and mortality, creativity and frailty. The greatest danger of modern ideologies—whether fascist, communist, liberal, or ethnonationalist—is that they seek to compensate for the partiality and provisionality of human existence with oversimplified, grandiose conceptions of social unity and unquestioning conceptions of political identity. Although they worship different deities—Volk, History, Technology—these ideologies share a common refusal to take into account the recalcitrance of the world, the fact that there is more to the universe than was dreamt of in their philosophies. They lacked a healthy sense of moderation and of what the ancient Greeks called *nemesis*.

Arendt's model of politics is thus anti-ideological in its rejection of totalizing visions of political organization or transformation. But it is visionary, indeed utopian, nonetheless. Arendt argued consistently for open, revisable, contestable political associations and communities, for a flourishing of *praxis*, the human ability to intervene creatively in the normal flow of events, to create new forms of solidarity and new ways of being. She supported an inclusive, participatory politics, yet not one limited by the model of mass suffrage. Her most notorious account of such a politics appears in *On Revolution*, where she criticizes the principle of universal suffrage, not because it includes those who should be excluded but because it homogenizes and eventually evaporates political energies. She proposes instead an "aristocratic" elite "that is chosen by no one but constitutes itself" and can drive a politics based upon voluntary associations, "islands in the sea" of mass politics.[45]

Many have been rightly troubled by this account, more for what it leaves out than for what it says. But two things seem clear. First, Arendt did not believe that this politics of elites can, will, or should completely supplant universal suffrage and representative government so much as she hoped that it might energize and complement more "normal" forms of modern politics. Second, her "elites" are not conventional elites at all. They occupy no special privilege, and they draw their power from nothing other than their decision to act in concert with their fellows; they are completely self-selecting. As she puts it, we need "a completely different principle of organization, which begins from below, continues upward, and finally leads to a parliament. . . . Since the country is too big for all of us to come together and determine our fate, we need a number of public spaces within it."[46] Here she comes close to articulating a conception of "civil society" with deep affinities to the ideas of such writers as Václav Havel and George Konrad. For Arendt as for them, the principle extends "upward," beyond the boundaries of states themselves, to encompass new forms of federation and new forms of international responsibility, solidarity, and accountability.

This model of politics is "communitarian" insofar as it endorses multiple forms of public participation and empowerment that challenge the privatism and indifference so typical of modern society. But insofar as these forms are irreducibly multiple, Arendt's vision leaves room for things that often get short shrift in communitarian accounts: antagonism, conflict, even violence itself. Arendtian politics is thus fractious and agonistic even as it supports efforts to establish broader forms of public identity and power. It is also "existential" insofar as it seeks to multiply the opportunities for individuals to enrich their lives through public "performances" in concert with others, and to create themselves anew through their commitments and their deeds.

And yet it is not a politics of "authenticity," if by this we mean an effort to find our "true selves," to manifest our deepest individual longings, to surpass our "alienation." For Arendt, to act politically—indeed, to act at all, in any capacity and in any circumstance—is to enter a complex web of interrelationships, conventions that preexist our action and often elude our understanding, and consequences that invariably escape our control. Political life, although it affords empowerment, is thus a profoundly partial form of existence which can provide no ultimate satisfaction or validation. Politics is indeed characterized above all by difference and dissonance, by the copresence of others with alternative understandings and competing projects, others from whom one cannot escape and with whom one must share the world. To ignore this is to suffer from *hubris,* to imagine that politics can offer the kind of total identification or satisfaction that can only be found, perhaps, in death. To recognize this is to see that otherness and the respect for it are central to any decent and free politics. This is why Arendt endorses the idea of "representative thinking"—the idea that "the more people's standpoints I have present in my mind while I am pondering a given issue, and the better I can imagine how I would think and feel if I were in their place . . . the more valid my conclusions, my opinion."[47]

Here we return to the guiding thread of Arendt's dissenting attitude: her refusal of a monologic politics that is incapable of projecting beyond the subject—whether nation, class, party, or race—and an equally insistent refusal of its outgrowth: a polarizing politics in which the Other becomes simply a projection of one's own obsessions and fears, a silent interlocutor in a contest whose outcome can only be statis or contending ruin. In place of such a politics, epitomized by the mutual balance of terror and conformity that held the world in its grip for almost five decades, Arendt offered the vision of a politics always alive to difference, novelty, and particularity, one that refuses to force issues into the straitjackets of ideological labels and vigorously supports the freedom to be different from the way such labels demand that we be, yet at the same time seeks to promote new forms of solidarity and commonality.

This vision is as relevant now as it was during Arendt's lifetime. We are no longer caught in the ideological deep freeze of the Cold War, and we confront a situation in many ways more open, and more hopeful, than the moment in which Arendt wrote. But we face our own forms of dogma and our own exclusive truths—no less disturbing because they lack the poignancy associated with mutually assured destruction. Indeed, the post–Cold War moment in which we live seems to be a time of proliferating antagonisms and competing monologues—whether they be the certainties associated with resurgent racism and nativism, with Afrocentrism and militant religious fundamentalism, or with a belief in a postindustrial, postideological utopia of global markets and global communications. In such a world, pulled apart by the competing (and often reinforcing) logics of meanness and marketization, the iconclastic vision presented in Arendt's political writings is both an inspiration and a resource for our own efforts to reconsider what it means to think politically.

Notes

1. The classical reading of Arendt is nicely stated in John Gunnell, *The Descent of Political Theory* (Chicago: University of Chicago Press, 1994). This view is still quite prominent, especially among nonpolitical theorists unfamiliar with the nuances of Arendt's texts, but it has recently come under fire. See, e.g., Dana Villa, "Beyond Good and Evil: Arendt, Nietzsche, and the Aestheticization of Political Action," *Political Theory* 20 (1992): 274–308; and the criticisms offered in Bonnie Honig, "The Politics

of Agonism," and my own "Situating Hannah Arendt on Action and Politics," both in *Political Theory* 21 (1993): 528–40. A number of recent books situate Arendt in the twentieth-century context. See Elisabeth Young-Bruehl's authoritative biography, *Hannah Arendt: For Love of the World* (New Haven, Conn.: Yale University Press, 1982); Dagmar Barnouw, *Visible Spaces: Hannah Arendt and the German-Jewish Experience* (Baltimore, Md.: Johns Hopkins University Press, 1990); Margaret Canovan, *Hannah Arendt: A Reinterpretation of Her Political Thought* (Cambridge: Cambridge University Press, 1992); Jeffrey C. Isaac, *Arendt, Camus, and Modern Rebellion* (New Haven, Conn.: Yale University Press, 1992); and Richard Bernstein's recent *Hannah Arendt and the Jewish Question* (Cambridge, Mass.: MIT Press, 1996).

2. Joanna Vechiarelli Scott, "The Methodology of Reaction: Hannah Arendt and the Uses of History" (paper presented to the 1988 meeting of the American Political Science Association, Washington, D.C.), 12; Alexander Bloom, *Prodigal Sons: The New York Intellectuals and Their World* (New York: Oxford University Press, 1986), 220.

3. Alan Wald, *The New York Intellectuals: The Rise and Decline of the Anti-Stalinist Left from the 1930s to the 1980s* (Chapel Hill: University of North Carolina Press, 1987), 269.

4. Hannah Arendt, "On Hannah Arendt," in *Hannah Arendt: The Recovery of the Public World*, ed. Melvyn A. Hill (New York: St. Martin's Press, 1979), 334.

5. Albert Camus, "Return to Tipasa," in *Lyrical and Critical Essays* (New York: Knopf, 1968), 165.

6. Irving Howe, "This Age of Conformity," *Partisan Review* 21 (January–February 1954): 8.

7. On Macdonald, who was at the center of the intellectual circles in which Arendt moved and her close friend, see Gregory Sumner, *Dwight Macdonald and the "Politics" Circle* (Ithaca, N.Y.: Cornell University Press, 1996).

8. See Peter Clecak, *Radical Paradoxes: Dilemmas of the American Left, 1945–1970* (New York: Harper & Row, 1973).

9. See Maurice Isserman, *If I Had a Hammer: The Death of the Old Left and the Birth of the New Left* (New York: Basic Books, 1987), 77–124.

10. Young-Bruehl recounts this incident in *Hannah Arendt*, 308–18. For further discussion, see Hannah Pitkin's brilliant essay "The Return of 'The Blob,'" in *Feminist Reinterpretations of Hannah Arendt*, ed Bonnie Honig (College Park: Pennsylvania State University Press, 1995).

11. See James Bohman, "The Moral Costs of Political Pluralism: The Dilemmas of Difference and Equality in Arendt's 'Reflections on Little Rock,'" in *Hannah Arendt: Twenty Years Later*, ed. Larry May and Jerome Kohn (Cambridge, Mass.: MIT Press, 1996).

12. See Herbert J. Spiro and Benjamin R. Barber, "Counter-Ideological Uses of 'Totalitarianism,'" *Politics and Society* (November 1970): 3–23; and Les K. Adler and Thomas G. Patterson, "Red Fascism: The Merger of Nazi Germany and Soviet Russia in the American Image of Totalitarianism, 1930s–1950s," *American Historical Review* 75 (April 1970): 1046–64

13. The following arguments draw from Jeffrey C. Isaac, *Arendt, Camus, and Modern Rebellion* (New Haven, Conn.: Yale University Press, 1992), chap. 2.

14. On this theme, see James D. Wilkinson, *The Intellectual Resistance in Europe* (Cambridge, Mass.: Harvard University Press, 1981).

15. Trotsky's essay is discussed in Dwight Macdonald, "The Root is Man," *Politics*, April and July 1946, 97–115 and 194–214.

16. Many of its themes can be discerned in Hannah Arendt, "Organized Guilt and Universal Responsibility," *Jewish Frontier*, January 1945, 19–23. This essay strongly influenced Dwight Macdonald's

famous "The Responsibility of Peoples," *Politics*, March 1945, rpt. in his *Memoirs of a Revolutionist* (New York: Meridian Books, 1958), 33–72.

17. Hannah Arendt, *The Origins of Totalitarianism* (New York: Harcourt Brace Jovanovich, 1973), vii.

18. See Robert Booth Fowler, *Believing Skeptics: American Political Intellectuals, 1945–1964* (Westport, Conn.: Greenwood Press, 1978).

19. Arendt, *Origins*, 460.

20. Ibid., 267.

21. Ibid., xviii.

22. Ibid., 269, ix.

23. See her paraphrase of Constant's remark about Rousseau, published in 1958, hardly a moment hospitable to Marxist ideas in the American academy: "Certainly, I shall avoid the company of detractors of a great man. If I happen to agree with them on a single point I grow suspicious of myself; and in order to console myself for having seemed to be of their opinion . . . I feel that I must disavow and keep these false friends away from me as much as I can" (Hannah Arendt, *The Human Condition* [Chicago: University of Chicago Press, 1958], 79).

24. Young-Bruehl, *Hannah Arendt*, 274–92.

25. Hannah Arendt, "The Ex-Communists," *Commonweal*, March 20, 1953, 596.

26. Ibid., 599. For parallel, see Henry Steele Commager, *Freedom, Loyalty, Dissent* (New York: Oxford University Press, 1954), esp. 58.

27. Young-Bruehl, *Hannah Arendt*, 287.

28. See Peter Coleman's useful if uncritical *The Liberal Conspiracy: The Congress for Cultural Freedom and the Struggle for the Mind of Postwar Europe* (New York: Free Press, 1989), 15–32.

29. Hannah Arendt, "The Aftermath of Nazi Rule: Report from Germany," *Commentary* 10 (October 1950): 342–53.

30. Hannah Arendt, "Dream and Nightmare," *Commonweal*, September 10, 1954, 553.

31. For an interesting reconstruction of the ideological temper of this moment, see Tony Judt, *Past Imperfect: French Intellectuals, 1944–1956* (Berkeley: University of California Press, 1992).

32. Arendt, "Dream and Nightmare," 578–80. See also Karl Jaspers, *The Future of Mankind* (Chicago: University of Chicago Press, 1961). Jonathan Schell's important *The Fate of the Earth* (New York: Knopf, 1982), esp. 118–78, sounds Arendtian themes.

33. Hannah Arendt, "The Cold War and the West: An Exchange," *Partisan Review* 29 (Winter 1962): 11–12.

34. Ibid., 12–13.

35. Ibid., 19.

36. Quoted in Young-Bruehl, *Hannah Arendt*, 208.

37. Daniel Boorstin, *The Genius of American Politics* (Chicago: University of Chicago Press, 1958).

38. Hannah Arendt, *On Revolution* (Harmondsworth, Eng.: Penguin Books, 1977), 215–82.

39. Hannah Arendt, *Crises of the Republic* (New York: Harcourt Brace Jovanovich, 1972), 39–40.

40. Ibid., 173.

41. For incisive elaborations on this theme on the part of postcolonial writers, see Kwame Anthony Appiah, *In My Father's House: Africa in the Philosophy of Culture* (Oxford: Oxford University Press, 1992); Kanan Makiya, *Cruelty and Silence: War, Tyranny, Uprising, and the Arab World* (New York: Norton, 1993); and Wole Soyinka, *The Open Sore of a Continent: A Personal Narrative of the Nigerian Crisis* (Oxford: Oxford University Press, 1996).

42. Arendt, *Crises of the Republic,* 105–11.

43. Ibid., 116, 118.

44. Ibid., 89.

45. Arendt, *On Revolution,* 278.

46. Arendt, "Thoughts on Politics and Revolution," in *Crises of the Republic,* 232.

47. Hannah Arendt, "Truth and Politics," in *Between Past and Future* (Harmondsworth, Eng.: Penguin Books, 1977), 241–42.

Chapter 14

William Appleman Williams:
Grassroots against Empire

Paul Buhle

William A. Williams remains the preeminent critic of empire in the second half of the twentieth century, casting a long shadow over the attempted recuperation of Cold War rationale by Arthur Schlesinger Jr. and many others.[1] As the cumulative effects of the planetary arms race and accompanying ecological degradation diminish hopes of dignified escape from the Cold War's aftereffects and underline an infrastructural economic decline, the tragedy of lost opportunities becomes increasingly apparent.[2] But a paradox also lurks here. Williams devoted only a minor fraction of his work to the Cold War, and even his critique of empire presupposed an unstated alternative. To understand the great historian's full perspectives, we must explore the personal sources of his world view, examine the intellectual context of his development, and capture his sometimes curious vision of a community-based movement that could displace "empire" as the central organizing category for American life.

Williams's success in theorizing the overseas American empire can be traced to the twofold process of "reading America from the outside in," as Bruce Cumings recently put it, and, conversely, analyzing diplomacy through a cogent critique of the expanding megastate at home.[3] This innovative approach is sui generis, yet it can be understood in two large ways. First, Williams mirrors or inverts the dominant mode by reading liberalism as the suffocating ideology that preempts both solid radicalism and thoughtful conservatism. The frontier that furnished the material for the American success story becomes the source of our collective corruption. Second, although altogether original in his argument, Williams draws upon a neglected tradition of communitarianism. Based in an immanent critique of national history, and updated to the shifting conditions from the 1910s to 1950s, this perspective passed from such historically minded grassroots socialists as A. M. Simons to progressives like Charles Beard, to environmentalists like Louis Mumford, and to the Wisconsin milieu around the young Williams of the later 1940s. Far from being exhausted by the dramatic changes in American society, this tradition is more fundamental and long-range than the particular problems posed by the Cold War era.

New or previously unavailable documents (along with extensive personal interviews) permit a look at the William Appleman Williams that his students, devotees, and critics only glimpsed from his occasional interviews and passing comments. Williams's own self-presentation went far to emphasize those elements of his background and personal development which best demonstrated his often embattled (and just as often idiosyncratic) political conclusions, passing over otherwise revealing episodes and relations.

Williams interpreted his life against the context of late 1960s counterculture in particular and the charge of "un-Americanism" thrown at radical critics more generally. He depicted himself as a perfectly ordinary American from a cohesive middle-class or lower-middle-class, relatively egalitarian, Depression-era culture of the small town. Unlike most American radicals who grew out of nonradical backgrounds, he admitted to no "conversion experience." He had no need, he insisted, to break from the sense of community that he had achieved, because his radicalism stemmed from his positive experiences in it. Schooling and personal experience in a Missouri military academy and at Annapolis had challenged him to do his best in his chosen tasks. War duties strengthened his sense of the necessity for community, his confidence in his own abilities, and the seriousness of his undertaking. From that point, his life was the straightforward tale of socialist and scholar—or so he believed.[4]

Much is absent from this account because it is so uniform in its claims. Son of a World War I pilot who was unable to settle down to daily life in a small Iowa town, Williams suffered terribly from his father's sudden accidental death, in army war games, when the boy was only eight. An only child raised by grandparents and a mostly absent mother who could be cold and demanding, he retained a deep emotional insecurity beneath his air of almost military self-confidence. In the small and deeply conservative commercial town of Atlantic, he raised himself up through acts of will. Short in stature and economically hard-pressed, he nevertheless became a basketball star and school journalist—in all, a popular local figure. After two years of a basketball scholarship at the military academy, he received an appointment to Annapolis (which he had not particularly wanted to attend), where he nearly flunked out because of restlessness and boredom.[5] Academy classmates remember the boy as unusually serious, bookish (especially compared with the normal run of athletes and pranksters), badly missing home and his fiancé.[6] At this moment of soul-searching, political questions became important to him for the first time in his life.

But no one at the time would have regarded his response to war events as especially unusual. The antifascist rhetoric of the war and a wave of sympathy for the Russians after their victory at Stalingrad inspired sentiments far beyond empathy with their suffering. On this point Williams became, willy-nilly, a small part of a large potentially leftward inclination. Like many officers as well as enlisted men and women, he also picked up discussions carried over from the Depression years about the seemingly intractable economic problems of peacetime capitalism and the possibilities of a different world after the war. Commander of a Landing Craft Medium (LCM) in the Pacific until he suffered a debilitating spinal injury, Williams claimed to have learned more on shipboard from Karl Marx than from Alfred Mahan, the admiral (and creator of the Naval War College) whose historical studies, generations earlier, had argued the supreme importance of a strong navy. And yet Williams experienced in the navy a camaraderie and a sense of responsibility in power that remained with him. Proposed fancifully by his Annapolis classmates as a future member of the Joint Chiefs of Staff, he had the bearing of a well-organized patriot who genuinely mourned a nation gone wrong.[7]

Williams's decisive political moment occurred while he was still in the service, shortly after the war. Stationed in Corpus Christi during 1946, he and his former high school sweetheart joined a small group of out-of-towners and the black community to press various integrationist goals. Made editor of the *Corpus Crisis*, the local NAACP newsletter, Williams found himself working alongside hard-bitten left-wing veterans of southern racial struggles. He joined no radical organization, but he did forcefully resist redbaiting by local Catholic Church officials. For this unbending posture he was personally assailed as an "outsider," altogether too close to the "reds."[8] As Cold War broke out and the Truman administration threatened dissenters of all kinds, Williams knew better than to identify with the wrong side, but he set himself to find ways to understand and explain what had happened to the promise of world amity. As he ruminated, he felt more and more drawn to the study of history.

The Williams who arrived in Madison in 1947 to attend the University of Wisconsin seemed at first glance an improbable socialist. A registered Republican, he would soon become a church-going Presbyterian. But Madison's isolationist, progressive, and socialist traditions blended into the postwar unrest to legitimate a particular kind of dissent. Discharged GIs and other students voted down conscription in a straw poll and flocked to hear the campus address of Idaho's folk-singing Senator Glen Taylor, Henry Wallace's running mate in 1948. American historians at the university had by that time become famous or notorious as opponents of the behemoth state, suspicious of its origins all the way back to the Constitutional Convention, and skeptical of motives behind great military crusades.

Williams devoted his personal energies to getting through graduate school and making up for time lost to war. Yet he probed cultural theory with exiled Frankfort School sociologist Hans Gerth while learning the basics of progressive history with Merle Curti, Merrill Jensen, Fred Harvey Harrington, and others. For his master's thesis he made a careful study of the *Chicago Tribune's* response to World War I, and his Ph.D. dissertation profiled Raymond Robins, a leading Progressive politician who resisted anticommunism and sought to promote reconciliation of the United States and the Soviet Union at upper council levels. Williams also took the time, in his last year on campus, to preach a sermon or two at the university's Unitarian Center.[9]

These experiences help to explain his approach to his particular historical interests. An unelaborated passage in his major study, *Contours of American History,* notes that a passing phrase in a letter by Marx on the concept of "feudal socialism" inspired the book.[10] What Williams probably meant was that his introduction to Marxism had confirmed his own deepest inclinations. Capitalism could be seen as a systemic inculcation of the idea that economic growth—with all its incidental human costs—was the main motive force of human progress. Capitalism had done its part in creating the potential for abundance, but its continuation now threatened to destroy everything humanity had attained. Liberalism supplied the ideology that justified accelerated expansionism as a gift of the West to benighted humanity.

The struggle for an alternative meant, in part, an attempted return to an older collective or community ethic, an escape not only from capitalism as such but from undemocratic centralizing impulses of every kind. This theme had been an important undercurrent in 1930s thought, articulated by writers such as Lewis Mumford, who also decried the passing of community. Decimated by the wartime experience, more honored on the right than on the left (where liberals and communists tended to share enthusiasms for the big state), even the vision of community had disappeared. Recuperation of its possibility meant, in the short term for Americans, a forceful resistance to the worst impulses of their own society in the modern age: war and preparations for war, serving the Moloch of perpetual expansion.[11]

Spending several months in England in 1949, when the Labour Party was still seriously talking about democratic control over the means of production, Williams found an explicitly socialistic version of what he was seeking. The "Guild Socialism" of G.D.H. Cole, more de-centralized and ethical than class-oriented, might easily be traced back to Cole's own inspiration: the utopian novelist, poet, designer, and agitator-romantic, William Morris.[12] Returning home, Williams embraced a politics that could be called anticentralist and anti-anticommunist. It was a view both spare in particulars and in many ways more economistic than its articulators would have chosen, better at denouncing power (as it did in the hands of the sociologist C. Wright Mills) than at offering alternatives. In the circumstance, it was nevertheless a remarkable testament of determination, and a building block for the next dissenting generation. By no accident, Williams's teachers and admirers described *him* as a Romantic.

Williams moved swiftly toward a teaching career and penned his first book. The earliest scholarly effort to reveal the unexamined historical assumptions that lay behind the U.S. opposition to Russian policies long before the Bolshevik Revolution, *Russian-American Diplomacy* (1953) also challenged George Kennan's theses on the current Russian threat. Williams came within a hairsbreadth of publishing an epilogue to his book in the journal *Foreign Affairs*. After several false starts in academic life, he secured a regular position at the University of Oregon, where he produced some of his finest early academic work (including the massive two-volume documentary text *The Shaping of American Diplomacy*) and a series of controversial anti–Cold War essays for the *Nation*. He had emerged a most unusual crusader against empire.

* * *

A series of ostensibly unrelated developments in American intellectual life meanwhile proved decisive for Williams's evolution. If Cold War liberalism was the dominant intellectuals' credo of the day, its proponents nevertheless had important methodological differences, which critics of various kinds frequently overlooked. The same critics, unable to escape the logic of the mainstream, also seemed unwilling or unable to see their own common ground. By leaping over the usual boundaries and training fire on Cold War liberalism from several directions simultaneously, Williams established a unique place for himself and his writings.

On the contemporary cutting edge of the intellectual-political debates stood Williams's bête noire, Arthur Schlesinger Jr. Drawn to moderate versions of radicalism (and radical teachers) in his youth, the ardent liberal Schlesinger dramatically took the lead after World War II in calling for the isolation and eradication of communist influence. Asserting the archaism of Marxist theory and the inadequacy of ordinary people to bring about fundamental change, he proposed that intellectuals themselves could ride the beast of history by mastering the state. Communism had to be reined in, the working-class threat of disorder transformed into loyalty through union jobs for military spending, and the Democratic Party reoriented at large toward domestic intervention and military buildup. Truman, who first appeared too oafish to accomplish these goals, successfully created the magnum-scale security state suitable to Schlesinger's purposes, even though the Korean stalemate and the popularity of Dwight Eisenhower kept the liberals from the seats of power until the Kennedy administration.[13]

U.S. history offered the scholar in Schlesinger an arena in which to project a past appropriate to the future. His *Age of Jackson* (1945) had proposed in Andrew Jackson a Franklin Roosevelt-like figure, too personally strong to be held back by Congress and wise enough to bring reformers, intellectuals, and workers together with businessmen in a coalition hitched to expansionism. Schlesinger put aside, as far as possible, Jackson's pro-slavery views and his personal role in the expropriation and extermination of Indians. *The Vital Center* (1950), however, insisted that those who opposed the program of expansionist democracy had been enemies of democracy, naysayers on the right or left. To raise questions of legitimacy or morality in treatment of Mexicans and Indians, for instance, was tantamount to questioning America's material progress and its leadership role in the free world. Liberalism, heart of the "Vital Center," was the Manifest Destiny (although Schlesinger did not put it this way) of the modern world order—if only communism could be crushed.[14]

Much of Schlesinger's historiographical animus had been directed not at communists (apart from the leftish W.E.B. Du Bois, whose work was studiously ignored, they played little role in this world) but implicitly at the leading historian of the 1920s and 1930s, Charles Austin Beard. The masterful synthesizer of large themes, Beard and his wife, Mary Ritter Beard, had written the best-selling *Rise of American Civilization* (1930). Beard himself stood at the leftward edge of the mainstream, having resisted World War I by resigning from Columbia University to protest the firing of colleagues, calling attention to the need for dramatic economic reform (but not socialism), and above all resisting the national drift toward war during the 1930s. Assailing Franklin Roosevelt's lack of candor and attacking the further centralization of the wartime state and economy, Beard drew upon himself the extreme hostility of the newer liberal historians. During his last years of life Beard saw himself displaced and his former prestige disparaged by the Young Turks of the profession, the intellectual-history-minded East Coast scholars. His whole way of viewing history—as if through the lenses of a democratic frontier society that had gone wrong, turned toward reform, and gone wrong again—seemed to them an intolerable concession to national self-criticism.[15]

The Cold War historians' move was also part of a larger interdisciplinary paradigm shift. Like most other interwar liberals, Charles Beard had been strongly affected by the "cultural relativism" of the anthropologists. They still envisioned "higher" and "lower" civilizations, judged by the existing standards of economic and social organization. But they had good reasons to see many qualities of the so-called "lower" civilizations as preferable to or at least no worse than those of the "higher." This view added a new, emancipating dimension to liberalism, making it more democratically international, more inter-racially minded, and more open to the changing roles of women. Americans, many concluded, had special experiences, but they also had every reason to learn from others. The intolerance and open racism of the Nazis also seemed to demand a defense of pluralism and self-definition by those who opposed fascism.

But the Cold War vision, in its sophisticated forms a liberals' outlook stretching across disciplines from the social sciences to the humanities, replaced this flexible scale with a distinction between "free" and "unfree," in which the very concept of relativism became hateful. America in this construction was the normative or ultimate "free" society against which all others would be measured, tested, and judged. In order to stay free, it had to uproot the sources both of disorder and of utopianism, whether challenges to sex role differentiations (as Talcott Parsons saw the matter), or the dangerous notion of human perfectibility, which the theologian and neoconservative mentor Reinhold Niebuhr pinpointed as the great error of socialism.[16]

The bruising ethnocentrism (and misogyny) in this patriotic hyperbole arguably delayed the development of a humane or realistic U.S. history for decades, shunting aside much of the creative scholarly impetus of the 1930–1940s generation. Political insurgents challenging business or empire came to be seen as deviants from appropriate social norms; social classes outside the leadership of the market economy—including African Americans, Indians, Mexican Americans, Asian Americans, and women—seemed of no great historical interest. Until the 1960s, and notwithstanding a wave of both civil rights activities and revisionist popular culture, major survey textbooks described slaves as childlike figures and Indians as temporary obstacles to "American" society's proper development.[17]

But the steady impact of the Cold War provoked a gradual rethinking of critical positions as well. Diplomatic history became mainstream, and more acute minds began to turn over the dark side of an American consensus. The powerful bloc of "New York intellectuals" that emerged at the center of cultural discussion during the early 1950s played strangely into this paradigm shift. They certainly shared Schlesinger's political animus and elaborated a particular cultural version of the European legacy to be protected against the modern barbarians.[18] Yet from a methodological view, several tendencies within and around this circle tended to undercut the triumphalist Cold War liberalism that Schlesinger expounded. From a strictly cultural point of view, as Freud replaced Marx in the reading lists and consumer society increasingly seemed to marginalize high culture, some of the most interesting and ultimately most influential figures placed large question marks over the happy age that Americans had presumably reached. Sociologists warned widely against anomie and described the parallel effects of commercialization and bureaucratization in creating a ubiquitous, weak-willed, "other-directed" personality.

From a historiographical standpoint, the spread of "consensus history," flattening the patterns of conflict so as to stress near-universal agreement on means and ends, tended to undercut the very dynamic of the Schlesingerian narrative. A profoundly conservative vision in many ways, it nevertheless badly diminished, from an unexpected direction, the heroic status of such presidential warriors as Andrew Jackson, Woodrow Wilson, and Franklin Roosevelt. Award-winning historian Richard Hofstadter and historically minded political scientist Louis Hartz captured wide public attention by respectively puncturing some favorite liberal myths and describing consensual liberalism as ill preparing Americans for the complexities of the world they lived in.

It would be tempting to view Williams as a simple mirror image of these intellectual trends. The New York intellectuals, mostly second-generation Jewish Americans who gained acceptance in the dominant order by taking the political assumptions of Cold War liberalism at face value, had themselves escaped the communitarian impulse (and now unwanted taint) of a once powerful Jewish radicalism.[19] By contrast, Williams—all-American boy, sports star, and navy man—asserted his legitimacy as a small-town citizen to address grave errors of the nation.

He understood sympathetically the impulses toward conformity as the actions of a confused and misled people unable to address the steady drift toward disaster. He claimed to propose radical solutions not because they suited his own traditions but because nothing less would succeed.

The mirror-image temptation should be resisted, however, because Williams also placed himself unexpectedly among these developments. Charles Beard he admired as a model public citizen and scholar, and he regarded with special contempt the liberals who disgraced (or refused to defend) Beard. But the chief victims of the Cold War as well, communists and their allies, had no particular love for Beard and shared Schlesinger's fondness for the New Deal, however they disputed its successor regimes. When Williams struggled to explain his views, he therefore often found himself looking toward the "isolationist" conservatives and Republican liberals as near-heroic figures who had resisted the drift toward the military-industrial complex and managed to hold on to their constituents—perhaps the best that could be done in the situation at that time. Given his own Iowa Republican background, this was not surprising. But he also found himself drawn to certain elements of the views set forth by Hofstadter and Hartz. Perhaps the "consensus" that Hofstadter described as the character of U.S. society had a further, hidden meaning.

* * *

William Appleman Williams's breakthrough text, *The Tragedy of American Diplomacy* (1959), should be read with a special emphasis on the first noun of the title. Williams assumed that even the worst, most degrading, and dangerous foreign policies had to be explained historically by the presence of a community of perceived interests (or *Weltanschauung*, the word he borrowed from William Dilthey's writings) which had at once unified and misled Americans. That perceived interest must be found in the national background: the internal expansion represented by the ever moving frontier.

For Williams, the contemporary Cuban crisis exemplified the self-destructive character of American perspectives. Upholding the right to revolution in the abstract, the nation punished peoples who took the rhetoric seriously. Looking back in history, "imperial anticolonialism" and "imperial idealism" had marked the rise of an armed logic of expansionism. The New Deal, which a generation of liberal historians had regarded as the happy culmination of all U.S. developments, looked to Williams more as it did to Old Right conservatives: an evasion of problems falsely resolving itself through world war. The "Nightmare of Depression and the Vision of Omnipotence," as he titled the penultimate chapter of his *Tragedy,* recounted the willingness of American leaders to promote a dangerous and destructive arms race and permanent tension in order to secure the hegemony over the planet that they believed it was the right and duty of the United States to exercise into the unforeseeable future. Imperial chutzpah in the nuclear age was catastrophic, but the whole saga had the makings of Greek tragedy. If Americans could withdraw from their Armageddon-chasing, they could survey the failings in their own society and begin to make themselves anew. Enlightened conservatives were the ones placed to make that reconsideration possible.

Whereas *Tragedy* has been described by a Williams student as so Beardian that it demanded a minimum of Williams himself, *Contours of American History* (1961) is Williams's startlingly original work.[20] It might be described as the author accepting the logic of consensus and turning its implications around 180 degrees. Here, he sees power more than liberty—or perhaps liberty in a special sense, defined by those in power to embrace imperial prerogatives—as having been the working principle of European and post-European expansion. The children of power, including the lower classes of whites, had advanced, literally and without serious moral compunctions, over the bones of destroyed cultures. U.S. foreign policy, which in *Contours* Williams took to be guided by the aim of replacing the frontier, he later saw as the logical extension of the frontier.[21] Conquest of world power and world markets emerged, at last, as the essence of the inner logic and world horizon of capital.

This motif in Williams's work emerges most clearly at the beginning of *Contours*, in a long look backward to medieval life and medieval Christianity. Writing in a framework familiar to readers of Lewis Mumford, Williams highlights what Mumford called the "breakdown of the medieval synthesis" as the process that set the modern demons loose. Mercantilism became a world view of those who sought to retain and adapt an original Christian morality during the dynamic secularization of a religious outlook, as an agrarian society was transformed into one of commerce and industry. Corrupted by its own acceptance of empire, mercantilism yielded to liberalism in a "triumph of laissez-faire individualism over corporate Christianity." As a tragic consequence of the bourgeois revolution, "the gradual secularization of the religious concept of a corporate society weakened the sanction for the ideal of a common good."[22] But the original "heresy," individualism, evoked in response a renewal of the "original idea" of property's responsibility. In this struggle for renewal, he insists, can be found "one of the basic explanations of socialism's persistent relevance and appeal in the 20th century."[23] Modern liberalism, in this light, represents the kind of failure of moral imagination which prompted Arthur Schlesinger Jr. to argue that there are no real solutions, but that buttressing the corporate state with economic integration and social planning is the obligatory next best thing.[24]

Seeking predecessors in the Anglo-American vein, Williams hints at his fondness for Ruskin and Carlyle and the intellectual mood of eclectic Anglo-American socialists during the late nineteenth century, when capitalism was very often seen as a perhaps inevitable but still monstrous interruption of historical collectivity. Even as Marx urged the progressive effects of capitalism, ordinary socialists and intellectuals such as Morris emotionally resisted the implications. The price, in the world they saw around them, was already too heavy. Many of them feared, quite understandably, that the destruction of badly severed social relations had already gone too far. For these militantly free-thought socialists, religion was more than a background and a metaphor; its traditions of solidarity remained central, despite the uses religious authorities had made of order. Williams reaches back through scholarly observation and his own experience for something similar.

His perspective has much in common with the two most read American socialist historians (with the possible exception of W.E.B. Du Bois) who preceded him. The first, C. Osborne Ward, was brother to the famed sociologist Frank Lester Ward and a member of the "American" or anti-Marx faction of the First International. In 1879 he published in two giant volumes, *The Ancient Lowly,* an extraordinarily creative reading of available documents, attempting to prove that Christianity had arisen from communal artisan institutions and was corrupted into a conservative religion of the rich only when its supporters and corrupters attained state power in Rome. The road back, Ward emphasized, would be to that sweet, voluntary ethical socialism. Republished repeatedly after the turn of the century, *The Ancient Lowly* remained a Bible to generations of religious-minded radicals.[25]

The second historian, Algernon M. Simons, came out of University of Wisconsin training as a student of Frederick Jackson Turner, just slightly more than a half-century before Williams entered the graduate program. Simon's *Class Struggles in America* (1907; expanded as *Social Forces in American History,* 1912) was Beardian in its assumptions about the farmer's democratic instincts. But it was overlaid with a heavy sense of the whites having destroyed communal institutions of Indians, and of chaotic individualism as well as the wealth of the cities having drained off the reputation and energies of the yeoman culture. Simons, against all the weight of Second International orthodoxy, sought to appeal morally to the small farmer to cling to his land and join up with socialism. Perhaps five thousand socialist reading clubs, particularly in the Midwest and plains states, formed to study Simons's historical works.[26] The tradition thinned afterward, yet history alone found a continuing popular audience for socialist writings, and its various scholars (including

Matthew Josephson, Granville Hicks, and historical novelist Upton Sinclair) all made an argument that some kind of special American experience had been corrupted or overturned by the rise of big business. Even Du Bois in *Black Reconstruction,* arguing in biblical language that Reconstruction had presented a unique opportunity that a sinful America cast aside, was not far from this conception.

Like these predecessors, Williams remained a Christian Socialist without a clearcut theology. Responding to his critics and to his own inner urgings, he attempted repeatedly after *Contours of American History* to approach the question of community from a more positive or constructive position. *The Great Evasion* (1963), arising out of a graduate seminar and renewed intensive reading in Christian Socialist texts (also possibly Williams's return to churchgoing), foresaw a dialogue "to convince those vast number of Americans that we can take the productive apparatus of mature capitalism and reorganize it for their benefit"[27]—but not even favorable critics considered it persuasive. In his textbook survey of U.S. history, *Americans in a Changing World: A History of the Twentieth Century* (1975), Williams sought to fill in many of his earlier lapses, describing socialist, women's and African American movements, plus popular culture and fine literature, as making contributions to a better, more realistic and humane, view of America. In another intended survey, *America Confronts a Revolutionary World* (1976), Williams wrote at some length about Indians, the "First Americans," and their stewardship of the land. At the end of the story he proposed that the United States could return to a sort of Articles of Confederation government, breaking down the nation into governable units with citizens' control over their own regions. Few of his devotees, let alone his critics, considered these efforts on a par with his important books.

But this envisioned alternative remains the undeveloped side of his socialist argument. In an early essay on Brooks Adams, Henry Adams's brother, Williams places his keenest perspective in the eye of the ironic, upper-class radical or at least clear-eyed observer.[28] The "Tory radical" (an honorific taken from the nineteenth century Englishman outraged at industrialism's baneful results) and dirt-farmer egalitarian, in Williams's mind, share a crucial opposition to the emerging liberal modus operandi. Grassroots socialism, if it can find its way, will arise from the possibility of a coalition led by modern Tory radicals, intellectuals, political professionals or even, conceivably, humanitarian business leaders who can see the working of the system from the top down and judge the realistic alternatives. The working and middle classes will respond, he believes, to a realistic, reasonable program when they see it offered.

Lord Shaftsbury, his favorite historical figure in *Contours* (and perhaps in all his works), provides the chronological first in a series of elites whom Williams views as conscientious and capable managers of the commonweal. Williams is moved by Shaftsbury's knowledge, insight, and grace; he will be similarly moved by John Quincy Adams. Williams's seemingly eccentric choice of Herbert Hoover as the best modern president reflects not only disdain for the New Deal lack of vision, and real sympathy for the historic scapegoat of the Depression, but also admiration for the planner and visionary who tried to make capitalism work in a rational way. Shaftsbury and Hoover, he seems to argue, could not personally have been socialists; but if they *had* been socialists, they would have known how a different kind of system might work and how to appeal to the good common sense of people around them.

* * *

In *The Roots of the Modern American Empire* (1969), Williams's only major work after *Tragedy* and *Contours,* he looks at the problem of empire from a different standpoint and seeks to make his subject collective. To achieve his aim, he drops out almost everything that social history contributed to the picture of a deeply conflicted and frequently violent late nineteenth-century society: Radical Reconstruction's sheer force and international implications; the labor movement of the 1880s, which also sent out ripples around the world; and the almost apocalyptic side of Populism. All these shrink in a common acceptance of the necessity of expanding economic horizons by large segments of labor, farm, and citizen leadership. Farmers make a market-smart choice, albeit one morally disastrous; to understand their inner logic is to see how, presented with better alternatives, they—and more important, their descendants—might make a very different choice.[29]

This essentially tragic view of western farmers drawn to market solutions with catastrophic long-run consequences points to an important element of Williams's lasting significance, quite apart from his undeniably central role in reshaping diplomatic history. It was not one that he had anticipated, but it lay clearly within the compass of the Madison trajectory and demonstrated that Williams had made himself the most prominent part of a tradition, even as he set off on his own personally unique quest.

The Vietnam War vindicated his longstanding critique of U.S. policies' historical roots and immensely widened the influence of his students and indirect disciples. But another influence, little suspected at the time, was on a fresh generation of scholars in Western history who, confronted with a virtual vacuum of acceptable interpretations, found in Williams a guide to a new and drastically different view of America.

John Mack Faragher, the award-winning biographer of Daniel Boone, perhaps tells the personal story best. Like many others in graduate school during the Vietnam days, he had been struck by Williams's perceptive view, in *Contours*, of continental expansion as a substitution of Manifest Destiny for the vision of Christian Commonwealth. *Roots of the Modern American Empire*, however, made the connection between continental and overseas expansion explicit. The problem of expansion and its implications for community, as described and analyzed by Williams, became the springboard for some of the most influential and most radical scholarship of the next twenty years.[30]

Williams did not set the course for this historical study, as he did in diplomacy. But his provocation came at just the right moment to prompt young scholars in a direction that was calling them and to give them what their own predecessors in Western history palpably lacked: a view both personally sympathetic to and realistically (even harshly) critical of the consequences. Without any particular stress upon the fate of Mexican Americans, Indians, or the land, Williams had made it possible for them to pursue all these logical concerns.

Williams's own intellectual lineage can also be usefully traced in this regard. David Noble has suggested that his graduate classmate's true importance can be understood best by reexamining the problems for U.S. history which Frederick Jackson Turner articulated in 1893. If the frontier was the key to American specialness and success, what would happen when the frontier was closed? Warren Susman, Williams's intimate friend, saw the continual scholarly re-evaluation of Turner as the clearest symptom of changing attitudes toward American life, attitudes that tended nevertheless to return to the same, almost obsessive questions about expansion.[31] Williams discerned in Turner less the master scholar than the essayist looking for a grand metaphor; perhaps Williams understood this best because it so matched his own temperament. Among all those who spoke to that continuing controversy about the frontier, Williams offered the freshest insights of any historian for generations.

How, Noble asks provocatively, can we explain the impact of a youngish scholar like Patricia Limerick, whose *Legacy of Conquest* may be said more than any other work to have precipitated the change in the way the history of the American West is taught? Limerick's innovation was, foremost, in periodization: The history of the West does not begin in the eighteenth century and end in 1890 but must be seen within a continuous history of conquest by Euro-Americans. The study of contestation, in Limerick's work, becomes a reconceptualizing of that history as a running story where a fragmented narrative becomes whole again.[32] She does not herself invoke Williams and has no need to do so, for Williams shaped the background upon which scholarship's patterns now move.

Noble argues what Faragher affirms, that by drawing domestic conclusions from diplomatic history, and by perceiving the limits of earlier progressive history, Williams cut the famous nexus of 1890 (or thereabouts) which had bedeviled Beard with conflicting contemporary impulses of democracy and empire. Already in *American-Russian Relations* and *The Tragedy of American Diplomacy*, Williams assumed that a kind of community of interests or at least a *Weltanschauung*—to repeat one of his favorite words—unified America.[33] His final volume, *Empire as a Way of Life* (1981), drove home the lesson one final time. There he shows readers the ugly side of market choices and reveals the wages of conquest as stealing from conqueror and conquered alike the possibility of higher purpose.

We have today no great evidence at hand to refute the confidence of all-conquering capital and its successful pursuit of further markets, whatever the cost to peoples and the planet. But Williams's tragic view helps bring careful readers toward the kernel of his socialistic notions, which lies at the grassroots of a once green continent. If the current moves toward consolidation of the new world order are unsuccessful because the imperial grasp outreaches its capacities to secure and hold without destroying, and if a democratic response can be made to limit the destruction, then Williams's contributions will provide an immensely useful way to see the modern world. This political contribution, however delayed, would match the scholarly contribution that has allowed so many historians to see U.S. history in a new light. He offers no complete world view, but his work has been and continues to be immensely influential. More would not have been asked by Bill Williams himself, who took justifiable pride in understanding the role of historical figures, including the greatest of intellectual figures, as part of their own age.

Notes

Acknowledgments: This essay has been revised extensively from its original conference presentation with the assistance of comments by Allen Hunter and in the process of coauthoring, with Edward Rice-Maximin, *William Appleman Williams: The Tragedy of Empire* (New York: Routledge, 1995). Special thanks go to the Williams families; to the librarians in charge of the Williams Papers at Oregon State University; and, for their insights, to many friends, including Henry Berger, Ed Crapol, Saul Landau, the late Merle Curti, Fred Harvey Harrington, and Warren Susman.

1. See Bruce Cumings, "'Revising Postrevisionism,' or The Poverty of Theory in Diplomatic History," *Diplomatic History* 17 (Fall 1993): 539–69.

2. See, e.g., the vindication of Williams's general view in two well-received recent texts: H. W. Brands, *The Devil We Knew: Americans and the Cold War* (New York: Oxford University Press, 1993); and Edward Pessen, *Losing Our Souls: The American Experience in the Cold War* (Chicago: Ivan R. Dee, 1993).

3. Bruce Cumings, "Global Realm With No Limit, Global Realm with No Name," *Radical History Review*, no. 57 (Fall 1993), 55.

4. See, e.g., William Appleman Williams, "My Life in Madison," in *History and the New Left: Madison, Wisconsin, 1950–1970*, ed. Paul Buhle (Philadelphia: Temple University Press 1990), 264–74; and "William Appleman Williams," in *Visions of History*, ed. Henry Abelove *et al.* (New York: Pantheon, 1983), 123–46, an interview conducted by Michael Wallace.

5. His family memoir, "A Good Life and a Good Death: A Memoir of an Independent Lady," (in the William A. Williams Papers, Ava Helen and Linus Pauling Collection, Oregon State University, Corvallis), is a reliable guide to Williams's own perceptions of family and social relations. I have been greatly aided in untangling the complications by Jeannie Williams, his wife of 1946 to 1955.

6. "William Appleman Williams," Naval Academy yearbook, 1944; and telephone interview with John Pirro, November 15, 1993.

7. Williams to Donald McIlvane, April 19, 1983, Williams Papers.

8. *Corpus Crisis,* May 9 and 17, 1946; Msgr. John F. Basso to Dr. Boyd Hall, May 15, 1946, and Teresa Grace Herald to Boyd Hall, May 15, 1946, in NAACP Papers, Corpus Christi file, Library of Congress. I am greatly indebted to Scott McLemee for assistance in uncovering these materials. Jeannie Williams and Charlotte Gilmor, fellow participants in the Corpus Christi events, were also very helpful.

9. Williams's interview with Warren Susman, September 1982, published in part as "The Smoking Room School of History," in Buhle, *History and the New Left*, 43–46.

10. William Appleman Williams, *Contours of American History* (Cleveland, 1961), 490–91.

11. In a letter during his last year of life, Williams confirmed a number of these perspectives in his intellectual development. "Dear Jim," July 22–23, 1989, Williams Papers. On Mumford's circle, see John L. Thomas, "Lewis Mumford, Benton MacKaye, and the Regional Vision," in *Lewis Mumford: Public Intellectual,* ed. Thomas P. Hughes and Sara Hughes (New York: Oxford University Press, 1990), 71–110.

12. See Luther P. Carpenter, *G.D.H. Cole: An Intellectual Biography* (Cambridge: Cambridge University Press, 1973). The politics of Morris continued to inspire youngsters such as the young war veteran E. P. Thompson, drawn like Williams to historical studies but (more logically in the British context) also to a Communist Party group of Marxist historians, most of them destined to break with Communism in 1956. Williams made frequent later references to his indebtedness to Cole.

13. Michael Wreszin, "Arthur Schlesinger, Jr., Scholar-Activist in Cold War America: 1946–1956," *Salmagundi,* nos. 63–64 (Summer 1984): 255–85; Arthur Schlesinger Jr., "The Future of Socialism, III," *Partisan Review* 14 (May–June 1947): 229–42.

14. Wreszin, "Arthur Schlesinger, Jr.," and Arthur Schlesinger Jr., *The Vital Center* (Boston:Houghton Mifflin, 1949). Warren Susman's graduate school critique of Schlesinger, written thirty-five years before Wreszin's but not outdated by any subsequent material, was published for the first time as "Appendix One: The Historians' Task," in Buhle, *History and the New Left*, 275–84.

15. See, e.g., the perceptive comments about Schlesinger's spiritual guide, Reinhold Niebuhr, in David W. Noble, *The End of American History: Democracy, Capitalism, and the Metaphor of Two Worlds in Anglo-American Historical Writing, 1880–1980* (Minneapolis: University of Minnesota Press, 1987), 65–89.

16. See Edward A. Purcell Jr., *The Crisis of Democratic Theory: Scientific Naturalism and the Problem of Value* (Lexington: University of Kentucky Press, 1973), 138, 210–11.

17. One of Williams's most decisive commentaries on this historical style at large is his review es-

say "Schlesinger: Right Crisis—Wrong Order," reprinted from the *Nation*, March 23, 1957, in William Appleman Williams, *History as a Way of Learning* (New York: New York Viewpoints, 1973), 203–12. See also "The Age of Re-Forming History," a critique of Richard Hofstadter's *Age of Reform*, reprinted from the *Nation*, June 30, 1956, in *History as a Way of Learning*, 161–68, in which Williams argued that Hofstadter's psychological overlay, through which radical dissenters such as Populists were caricatured as inherently irrational, was both silly and unworthy of Hofstadter's own talents—notwithstanding the high marks it received in the *New York Times* and within the profession. Discussions with Merle Curti have clarified, for my purposes, the popularity Hofstadter gained through articulating precisely such views during this period for a New York intellectual milieu eager to believe them, and his later second thoughts about them.

Samuel E. Morison, the most unembarrassedly racist of the major textbook authors, privately defended his characterizations as appropriate to African Americans because of the "essential docility in their character." Criticisms of his *Growth of the American Republic* (coauthored with the distinguished civil libertarian Henry Steele Commager) were characteristically brushed off as communist-influenced. See Peter Novick, *That Noble Dream: The "Objectivity" Question and the American Historical Profession* (Cambridge: Cambridge University Press, 1988), 350 n. 46.

18. As is well known, future neoconservative savants not only praised an aggressive foreign policy, but labored covertly with the Central Intelligence Agency on the American wing of the Congress for Cultural Freedom, publisher of the politically hardline *Encounter* magazine. Alan Wald, *The New York Intellectuals: The Rise and Decline of the Anti-Stalinist Left from the 1930s to the 1980s* (Chapel Hill: University of North Carolina Press, 1987), chap. 11.

19. Novick captures this spirit in *That Noble Dream*, 340–41; Wald is more precise in *New York Intellectuals*, chaps. 9–10.

20. Edward Rice-Maximin's interview with Thomas McCormick, June 1993.

21. This was pointed out to me in a communication from David W. Noble (who in 1949 was Williams's graduate school classmate), June 10, 1993.

22. Williams, *Contours*, 48.

23. Ibid., 38.

24. Williams, "Schlesinger: Right Crisis—Wrong Order," 209.

25. C. Osborne Ward, *The Ancient Lowly*, 2 vols. (1879; Chicago: Charles H. Kerr 1902). I wish to credit my interviews with the late Christian Socialist notable Willard Uphaus for a discussion of Ward's continuing significance into the 1910s–1930s.

26. Algernon M. Simons, *Social Forces in American History* (New York, 1912). So close did the ties remain that Simons, who had taken classes with Frederick Jackson Turner and faithfully published his mentor's famed "Frontier" essay in the *International Socialist Review*, also thanked his former and current Madison professors, Richard T. Ely and John R. Commons respectively, for allowing him to use research materials from their volumes that would appear shortly as *Documentary History of American Society* (Cleveland: A.H. Clark, 1910–11). Simons, *Social Forces*, xi.

27. William Appleman Williams, *The Great Evasion* (Chicago: Quadrangle Books, 1964), 48.

28. William Appleman Williams, "Brooks Adams and American Expansionism," *New England Quarterly* 25 (June 1952), 123–28.

29. It is worth noting that much of the advanced Italian New Left thought of the 1970s argued that modern capitalism had required the participation of workers as consumers and so—although at first almost entirely against the will of individual capitalists themselves—the system's leaders finally accepted the industrial trade union as a higher interlocking mechanism within the system. Williams's stu-

dents had, decades earlier, made this argument—if less theoretically and more historically—in various issues of the journal *Studies on the Left.* The most available version of the Italian variant can be found in Antonio Negri, *Marx beyond Marx: Lessons on the Grundrisse,* trans. Harry Cleaver, Michael Ryan, and Maurizio Viano (South Hadley, Mass: Bergin & Harvey, 1984).

30. John Mack Faragher, to Paul Buhle, December 25, 1993.

31. David W. Noble, "The American Wests: Refuge from European Power or Frontiers of European Expansion," in *The American West as Seen by Europeans and Americans,* ed. Rob Kroes (Amsterdam: Free University Press, 1989). Also see Warren Susman, "The Frontier Thesis and the American Intellectual," in Susman, *Culture as History: The Transformation of American Society in the Twentieth Century* (New York: Pantheon, 1985).

32. Noble, "The American Wests," 31. For Patricia Limerick's own account, see her introduction to *The Legacy of Conquest: The Unbroken Past of the American West* (New York: Norton, 1987), 17–32.

33. No wonder Oscar Handlin described *Contours of American History* as the product of an unbalanced mind: To think as Williams did was not merely deplorable but incredible to those who believed that they had settled the main lines of U.S. history for the foreseeable future. See Bradford Perkins, "'The Tragedy of American Diplomacy' Twenty-Five Years After," reprinted from *Reviews in American History* in *Redefining the Past: Essays in Diplomatic History in Honor of William Appleman Williams,* ed. Lloyd C. Gardner (Corvallis: Oregon State University Press, 1986), 21–34.

About the Contributors

Michael A. Bernstein is Associate Professor and Chair of the Department of History and Associated Faculty Member in the Department of Economics at the University of California, San Diego. He is the author of *The Great Depression: Delayed Recovery and Economic Change in America, 1929–1939* (1989), *Understanding American Economic Decline* (1994), and numerous articles on the history of economic thought and the economic and political history of twentieth-century America.

Shannon Lindsey Blanton is Assistant Professor of Political Science at Southern Illinois University. She received her Ph.D. in international studies from the University of South Carolina and has published articles on such topics as U.S. foreign policy, human rights, and the arms trade.

Paul Buhle, great-grandson of an abolitionist, teaches in the American Civilization Department at Brown University. He has authored, coauthored and coedited numerous books including *The Tragedy of Empire: A Biography of William Appleman Williams* (1995), *History and the New Left: Madison, Wisconsin, 1950–1970* (Temple, 1990), *Marxism in the United States* (1987), and *C.L.R. James: The Artist as Revolutionary* (1988).

Michael Cox is Professor of International Politics at the University of Wales, Aberystwyth. His latest book is *U.S. Foreign Policy after the Cold War: Superpower without a Mission?* (1995). He is the editor of *Irish Studies of International Affairs* and *Review of International Studies* and deputy editor of *Critique*.

Carolyn Eisenberg is Associate Professor of U.S. Foreign Policy in the History Department of Hofstra University. She is the author of the book *Drawing the Line: The American Decision to Divide Germany, 1944–49* (1996) and has published articles in *Diplomatic History, Science and Society, Radical History Review,* and most recently in Michael Ermarth, ed., *America and the Shaping of Germany* (1993).

Cary Fraser teaches in the Department of African and African-American Studies at the Pennsylvania State University. He is the author of *Ambivalent Anti-Colonialism: The United States and the Genesis of West Indian Independence, 1940–1964* (1994). His current work involves the impact of the Civil Rights Movement on U.S. foreign policy.

Harriet Friedmann is Professor of Sociology at the University of Toronto. Her research explores food in all its dimensions from human and ecosystem health to international regulation. She has studied and compared regional food systems in various parts of the world. She is currently investigating the agrofood sector of world, national, and regional economies as a window on histories of power and property and realistic possibilities for transformation.

Allen Hunter is Administrative Director of the A. E. Havens Center for the Study of Social Structure and Social Change in the Sociology Department of the University of Wisconsin. He has written about social movements of the right and left in the United States, transnational movements, and social theory. With Michael Bernstein he coedited a special issue of *Radical History Review* (Fall 1995) on "The Cold War and Expert Knowledge." He chairs the advisory board of the Progressive Media Project, which generates and distributes op-ed pieces to newspapers around the country.

Jeffrey C. Isaac is Professor of Political Science at Indiana University. He is the author of *Power and Marxist Theory: A Realist View* (1987), *Arendt. Camus, and Modern Rebellion* (1992), and *Democracy in Dark Times* (1997). He has published numerous articles and essays in journals including the *American Political Science Review, Political Theory, Salmagundi,* and *Dissent*.

Mary Kaldor is Jean Monnet Reader in Contemporary European Studies at the

Sussex European Institute, University of Sussex. She is also co-chair of the Helsinki Citizens Assembly, a peace and human rights network committed to the construction of a Pan-European civil society. Her books include *The Baroque Arsenal* (1982) and *The Imaginary War: Understanding the East-West Conflict* (1991).

Charles W. Kegley Jr. is Pearce Professor of International Relations at the University of South Carolina and former president of the International Studies Association (1993–94). His research interests center on the comparative study of foreign policy, international norms, and the correlates of peace. He recently published *Controversies in International Relations Theory: Realism and the Neoliberal Challenge* (1995).

Walter LaFeber is Noll Professor of History at Cornell University. His books include *The New Empire: An Interpretation of American Expansion* (1967), *America, Russia, and the Cold War, 1945–1996* (1997), *The American Age: U.S. Foreign Policy at Home and Abroad, from 1750 to the Present* (1989), and *The Clash: U.S.-Japan Relations from the Beginnings to the Present* (1997).

Thomas D. Lairson is Professor of Politics at Rollins College and in 1994 was the first Ford Foundation Professor of International Politics at the Institute for International Relations in Hanoi, Vietnam. He coauthored *International Political Economy: The Struggle for Power and Wealth* (1996), and he is currently writing a book on the globalization of the world economy.

Ronen Palan is Lecturer in International Relations at the University of Sussex and coeditor of the *Review of International Political Economy*. He coauthored, with Jason Abbott, *State Strategies in the Global Political Economy* (1996) and coedited, with Barry Gillis, *Transcending the State Global Divide* (1994).

Brenda Gayle Plummer is Professor of History and Afro-American Studies at the University of Wisconsin-Madison. Her research focuses on the connections between race and the history of U.S. foreign relations. She is the author of the books *Haiti and the Great Powers, 1902–1915* (1988) and *Rising Wind: Black Americans and U.S. Foreign Affairs, 1935–1960* (1996). Her essays have appeared in such journals as *Diplomatic History, Phylon,* and *Latin American Research Review.*

Ian Roxborough is Professor of Sociology and History at the State University of New York, Stony Brook. He edited, with Leslie Bethell, *Latin America between the Second World War and the Cold War, 1944–48* (1992). He is currently researching the U.S. military's post–Cold War debates on the likely nature of future wars.